# Viking Worlds

## Things, Spaces and Movement

Edited by

*Marianne Hem Eriksen*
*Unn Pedersen*
*Bernt Rundberget*
*Irmelin Axelsen*
*Heidi Lund Berg*

OXBOW | books
Oxford & Philadelphia

First published in the United Kingdom in 2014. Reprinted in paperback in 2019 by

OXBOW BOOKS
The Old Music Hall, 106–108 Cowley Road, Oxford, OX4 1JE

and in the United States by

OXBOW BOOKS
1950 Lawrence Road, Havertown, PA 19083



Paperback Edition: ISBN 978-1-78925-210-1
Digital Edition: ISBN 978-1-78297-728-5 (epub)

A CIP record for this book is available from the British Library

Library of Congress Cataloging-in-Publication Data

Viking worlds : things, spaces and movement / edited by Marianne Hem Eriksen, Unn Pedersen, Bernt Rundberget, Irmelin Axelsen, Heidi Lund Berg. -- Hardcover edition.
pages cm
Based on papers presented at the international conference "Viking Worlds," held at the University of Oslo in March 2013.
Includes bibliographical references.
ISBN 978-1-78297-727-8
1. Vikings. 2. Viking antiquities. I. Eriksen, Marianne Hem, editor.
DL65.V548 2014
948'.022--dc23
2014040011



For a complete list of Oxbow titles, please contact:

UNITED KINGDOM
Oxbow Books
Telephone (01865) 241249
Email: oxbow@oxbowbooks.com
www.oxbowbooks.com

UNITED STATES OF AMERICA
Oxbow Books
Telephone (610) 853 9131, Fax (610) 853-9146
Email: queries@casemateacademic.com
www.casemateacademic.com/oxbow

Oxbow Books is part of the Casemate group

*Front cover: Doorway from the reconstructed Iron-Age longhouse at Ullandhaug, Stavanger, Norway. Photo © Marianne Hem Eriksen.*
*Back cover: Proposed reconstruction of the courtyard site at Hjelle, Stryn, Sogn og Fjordane. Produced by Ragnar Børsheim, © Arkikon AS, Bergen.*

# Contents

# List of contributors

*Albris, Sofie Laurine*
The Danish National Museum
Frederiksholms Kanal 12
DK 1220 Copenhagen
Denmark
E-mail: sofie.albris@natmus.dk

*Axelsen, Irmelin*
Linderngata 8
0455 Oslo
Norway
E-mail: irmeax@gmail.com

*Berg, Heidi L.*
Eugenies gate 8 C
0168 Oslo
Norway
E-mail: h.berg87@gmail.com

*Bruen Olsen, Asle*
University Museum of Bergen
Pb. 7800
5020 Bergen
Norway
E-mail: asle.olsen@um.uib.no

*Butler, Joanne Shortt*
Department of Anglo-Saxon
Norse and Celtic
University of Cambridge
Cambridge
E-mail: js616@cam.ac.uk

*Carstens, Lydia*
Centre for Baltic and Scandinavian
Archaeology
Schloss Gottorf
D-24837 Schleswig
Germany
E-mail: lydia.carstens@schloss-gottorf.de

*Cartwright, Ben*
The Material Culture Laboratory
Department of Archaeology
Jesus College
Cambridge
CB5 8BL
E-mail: bhjc2@cam.ac.uk

*Eriksen, Marianne Hem*
Dept. of Archaeology, Conservation
and History
University of Oslo
PO Box 1019 Blindern
0315 Oslo
Norway
E-mail: m.h.eriksen@iakh.uio.no

*Gardeła, Leszek*
Institute of Archaeology
University of Rzeszów
st. Moniuszki 10
Hoffmanowej 8
35-015 Rzeszów
Poland
Email: leszekgardela@archeologia.rzeszow.pl

*Gaut, Bjarne*
Postboks 1200 Sentrum
0107 Oslo
Norway
E-mail: bjarne.gaut@akershus-fk.no

*Hauptmann, Andreas*
Deutsches Bergbau-Museum Bochum
Herner Straße 45
D-44787 Bochum
Germany

*Hedenstierna-Jonson, Charlotte*
Swedish History Museum
Department of Cultural History and Collections
PO Box 5428
114 84 Stockholm
Sweden
E-mail: charlotte.hedenstierna-jonson@historiska.se

*Hilberg, Volker*
Stiftung Schleswig-Holsteinische Landesmuseen
Schloss Gottorf
24837 Schleswig
Germany

*Kupiec, Patrycja*
Department of Archaeology
School of Geosciences
University of Aberdeen, St Mary's
Elphinstone Road
Aberdeen
AB24 3UF
UKE-mail: r01pmk12@abdn.ac.uk

*Lehmann, Robert*
Institut für anorganische Chemie
Leibniz Universität Hannover
Callinstr. 9
D-30167 Hannover
Germany

*Merkel, Stephen*
Deutsches Bergbau-Museum Bochum
Herner Straße 45
D-44787 Bochum
Germany
E-mail: StephenWilliam.Merkel@bergbaumuseum.de

*Milek, Karen*
Department of Archaeology
School of Geosciences
University of Aberdeen, St Mary's
Elphinstone Road
Aberdeen
AB24 3UF
E-mail: k.milek@abdn.ac.uk

*Pedersen, Unn*
Department of Archaeology, Conservation and History
University of Oslo
PO Box 1019 Blindern
0315 Oslo
Norway
E-mail: unn.pedersen@iakh.uio.no

*Price, Neil*
Dept. of Archaeology and Ancient History
Uppsala University
Box 626, 751 26 Uppsala
Sweden
E-mail: neil.price@arkeologi.uu.se

*Rundberget, Bernt*
Museum of Cultural History
University of Oslo
PO Box 6762
St Olavs plass
0130 Oslo
Norway
E-mail: bernt.rundberget@khm.uio.no

# Exploring Viking worlds

*Marianne Hem Eriksen, Unn Pedersen, Bernt Rundberget, Irmelin Axelsen and Heidi Lund Berg*

This book explores a plurality of approaches to the Viking past, both in Scandinavia and in the Viking diaspora. It is based on papers presented at the international conference 'Viking Worlds', held at the University of Oslo in March 2013. The conference was particularly focused towards postgraduates and early career researchers, in the realisation that there are few open and international forums for a new generation of Viking scholars. The conference seemingly struck a chord with the research community, and we received numerous paper proposals, also attracting the interest of recognised researchers. Thus, the edited volume constitutes a mix of new and established voices in the worlds of Viking research, asking new and different questions and using innovative methods and theories.

The conference was the third in a series organised by early career researchers and graduate students at the Department of Archaeology, Conservation and History; the two previous volumes – on the Roman Iron Age and the Neolithic respectively – published as conference proceedings by the in-house journal *Nicolay* (Gundersen and Eriksen 2010; Solberg *et al.* 2012). For *Viking Worlds* it was decided to ensure international availability by using English as the language of the conference, and to publish an edited volume with an international publisher.

*The Viking World* (Simpson 1980), *The Viking World* (Graham-Campbell 1980, 2nd edn 1989, 3rd edn 2001), *Vikingernes verden* ('The world of the Vikings') (Roesdahl 1987 and eight subsequent editions), *The Viking World* (ed. Brink and Price 2008): old and new classics in Viking archaeology and Viking studies. We have chosen to allude to this well-established title, but with a twist. By stressing the plural form, *Viking Worlds*, our idea is to emphasise the varied and eclectic Viking past, opening for studies of the particular and the individual.

Although the main point of departure is the archaeology and thereby the *materiality* of the Vikings, the Viking period has always invited inter-disciplinarian approaches, and this volume is no exception. Certainly including traditional inter- or multi-disciplinarian perspectives such as using historical sources, Icelandic sagas and Eddic poetry; the anthology also contains papers using perspectives from place-name research, history of religion, and technological advancements, such as isotope analysis. Bringing particular studies of specialised methodologies and/or empirics together can generate new insights of the technology, social organisation and mentality of the worlds of the Vikings.

In terms of geography, the contributions of this volume range from Iceland through Scandinavia to the Continent. The book furthermore brings Scandinavian, British and Continental Viking scholars together, in an internationally accessible form. The papers challenge established truths, present new definitions and discuss old themes from new angles. Topics discussed include personal and communal identity; gender; relations between people, artefacts, and places/spaces; rules and regulations within different social arenas; processes of production, trade and exchange, and transmission of knowledge within both past Viking-Age societies and present-day research. Studies include investigations of coins, ornamental metalwork, textile tools, door rings, halls, courtyard sites, manors and markets. Displaying thematic breadth as well as geographic and academic diversity, the articles may foreshadow up-and-coming themes for Viking-Age research.

For the conference, an open call for papers on new perspectives on the Viking Age was issued. However, as it turned out, several of the papers interlinked in terms of subjects and/or approaches. Thus, the book is organised around three main topics.

As an introduction, Neil Price shares some of his thoughts on the development of Viking archaeology in later years, *e.g.* examining the notion of women with weapons, or Vikings who manipulated their appearance by filing their teeth, or the unnerving 'otherness' of the Vikings that we are just beginning to grasp. As he points out, the Vikings we study today are very different than the Vikings studied a few decades ago.

Subsequently, Part I, *Real and ideal spaces* focuses on architecture, settlements and landscapes of the Viking era. Three of the articles in this section deal with aristocratic architecture from different perspectives (Carstens, Albris, Shortt Butler), while the remaining two focus on judicial arenas and artefacts of the Viking Age (Olsen, Eriksen).

Part II, *Gendered things, gendered spaces?* provides thought-provoking and critical papers on gender through three cases: the burial and social biography of a particular individual from Birka (Hedenstierna-Jonson); the tradition of regulating shielings as gendered spaces in Iceland (Kupiec and Milek); and a reassessment of keys as gendered objects in Viking-Age Norway (Berg).

The third and last section of the book is titled *Production, exchange, and movement.* This section consists of studies examining craft and production (Cartwright, Pedersen), trade and exchange (Gaut, Merkel), and mobility and movement through a critical perspective on Vikings in Poland (Gardeła).

Together, the articles present studies that emphasise the plurality of the Viking past; shedding light on parts of the Viking worlds that have largely been left undiscovered or undebated, while also putting forth new perspectives on (until recently) established views.

The editors would like to thank the following institutions for financial contributions to the conference and the edited volume: Department of Archaeology, Conservation and History, Museum of Cultural History, Vestfold County Council, Vest-Agder County Council and Norsk arkeologisk fond (Norwegian Archaeological Association). We are also very grateful to our external peer reviewers for taking the time to evaluate the articles of this book.

Our hope as editors is that the 14 contributions of this volume – while rooted in different traditions, using diverse methods and exploring eclectic material – nonetheless will provide the reader with a sense of current and forthcoming issues, debates and topics in Viking studies, and give insight into a new generation of ideas and approaches which will mark the years to come.

*Oslo, February 2014*

## References

Stefan Brink and Neil Price
2008. *The Viking World.* Routledge, London.
Graham-Campbell, James
1980. *The Viking World.* Frances Lincoln, London.
Gundersen, Ingar M. and Marianne Hem Eriksen (eds)
2010. På sporet av romersk jernalder: artikkelsamling fra romertidsseminaret på Isegran 23.–24. januar 2010. *Nicolay Skrifter 3*, Oslo.
Roesdahl, Else
1987. *Vikingernes verden: vikingerne hjemme og ude.* Gyldendal, København.
Simpson, Jacqueline
1980. *The Viking World.* Batsford, London.
Solberg, Annette, John Atle Stålesen and Christopher Prescott
2012. Neolitikum: nye resultater fra forskning og forvaltning. *Nicolay Skrifter 4*, Oslo.

*Chapter 1*

# From Ginnungagap to the Ragnarök. Archaeologies of the Viking worlds

*Neil Price*

*Abstract*

The *Viking Worlds* conference marks a landmark in interdisciplinary Viking studies, with the birth of what will hopefully become a regular open-access forum for all researchers – and especially those at an early stage of their careers – to exchange ideas and build collaborative projects. It also comes at a time when our perspectives on the Viking worlds (definitely in the plural) are changing dramatically. This paper briefly charts some milestones in that process, with a focus on Norse conceptions of the realities within which they understood themselves to move. These transformations in our understanding of the Viking Age will be considered primarily through their material reflection in the archaeological record: as ideas made manifest through social action, they are no longer marginalised as imaginative codas to settlement studies and art history, but co-exist with them as varied points of access to the Viking worlds in every sense of the term.

## Introduction

One thing must be admitted about the Vikings: they've come a remarkably long way in a relatively short space of time.

A hundred years ago, and for a century before that, they were the Nordic archetypes of choice. As blond supermen (definitely men) with horned helmets, they terrorised the world in their dragon ships, but somehow – strangely to us – in an admirable and heroic way. They were seen to have laid the foundations of modern Scandinavia and were pioneers of northern Christianity, though in a fashion that nonetheless permitted the remembrance of their excitingly savage paganism. Romance was blended with nationalism that manipulated a blurred sense of emergent identity, supposedly rooted in the deep past.

Eighty years ago, as Europe fell to fascism, these fictions of a racially pure North took on a still darker tone, and Viking studies would take decades to recover from the contamination. In the post-war years there was a resulting emphasis on data collection above interpretation, the latter being deemed still too risky, and our knowledge base grew while our understanding remained largely static. By the 1970s and '80s, the Vikings began to revive but in a new and more peaceable incarnation, their warrior stereotypes not exactly forgotten but instead giving way to a cosmopolitan population of traders, crafts-workers, travellers and poets.

Until about 25 years ago – with some notable exceptions – the notion of the female Viking was a contradiction in terms, and the unquestioningly androcentric view of the period took a very long time indeed to be engendered.

In more recent years, the violent Vikings have begun to return, albeit contextualised. We are also becoming increasingly interested in the contents of their minds as well as the substance of their actions, creations and landscapes.

A review of current perspectives on the early medieval Scandinavian world shows them to be numerous, pluralistic and in constant flux (Price 2005, 2014). Archaeologists share the field with historians, linguists, textual scholars, students of comparative religion, runologists, anthropologists, and specialists from the full spectrum of natural, physical and biological sciences (Brink and Price 2008). Very little has actually been left behind, and instead the traditional views of the Viking Age are being expanded and nuanced with other, more cognitive readings, which are in turn feeding back into new studies of materiality, of things.

To some extent it even comes as a surprise that the Viking Age is still a viable concept, because there have been serious challenges to that. The time of the Vikings has been dismissed as an imperial, nationalistic construct artificially combining ethnic identities that were in reality distinctive and separate (Svanberg 2003), and reconfigured as a mere component of a general Continental shift in economic strategies balanced against the Arab world (Hodges 2006). There is truth in this. The societies of what is now Scandinavia, from the mid-8th to the late 11th centuries CE, *were* indeed heterogeneous, varied and changeable, dynamic rather than static or monolithic. As we have seen, a millennium after their time those same societies *were* undoubtedly appropriated in the cause of imperialising agendas, and worse. But all this is to ignore the very real cultural (and linguistic) continuity from the Danish border to the high arctic, over and above regional variation. Similarly, we cannot overlook the genuinely significant social changes that took place during these three centuries that were so different from what came before and after. In acknowledging that the Vikings have fascinated a long line of colonial agents, from the Victorians to the Nazis, we must have the confidence to assert our own right to study them without being influenced or steered by past prejudice.

## Viking worlds

There is, however, one truly fundamental change. As scholars of the early medieval North we have had *a* 'Viking world' for a very long time, a singular concept perpetuated in numerous books bearing variants of that title, a trend to which I myself have certainly contributed. And this brings us to the present volume, and the meeting on which it is based. It was both a pleasure and privilege to deliver the keynote opening address in Oslo, at the start of the first Viking Worlds conference, and that pluralism – *worlds* – is important. Part of my purpose with this paper, deliberately retaining something of the flavour of my oral delivery from the day, is to explain just why I think this development is so timely.

Viking studies has been in great need of a regular, large-scale international forum for new research, open to all, in particular to provide a general platform for the work of younger, early career scholars rather than the Usual Suspects (a term I use with no disrespect as I suppose, alas, that I'm one of them). A glance at the list of authors for this volume reinforces the point, a new generation with new ideas: and what a lot there has been to learn about even in recent years, the timeframes of many of the contributors' PhDs.

In expanding our existing horizons, there has been a host of new work at familiar places, including the major projects underway at Kaupang (Skre and Stylegar 2004, and the ongoing *Norske Oldfunn* report series), Hedeby (Maixner 2012), Birka (Hedenstierna-Jonsson 2013), Oseberg and Gokstad (Bill and Daly 2012), at the Danish circular fortresses (Dobat 2013 and the forthcoming Aggersborg publications), and many key sites. Several of these also feature as the subject of specific, focussed research, such as the new pathologies emerging from the Norwegian ship burials (Holck 2009).

More generally, we may think of all the studies of coinage, hoarding and economy; of manufacturing and craftwork; of trade and economics. This is supported by research on material culture of every kind; all the studies of dating, origin, and movement. An emerging field, with links to more mainstream archaeological theory, is the exploration of networks and the agents within them, building on long-standing research into studies of acculturation, ethnicity and identity. Power and the nuanced study of state formation continue to occupy a central role in Viking scholarship, as does the ever-expanding interest in religion and spirituality, symbolism and the mind.

And then there's the new, *really* unexpected stuff. The papers in this book take up many of the developments of recent years and present the latest research, but it is worth pausing before some recent breakthroughs. Who would have thought we would learn that a significant proportion of Viking-Age men filed their teeth (Ahlström Arcini 2011; Arcini 2005)? Or that we could trace the movements of Norwegians through the genetic signals of the mice that came with their ships (Jones *et al.* 2012)? Or that the men in the Trelleborg cemetery largely came from Germany (Price *et al.* 2011)? Or that we would find a sacred hall decorated with sacrificial heads at Hofstaðir (Lucas 2009)? Or (one for me) that a sorceress had white facepaint like a geisha, a blue dress of translucent linen, and may have swallowed balls of human ash and fat (Pentz *et al.* 2009)? Or that we would find a Viking mass grave from Ridgeway Hill in Dorset, where isotopes tell us that a raiding party came from all over Scandinavia, including north of the arctic circle (Loe *et al.* 2014)? Or – perhaps the most spectacular of all – that two ship burials with more than 40 battle casualties would be found on an Estonian island, a site now dated to *c.* 750 and thus a pretty good candidate for the earliest archaeological evidence of properly Viking raids (Peets 2013)?

Some of the most intriguing discoveries are so recent that they are as-yet (July 2013) unpublished even in popular form, though with a strong online presence. The replica of Valhöll that was built on the royal terrace at Gamla Uppsala, with spears for doors; and the discovery that King Harald's Jelling was bigger than we ever expected.

Then there are the individual unparalleled finds, many of them emerging through new collaborations with metal detectorists. What are we to make of the figurine from Uppåkra (Helmbrecht 2013), that due to its specific iconography we really can identify as Völundr in his flying suit? And there are so many more of these kinds of things, feeding into a public interest that remains unabated, as we see in the success of the latest major international exhibition (Williams *et al.* 2013).

## Popular Vikings

Popular fascination takes other shapes too, one of which has been a surprisingly long time in coming: after years of waiting, the Vikings have finally made it to Hollywood in not too disgraceful a form. The American cable channel History has started drama programming alongside its documentaries, and in early 2013 launched the nine-part series *Vikings*, based (loosely) on the story of Ragnarr Loðbrók. Written by the creator of *The Tudors*, the series had a budget of $40 million – a fact that all Viking scholars would do well to digest, in view of the show's impact and the material on which its look is inevitably based, otherwise known as our work. A month after the first installment was screened, *Vikings* was renewed for another ten commissioned episodes, and we should take that very seriously indeed.

For the most part the series manages to avoid the traditional clichés. The material culture is pretty good, and some of the new Viking archaeology has made it in there, slipped past the stereotypes in a way that does more to inform the public than we might realise. By way of example, over the past few months I've been asked many, many times whether Vikings *really* wore what appears to be eyeliner and mascara, and the answer is, yes, they did. This is where our research makes a difference, however subtle, because someone involved with that series must have read the new commentaries on Ibrahim ibn Yaqub al-Tartushi, who wrote of both sexes' beauty being enhanced by eye make-up as he witnessed during his visit to Hedeby around 950. A small thing perhaps, but Vikings with guyliner would have been pretty much unthinkable 20 years ago, despite the fact that al-Tartushi's words were there for all to read.

Another positive aspect of the *Vikings* series is the presence of female warriors, and as major characters too. Nor are they ridiculous Wagnerian clones, but recognisable women with weapons. This admittedly plays to a stereotype of sorts (shield maidens and so on), but still, it is encouraging because if I had to isolate one single development of recent years more important than all the others, something I deliberately have not mentioned much so far, I would choose the slow recognition of women in the Viking Age.

## Women with weapons

In a sense, of course, women have always been topics of discussion in Viking research, especially in relation to their supposed receptiveness to Christianity and their presence in rune stone inscriptions. However, a far more prominent aspect of Viking-Age women was unfortunately another cliché, one of relative emancipation combined with a hint of warlike ferocity. The idea that Nordic women enjoyed greater social independence than most of their European sisters has been around almost as long as the myth of the Viking warrior, a kind of arc from the Noble Savage to the Noble Housewife. As with many stereotypes there is some core of fact in this, but it may owe more to the spirited female characters of the medieval sagas than to any Viking-Age reality, supported by the equally fantastical qualities attributed to supernatural warrior women such as the valkyries. In everyday life, notwithstanding the independent rights of divorce and the possibility of personal landholding and inheritance, it seemed that women were still socially subordinate to men. However, here as in other areas of Viking research, new vistas are opening up in our points of view.

On a serious scale the turnabout began with a number of fundamental works in the 1990s (*e.g.* Jesch 1991; Clover 1993; Jochens 1995, 1996), but over the last 15 years or so this research has developed incrementally in two directions. The first of these has seen new and nuanced studies of Viking-Age female lives and lifestyles (*e.g.* Magnúsdóttir 2001; Norrman 2008), while the second broadens this approach into wholly gendered readings of the period, including some surprising strands of enquiry and conclusion (*e.g.* Arwill-Nordbladh 1998; Back Danielsson 2007; Moen 2012). It is particularly encouraging that the works I cite as examples here are but the tip of the iceberg, and that an integrated concern for humanity regardless of sex is now the rule rather than the exception in Viking studies.

A particularly strong strand of this research has been the clear association of women with power, not just in the household but also in the context of ritual and the supernatural. With regard to the latter, it seems that women may have in fact played *the* leading role in magical and cultic communications between Viking-Age people and the invisible population of spirits and other beings with whom they believed they shared the world (*e.g.* Price 2002). Archaeologically, we could find these women in special categories of excavated data, such as the possible 'sorceress' graves that I discussed in my 2002 book. More importantly however, we find them in increasing numbers of remarkable female burials across the social spectrum, coming to light either as new discoveries or as newly acknowledged reassessments of earlier finds. Not least, these graves are now being interpreted in their own, unique terms rather than as reflections of male ritual (for example the extraordinary burial A505 from the cemetery at Trekroner-Grydehøj near Roskilde, Ulriksen 2011). These women appear in other media too, and may straddle the boundary between the human and otherworldly spheres, as in the strange seated figure on its chair from Lejre (Christensen 2009; with all respect to the Odinnic interpretations of that author, this figure wears clothes that in almost any circumstances would clearly be interpreted as female dress).

Most dramatically of all, we have a whole group of unusual finds that breathe new life into an old image – that of the woman with weapons. In the past ten years a number of metalwork mounts and pendants have been recovered through metal detection from sites in Denmark and England, depicting female figures either standing or mounted, bearing combinations of shields, helmets, swords and lances (see Williams *et al.* 2013). Their postures are precise, including such gestures as shields held against the body with the reverse, grip-side outwards, and clearly have meaning; the consistency of pose and iconography between widely-distributed figures also suggest that a specific motif was intended. Unique though these images are, they

*Fig. 1.1. The most exciting Viking-Age discovery of recent years? I think so. The armed female figurine, gilt silver and 3.4 cm tall, found at Hårby on Fyn, Denmark. Photo: John Lee, © National Museum of Denmark, used by kind permission.*

have been unexpectedly surpassed in clarity by what I would rate as the most exciting single Viking-Age find of recent years: a three-dimensional silver-gilt version of the armed, standing female, discovered at Hårby on Fyn, Denmark in December 2012 (Henriksen and Petersen 2013) I choose this as my only illustration, to stand as representative for what I personally see as the core of the new direction in Viking studies (Fig. 1.1).

Who are these warrior women? Almost everyone who has commented in print (I shall not name them) has come to the same, automatic conclusion: that they are valkyries. The reasons are obvious and understandable, but we must be careful. I have earlier warned about the dangers of easy attributions, the problems of labelling that which is in fact ambiguously anonymous (Price 2006). Yes, they may be valkyries; they may be *dísir* or *fylgjur* or goddesses or any number of other female figures who for whatever reason in whatever circumstances may have borne weapons and been thought worthy of meaningful depiction in metal. Not least, they may be human, and the thought of genuinely armed and armoured women should not surprise us: the numerous female burials that include weapons have in the past been interpreted with consistent bias, and there are even independent eye-witness accounts of Scandinavian women fighting on the battlefield in the 970s (Price 2002: ch. 6). The figures may be warrior women of fact and not fantasy. What *is* clear is that the image of female fighters is not an invention of the medieval saga-writers and poets – it was definitely, unequivocally *there* in the Viking mind. After all this time, at last, we really do have female Vikings.

## Vikings and strangers

That is a good image to have in our thoughts, because I suppose what I'm really trying to do in this introduction is convey how *different* I think the Vikings have become in the last couple of decades. They are no longer like the people we used to study; they are certainly no longer the people I was taught about at college. They have grown. They have gained more depth and more resolution.

This part is hard to explain. I think this difference, this strangeness, also returns to the Vikings something that I believe they possessed in their own lifetimes, in their interactions with peoples other than themselves (and let us be clear, those interactions are one of the main things that characterise this time we call the Viking Age). Interestingly – and I have no idea whether readers will agree with this – I think that their contemporaries perhaps knew or suspected this strangeness long before we did. Part of the familiar 'shock and awe' attitude to the raids comes to us through the Christian chroniclers and their evident fear of the Vikings – a fear prompted, we are usually told, by their paganism (the violence itself can hardly have been novel in the 8th century). I can see that, of course, but what do we mean by 'paganism'?

I will not rehearse the arguments of the last decade, other than to say that it is not often now we speak of a pre-Christian Viking 'religion' at all – it was far more than that: a total view of the world, a complete, and very different, understanding of the nature of reality itself (*e.g.* Schjødt 2012). *That* was what the Vikings' victims were afraid of, and it is also what we are starting to really get to grips with. But there is something more.

I think that fear of the Vikings not only arose because they were so different, but because in that difference lay some horribly unnerving kind of familiarity. The Anglo-Saxons, for example, knew that this Viking world-view was not so far removed from what theirs had been not so long before, and maybe, under the surface, still was – and I think that realization frightened them. The Vikings were not only conventionally terrifying, they were also a dark mirror held up to the image of what the English needed to believe themselves to be. The same probably applied to the Franks and the other Continental peoples.

Can we recapture that feeling? A century or so ago, it was easier. You can see it in the writings of the more enlightened colonialists, for all the unpleasant freight that they carry today. Here's Joseph Conrad in his *Heart of Darkness,* scaring himself with what he thought he saw on a journey up the Congo, as the local tribes danced and sang on the river bank:

> [...] but if you were man enough you would admit to yourself that there was in you just the faintest trace of a response to the terrible frankness of that noise, a dim suspicion of there being a meaning in it which you – you so remote from the night of first ages – could comprehend [...]. (Conrad 2002 [1902]: 40–41, based on his journey of 1890, as detailed in *The Congo Diary* and *Up-river Book* (Conrad 2002 [1890])

Over more than two decades of research into the Viking mind, I've become more than ever convinced (with all the intellectual pitfalls thus implied) that there was a similarly dislocating sense of unreality about the Vikings *in their time*, to their contemporaries. And to be clear, not just the 'proper', raiding kind of Vikings, but all of them, everyone from 'thereabouts' who shared some aspect of that understanding of the world.

With some crucial implications for our archaeological possibilities of access, much of that world-view was concerned with the dead, about what it meant to *be* dead, in relation to what it meant to be alive. Returning again to the cognitive studies I have addressed before, this links productively to all the ongoing work on mortuary behaviour, on symbolic landscapes, on ritual sites, on the numinous qualities of the everyday world, and the meaning content of material culture, all of it. And that 'all of it' brings back the rest of archaeology, the settlements, the urban processes, the state formation, the systems of economic exchange and production – they are 'all of it' too. We are rediscovering that Viking difference.

The reconstruction drawings of Viking warriors produced today are very rarely prone to the same stereotypes as once were common. Enough about dress and equipment is known, and published in accessible form, for artists to create a pretty good image of the material culture. There are no horned helmets, no rubbish: such pictures generally represent a fairly solid guess as to what those monks of Lindisfarne really saw on 8 June 793. But what has changed, for us, is that we now have a very different understanding of what was in these Vikings' heads, and in the heads of their contemporaries at home.

And the point is that it was *all* in there: from the creation, from the very beginnings in Ginnungagap, the ultimate void, all the way to the Ragnarök, the ice and fire at the end ('a *real* end, *the* end' as rightly emphasised in A. S. Byatt's wonderful new retelling from 2011). From the beginning to the end of all the Viking worlds really is our new span of research – all that this encompassed is now on the table (or in the lab, or in the trench) for us to work on. Think of all the places that can lead, how interconnected it all is.

Never before have Viking studies occupied a bigger room, and the authors setting out their ideas in the following pages are making themselves at home. Here's to them.

*Acknowledgements*

Thanks to Marianne Hem Eriksen, Unn Pedersen and the organising committee of *Viking Worlds* for their kind invitation to the conference and this volume. I wish future organisers every success in ensuring the regular and fruitful continuation of this important initiative.

*References*

Ahlström Arcini, Caroline
2011. *The Viking's Grim Grin.* Fornsalen, Visby.

Arcini, Caroline
2005. The Vikings bare their filed teeth. *American Journal of Physical Anthropology* 128(4): 727–733.

Arwill-Nordbladh, Elisabeth
1998. *Genuskonstruktioner i Nordisk Vikingatid: Förr och Nu.* Göteborg University, Göteborg.

Back Danielsson, Ing-Marie
2007. *Masking Moments: the Transitions of Bodies and Beings in Late Iron Age Scandinavia.* Stockholm University, Stockholm.

Bill, Jan and Aoife Daly
2012. The plundering of the ship graves from Oseberg and Gokstad: an example of power politics? *Antiquity* 86: 808–824.

Brink, Stefan and Neil Price (editors)
2008. *The Viking World.* Routledge, London.

Byatt, Antonia S.
2011. *Ragnarok: the End of the Gods.* Canongate, Edinburgh.

Christensen, Tom
2009. Odin fra Lejre. *ROMU* 2009: 7–25.

Clover, Carol
1993. Regardless of sex: men, women and power in early northern Europe. *Speculum* 68: 363–387.

Conrad, Joseph
2002. [1890, 1902] *Heart of Darkness* with *The Congo Diary* and *Up-river Book.* Hesperus, London.

Dobat, Andres (editor)
2013. *Kongens borg: rapport over undersøgelserne 2007–2010.* Jysk Arkæologisk Selskab, Aarhus.

Hedenstierna-Jonson, Charlotte (editor)
2013. *Birka nu: pågående forskning kring världsarvet Birka-Hovgården.* Historiska Museet, Stockholm.

Helmbrecht, Michaela
2013. Smeden, der fløj. *Skalk* 3: 3–7.

Henriksen, Mogens Bo and Peter Vang Petersen
2013. Valkyriefund. *Skalk* 2: 3–10.

Hodges, Richard
2006. *Goodbye to the Vikings? Re-reading Early Medieval Archaeology.* Duckworth, London.

Holck, Per
2009. *Skjelettene fra Gokstad- og Osebergskipet.* Oslo University, Oslo.

Jesch, Judith
1991. *Women in the Viking Age.* Boydell, Woodbridge.

Jochens, Jenny
1995. *Women in Old Norse Society.* Cornell University Press, Ithaca, NY.
1996. *Old Norse Images of Women.* University of Pennsylvania Press, Philadelphia.

Jones, E. P., K. Skirnisson, T. H. McGovern, M. T. P. Gilbert, E. Willerslev and J. B. Searle.
2012. Fellow travellers: A concordance of colonization patterns between mice and men in the North Atlantic region. *BMC Evolutionary Biology* 12: 35.

Loe, L., A. Boyle, H. Webb and D. Score
2014. *'Given to the Ground': A Viking Age Mass Grave on Ridgway Hill, Weymouth.* Oxford Archaeology and Dorset Natural History and Archaeological Society, Oxford.
Lucas, Gavin
2009. *Hofstaðir: Excavations of a Viking Age Feasting Hall in North-Eastern Iceland.* Institute of Archaeology, Reykjavík.
Magnúsdóttir, Auður
2001. *Frillor och Fruar: Politik och Samlevnad på Island 1120–1400.* Göteborg University, Göteborg.
Maixner, Birgit
2012. *Haithabu: Fernhandelszentrum zwischen den Welten.* 2nd ed. Wikinger Museum Haithabu, Schleswig.
Moen, Marianne
2012. *The Gendered Landscape: a Discussion on Gender, Status and Power in the Norwegian Viking Age.* Archaeopress, Oxford.
Norrman, Lena
2008. *Viking Women: the Narrative Voice in Woven Tapestries.* Cambria Press, Amherst, NY.
Peets, Jüri
2013. Salme ship burials. *Current World Archaeology* 58: 18–24.
Pentz, Peter, Maria Panum Baastrup, Sabine Karg and Ulla Mannering
2009. Kong Haralds vølve. *Nationalmuseets Arbejdsmark* 2009: 215–233.
Price, Neil
2002. *The Viking Way: Religion and War in Late Iron Age Scandinavia.* Uppsala University Press, Uppsala.
2005. Cognition, Culture and Context: Observations on the 'New' Viking Archaeology. In *Viking and Norse in the North Atlantic. Select Papers from the Proceedings of the Fourteenth Viking Congress, Tórshavn, 19–30 July 2001*, edited by Símon Arge and Andreas Mortensen, pp. 375–382. Føroya Fróðskaparfelag, Tórshavn.
2006. What's in a name? An archaeological identity crisis for the Norse gods (and some of their friends). In *Old Norse religion in long-term perspectives*, edited by Anders Andrén, Kristina Jennbert and Catharina Raudvere, pp. 179–183. Nordic Academic Press, Lund.
2014. Viking Archaeology in the 21st century. In *40 Years of Medieval Archaeology*, edited by Mette Kristiansen, Else Roesdahl and James Graham-Campbell. Aarhus University Press, Aarhus.
Price, T. Douglas, Karin M. Frei, Andres S. Dobat, Niels Lynnerup and Pia Bennike
2011. Who was in Harald Bluetooth's army? Strontium isotope investigation of the cemetery at the Viking Age fortress of Trelleborg, Denmark. *Antiquity* 85: 476–489.
Schjødt, Jens Peter
2012. Reflections on aims and methods in the study of Old Norse religion. In *More than Mythology. Narratives, Ritual Practices and Regional Distribution in pre-Christian Scandinavian Religions*, edited by Catharina Raudvere and Jens Peter Schjødt, pp. 13–46. Nordic Academic Press, Lund.
Skre, Dagfinn and Frans-Arne Stylegar
2004. *Kaupang: the Viking Town.* Oslo University, Oslo.
Svanberg, Fredrik
2003. *Decolonizing the Viking Age.* 2 vols. Stockholm, Almqvist and Wiksell.
Ulriksen, Jens
2011. Spor af begravelseritualer i jordfæstegrave i vikingetidens Danmark. *KUML* 2011: 161–245.
Williams, Gareth, Peter Pentz and Mattias Wemhoff (editors)
2013. *Viking.* National Museum of Denmark, Copenhagen.

# PART I

# REAL AND IDEAL SPACES

*Chapter 2*

# Powerful space. The Iron-Age hall and its development during the Viking Age

*Lydia Carstens*

*Abstract*

The article is about the hall: A building from the Scandinavian Iron Age which is frequently mentioned as ON 'hǫll' in medieval written sources. Many articles have been written about the subject, and an archaeological definition was established in the 1990s. Since then many buildings have been unearthed, while the definition has remained unchanged. Other sources, such as word etymology, have been largely ignored, which has led to a rather generalized picture of Iron-Age halls.

The aim of this article is to present a new, comprehensive definition of the Iron-Age hall which is based on a comparison of the archaeological finds to word etymology and medieval literature. The second aim is to find out if the concept of the hall remained unmodified during all of the Scandinavian Iron Age, or if some changes in hall fashion could be observed. Special attention is directed toward the Viking Age – a period that saw important societal changes.

## Prologue

Terms like 'king', but also 'nobility' and 'lordship' are rather problematic in the Scandinavian Iron Age, because it is still a matter of debate when king and royalty were introduced. Nevertheless the word 'king' (ON *'konungr'*) occurred on several runic inscriptions from the Viking Age (*e.g.* stones from Adelsö or Hedeby), which means that the most influential magnates of the Viking Age wanted to be memorialized as kings. They were the people who built the halls as tools of self-display. How closely this 'king' was comparable to other kings of the same period in different regions is not the topic of this article.

## Introduction

An ambassador from the South would need at least a second glance to distinguish the Viking king's home from any rural farmstead in the North. In their outer appearance both were more or less large wooden buildings, accompanied by minor huts and houses, eventually surrounded by a fence. The most obvious difference was the length of the royal building and its exclusive usage. Using the traditional building fashion of the three-aisled longhouse, halls were fully developed in the Roman Iron Age and they remained until the Middle Ages, when the royal seats of power moved into the newly established towns. There the stone built multi-storey halls were reminiscent more of the continental seats of power than their wooden predecessors, which formed the cultural conscience of the Scandinavian elite for more than 1000 years.

This article is a very abridged study of some aspects from a larger multidisciplinary research project about the Iron-Age halls, which will be fully published in the near future (Carstens in prep.). The results are based on a close investigation of all hall findings from Scandinavia (including Iceland and Greenland) which have been published so far. Seventy-five different places have been studied, covering the time frame from the earliest so-called Proto-halls (Løken 2001) of the Pre-Roman Iron Age (*e.g.* Forsand/N) to the medieval stone built halls of the 13th century (*e.g.* Bergen/N) and the so-called Greenlandic chieftains halls of the 13th and 14th century (*e.g.* Brattahlid/G). This makes the project one of the largest-scale comparative analyses of hall buildings to date. The aim of the project has been to summarize the current state of research, to review and perhaps even alter the common hall definition and to compare the archaeological findings with linguistic and literal evidence.

This article will use the extensive abovementioned material as the basis of the project, but can only concentrate on two main questions: The basic question has to be 'What is a hall?' and will result in a new and comprehensive list of hall indicators. The second question is about the development of the hall and asks if halls remain unchanged during the whole period. According to the theme of this volume, emphasis will be laid on the Viking-Age development.

### Some basic information about halls

Iron-Age halls are a prominent field of research among archaeologists and a lot of work has been carried out on the subject. The investigation of hall-like buildings is closely associated with what is known as central-place archaeology, which follows earlier geographical research (Christaller 1933) in an attempt to demonstrate the existence of networks of neighboring seats of power (Lund Hansen 2001; Steuer 2007). The excavation of a hall of the late Roman period at Gudme in Denmark (Østergaard Sørensen 1994, 2010) and, simultaneously, halls of the 5th–10th century at Borg in northern Norway (Fig. 2.1; Stamsø Munch *et al.* 2003) in the late 1980s and early 1990s gave renewed impetus for a new wave of central-place research (see *e.g.* Böhme 2001; Callmer 1997; Näsman 2011). Large-scale excavations and increasing use of the metal detector has led to several new discoveries in the last 20 years, and there has also been a renewal of interest in the historically known princely residences like Gamla Uppsala (Ljungkvist *et al.* 2011) and Lejre (Christensen 2010). Numerous works (mostly articles and conference proceedings) have been published, but most of them concentrate on individual find spots. Curiously enough, comprehensive studies, comparative analyses and new definitions are still lacking.

*Fig. 2.1. The reconstructed hall in Borg/Norway. Photo: © Lydia Carstens.*

## *Defining the hall*

The currently used definition of the hall was brought up by the archaeologist Frands Herschend in 1993, who also made several in-depth studies of the Iron-Age hall in general (*e.g.* Herschend 1993, 1997, 1999). According to him, the halls belonged to big farms, consisted of one room with a minimum of posts, were singled out by their position on the farm, their hearths were not used for cooking or for handicraft and the artifacts found in the house had to be different from those in the dwelling part of the house or the rest of the farm (Herschend 1999: 415). Today more than 70 so-called halls have been excavated in Scandinavia, but only a few of them to the level of detail that the abovementioned criteria could be tested properly. In practice, it was mainly the length which led scholars to label a freshly excavated building as a hall. This has caused some reasonable criticism in recent years, as it has been convincingly argued that not every large house necessarily had to be a hall (Andersson 2001; Norr 2006). There is a need for an extension of the current hall definition, which should be based on concrete archaeological findings.

I would therefore like to propose a list of criteria which extend Herschend's definition. The list is divided into three parts (the building, the place and the objects) and it goes without saying that not all criteria have to be fulfilled in every single case. There were no DIN standards and no building authorities, but there was some kind of consensus on how to build a proper residence. This seemed to include the following criteria, which were of course also depending on personal taste as well as on the terrain, the surrounding area and the amount of resources. The list of criteria is made up on the basis of all the 75 Scandinavian hall findings from the Roman Iron Age to the Middle Ages. The findings are not evenly distributed (Sweden: 34, Norway: 24, Denmark: 12, Greenland: 4, Iceland: 1) and the medieval finds have turned out to be slightly different from the average halls, which makes this list most suitable for the findings from the 3rd to the 11th century. The development of the hall and changes of hall customs will therefore be discussed separately later in this article.

### *A new list of criteria*

1. The building itself: Appearance and conception
   a. Of unusual length (30–50 m)
   b. Without a byre (exceptions because of hard weather conditions possible, which increases the length of the building even further, *e.g.* Borg/N)
   c. Wide internal space (indicated by a larger space between the posts)
   d. More than two entrances and/or unusually broad entrances
   e. Large central fireplace (often extended by one or two minor cooking pits at the gable ends of the building)
   f. Of unusual height (indicated by massive posts)
2. The place: Location and surrounding
   a. Part of a settlement complex
   b. Located in an elevated position (either on a natural or a man-made plateau overlooking the settlement)
   c. Close to fresh water
   d. Overlooking land and sea routes
   e. Not directly on the coast
   f. Places for cultic worship close by
   g. Large grave mounds (often from the Bronze Age) or notably rich graves (often from older periods)
   h. Heaps of fire cracked stones and several large open-air fireplaces
   i. Workshop area with high status crafting (*e.g.* fine metal, glass, gemstone)
   j. Special place names (often theophorical)
3. Finds and objects
   a. Either very exclusive finds or no finds at all (cleansing)
   b. Traces of cultic worship (*e.g.* amulets, depositions, a smaller 'cult house' or fenced cultic area)
   c. High status artifacts, especially glass and fine metal (*e.g.* small gold foils)
   d. Depositions in connection to the posts
   e. A special way of handling the building after the end of its use (*e.g.* deposition of artifacts, scattered bones, sealing with clay, burning, removal of posts)

Interestingly, neither the quality of arable land nor the orientation of the building seemed to be important for the choice of a suitable location for a hall. The orientation followed the shape of the chosen ridge, but if possible an east–west orientation was preferred. The same counted for arable land, which was preferred but not absolutely necessary.

The abovementioned characteristics give the impression that the Iron-Age hall was part of an older building tradition, which was complemented by several elements to support a distinct message. In most illiterate societies (apart from shorter runic inscriptions, which, at least before the Viking Age, were not meant for everyday communication, there are no hints that the Iron-Age people were literate in larger scale) messages were spread with the help of visible monuments like, for example, large grave mounds. With their distinct features and the long-term perspective it seems as if halls were also part of this monumental communication system. Judging from the archaeological remains, Iron-Age halls can be interpreted as statements of power. The most obvious sign of this was their elevated position: The halls were singled out from the settlement, they were visibly separated by this special location and they were visually exalted (*e.g.* Gamla Uppsala/S). Transferred into social terms this would mean that the owners of the building saw themselves in a higher social position than everyone else. Such a sign of power and dominance was not only visible to the locals but to everyone who visited. Because most of the halls were visible from important sea and land routes, they were also marks of power and ownership for foreigners and possible raiders.

The height contributed to the grand impression and supported the exalted and dominant placement of the building. Along with the large internal space between the posts, the height created an even larger room than expected from the outside (large internal space *e.g.* in Tissø/Dk, large posts *e.g.* in Borg/N). Such a room might have made the same impression as a cathedral, where height, grandness and space were also of special importance. It made the building visible and created a very special atmosphere, where a visitor might feel smaller than he actually was. A grand room appeared to be intimidating especially to people accustomed to much smaller homes and buildings, as the retainers usually were.

Other features were similar to those in the later conception of a church, such as the many entrances of the hall. As an example the typical Norwegian Viking-Age longhouse had one or two entrances placed on the long walls (Eriksen 2013), while churches had different entrances for men, women, the ruler and the priest. It might be possible that the many entrances of the hall served a similar purpose. It was perhaps part of the 'entrance ritual' that the hall owner used a different entrance than his retainers and possibly guests had to use another entrance as well (see also Eriksen this volume on the ritualisation of doors). We can only speculate about the function of the various entrances, but excavation plans make it plain that several entrances lead to one large room – this must have had some kind of meaning. In the cold and windy North, every additional door made it more difficult to keep up the temperature in the room.

Feasting, indicated by the remains of glass beakers and large quantities of animal bone, was an important social act between the ruler and his retinue (*e.g.* Enright 1988; Vierck 1991), but was also used to welcome and introduce foreigners and possible allies. It was an act of hospitality, but also a way of political governance. Such feasts were accompanied by the exchange of gifts, and some precious foreign artifacts in the halls might have functioned as gifts either for the ruler himself or for his retinue (Lönnroth 1997). But they might also reflect war booty and precious items, which have been part of some sort of sacrifice – to the gods or to the ruler himself. We do not know the relationship between feasting remains and the precious foreign or the obviously cultic artifacts (*'guldgubber'*, amulets, *etc.*), but both events – if they should be seen separately – were carried out in the hall. It is highly possible that some sort of cultic activity followed or was even part of a feast.

One of Herschend's hall criteria was the fireplace, which was not used for cooking. It is difficult to find traces of cooking (*e.g.* scattered animal bones) because the fireplaces might have been cleansed afterwards or the cooking had not left visible traces at all. They also would have been cleared out regularly to remove the build-up of ashes, which may have been dumped outside. A possible indication for the lack of cooking in the hall might be the number of fireplaces: Usually the hall has one central long fire and additional round fire pits at one or both ends of the hall. The central long fire in the middle might have been solely used for light and heating, while the smaller fire places were used for cooking. They were probably separated from the main feasting room in order to avoid smoke and stench. Stench was one of the reasons why animals were no longer accommodated in the building. But it was also a sign of wealth if the heat of the animals was not needed to keep the large house warm. And, of course, it was also a sign of prosperity that all of the space could be used for feasts and representation.

The traces of feasting activities in the house might also explain the many open-air fireplaces and heaps of fire cracked stones outside, which were discovered at many hall sites all over Scandinavia (*e.g.* in Åker/N, Tissø/Dk or Uppåkra/S). These might also derive from such feasts: Guests might have brought their retinue with them, and if there was not enough space in the hall, or if it was only reserved for the most important followers, the guest's retinue could be served and entertained outside. The retinue of guests as well as visitors for annual cultic feasts had to camp outside the hall where they needed food, light and warmth.

The evidence for cultic worship is an important hall feature. Either there are traces of additional buildings (*e.g.* Gudme/Dk, Uppåkra/S), a fenced area (Tissø/Dk, Toftegård/Dk), a cultic area close by (Helgö/S, Lunda/S) or depositions of bones, amulets and other kinds of objects indicating cult activity. It becomes obvious that the ruler had some affiliation to the cult, and even if he was not the cult leader himself, his contacts to the gods were obvious: It was on his property that the gods were worshipped, and it was him who could order and host cultic events. But it was also his property to which people had to gain access if they wanted to use the consecrated areas, and it was he who could give permission for that or reject it. With the cult so close to the ruler's residence, his power increased considerably.

Specialized craftsmen were probably there mainly because the ruler with his armed retinue could guarantee protection for the precious raw materials. But it was also the ruler who was rich enough to purchase the raw materials and to order the artifacts. The craftsmen in return had the ability to form objects which the ruler needed to display his power, and they might also have played some role in the cultic aspect of the hall (Pesch 2012). They could produce the ruler's regalia, his weapons and the gifts, which he handed over to create bonds and allies.

In connection to large grave mounds and older richly furnished graves, the owner of the hall positioned himself among great ancestors and made plain his claim to land and power. With the large and eye-catching grave mounds, the hall stood in a line of monumental self-display, which was, among others, remarkably implemented in Gamla Uppsala (Fig. 2.2).

*Fig. 2.2. The restored Håkonshallen in Bergen, built in the 13th century. Photo: © Lydia Carstens.*

### The meaning of the hall – and some literary examples

To close this survey of hall features, it is interesting to note that most of the halls received special treatment after their abandonment. The long life of the halls is part of their composition idea – they were intentionally built to last – and some lasted for a remarkable period (Söderberg 2003: Järrestad/S with 250 years). This suggested stability, ruling continuity and identity for the locals and the retainers (Ängeby 1999). But some halls were abandoned and some suffered one or even several attacks, which is indicated by the high number of burned halls (Bejsebakken/Dk, Gamla Uppsala/S, Högom/S). Some were restored after the fire (Valum/N) while others were not (Uppåkra/S) – at least not directly on the spot. The treatment of the older hall from Uppåkra makes it clear that the hall burning was a targeted act to harm the ruler and not the settlement itself: The hall burned down, while the settlement itself and the 'cult house', which was only some metres away from the burning hall, remained unharmed (Larsson and Söderberg 2012). The act of burning the hall might have a very special meaning; an explanation for this might be preserved in the medieval mythological poems: Hall burnings often occur in the poems of the Poetic Edda (12th century, Iceland) and they usually describe the end of a king's dynasty and his family's rule (see *e.g.* the poem *Atlakvíða*). Even one hall of the Norse Gods is set alight (see the poem *Lokasenna*), which among others marks the beginning of *Ragnarǫkr*, the world's demise. But when the world rises again it is centered on the hall called *Gimlé*, a hall that

*Fig. 2.3. The monumental mounds in Gamla Uppsala and the church today. The halls are situated on the plateaus behind the church and might have been visible from this direction as well. Photo: © Lydia Carstens.*

cannot burn (see the poem *Vǫluspá*). Hence it is the undestroyed hall that makes up the picture of eternal paradise in the North.

So it was probably not by accident that a burned hall was restored at Lejre using exactly the same post holes as the old building (Christensen 1991). The rebuilders probably tried to show that nothing had happened – that the hall and, therewith, the ruler stood as before. If the burning of the hall in Uppåkra would have been an 'ordinary' attack on the settlement as a whole, all buildings would have shown traces of burning. But it was only the hall, and additionally three dead were left unburied in the ruins, while the settlement continued on right beside it. At least they might have been buried properly, unless somebody wanted to make an example: Here the ruling family might have suffered a defeat and new rulers built a new hall in Uppåkra, while they continued to use the cult building and the settlement.

In a society that was so dependent on the visual effects of monuments, halls can be conceived of as monuments as well as full of symbolic meaning. It is obvious that the hall was chosen as a strong symbol for power. If the hall stood and prospered, so did its owner. If the hall was targeted and destroyed, the ruler tried to restore it on the spot. If he was defeated the ruins were left as a mark of failure. In some cases halls were even buried under a layer of burned clay and bones (Gamla Uppsala/S), and sometimes bones were scattered over the remains (Åker/N, Alby/S, Ströja/S). The hall in Högom was actually covered with a large mound. Halls were the foremost representations of the claim to rule: The possession of a hall and the grandness of it indicated the ability of its owner. The king without the ability to defend his hall was no longer strong enough to rule his land; a burned hall equaled a defeated king.

### The Viking Age: Continuity or change?

The abovementioned hall criteria and the interpretations implying a symbolic and monumental use of the hall were made on the basis of the study of 75 halls from all over Scandinavia and from the whole Scandinavian Iron Age. This period lasted for a millennium. During this period several important changes took place in the North: The period of war booty sacrifices ended, the runic alphabet was introduced and changed considerably during the Migration period, the decline of the Roman empire and the rise of the Frankish and Ottoman kings opened new contacts and trading partners, the discoveries and land-taking in the east and west opened the trade even further, the change of belief and the introduction of a written law, and finally, the consolidation of the three Scandinavian kingdoms under powerful sole ruling kings are only some of the great events that took place. It is unlikely that something which is so important and so close to power remained unchanged during all these processes. I would therefore like to take a look into the Viking-Age development of halls, to see if the halls were elements of continuity throughout the period or if they were somewhat altered and affected during the cause of events.

The obvious change in the hall tradition is marked by the end of the Viking Age, when the wooden king's hall disappeared (about a possible continuity of hall features into the Middle Ages see Gansum 2008). At this stage the newly established kingdoms were governed from royal residences in the new towns. These medieval residences often contained a hall as well, which, according to continental fashion, was now part of the stone built multi-storey residential building (in most cases the hall was situated on the first floor, see *e.g.* Håkonshallen in Bergen (Fig. 2.3)). While the interior might have been quite similar to the wooden halls, the outward appearance was not. Now it was the castle which represented the social status of its owner: Large towers, defensive works and the church were now the eye-catching factors of noble self-display from the outside, while the hall was only a representative room and only seen by those who were able to access the castle.

Today, 16 halls are known from the Viking Age, some of them succeeding older halls (Alby/S, Bejsebakken/Dk, Borg/N, Gamla Uppsala/S, Järrestad/S, Lejre/Dk, Sanda/S, Tissø/Dk, Uppåkra/S), and some of them newly established (Åker/N, Boeslunde/Dk, Fornsigtuna/S, Lisbjerg/Dk, Skiringssal/N, Slöinge/S, Toftegård/Dk). This number reflects the current state of research. More Viking-Age halls might be detected in the future, older halls might be re-dated, and some Viking-Age halls might never be found, because they are covered by modern structures (*e.g.* Alrekstaðir in Bergen, Hlaðir in Trondheim *etc.*). Nevertheless, comparing them with the characteristics of earlier halls in Scandinavia leads to the result that halls seem to become more and more uniform over time. In the Viking Age *all* halls were raised on elevated positions. The most outstanding halls (Gamla Uppsala/S,

*Fig. 2.4. A detail from the reconstructed hall in Borg/Norway. Photo: © Lydia Carstens.*

Lejre/Dk, Tissø/Dk, Uppåkra/S) seem to be fixed around 50 m in length during the entire Viking Age, while in other places the average length of the building increased from 34 m in the 8th century to 40 m in the 9th century, and 45 m in the 10th century. Most of the above mentioned characteristics count for the Viking-Age halls as well, but three things seem to change:

1. A smaller proportion (¼ instead of almost ½) burned down
2. The cultic aspect seems to grow stronger
3. Workshops become even more important

The reduced number of burned halls in the Viking Age could be a sign of a less violent period than the centuries before. Considering the smaller number of halls on the whole it could as well be a first sign of consolidation, where power structures were starting to become fixed and established. In the centuries before, new chieftains arose constantly with their own hall and a claim for power. These claims caused struggles and violent attacks, which often resulted in the burning of the opponent's hall. While the Viking-Age raiders caused trouble elsewhere, their homelands seem to become less violent and more stable, probably through stabilized power structures, fewer opponents and strong alliances.

In all Viking-Age halls, apart from Boeslunde/Dk, either traces of a possible cultic worship in or directly beside the hall were physically recorded (*e.g.* grounded bones, folded weapons), or the cultic function was ascribed to them in medieval written sources (Gamla Uppsala/S, Fornsigtuna/S). Six out of the eight known cult houses that were found beside halls are from the Viking Age (Järrestad/S, Lejre/Dk, Sanda/S, Tissø/Dk, Toftegård/Dk, Uppåkra/S [+ Lunda/S and Gudme/Dk]). It seems as if the cult became more and more tied to the place in which the secular power was already based, a development which was firstly proposed by Fabech in 1991 and described in detail by Jørgensen in 2009. The cultic aspects seem to become more important over the course of time and culminate in church buildings, which were often donated by magnates as a sign of piety and power (see *e.g.* Anglert 1989). Ruler and religion united, probably influenced by the Continent, where the church supported the kings and the king's power increased as he was claimed to be chosen by God.

There is no Viking-Age hall without a workshop area (except for the Alby hall, which is only preliminarily published), and all other Viking-Age halls show evidence for fine metal workshops. Moulds and casting debris were also found in the halls themselves, suggesting that some of the metal working was carried out inside – either as work under the watchful eyes of the ruler or perhaps even as some sort of entertainment or for cultic purposes (see Blankenfeldt and Pesch 2012). While in former times craft specialists often seem to visit the ruler and work in the vicinity of his hall, in the Viking Age every ruler seemed to have his own mastersmith. The role of the smith became more important when the king needed artifacts of self-display to legitimate his power. Old symbols were slowly abandoned, the forefathers' grave mounds with rich gifts lost their importance and new ways of remembrance were introduced (*e.g.* thousands of memorial rune stones, see Klos 2009). The importance of the mastersmith for the ruling dynasty is mirrored by Norse Mythology (*e.g.* the poem *Vǫluspá*), in which the gods themselves were able to work metal but were nevertheless dependent upon the skillful dwarf smiths to make their most precious artifacts (Carstens 2012). The increasingly fine metalwork in and around the hall is another hint of the emergence of a stable ruling dynasty, which enlarged its retinue with the skillful mastersmith.

When compared to older halls these differences point toward an increasing concentration of various social aspects around the seats of power. More and more actions apart from political governance and representation such as religious service, craftsmanship, and economy became centered on the hall. The ruler became more and more engaged in different spheres and increased his demand for absolute control and power.

But it is important to emphasize that although many things changed during the Viking Age, the buildings themselves stayed almost the same. Scandinavian longhouses date back to the transition between the Stone and the Bronze Age (*e.g.* Carlie *et al.* 2005), and halls were founded on the basis of these rural dwellings. The oblong shape of the house, posts carrying the roof, and wood as the foremost building material were traditional building features. Changes to these traditions took place because representation and prestige started to take precedence over practical considerations. The use of the traditional longhouse instead of a new type of residential building indicates that past traditions were important anchors in times of change.

## The etymology of '*hǫll*' and '*salr*'

Another hint of change during the Viking Age is the word 'hall' itself. In the Old Norse language it appeared as *'hǫll'* – the close relation to our modern word is obvious. A closer look into the history of the Old Norse word reveals that it seems to be a rather young term. The first mention was the name *Valhǫll* in Eyvindr skáldaspillir Finnsson's poem *Hákonarmál* from 961 (see the Skaldic project homepage [http://abdn.ac.uk/skaldic/db.php] for more information, all dating were taken from their publications). Only a few other sources contain the word in the 10th and 11th centuries, while it appears more frequently from the 12th century onward. Interestingly, the term *'hǫll'* has a counterpart with exactly the same meaning, namely the word *'salr'*. In some cases both words occur in the same story describing exactly the same building. The only difference is that *salr* is mostly used in poetry, while *hǫll* was used in the prose sections. This indicates *salr* to be the older term. The poetical form of the poems was important: As skaldic verse was based on alliteration and a fixed number of syllables per verse, words could not be easily replaced. Therefore, the skaldic language retained ancient terms, while the prose text made use of the words which were common in the times of text transmission.

This idea is further supported by the fact that the earliest sources for the Old Norse language use *salr*, while *hǫll* is noticeably absent: This is true for runic inscriptions as well as place names. A *salr* is mentioned as *'salagastiR'* (guest of the hall) on the Migration-period stone from Berga in Sweden (Sö 24) and as *'salhaugr'* (the hall barrow) on the 10th century Danish stone from Snoldelev (DR 248). In place names *salr* is spread all over Scandinavia (*e.g.* Upp-sala, On-sala, Sala), while *hǫll* is not even recorded. Furthermore, *salr* was used in the oldest known skaldic poem *Ragnarsdrápa* by Bragi Boddason from the 9th century, and in several other early poems as well. The dwellings of all Norse gods except Oðinn were called *salr*.

The complicated deliverance of Old Norse texts leads to an apparent contemporaneous use of both *hǫll* and *salr*, but a closer investigation reveals a change of words during the Viking Age. In the time of saga writing, *salr* was already out of fashion and only used as part of the skaldic language to keep the alliteration. During the Viking Age, an increasing influence from for example the British Isles lead to the introduction of the term *'hǫll'*, possibly in an attempt to copy their royal residences. This was probably accompanied by a new understanding of the hall in the Viking Age in accordance with the findings. The hall slightly changed from the place of worldly dominance and power to the universal 'centre of the world' with cult and economy directly associated. Changes are visible in the archaeological findings, and the change of terminology supports this, indicating that the Viking Age indeed was a time of change.

This example shows that word etymology should not be underestimated. Another important result from the linguistic survey, which cannot be presented here in full (see Carstens 2014), was the apparent differentiation between the king's hall (as *salr* and *hǫll*) and the retainer's *skáli*, which was the common term for the longhouse: Several times it is stated that people were not allowed to own a hall if they were not the king (*e.g.* in the 13th century *Knýtlinga saga*). Consequently, in Iceland and Greenland, where there was no king, there were no halls but only *skálar*. The term was known in Iceland and even frequently mentioned in the Sagas of the Icelanders, but only to describe the halls of the Scandinavian and British kings. There was an obvious awareness that the houses of the Icelandic chieftains – even if they were quite large – were different from the royal halls. As a consequence of this the halls from Iceland (Hofstaðir) and Greenland (Brattahlið, Garden under Sandet, Garðar and Hvalsey) have to be taken out of the abovementioned material basis, which reduces the number of Scandinavian halls to 70.

## Summary and conclusion

On the basis of a comparative analysis of 70 Scandinavian hall buildings from the Iron Age, this article extends the well-known 'Herschend definition' with a catalogue of hall criteria which are based on the archaeological findings. These criteria can furthermore show that halls were more than royal dwellings: They had a very special symbolic meaning and they were used as signs throughout the whole Iron Age. The idea behind the chosen place, shape and the surrounding was to portray power and dominance. The burned halls of archaeology have direct parallels in the written sources and both were signs of total loss and defeat. During the Viking Age, halls became more uniform, and altogether there was a lesser number of halls. Economy and cult were added to the ruler's range of duties and the hall changed its term from *salr* to *hǫll*. The Viking-Age kings wanted to be different from their forefathers, but at the same time they kept to old traditions until they finally gave up the wooden residence in favor of a royal complex in stone. This among others marked the end of the Viking Age and the beginning of a new era.

### *Acknowledgements*

This article was made possible through generous funding by the German research council (DFG) and the project 'Halle und Herrschaft' (Kl 2426/1-1). I would like to thank Dr Griffin Murray and Dr Elizabeth Pierce for revising my English and Dr Oliver Grimm, Schleswig, for stimulating discussions and helpful remarks. All remaining errors are, of course, mine.

### *References*

Ängeby, Gisela

1999. Långhusets livstid – en diskussion kring järnåldershusets brukningstid och sociala funktioner utifrån ett månghundraårigt halländskt exempel. In *Kring Västsvenska hus – Boendets organisation och symbolik i förhistorisk och historisk tid*, edited by Tore Artelius, Eva Englund and Lars Ersgård, pp. 9–26. Gotarc, Series C. Arkeologiska Skrifter, Vol. 22. Institutionen för arkeologi, Göteborgs universitet, Göteborg.

Andersson, Maud Cecilia

2001. Om problemet att lokalisera hallar. In *Uppåkra. Centrum och sammanhang*, edited by Birgitta Hårdh, pp. 71–86. Uppåkrastudier, Vol. 3. Almqvist and Wiksell, Stockholm.

Anglert, Mats
1989. Den kyrkliga organisationen under äldre medeltid. In *By, huvudgård och kyrka. Studier i Ystadsområdets medeltid*, edited by Hans Andersson and Mats Anglert, pp. 221–242. Lund Studies in Medieval Archaeology, Vol. 5. Almqvist and Wiksell, Stockholm.

Blankenfeldt, Ruth and Alexandra Pesch
2012. *Goldsmith Mysteries. Archaeological, Pictorial and Documentary Evidence from the 1st Millenium AD in Northern Europe. Papers Presented at a Workshop Organized by the Centre for Baltic and Scandinavian Archaeology (ZBSA), Schleswig, October 20th and 21st, 2011.* Schriften des Archäologischen Landesmuseums, Vol. 8. Wachholtz Verlag, Neumünster.

Böhme, Horst Wolfgang
2001. Gedanken zu den frühen Markt- und Handelsplätzen in Südskandinavien. In *Archäologisches Zellwerk. Beiträge zur Kulturgeschichte in Europa, und Asien (Festschrift für Helmut Roth zum 60. Geburtstag)*, edited by Helmut Roth, Ernst Pohl, Udo Recker and Claudia Theune, pp. 483–498. Internationale archäologie: Studia honoraria, Vol. 16. M. Leidorf, Rahden/Westfalen.

Callmer, Johan
1997. Aristokratiskt präglade residens från yngre järnålder i forskningshistorien och deras problematik. In *"...gick Grendel att söka det höga huset..." Arkeologiska källor till aristokratiska miljöer i Skandinavien under yngre järnålder. Rapport från ett seminarium i Falkenberg 16–17 november 1995*, edited by Johan Callmer and Erik Rosengren, pp. 11–18. GOTARC, series C, Vol. 17. Hallands länsmuseer, Halmstad.

Carlie, Lennart, Jørgen Lund and Trond Løken
2005. Siedlungs-, Gehöft- und Hausformen. In *Seddin – Skíringssal*, edited by Heinrich Beck, Dieter Geuenich and Heiko Steuer, pp. 282–314. Reallexikon der Germanischen Altertumskunde, Vol. 28. DeGruyter, Berlin.

Carstens, Lydia
2012. Might and Magic. The smith in Old Norse literature. In *Goldsmith Mysteries. Archaeological, Pictorial and Documentary Evidence from the 1st Millenium AD in Northern Europe. Papers Presented at a Workshop Organized by the Centre for Baltic and Scandinavian Archaeology (ZBSA), Schleswig, October 20th and 21st, 2011*, edited by Ruth Blankenfeldt and Alexandra Pesch, pp. 243–270. Schriften des Archäologischen Landesmuseums, Vol. 8. Wachholtz Verlag, Neumünster.
2014. Lordship, symbols, memory: The large house in Runsa from a philological point of view. In *Runsa Borg – Representative Lifestyle and Specialized Handicrafts on a Hilltop Site from the Migration Period, a Scandinavian Perspective* (Publications from the Runsa Borg Project Nr 2), edited by Michael Olausson, Stockholm.
In prep. *Halle und Herrschaft. Zur symbolischen Bedeutung der Halle im frühgeschichtlichen Nordeuropa.*

Christaller, Walter
1933. *Die zentralen Orte in Süddeutschland: eine ökonomisch-geographische Untersuchung über die Gesetzmäßigkeit der Verbreitung und Entwicklung der Siedlungen mit städtischen Funktionen.* Verlag von Gustav Fischer, Jena.

Christensen, Tom
1991. *Lejre – syn og sagn.* Roskilde museums forlag, Roskilde.
2010. Lejre beyond the legend – the archaeological evidence. In *Gedächtnis-Kolloquium Werner Haarnagel (1907–1984): Herrenhöfe und die Hierarchie der Macht im Raum südlich und östlich der Nordsee von der vorrömischen Eisenzeit bis zum frühen Mittelalter und zur Wikingerzeit; 11.–13. Oktober 2007, Burg Bederkesa in Bad Bederkesa = Memorial Colloquium Werner Haarnagel (1907–1984)*, edited by Niedersächsisches Institut für historische Küstenforschung (=Lower

Saxony Institute for Historical Coastal Research), pp. 237–254. Siedlungs- und Küstenforschung im südlichen Nordseegebiet, Vol. 33. Marie Leidorf, Rahden/Westfalen.

Enright, Michael
1988. Lady with a Mead-Cup. *Frühmittelalterliche Studien* 22: 170–203.

Eriksen, Marianne Hem
2013. *On the Threshold. The Social, Spatial and Ritual Significance of Doors in Late Iron Age Scandinavia.* Poster presented at the 17th annual Viking Congress, Lerwick.

Fabech, Charlotte
1991. Samfundsorganisation, religiøse ceremonier og regional variation. In *Samfundsorganisation og Regional Variation. Norden I romersk jernalder og folkevandringstid, Beretning frs 1. Nordiske jernaldersymposium på Sandbjerg Slot 11–15 april 1989*, edited by Charlotte Fabech and Jytte Ringtved, pp. 283–303. Jysk Arkæologisk Selskabs Skrifter, Vol. XXVII. Aarhus Universitetsforlag, Aarhus.

Gansum, Terje
2008. Hallene og Stavkirkene – Kultbygninger i en overgangstid. In *Facets of Archaeology. Essays in Honour of Lotte Hedeager on her 60th Birthday*, edited by Konstantinos Chilidis, Julie Lund and Christopher Precott, pp. 199–213. OAS, Vol. 10. Unipub, Oslo.

Herschend, Frands
1993. The Origin of the Hall in Southern Scandinavia. *TOR* 25: 175–199.
1997. *Livet i Hallen. Tre fallstudier i den yngre järnålderns aristokrati.* OPIA, Vol. 14. Institutionen för arkeologi och antik historia, Uppsala universitet, Uppsala.
1999. Halle. In *Greifvögel – Hardeknut*,edited by Heinrich Beck, Dieter Geuenich and Heiko Steuer, pp. 414–425. Reallexikon der Germanischen Altertumskunde, Vol. 13. DeGruyter, Berlin.

Jørgensen, Lars
2009. Pre-Christian cult at aristocratic residences and settlement complexes in southern Scandinavia in the 3rd–10th centuries AD. In *Glaube, Kult und Herrschaft. Phänomene des Religiösen im 1. Jahrtausend n. Chr. In Mittel- und Nordeuropa*, edited by Uta von Freeden, Herwig Friesinger, Egon Wamers, pp. 329–354. Habelt, Bonn.

Klos, Lydia
2009. *Runensteine in Schweden. Studien zu Aufstellungsort und Funktion.* Ergänzungsband zum Reallexikon der Germanischen Altertumskunde, Vol. 64. DeGruyter, Berlin.

Knýtlinga saga
[1982] Translated by Bjarni Guðnason. In *Danakonunga sǫgur. Skjǫldunga saga, Knýtlinga saga, Ágrip af Sǫgu danakonunga.* Íslenzk Fornrít, Vol. XXXV. Hið íslenzka fornritafélag, Reykjavík.

*Vǫluspá, Atlakvíða, Lokasenna*
[1983] *Edda.* Kuhn, Hans and Gustav Neckel Die Lieder des Codex Regius nebst verwandten Denkmälern. I. Text, Heidelberg.

Larsson, Lars and Bengt Söderberg
2012. Bland mordbrännare och flygande smeder. En sekvens av hallbyggnader i Uppåkra. *ALE. Historisk Tidsskrift för Skåne, Halland och Blekinge* 4: 1–15.

Ljungkvist, John, Per Frölund, Hans Göthberg and Daniel Löwenborg
2011. Gamla Uppsala – Structural development of a centre in Middle Sweden. *Archäologisches Korrespondenzblatt* 4 (41): 571–585.

Løken, Trond
2001. Oppkomsten av den germanske hallen – Hall og sal i eldre jernalder i Rogaland. *Viking* 64: 49–86.

Lönnroth, Lars
1997. Hövdingahallen i fornnordisk myt och saga. Ett mentalitetshistoriskt bidrag till förståelsen

av Slöingefundet. In *"...gick Grendel att söka det höga huset..." Arkeologiska källor till aristokratiska miljöer i Skandinavien under yngre järnålder. Rapport från ett seminarium i Falkenberg 16–17 november 1995*, edited by Johan Callmer and Erik Rosengren, pp. 31–37. GOTARC, series C, Vol. 17. Hallands länsmuseer, Halmstad.

Lund Hansen, Ulla
2001. The nature of centres. In *Military Aspects of the Aristocracy in Barbaricum in the Roman and Early Migration Period*, edited by Birger Storgaard, pp. 113–118. Publications of the National Museum, Studies in Archaeology and History, Vol. 5. National Museum, Copenhagen.

Näsman, Ulf
2011. Central Places in South Scandinavia – A transformation twenty years after. In *Transformations in North-Western Europe (AD 300–1000). Proceedings of the 60th Sachsensymposion 19.–23. September 2009 Maastricht*, edited by Titus A. S. M. Panhuysen, pp. 185–193. Niedersächsisches Landesmuseum, Hannover.

Norr, Svante
2006. *Långa och ännu längre långhus från romersk järnålder*. Electronic document, http://www.norn.se/AKWeb.nsf/0/a4e5571c859b3f97c12571d100303b97/$FILE/L%C3%A5ngaHus.pdf, accessed 11 december 2013.

Østergaard Sørensen, Palle
1994. *Gudmehallerne. Kongeligt byggeri fra jernalderen.* Nationalmuseets Arbejdsmark, Copenhagen.
2010. The political and religious centre at Gudme on Funen in the late Roman and Germanic Iron Ages – settlement and central halls. In *Gedächtnis-Kolloquium Werner Haarnagel (1907–1984): Herrenhöfe und die Hierarchie der Macht im Raum südlich und östlich der Nordsee von der vorrömischen Eisenzeit bis zum frühen Mittelalter und zur Wikingerzeit; 11.–13. Oktober 2007, Burg Bederkesa in Bad Bederkesa = Memorial Colloquium Werner Haarnagel (1907–1984)*, edited by Niedersächsisches Institut für historische Küstenforschung (=Lower Saxony Institute for Historical Coastal Research, pp. 225–236. Siedlungs- und Küstenforschung im südlichen Nordseegebiet, Vol. 33. Marie Leidorf, Rahden/Westfalen.

Pesch, Alexandra
2012. The goldsmith, his apprentice and the gods. A fairy tale. In *Goldsmith Mysteries. Archaeological, Pictorial and Documentary Evidence from the 1st Millenium AD in Northern Europe. Papers Presented at a Workshop Organized by the Centre for Baltic and Scandinavian Archaeology (ZBSA), Schleswig, October 20th and 21st, 2011*, edited by Ruth Blankenfeldt and Alexandra Pesch, pp. 37–48. Schriften des Archäologischen Landesmuseums, Vol. 8. Wachholtz Verlag, Neumünster.

Söderberg, Bengt
2003. *Järrestad. Huvudgård i centralbygd.* Riksantikvarieämbetet Arkeologiska undersökningar Skrifter, Vol. 51. Riksantikvarieämbetets förlag, Stockholm.

Stamsø Munch, Gerd, Olaf Sverre Johansen and Else Roesdahl
2003. *Borg in Lofoten. A chieftain's farm in North Norway.* Arkeologisk Skriftserie, Vol. 1. Lofotr – Vikingmuséet på Borg, Bøstad.

Steuer, Heiko
2007. Zentralorte. In *Wielbark-Kultur – Zwölften*, edited by Heinrich Beck, Dieter Geuenich and Heiko Steuer, pp. 878–914. *Reallexikon der Germanischen Altertumskunde*, Vol. 34. DeGruyter, Berlin.

Vierck, Hayo
1991. Hallenfreude. In *Feste und Feiern im Mittelalter. Paderborner Symposium des Mediävistenverbandes*, edited by Detlef Altenburg, Jörg Jarnut, Hans H. Steinhoff, pp. 115–124. Thorbecke, Sigmaringen.

*Chapter 3*

# *Húsdrápa*. A skaldic poem in context

*Joanne Shortt Butler*

*Abstract*

*Húsdrápa* is a skaldic poem said to have been composed at the end of the 10th century. Its subject matter – or what survives of it in *Snorra Edda* – describes a number of myths and uses language typical of encomiastic compositions. Because of a passage in *Laxdœla saga* concerning the performance of the poem, it has traditionally been assigned to the genre *'billedbeskrivende dikt'* ['picture-poetry'], and it has been taken as fact that the poem was composed to describe carvings present in a Viking-Age hall. This article re-examines the subject matter of the poem through categories representing the language of visual expression and ekphrasis. In this analysis the poem is kept separate from the context given in *Laxdœla saga* before the account of the saga itself is examined. By looking at the two sources separately, this article describes what value each source has for the other.

## Introduction

*Húsdrápa* is a Viking-Age poem by the Icelander Úlfr Uggason. It is now partially preserved in the 13th century guide to skaldic poetry *Snorra Edda*, whilst *Laxdœla saga* gives an account of the poem's 10th century composition. It is recounted that in *c.* 985 Úlfr recited the poem at a wedding that took place at Óláfr pái Höskudsson's farm, Hjarðarholt; *Húsdrápa* ['House-poem'] commemorated the elaborate carved decoration within the *eldhús* ['main-room'] of the farm. Thus this poem has long been held up as an example of the materiality of Viking culture, as *billedbeskrivende dikt* ['picture-poetry'] that celebrates and alludes to now lost Viking-Age artwork. This article gives a partial survey of ways in which *Húsdrápa* can be approached, from modern methods of understanding its function and artistry to its treatment in the medieval sources which preserve it and its context. It will be argued that it is important to explore various ways of interpreting *Húsdrápa*, as its partial preservation leaves us with very little evidence with which to conclusively describe its origins or function. Owing to this partial preservation, the present article takes the expansionist view of the poem as laid out by Edith Marold in her forthcoming edition for volume three of the *Skaldic*

*Poetry Project* (in Gade and Marold in prep.); Marold's edition follows the numbering and attribution of stanzas given in *Skjaldedigtning* (Finnur Jónsson 1912–15). All references to *Íslendingasögur* and *Landnámabók* are from the *Íslenzk fornrit* series.

### Approaches to Húsdrápa

*Húsdrápa* may be approached within its context in *Snorra Edda*, or that of *Laxdœla saga*; it may be approached as a poem in its own right, either as a hypothetical complete composition that no longer survives, or as a collection of loosely related stanzas and half-stanzas. In terms of its content, it may be approached as praise-poetry, *billedbeskrivende dikt*, or, through Kate Heslop's innovative methodology it may be explored as an example of striking, visually-charged rhetorical composition, termed 'ekphrasis' (Heslop 2009). As part of this volume's interest in the materiality of the Vikings, this article focuses on approaches that relate to *Húsdrápa*'s alleged connection to Viking-Age artwork. Therefore it will examine the surviving material of the poem separately from its specialised, literary context in *Snorra Edda*, applying criteria that aim to discern a visualising style of composition and questioning the evidence for the poem's association with Viking-Age carvings. Following this, the account in *Laxdœla saga* will be assessed separately from the poem, and the connection between the two works will be placed in context.

### A note on chronology

It is not my intention to lay out a chronology for the written sources relating to the poem, as the comparative dating of many of these texts remains highly subjective. The poem is preserved by a 13th century source; *Laxdœla saga* survives as a 13th century account; the current form of other sagas and sources concerning Úlfr Uggason also date broadly to the 13th century. Beyond this I am loath to say which may have influenced which as a text: without evidence for direct textual borrowing we cannot say which sources were known to which compilers. This is in part due to the oral-literate continuum that existed in Iceland at the time, and this article upholds a view of oral traditions in Iceland that is heavily indebted to the work of Gísli Sigurðsson (2004).

Whilst this article is only concerned with the surviving portion of the poem and does not seek to reconstruct lost material, a premise of this study is that the material preserved in *Snorra Edda* does represent part of an earlier composition that was preserved by oral transmission. A lack of both scholarly consensus and evidence ensures that it is impossible to establish who was responsible for the oral transmission of skaldic poetry (as opposed to saga content), therefore it cannot be claimed that *Húsdrápa* survives only because of the interests of the élite compilers of *Snorra Edda*. Such a statement ignores the vast amount of material that has been lost, as well as the clear interest in skaldic poetry displayed within the narratives of many sagas, including that of *Laxdœla saga* itself (see Quinn 2000: 41–6). There is therefore no barrier to an approach that allows for a broad medieval awareness of Úlfr Uggason and his works beyond the audience of *Snorra Edda*. In other words, I do not believe that a 13th century audience would have needed to be familiar with *Snorra Edda* in order to have been familiar with *Húsdrápa.*

## Outline of the surviving poem

The term *drápa* is commonly translated as 'long poem with a refrain' and describes elaborate, courtly compositions. We cannot say how long *Húsdrápa* originally was, but given that most of the surviving material exists as ten separate half-stanzas scattered throughout *Snorra Edda* it is clear that at least 40 lines of the poem have been lost. As well as these ten half-stanzas, two complete stanzas of eight lines survive (whether *Húsdrápa* 6 is a whole or should be treated as two half-stanzas remains open to debate, but is not relevant to this study). The subjects are overwhelmingly mythological, meaning that much of the alleged material inspiration for the poem remains unattested in surviving Viking-Age art (Þórr's fishing expedition being the obvious exception, see Meulengracht Sørensen 1986).

The subjects of *Húsdrápa* are: the funeral of the god Baldr, Óðinn's son (five half-stanzas [*Húsdrápa* 7–11]); verses apparently concerning Þórr's pre-Ragnarǫk encounter with Miðgarðsormr, in which the cowardly giant Hymir accompanies him on a fishing expedition (three half-stanzas; one stanza [*Húsdrápa* 3–6]); a contest between the gods Loki and Heimdallr (one stanza: [*Húsdrápa* 2]); and authorial presence, that is the poet's exposition and appeals his patron (two half-stanzas [*Húsdrápa* 1, 12]). The cohesiveness of this subject matter supports the view that all of these verses are from *Húsdrápa.*

Finally, this article follows Edith Marold's interpretation of *Húsdrápa* 2, eschewing its traditional association with the necklace Brísingamen in favour of reading it as a struggle between the gods over a certain island (Gade and Marold in prep.). Quotes here follow the prose-order in Marold's edition with constituent parts of kennings in small capitals; translations generally give only the referent of the kenning, also in small capitals.

## Approaching the materiality of Húsdrápa

The surviving poem makes no overt statement regarding the circumstances of its composition. For this reason, in order to corroborate the account in *Laxdœla saga*, attempts to establish its connections with material, carved artwork have had to use certain other criteria. We have largely moved on from interest in the 'absent objects and lost moments' (Heslop 2009: 2) that characterised the early study of *billedbeskrivende dikt*, however, a fascination with the connection between the material and the poetic remains.

Margaret Clunies Ross (2007) has set out 'stylistic definers' for *billedbeskrivende dikt*, taking the account of *Laxdœla saga* at face value and including *Húsdrápa* as an established poem from this genre. She uses the term 'ekphrasis' to describe the genre of picture-poetry, but this usage is imprecise, as described below, so I will refer to the genre as *billedbeskrivende dikt*. By examining poems from this genre, she aimed to develop criteria for recognising further examples of *billedbeskrivende dikt*. This involves asking whether the poem refers to the images it allegedly describes; whether it refers to a patron; whether it makes use of deixis; whether it makes use of a visualising style; and what is the nature of the verbs used. The surviving lines of *Húsdrápa* fulfil different combinations of these criteria by subject matter, although internal evidence for *Húsdrápa* as *billedbeskrivende dikt* is only 'suggestive' in the context of *Laxdœla saga*'s account (Clunies Ross 2007: 174–175). Whether the poem provides evidence for a material connection without the context provided by *Laxdœla saga* will be explored below.

Whilst *Húsdrápa*'s connection with the material Viking Age has undoubtedly contributed to interest in the poem, in this context it is nevertheless often neglected in favour of the 'shield-poems' *Haustlǫng* by Þjóðólfr ór Hvini and *Ragnarsdrápa* by Bragi Boddason. It is for this reason that I intend to explore a further approach to *Húsdrápa* that stems from ongoing research by Kate Heslop. *Billedbeskrivende dikt* has been conflated in recent years with the Greek rhetorical device known as 'ekphrasis', which some term a genre akin to picture-poetry; it has been demonstrated, however, that the word ekphrasis refers to a technique rather than a genre (Webb 1999). This technique had no specific connection with *objects d'art* or material artefacts; however it encouraged vivid mental pictures and blurred the lines between our modern notions of description and narration. Using criteria drawn from ancient Greek sources and more recent studies of medieval ekphraseis (pl.), Heslop has sought to place emphasis upon the 'ekphrastic', visualising capacity of skaldic poetry over any alleged connection with material culture (Heslop 2009). In a volume dedicated to the materiality of the Vikings it strikes me as essential to explore this innovative research that has the potential to redefine the traditional association between materiality and poetry.

Heslop's 'significant points' of ekphrasis are drawn from a combination of sources, and whilst they overlap to a certain extent with Clunies Ross' criteria for *billedbeskrivende dikt*, they nevertheless offer different approaches to the material that they are applied to. As her research is ongoing (constituting progression towards a forthcoming publication, Heslop in prep.) I am hesitant to redefine her criteria, and choose for the purposes of this article to present them as in her 2009 paper, with the intention of providing new data that current research into ekphrasis in skaldic poetry can build upon. Heslop's significant points are as follows: *effect on the audience* (it should create a vivid mental image); *focus on the subject not the artwork* (portrayal of narrative background beyond basic description); *self-reflexive staging of the medium* (displaying a disjunction between the medium and what it depicts, awareness of the act of seeing). Additionally she examines the use of *memorial images* (references to memory and memorial content); *reflection of the epic narrative* (details align with themes in the wider narrative); *text-internal observers* (information about the setting is delivered by characters' reactions); the latter three criteria are based upon the work of Haiko Wandhoff (2003), the former upon classical rhetoric. Whilst they are not designed to demonstrate a direct link between classical ekphrasis and Viking Age and medieval Iceland, Heslop's research suggests a particular rhetorical function for poems such as *Húsdrápa* beyond the commemoration of material artwork.

**What motivates Húsdrápa, the material or the visual?**

In this section I will examine evidence for Heslop's criteria in the surviving lines of *Húsdrápa*. Clunies Ross' criteria that tie the poem to material inspiration will be borne in mind and addressed where relevant in the context of Heslop's criteria. By cataloguing the ekphrastic elements of *Húsdrápa* I intend to demonstrate that there is much in the poem that is of interest even when the material inspiration for its composition is cast into doubt. I will begin with the simplest criteria, before moving on to those which are more interconnected.

Whether the poem *reflects its epic setting* is difficult to discern; it reflects the wider concerns of *Snorra Edda* because what remains of it was chosen to fit that context (myths and skaldic descriptions of poetry and patrons). Its relationship with *Laxdœla saga* will be discussed below, but in any case the poem is not quoted there. We are not able to discern the 'epic setting' of *Húsdrápa* itself owing to its fragmentary preservation, so a search for reflections of the poem as a whole is unlikely to prove fruitful, especially as the order of the remaining material is uncertain.

In terms of the *self-reflexive staging of the medium*, there is no reference in the surviving material of *Húsdrápa* to material artworks. Whether 'images' are mentioned is a matter for a different category (addressed below), but there is certainly no mention of the medium of any such images. Without evidence of a material medium, we might ask whether the poem displays an awareness of the act of seeing, and indeed whether it implies seeing a material object or a clear view of a mental image. Hence self-reflexivity overlaps with the category of the *text-internal observer*, as both require the poet to reveal an awareness of the interaction between his words and the visual. The poet's voice is prominent in the surviving stanzas: the first-person singular is used in *Húsdrápa* 1, 2, 9, 10, and 12. One interjection reminiscent of a text-internal observer is found in 10, where the verb *hyggja* is used. However, *hyggja* is connected with internal processes such as thinking and believing and therefore lacks a clear visual element; it certainly does not support the notion of seeing a physical object.

In *Húsdrápa* 1 and 12 the poet is no mere observer, although the self-reflexivity of the poetic form is heightened in these half-stanzas on authorial presence. *Húsdrápa* 1 makes self-conscious references to the act of delivering praise through poetry, to the extent that the praise takes a back-seat to kennings for poetry: 'Telk hugreifum Áleifi LǪ GEÐFJARÐAR HILDAR HJALDRGEGNIS' ['I recite A POEM for the mind-happy Óláfr']; 'vilk kveðja hann at GJǪF GRÍMNIS' ['I want to summon him to A POEM']. Elsewhere, the poet's interjections are connected with speech rather than sight: 'kyndik áðr þǫttum mærðar' ['I revealed [that] earlier in the strands of the praise-poem', *Húsdrápa* 2] and 'hróðrmǫl líða of hvápta mér' ['praise-speeches flow through my mouth', *Húsdrápa* 9]. This language puts the emphasis firmly on the poet and his speech, reminding the audience that it is he who dictates what material is presented to them. The medium staged is overwhelmingly that of praise-poetry.

*Húsdrápa* 5 contains an unambiguous example of a text-internal observer, usually thought to be the giant observing Þórr's catch, but interpreted by Marold as Þórr observing the giant's fear (Gade and Marold in prep: *Húsdrápa* 5). Either way, the internal observer in this case tells us how comic an audience was meant to find Hymir. Very little trace exists of other text-internal observers; the poet does not appeal to his audience – his patron is greeted, but no action is explicitly required of him. A wider audience may be discerned in 'lofi þegna' ['praise of men', *Húsdrápa* 12] if we take it to mean that the poet offers the praise of a specific group, present at the moment of recital, yet the phrase works equally as a generalisation or kenning for poetry. Elsewhere, an aside in one of the Þórr verses may be a knowing nod to the audience: Þórr strikes a giant, and the poet comments 'þat vas ramt mein' ['that was a mighty injury', *Húsdrápa* 6]. This phrase appears as a continuous whole, in regular syntax that distinguishes it from its surroundings: whilst the rest of the half-stanza needed a degree of decoding by the audience (Heslop 2013: 3), this aside would immediately indicate that something dramatic was afoot. Text-internal observers are therefore the patron and perhaps a wider audience to whom 'þat vas ramt mein' may have been directed; this is what we would expect of a praise-poem, but does not demonstrate the highly self-conscious visual language of ekphraseis, nor does it tell us anything of the materiality of the poem's inspiration.

Two categories will now be discussed simultaneously as they affect similar verses and aspects of the poem: focus on the *subject not on an artwork* and the quality of having an *effect on the audience*. This will expand upon Clunies Ross' category of a 'visualising style', given that such a style would prove useful in the description of material images, yet it is also an important aspect of the effect of ekphrasis on an audience. It is already clear that *Húsdrápa* offers little evidence that it describes decorative art, so in order to define 'focus on the subject' (myth and encomiastic procedure) it might be considered what sort of narrative the poem presents. Ekphrasis involves an intertwining of our modern definitions of description and narrative, whereby an orator 'describes' a static image by 'narrating' the before and after of the moment portrayed (Webb 1999: 12). I will therefore ask whether *Húsdrápa* narrates myths that could not possibly be depicted, or whether its language reflects plausible descriptions of a static image.

As a skaldic poem it is heavily reliant upon kennings, which tapped into a cultural knowledge of myths whilst allowing the poet to devise new descriptions for familiar characters or items. Kennings in *Húsdrápa* are rarely directly relevant to the scene in which they appear (Table 3.1); rather they are attributes that could not be depicted in an image, and whilst they may therefore intensify the focus on the subject rather than a putative artwork, this to some degree detracts from 'visualising style' (Clunies Ross 2007: 180 n. 17). Despite this, the effect of kennings on an audience could be extremely potent: they are a part of the referential language of orally-derived literature (Foley 1991: 6–8), and referentiality was crucial to ekphrastic rhetoric (Webb 1999: 13–14). Hence they encapsulate a far larger story, and where one understands them they become keys to a wider body of myth: kennings have a panoramic effect on the poem's imagery, expanding the narrative into the past and future of mythic figures. They are not exclusive to *billedbeskrivende dikt*, however, so their ekphrastic value must be applied wherever they are found.

*Húsdrápa* does, nevertheless, also display language limited more or less to the events described, and where this is the case the visualising style increases, altering the nature of the effect on the audience. In *Húsdrápa* 2 abstract, non-visual kennings surround a carefully

| Mythological subject | Lines of verse | No. kennings | Referent of kenning | Translation (verse) | Visualising style/ relevance to scene |
|---|---|---|---|---|---|
| Baldr's funeral | 20 | 8 | Óðinn | Hroptatýr (9) | No |
| | | | | Victory-tree (10) | Tree relevant to carving? |
| | | | | Hroptr (11) | No |
| | | | Baldr | Óðinn's son (7) | No |
| | | | | Son of the raven-tester (8) | No |
| | | | Giantess | Mountain-Hildr (11) | No |
| | | | Ship | Sea-Sleipnir (11) | Maybe |
| | | | Sword | Helmet-fire (11) | Yes |
| Þórr | 20 | 12 | Þórr | Gods' friend (3) | No |
| | | | | Tester of the people of the bone of the land (4) | Yes; not directly relevant |
| | | | | Goat-user (5) | Yes; not relevant |
| | | | | Mountain-Gautr's killer (6) | Yes |
| | | | | Viðgymnir of Vímur-ford (6) | No |
| | | | Giant | Heavy-set one (5) | Yes |
| | | | | Tester of the bone of the reed (6) | Yes? Watery setting |
| | | | Miðgarðsormr | Earth's necklace (3) | Maybe |
| | | | | Stiff-cord (4) | Yes |
| | | | | Glittering adder (6) | Yes |
| | | | Eye | Forehead's interior-moon (3) | Yes |
| | | | Head | Ear's foundation (6) | Yes |
| Loki and Heimdallr | 8 | 4 | Heimdallr | Gods' defender (2) | No |
| | | | | Son of eight mothers and one (2) | No |
| | | | Loki | Fárbauti's son (2) | No |
| | | | Island | Sea-kidney (2) | Yes |

*Table 3.1. The relationship between kennings and a visualising style in Húsdrápa.*

described scene. The kennings invoke Heimdallr's role as protector of Bifrǫst and Loki's giant ancestry, reminding the audience which side to support whilst setting the action within the wider tradition. The action is not lost amidst the kennings, however: the verse describes a chronology of events from Heimdallr's victory over Loki to his rule of the *hafnýra*:

> RÁÐGEGNINN, FRÆGR VÁRI RAGNA bregðr rein við FIRNA SLŒGJAN MǪG FÁRBAUTA at Singasteini. MÓÐǪFLUGR MǪGR ÁTTA MŒÐRA OK EINNAR ræðr fǫgru HAFNÝRA' ['HEIMDALLR takes away a land-strip from LOKI at Singasteinn. HEIMDALLR rules the beautiful ISLAND', *Húsdrápa* 12].

It is impossible to know whether this chronology points to a narrative involving the subject or to inspiration from sequential images, although an example of chronological narrative elsewhere in the poem represents the former: 'goð hlóðu' ['gods erected', *Húsdrápa* 8] Baldr's pyre, presumably in the mythic past.

Another manifestation of a visualising style is simultaneity in the events described. This occurs largely in agonistic subject matter: *Húsdrápa* 11 (Baldr's funeral), 3, and 4 (Þórr). In 11 Hyrrokin pushes Baldr's funeral ship out to sea whilst her wolf-steed is killed; in 3 and 4 Þórr and Miðgarðsormr exchange baleful glares. The language of these episodes is rich with kennings, but they are kennings that are either appropriate to the scene at hand or produce a vivid visual image, for example Miðgarðsormr is 'stirðþinull' ['stiff-cord', *Húsdrápa* 4] and Þórr's eye 'innmáni ennis' ['interior-moon of the forehead', *Húsdrápa* 3]. Tension between the visual and the spoken does emerge in *Húsdrápa* 5, however, where Þórr's words evoke a vivid image of Hymir that nevertheless keeps the putative materiality of wood-carved images distant, as what is being described is reported speech and not presented as the poet's observation. Clunies Ross (2007: 171) saw agonistic subject matter as key to the poems she analysed, and the effect that this sort of narrative has on an audience has presumably changed little; the verse is dramatic and detailed, and humour lightens the action. Therefore, it is here that *Húsdrápa* conforms most to ekphrasis, with its focus on the subject described rather than a fixed scene, and its production of a strong effect on the audience.

Finally, we must address the *memorial content* of *Húsdrápa*; in doing so the traditional association between the poem's refrain and material images will be questioned. Because the refrain, 'hlaut innan svá minnum' [*Húsdrápa* 6, 10] is only one line, whereas refrains should have consisted of two lines in *drápur* (Fidjestøl 1993), it has been suggested that this is the remains of a *klofastef* ['split-refrain']. The first line of such a split-refrain would therefore have appeared in another stanza, but has since been lost (see Heslop 2013: 12 n. 90). The potential of missing information has encouraged scholars to view this line as a reference to images, translating it along the sense of 'thus it was decorated inside with memorable pictures' [*Húsdrápa* 6], where the subject of the sentence is taken to be the building described by *Laxdœla saga* (on which more below). The word *minni* is not especially associated with images, however; it is used of memorials such as runestones, and more commonly it just refers to 'memory' (Zoëga 2004: s.v. *minni*). The verb *hljóta* also lacks strict associations with the pictorial, making 'depict' a misleading translation. More accurately the refrain translates as '[it] allotted such memories from within'. Heslop interprets these 'memories' as the cultural memories that were preserved by the myths that *Húsdrápa* recounts. She cites examples from other *billedbeskrivende dikt* to show that these poems seem to have been aware of their conservationist, memorial function (Heslop 2013: 10–12). I would suggest that the *minni* in *Húsdrápa* can also function as communicative memory, if not in the instance of the poem's first performance, then at least through the generations of repetition that saw it eventually preserved in thirteenth-century texts. *Húsdrápa*'s transmission is connected not only to the preservation of mythological memories, but also to the memory of an event – its original performance. Recital of the poem provided a way of re-living the performance, or a way of experiencing it for those who were not present. The *minni* are not just evocative of cultural memory and myth, they are also memories within their bearer. The deictic 'þar' of *Húsdrápa* 10 could in this sense be interpreted as the mind or memory of the preserver of the poem: 'there I consider valkyries and ravens who accompany [Óðinn] [...] such memories were allotted within'.

Without the other half of the stanza this is simply conjecture, but the rest of *Húsdrápa* confirms that the poet understood the memorial value of myth well. Heimdallr and Óðinn are 'frægr' ['renowned', *Húsdrápa* 2, 9], and the word 'endr' in *Húsdrápa* 12, although meaning 'once more', also has the sense of 'in old times' (Zoëga 2004: s.v. *endr*). Thus the poet could be said to be handing out the 'praise of old times', aware of the gap between the mythological events that constitute his praise for Óláfr, and the time of recital (Heslop 2013: 11).

In summary, the poem resembles an ekphrasis through memorialising content, the production of a vivid mental image, and reference to a broad spectrum of mythic chronology. These categories are relevant to skaldic poetry as a whole, rather than just to examples thought to be *billedbeskrivende dikt*. The poem is obviously an example of praise-poetry, but its connection with material culture is impossible to establish from internal evidence. This by no means rules out such a connection – much of the poem has been lost after all – but we should be cautious of that fact that evidence of references to Viking-Age carvings in the poem appears to have been greatly exaggerated. Such exaggeration has been encouraged by the account of *Laxdœla saga*, so this passage will be examined next.

## The performance of Húsdrápa

*Húsdrápa* is one of only two praise-poems from an Icelandic setting. According to *Laxdœla saga*, Úlfr Uggason (*fl.* 1000) performed *Húsdrápa* for Óláfr pái Hǫskuldsson in celebration of carved decoration in his *eldhús* (*c.* 985). Úlfr appears in a number of other sources, but not in the thirteenth-century catalogue of court poets, *Skáldatal* – unusual for a poet quoted more than five times in *Snorra Edda* (Nordal 2001: 78).

Whilst *Snorra Edda* does not mention the context for the composition of *Húsdrápa*, it does name Úlfr's composition and provides some detail of the poem's content (although nothing beyond what has been preserved in the remaining verses). Elsewhere, Úlfr is recognised for his refusal to actively oppose the missionary Þangbrandr (*Kristni saga* II: 20–21; *Njáls saga*: 261–264), and his reluctance to participate in violence is underscored by an episode in which he refuses a duel (*Njáls saga*: 152). There is little detail concerning him in *Landnámabók* as he is only named in connection with his wife (*Landnámabók*: 111; see also Clunies Ross 1993). Despite this, the disparate subject matter speaks of a tradition concerning Úlfr that included and went beyond his composition of *Húsdrápa*.

Úlfr Uggason's presence in the traditions that lie behind our sources is relevant when we consider the plausibility of the performance context given by *Laxdœla saga*. Familiarity with this passage transforms the way in which we read *Húsdrápa* (Clunies Ross 2005: 56), so understanding it on its own terms is essential. Here I will assess the motives and language of the relevant passage as I assessed those of *Húsdrápa*. This will hopefully elucidate our understanding of how one source illuminates our understanding of the other.

*Laxdœla saga* revels in opulence, status and romance, but remains stylistically an *Íslendingasaga*. Its interest in the trappings of romance emerges only in specific areas, for instance in 'descriptions of customs, costumes and weapons' (Tómasson 1993: 388). Its fascination with Óláfr's new farm is evident:

> Þat sumar lét Óláfr gera eldhús í Hjarðarholti, meira ok betra en menn hefði fyrr sét. Váru þar markaðar ágætligar sǫgur á þilviðinum ok svá á ræfrinu; var þat svá vel smíðat, at þá þótti miklu skrautligra, er eigi váru tjǫldin uppi [...]. Þat boð var allfjǫlmennt, því at þá var algǫrt eldhúsit. Þar var at boði Úlfr Uggason ok hafði ort kvæði um Óláf Hǫskuldsson ok um sǫgur þær, er skrifaðar váru á eldhúsinu, ok fœrði hann þar at boðinu. Þetta kvæði er kallat Húsdrápa ok er vel ort. Óláfr launaði vel kvæðit. Hann gaf ok stórgjafar ǫllu stórmenni, er hann hafði heim sótt. Þótti Óláfr vaxit hafa af þessi veizlu (*Laxdœla saga*: 79–80).
>
> That summer Olaf had a fire-room built at Hjardarholt which was larger and grander than men had ever seen before. On the wood of the wainscoting, and the rafters, decorative tales were carved. It was so well crafted that it was thought more ornamental without the tapestries than with them [...]. A great number of people attended the feast as the fire-room was fully built by that time. Among the guests was a poet, Ulf Uggason, who had composed a poem about Olaf Hoskuldsson and the tales carved on the wood of the fire-room which he recited at the feast. It is called House Drapa and is a fine piece of verse. Olaf rewarded him well for the poem, and gave all the important people who attended the feast gifts, gaining considerable respect as a result (Kunz 1999: 39–40, with modifications).

Heslop (2009: 10) has suggested that this passage should not be taken at face value:

> [...] the decorative elements are a means of displaying the ideological commitments of the text-internal actors [...]. By insisting on the superiority of carvings and skaldic poetry with subjects from Norse mythology as aristocratic accoutrements, over the typical romance decor of tapestries, the saga has its Icelandic aristocrat outdo Continental varieties of courtly display.

Yet this conclusion should be repositioned. Tapestries are a familiar form of decoration in sagas; although reserved for special occasions, they are more commonplace than carvings in élite households (Roesdahl 1991: 43). By eschewing tapestries the saga does not prioritise native grandeur over foreign grandeur. In fact, the carvings locate Óláfr's spending decisively outside Iceland, as the wood for his hall came from Norway. Wood-carving is therefore the less-Icelandic form of decoration, given that the carvings described would have required significant amounts of Norwegian timber. The presence of the poet – a ubiquitous feature of the royal Norwegian court – reinforces the aspiration to mainland Scandinavian practices inherent in the building's decoration. Hence, Hjarðarholt is not demonstrative of the superior Icelandic lifestyle; rather Óláfr applies considerable royal splendour to his mid-Atlantic birthplace.

Úlfr himself is exclusively connected with Iceland, although his position in society remains opaque. In terms of discerning an 'immanent saga' we cannot say more than that he is portrayed as a cautious man who was unwilling to pursue his opinions forcefully (Clunies Ross 1993). The prestige that *Laxdœla saga* draws from the event evidently comes from the fact that a poet was there and he composed a *drápa*, not from who this particular poet was.

Moreover, in terms of romantic hyperbole, the scene is relatively restrained. Despite its desire

*Fig. 3.1. Two 12th-century panels from Flatatunga, Iceland, thought to have decorated the cathedral at Hólar.*
*Photo: © Þjóðminjasafn Íslands.*

to emphasise Óláfr's fantastical wealth, the descriptions of lavish objects are still couched in the terse language of the *Íslendingasögur*. Heslop compares ekphrastic flights-of-fancy from *riddarasögur* and travel tales to this passage, but they remain ideologically distinct (Heslop 2009: 7–9). *Laxdœla saga* retains an inherent 'believability' despite its very prominent aristocratic outlook.

Whilst we should not expect to find material traces of Hjarðarholt, we can imagine the scene quite clearly from our knowledge of Viking-Age housing. *Eldhús* indicates the main room of the farmhouse in *Íslendingasögur*, where everyday activities and social functions took place (Vidal 2013: 275). The open long-fire that gave the room its name would have adequately illuminated decorations, and the space would have contained ample surfaces for wood-carving. *Laxdœla saga* specifically mentions 'þilviðr' [wainscoting], which would have been a notable feature in its own right in a Viking-Age house, and would certainly have been familiar to a 13th century audience (Teva Vidal, personal communication 2013).

Unlike the decorated shields described by other *billedbeskrivende dikt*, there is evidence for wood-carving in medieval Iceland, although the Viking Age itself lacks examples, and none come from secular buildings (Magerøy 1993). When considering the flat surfaces of the wainscoting, the 12th century Flatatunga panels indicate a potential method of decoration (Fig. 3.1). These depict the Last Judgement, and were influenced by Byzantine portrayals of the scene (Jónsdóttir 1959). The style suits the thin panels, but is unlike any other medieval Icelandic decoration; their demonstrably Continental inspiration means that whilst they had the capacity to influence the imagination of a medieval audience, they tell us nothing about the 10th century. Nevertheless, relief-carving was practiced from the Iron Age to the medieval period, and thus it can be claimed that *Laxdœla saga*'s account, whilst lavish, would have been imaginable to its audience (Fig. 3.2).

Yet the probability is that different individuals in its 13th century audience imagined varying kinds of art, and the mention of wainscoting may just emphasise the vast amount of timber Óláfr imported. We are, as ever, hampered by a lack of evidence, but it cannot be doubted that every reader or listener exposed to this passage from *Laxdœla saga* may envisage something different. 'Envisaging' returns us of the techniques of ekphrasis and a text's effect on the audience. *Laxdœla saga* does not display any of the 'judicious choice of details' (Webb 1999: 14) that we ought to expect from a composition seeking to have a visualising effect on its audience. Its language is vague and non-specific; the pictures were 'ágætligar' [excellent] and 'skrautligar' [showy/ornamental]; the fire-room was 'meira' [bigger], 'betra' [better], 'vel smiðat' [well-crafted]. This achieves a general sense of splendidness, leaving the audience free to imagine any space they choose to, not a specific, vivid image. This vagueness naturally increases the 'believability' of the scene whoever the audience is: it is equally non-specific as a blueprint for lost buildings and as an ideological statement. Whilst 'the decorative elements are a means of displaying the ideological commitments of the text-internal actors' (Heslop 2009: 10), beyond their ostentatious display of wealth only the vaguest notion of the decoration is conveyed.

The detail that stands out in the passage is the mention of *Húsdrápa* itself. If the saga's audience knew the poem, then the broad descriptions offered by the prose could have contextualised imagery from the poem itself, as familiarity with medieval wood-carving would form a framework for imagining the *eldhús*. Thus by name-dropping *Húsdrápa* the saga does not need to quote it. Like kennings, it invokes the kind of referential language employed in orally-derived texts and ekphraseis. Quoting the poem at this point in the saga would not cause it to function as a reflection of the epic narrative, like ekphraseis in Continental romances (Wandhoff 2003: 42); the content of the remaining verses of *Húsdrápa* bears no relevance to the plot of *Laxdœla saga*. If the mention of the poem brought it instantly to the minds of the saga's audience it was only in order to elaborate upon the splendour of the scene.

## Concluding remarks

I hope in the short space allowed by this article to have demonstrated the extent to which *Laxdœla saga* and *Húsdrápa* are inter-dependent, and to have shown how different approaches to these texts can still provide new information. *Laxdœla saga* needs only to mention *Húsdrápa* to add luxury to the wedding scene and imply the grandeur of the building; medieval and modern audiences familiar with the poem itself may expand upon the information by imagining the detail of the carvings from their supplementary knowledge. However, even without a detailed idea of the poem's content an audience can still marvel at the unusual presence of a 'court poet' at an Icelandic farm. *Húsdrápa*, meanwhile, remains worthy of interest even when stripped of its context in *Laxdœla saga*: its surviving stanzas are vivid, dramatic and frequently epic, making it impressive even without affixing it to the materiality of Hjarðarholt.

*Húsdrápa* has a powerful effect on its audience, especially through kennings that expand the subject at hand into the wider field of mythology. The memorialising function of myth and kennings is an essential part of this, and it is a function aided by their position within the traditional referentiality of Old Norse orally-derived literature. These are techniques of

*Fig. 3.2. A 13th-century church door from Valþjófsstaðir, Iceland.*
*Photo: © Þjóðminjasafn Íslands.*

skaldic court poetry that are by no means exclusive to *billedbeskrivende dikt*, which should serve as a reminder that *Húsdrápa* is as much a praise-poem as a mythological poem. The poet mediates our experience of the myths recounted; even if this is a poem that commemorates another work of art, Úlfr Uggason ensures that he is the only artist remembered through the text of the poem itself. Nearly every surviving half-stanza contains at least one kenning that describes a myth that could not easily be shown pictorially, and *Húsdrápa* 2, 9, and 10 make it clear that we have the poet's perception of his source material, not a description of the source material itself.

*Húsdrápa* as *billedbeskrivende dikt* has been the focus of other studies, such as that by Margaret Clunies Ross, which show its potential in that regard. The survival of the poem is sufficiently fragmentary that *Laxdœla saga* has often been used as a 'way in' to the poem, whereby it is only commented on because of the certainty of its relationship to the decoration at Hjarðarholt. I hope that the rhetorical categories that Kate Heslop is currently working on will help to demonstrate that there is much of interest in *Húsdrápa* itself, and that approaches beyond that which is suggested by *Laxdœla saga* are worthwhile.

Heslop's approach is partially a reaction against attempts to fix a material reality to poems based on insufficient evidence. However, separating *Húsdrápa* from its carvings is not the same as separating shield-poems from their shields; they contain only internal indicators that they were inspired by objects, whereas *Húsdrápa*, crucially, has an external indicator. *Laxdœla saga* provides the kind of source that we do not have for other *billedbeskrivende dikt*. It demonstrates that a thirteenth-century audience found the connection between *Húsdrápa* and the carved decoration at Hjarðarholt plausible; its descriptions of the *eldhús* may be vague, but they are so vague as to be acceptable to any audience.

Another approach to these sources may therefore be to explore *Húsdrápa*'s language from the perspective of a 13th century audience familiar with *Laxdœla saga*. This allows us to view the poem as something that described carvings without commenting on whether the carvings were real or not, and the advantage of this is that ambiguous references to the visual in *Húsdrápa* need not be ambiguous when viewed through *Laxdœla saga*'s filter. The Viking world described by *Laxdœla saga* may have little or nothing to do with the Viking world from which *Húsdrápa* emerged, but whilst this world is now lost to us, *Laxdœla saga* provides the poem with a space in the medieval world and imbues its language with fresh significance.

*Acknowledgements*

This article uses unpublished material from Kate Heslop's Academia.edu page and is greatly indebted to her for her assistance in compiling references. Thanks are also due to Teva Vidal for sharing material from his recently completed thesis and to Edith Marold, for sharing her draft edition of *Húsdrápa*. Finally, I would also like to thank Judy Quinn and Edward Carlsson Browne for their advice and assistance in editing, Þjóðminjasafn Íslands for granting permission to use their images, and the organising committee of *Viking Worlds* 2013.

*References*

Clunies Ross, Margaret
1993. Úlfr Uggason. In *Medieval Scandinavia: an Encyclopedia*, edited by Philip Pulsiano and Kirsten Wolf, pp. 681–682. Garland Reference Library of the Humanities, Vol. 934 and Garland Encyclopedias of the Middle Ages, Vol. 1. Garland, New York.
2005. *A History of Old Norse Poetry and Poetics*. D. S. Brewer, Cambridge.
2007. Stylistic and Generic Definers of the Old Norse Skaldic Ekphrasis. *Viking and Medieval Scandinavia* 3: 161–184.

Fidjestøl, Bjarne
1993. Skaldic Verse. *Medieval Scandinavia: an Encyclopedia*, edited by Philip Pulsiano and Kirsten Wolf, pp. 592–594. Garland Reference Library of the Humanities, Vol. 934 and Garland Encyclopedias of the Middle Ages, Vol. 1. Garland, New York.

Finnur Jónsson (editor)
1912–15. *Den norsk-islandske skjaldedigtning*, A: *Tekst efter handskrifterne*, 2 vols; B: *Rettet tekst med tolkning*, 2 vols. Copenhagen, Gyldendal.

Foley, John
1991. *Immanent Art: From Structure to Meaning in Traditional Oral Epic*. Indiana University Press, Bloomington.

Gade, Kari Ellen and Edith Marold (editors)
in prep. *Poetry from Treatises on Poetics*. Skaldic Poetry of the Scandinavian Middle Ages, Vol. 3. Turnhout, Brepols.

Sigurðsson, Gísli
2004. *The Medieval Icelandic Saga and Oral Tradition: A Discourse on Method*. Publications of the Milman Parry Collection of Oral Literature, Vol. 2. Translated by Nicholas Jones. Harvard University Press, Massachusetts.

Heslop, Kate
2009. *What is Old Norse Ekphrasis For?* Paper presented at the Institute for Linguistic and Nordic Studies, University of Oslo, 30 October 2009.
2013. *Minni* and the Rhetoric of memory in eddic, skaldic, and runic texts. In *Minni and Munin: Memory in Medieval Nordic Culture*, edited by Pernille Hermann, Steven A. Mitchell, and Agnes S. Arnórsdóttir, pp. 1–23. Turnhout, Brepols.
In prep. *Hearing voices, seeing things: textual culture and poetic mediation in medieval Iceland*. TBA.
Jónsdóttir, Selma
1959. *An 11th-Century Byzantine Last Judgement in Iceland*. Almenna Bókfélagið Tómasson, Sverrir, Reykjavík.
Kunz, Keneva (translator)
1999. The Saga of the people of Laxardal. In *The Complete Sagas of Icelanders including 49 Tales* 1–120. Leifur Eiríksson, Reykjavík.
Magerøy, Ellen Marie
1993. Wood-carving. In *Medieval Scandinavia: an Encyclopedia*, edited by Philip Pulsiano and Kirsten Wolf, pp. 725–735. Garland Reference Library of the Humanities, Vol. 934 and Garland Encyclopedias of the Middle Ages, Vol. 1. Garland, New York.
Meulengracht Sørensen, Preben
1986. Þórr's fishing expedition. In *Words and Objects: Towards a Dialogue between Archaeology and History of Religion*, edited by Gro Steinsland, pp. 257–278. Norwegian University Press, Oslo.
Nordal, Guðrún
2001. *Tools of Literacy: The Role of Skaldic Verse in Icelandic Textual Culture of the Twelfth and Thirteenth centuries*. University of Toronto Press, Toronto.
Quinn, Judy
2000. From orality to literacy in medieval Iceland. In *Old Icelandic Literature and Society*, edited by Margaret Clunies Ross, pp. 30–60. Cambridge Studies in Medieval Literature, Vol. 42. Cambridge University Press, Cambridge.
Roesdahl, Else
1991 *The Vikings*. Translated by Susan M. Margeson and Kirsten Williams. The Penguin Press, London.
Tómasson, Sverrir
1993. Laxdœla saga. In *Medieval Scandinavia: an Encyclopedia*, edited by Philip Pulsiano and Kirsten Wolf, pp. 387–388. Garland Reference Library of the Humanities, Vol. 934 and Garland Encyclopedias of the Middle Ages, Vol. 1. Garland, New York.
Vidal, Teva
2013. *Houses and Domestic Life in the Viking Age and Medieval Period: Material Perspectives from Sagas and Archaeology*. Unpublished Ph.D. dissertation, School of English, University of Nottingham, Nottingham.
Wandhoff, Haiko
2003. *Ekphrasis: Kunstbeschreibungen und virtuelle Räume in der Literatur des Mittelalters*. Walter de Gruyter, Berlin.
Webb, Ruth
1999. Ekphrasis ancient and modern: the invention of a genre. *Word and Image* 15(1): 7–18.
Zoëga, Geir T.
2004. *A Concise Dictionary of Old Icelandic*. Dover Publications, Mineola, NY. Originally published 1910. Clarendon Press, Oxford.

*Chapter 4*

# Courtyard sites in western Norway. Central assembly places and judicial institutions in the Late Iron Age

*Asle Bruen Olsen*

*Abstract*

This paper presents four western Norwegian Iron-Age courtyard sites, of which three have been investigated during the last ten years. By comparing functional and contextual aspects of these sites it is argued that they represent central assembly sites in local communities. The coherent similarity of such complex physical structures across time is seen as an expression of strong social and ideological continuity in Iron-Age society from the Roman period until the process of territorial unification under kings with national ambitions that started in the late 9th century. With reference to the Icelandic analogy and the historical connection between Iceland and Western Norway in the Viking period it is also argued for the courtyard sites as an important institution (*þing*) in the pre-state judicial and political system.

## Introduction

The so-called courtyard site consists of a collection of house remains facing or surrounding a courtyard (Fig. 4.1). These sites are dated within the period AD 200–900. The courtyard site is a typical Norwegian phenomenon with no clear parallels outside the country border. The total number of 28 sites is distributed from Bjarkøy, Troms, in northern Norway to Spangereid, Lista, near the southernmost point in southern Norway. Most of the sites are located in south-western Norway (Rogaland) and northern Norway (Nordland/Troms). During the later years, Iron-Age research has focused on the courtyard sites as important contexts in the study of social and political organization in the late Early and Late Iron-Age society (Armstrong 2010; Brink *et al.* 2011; Grimm 2010; Grimm and Stylegard 2004; Kallhovd 1994; Olsen 2003; Olsen 2005, 2013; Storli 2000, 2001, 2006, 2010; Strøm 2010). Today it is agreed that the courtyard sites are gathering places and not settlements, but it is still debated as to whether they were built primarily for economic, religious, judicial,

*Fig. 4.1. Proposed reconstruction of the courtyard site at Hjelle, Stryn, Sogn og Fjordane. Produced by Ragnar Børsheim, © Arkikon AS, Bergen.*

military or other purposes. This paper will focus on the four sites discovered and investigated so far in western Norway (the counties Hordaland, Sogn og Fjordane and Sunnmøre, the southern district of the county Møre og Romsdal). From the location and construction of these sites it will be argued that the Norwegian courtyard sites reflect a polycentric structure of many small territories in which the courtyard sites served as central institutions for the gatherings of independent farmers in societies with a high degree of social equality. Inspired by the work of Morten Olsen (2003) it is further argued that they are the archaeological remains of a pre-state system of local assembly places, or *thing* assemblies, with judicial functions.

## The west Norwegian courtyard sites

The west Norwegian courtyard sites are all recorded under modern cultivation top soil, and appear in the subsoil mainly as house grounds with postholes, hearths and cooking pits. Most of the courtyard sites further north and south have been recognized by visible surface structures from the construction of outer earth and stone walls. This outer wall construction was not a part of the house-building tradition in western Norway. The four sites were all discovered by chance in connection with rescue excavation. This seriously questions to what degree the visible sites give a representative picture of density and distribution, and indicates that the courtyard sites may have been much more common than we can observe today.

West Norway is represented with three sites in Sogn og Fjordane county and one site

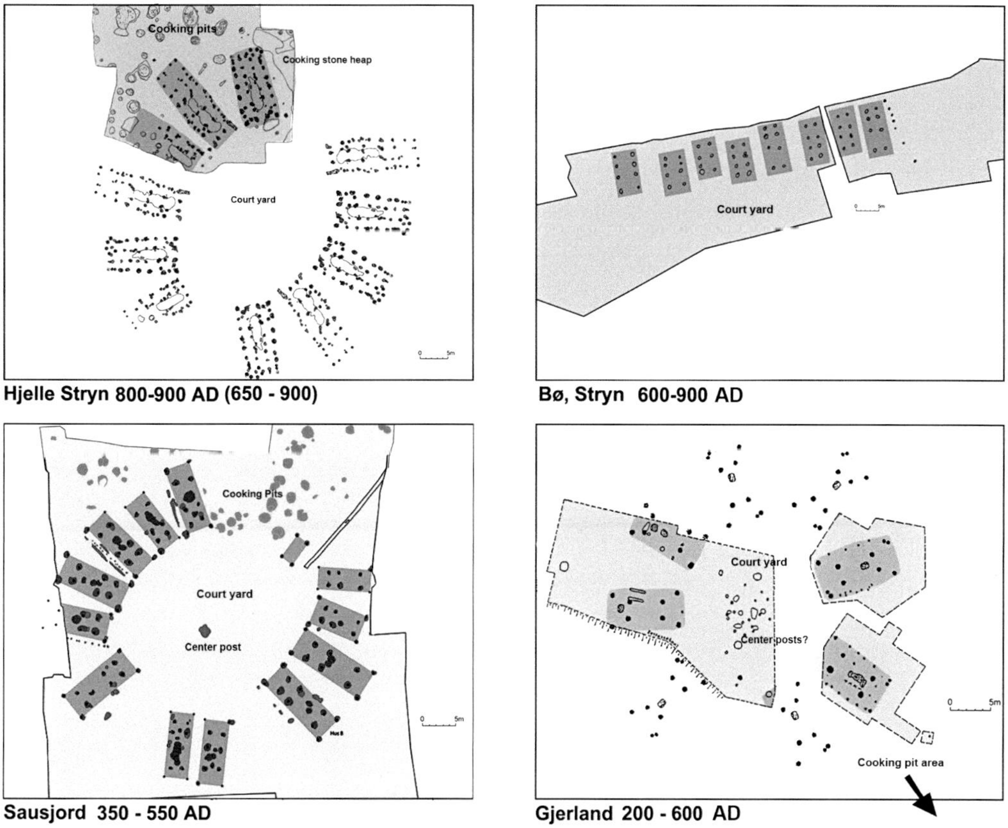


*Fig. 4.2. Plan drawings of the four courtyard sites in western Norway: Hjelle, Stryn (Olsen 2005: fig. 5), Sausjord, Voss (Olsen 2013), Bø, Stryn (Diinhoff and Bødal 2013) and Gjerland, Førde (Randers 1989: fig. 1).*

in Hordaland county: Gjerland, Førde, dated to the late Roman/Migration period (Myhre 1973; Randers 1989), Hjelle, Stryn, dated to the late Merovingian/early Viking period (Olsen 2004, 2005), Bø, Stryn, dated to the Merovingian/early Viking period (Diinhoff and Bødal 2013), and Sausjord, Voss, dated to the Migration period (Fig. 4.2; Hatling and Olsen 2012; Olsen 2013). Gjerland, Hjelle and Bø were not fully excavated, but the position of the uncovered house remains gives positive clues on real extensions and house frequencies. Sausjord was totally excavated, and constitutes the most completely investigated courtyard site in Norway. Gjerland, Hjelle and Sausjord are circular sites with the entrances facing an inner courtyard, thus falling into the common pattern of the Norwegian courtyard sites. Sausjord has 12 three-aisled houses, and it is likely that Gjerland has consisted of eight houses and Hjelle of 11 houses. Bø differs from the others by the linear position of eight exposed houses, and it can certainly be disputed as to whether this is a variant of the courtyard site or another type of gathering place. However, in Northern Norway courtyard sites with documented continuity in the late Early Iron Age and Late Iron Age show late extensions with more linear or irregular house rows (Berglund 1995: 63). There are also more linear structures in two of the three dated to the Late Iron Age in mid-Norway, Trøndelag (Stenvik 2001: 41, 2005: 133–145), indicating a larger variety in courtyard site construction in the Late Iron Age. Bø is therefore included here as a courtyard site.

### Finds and localization narrowing the frame of interpretation

Finds from postholes and hearths are few and scattered. At Hjelle the house floors were sunken and partly preserved under the topsoil, containing a relatively large sample of objects related to the court site activities. Among these is an Anglo-Saxon copper coin, *a styca,* embossed by the coin master Eanwin under king Eanred (Ethelred) in Northumbria in the period AD 810–840. The Hjelle material is dominated by small iron objects comprising several knives, arrowhead, scissor fragment, fish hook, key ring and a large number of rivets and nails, in addition to two beads of Viking-Age type, fire flints and stones for polishing. The three uncovered house grounds had almost identical find frequencies and distributions, with high densities in and near the entrances, lower around the house hearths and lack of finds in the inner space (Olsen 2005: 328–330). The Sausjord material contains a small Migration-period fibula, found in a posthole, one fibula needle pin of iron, two beads, two iron key fragments and a few rivets and nails (Olsen 2013: 98–100). Gjerland and Bø suffer from the lack of determinable artifact types (Diinhoff and Bødal 2013; Randers 1989: 16).

The absence of textile production tools, the most common find category in farm contexts, and the lack of finds that can be associated with military activities, strengthen the interpretation of the courtyard sites *as temporary assembly places constructed for peaceful activities*. This tendency in the composition of artifacts generally matches the inventories from investigated courtyard sites further north and south (Grimm 2010: 151–189; Johansen and Søbstad 1977). The peaceful aspect is also indicated by the fact that all the four sites lie on exposed, unsheltered places outside Iron-Age farmsteads and cultivation fields, located on what we may describe as 'neutral ground', but still in the vicinity of the settlements (Olsen 2005: 338, 2013: 103). This pattern also seems to characterize the layout of the sites in Southwest Norway (Grimm 2010: 44) and northern Norway (Storli 2010: 130–135).

### Common structural features and spheres of activity

The west Norwegian courtyard site houses vary in size between 8 m and 12 m in length and 4–5 m in width, and show no spatial or functional differentiation indicating that they have been built for main purposes other than the lodging of people at the assembly (Randers 1989: 5–6; Olsen 2005: 337, 2013: 103). This also seems to be the case for the other Norwegian sites, although it is better founded in the more thoroughly investigated sites in west Norway. The excavations in west Norway have to a larger degree than other court site investigations exposed areas in the front of and at the back of the house complexes.

Sausjord as the most completely uncovered site clearly constitutes a physical organization with an inner almost 'clean' courtyard, in which a posthole in the middle marks the center, and a high density of cooking pits are located between and behind the houses (Fig. 4.2). The excavations at Gjerland and Hjelle have also uncovered large concentrations of cooking pits outside the houses (Randers 1989: 19; Olsen 2005: 324). The courtyards of these two sites were only partially uncovered, at Hjelle only a small area without pits close to the houses. At Gjerland the excavation reached the center part of the courtyard, and here several small postholes were exposed, maybe the remains of shifting center posts or a light, wooden construction (Randers 1989: 6). At Bø, the area behind the houses remains unexposed. Here, a few cooking pits are documented at the side of the houses, but not in the front area (Diinhoff and Bødal 2013). Bø differs from the other sites, and one should be careful to draw conclusions about function at this stage. The features of the three *circular* courtyard sites seem to mark three main spheres of activity: One inner courtyard as the central space for gathering and dialogue, surrounding buildings for the lodging of those who met at the assembly, and behind the houses an area for the preparation of foods which most likely were consumed in the context of ceremonial and ritual actions that took place in the courtyard.

### The courtyard sites reflecting social equality

The courtyard sites reflect more clearly than any other types of archaeological sites the horizontal social dimension of Iron-Age society. This is indicated by both location and physical structure. Landscape analysis of the courtyard sites in Northern and Southwest Norway show a generally low affinity to farms which from the grave finds can be associated with chieftain farms (Grimm 2010: 44; Storli 2010: 130–136). This pattern can also be applied to the sites in west Norway, suggesting that the courtyard sites basically represent assembly places outside the control of individual power. Another argument for the same is that strong territorial chiefdoms hardly would have structured the exertion of power on collective gatherings as expressed by the courtyard sites. The horizontal dimension is also expressed in the physical organization of closely attached, identically constructed houses with only small internal variations in size. This uniformity is best illustrated at Sausjord as the only completely excavated courtyard (Olsen 2013: 92, 105). These aspects point to the courtyard sites as an institution grounded on a large degree of social equality between the people who met at the assembly, and, consequently, as an institution that served a society with strong egalitarian traits.

### General view on the courtyard site assemblies as an important structuring element of the pre-state society

The West Norwegian courtyard site dates, finds and locations picture a society which in the late Early Iron Age had grown dependent of neutral assembly places for peaceful collective gathering and dialogue. The main purpose of the gatherings can hardly be recognized from the finds and the physical structures, but the importance of this institution is underlined by its following long-lasting continuity across periods and through changes. In the perspective of the 700 year time span and the wide distribution of all the Norwegian courtyard sites as a body of similar, complex physical structures, they can be seen as an expression of a common social and political pre-state system established in the Roman period, and as an institution that served to maintain and reproduce the tribal structure of the northern Germanic society in Norway (*cf.* Olsen 2005: 341–352).

## Central assembly places in settlement territories

The farming district of Jæren in south-west Norway has the highest frequency of courtyard sites in Norway, all of them so far dated to the late Early Iron Age. Here the sites are situated close to the geographical center points of delimited Iron-Age settlement areas (Grimm 2010). This pattern is coherent with a polycentric social and political structure of small tribal territories with courtyard sites as central assemblies. Considering the landscape context of the west Norwegian sites, neither of these appear to be center points in larger regional networks. Gjerland is located in Haukedalen, a remote and rather isolated Iron-Age settlement area outside historically important communication lines in the region. The Late Iron-Age sites Hjelle and Bø are situated at knot junctions in the two adjacent districts Oppstryn and Nedstryn. Sausjord is located in the middle of the historically interconnected area of Vossestrand, north of the district Vangen in Voss, a densely populated area in the Iron Age (Olsen 2013: 104). The locations of the few known West Norwegian sites thus seem to reflect a structure of many small, more or less adjacent local communities organized around the courtyard site assembly (Fig. 4.3). This structure was established in the Roman period, possibly as a result of contact with and influence from southern Germanic tribes (Olsen 2005: 341–344). The Late Iron-Age continuity of sites implies that it was maintained, but interrupted in the end by the process of territorial unification under kings with national ambitions which started in the 9th century. However, it may have resolved at an earlier stage in certain areas. In Jæren, the absence of sites dated to the Late Iron Age can be seen as an indicator of a development towards territorial unification due to political events and structural change in the early Late Iron Age.

## The Icelandic thing as a reference for interpretation

The written Icelandic sources, especially The book of Settlements (*Landnámabók*) and The book of Icelanders (*Íslendingabók*) recount the stories of the first settlers, stories that give us a clearer picture of the Viking Age in Iceland than in the Scandinavian homelands of the emigrants. These stories have been important in the attempts of archaeologists and historians to understand and describe the pre-state society of Norway. The use of the so-called Icelandic analogy is problematic in many aspects, mainly because the stories were written down more than 200 years after the period of colonization. Linking the colonization to clearly interrelated archaeological features in the two countries has been a problem for

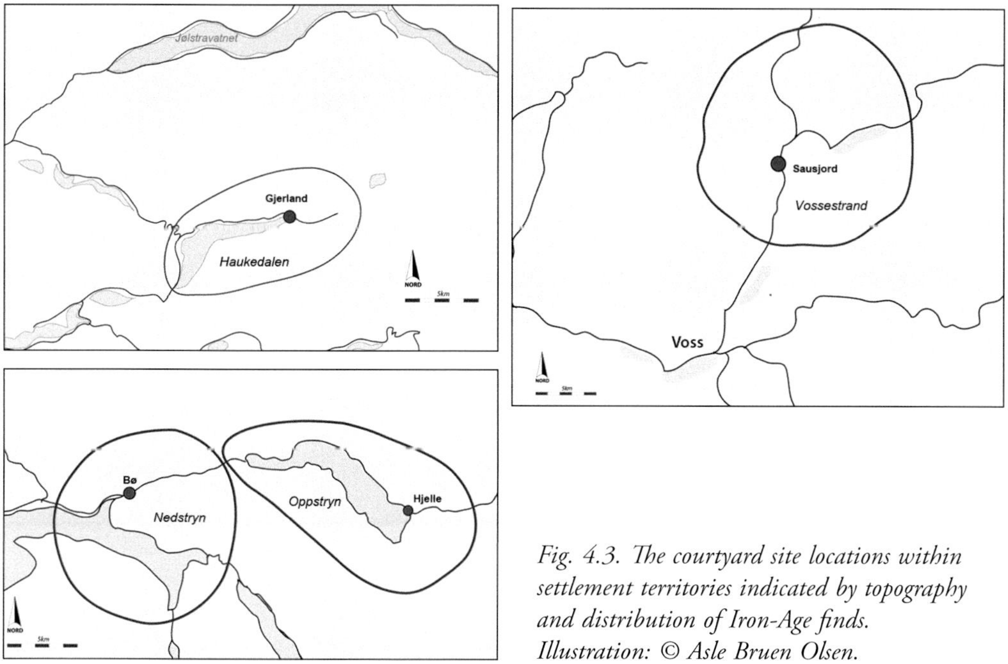


*Fig. 4.3. The courtyard site locations within settlement territories indicated by topography and distribution of Iron-Age finds. Illustration: © Asle Bruen Olsen.*

archaeologists. Contrary to earlier research, recent studies have focused more specifically on the Icelandic sources as a basis for interpreting the courtyard sites as *þing* assemblies (M. Olsen 2003; A. Olsen 2005, 2013; Storli 2010).

From the written sources it can be stated that the Viking-Age Icelandic thing was not an institution connected with chiefdom control and individual territorial supremacy. Within a basically tribal society the thing served two main purposes: First, to exercise law and rules in order to solve conflicts and to negotiate and secure collective and individual rights and interests, and, secondly, to regulate and control leadership through assembly election of leaders. Simplified, one can say that the Viking-Age population in Iceland was divided into two social categories, freeborn men and women and their slaves, and it was the freeborn, independent farmers that represented at the thing assemblies and elected the leaders (Eínarsson 1995: 64; Pétursdottír 2007: 3). The leaders, *i.e. goðar*, were recruited mainly within a social class of freeborn men with status linked to ancestry and wealth, and they formed a kind of aristocracy (Þorlaksson 2005: 120). But the position of the leaders was based less on wealth than on personal charisma, honour and reputation (Byock 2001: 120).

The Icelandic Althing (general assembly) governing system was established after the settlement period, around AD 930. This national system of political, judicial and social organization of the Icelandic society was a result of an autonomous historical development. The thing assembly itself was older, and may have originated from Norwegian territory. The oldest archaeologically known local site lies close to Elliðavatn at Krossnes in the vicinity of Reykjavik, commonly named *þingnes*. It has been partly investigated (1981–1986 and 2003 by Guðmundur Ólafsson), and consists of twelve 10–15 m long turf 'boots' built for the lodging of participants at the assembly. The boots are more irregularly scattered than the houses in most of the Norwegian courtyard sites, and less solid in construction (perhaps due to the limited availability of trees as house building material), but face a flat and open central area marked with a circular turf wall, 15 m in diameter, surrounding a small mound in the middle. Some of the structures are dated shortly after the 871±2 tephra settlement layer, probably around AD 900 (Ólafsson 1987: 41; Þorlaksson 2007: 40). *Þingnes* has a physical organization that resembles the Late Iron-Age courtyard sites in Norway, both in the cluster of houses obviously built for temporary lodging of many people and in the orientation of these houses with the entrances facing a central court area.

## Ingolfr Arnarsson

Within the research on the pioneer settlements (the *Landnám*) it is generally agreed that Iceland was settled mostly by Norsemen in the period AD 870–930, and that Ingolfr Arnarson from Western Norway, most probably with his homestead farm at Rivedal, Fjaler, Sogn og Fjordane, was the first settler. He established himself with farm and household in Reyjavik around AD 870. He may have emigrated because he was convicted of murder, but the written sources also indicate that he as well as many of his followers went to Iceland to escape from – or in opposition to – king Harald Fairhair, the most important actor in the events concerning the process of national unification (Olsen 2005: 52, Þorlaksson 2007: 52, 72). In the center of Reykjavik, a Viking-Age farm hall was excavated in 2001–2003 (today preserved and exhibited), situated on the historically largest farmstead in the area before the development of the city. This settlement was established around or immediately before a volcanic eruption tephra layer dated in glaciers to 871±2 (Stefánsson and Þorgímsdóttir 2007: 132). It is assumed to represent the farm of Ingolfr Arnarson. The farm confirms that written sources and archaeology are broadly consistent, and that Norse settlers came to Iceland around the time stated in old Icelandic writings (Gunnarsdóttir 2007: 9).

## The courtyard sites as thing assemblies based on their historical and chronological affinity to the early Icelandic thing

Stryn is an eastern municipality in the Fjordane district of Sogn og Fjordane. This district covers almost the same area as the Old Norse Firdafylkir, which also included Fjaler and the homestead of Ingolfr Arnarson. The late Merovingian and early Viking-Age settlements in Stryn are rich in grave finds. These are evenly distributed, and do not reflect a farm hierarchy (Olsen 2005: 252). Together with the location of the Hjelle and Bø courtyard sites, this indicates that the sites functioned as local assembly places in a pre-kingdom society of basically egalitarian farmers. Thus, Hjelle and Bø represent an institution with potential affinity to the early Icelandic society, both in time, organization and in terms of their geographical location in one of the supposed core areas of emigration to Iceland.

The Fjordane district has the densest concentration in Norway of Irish and Anglo-Saxon

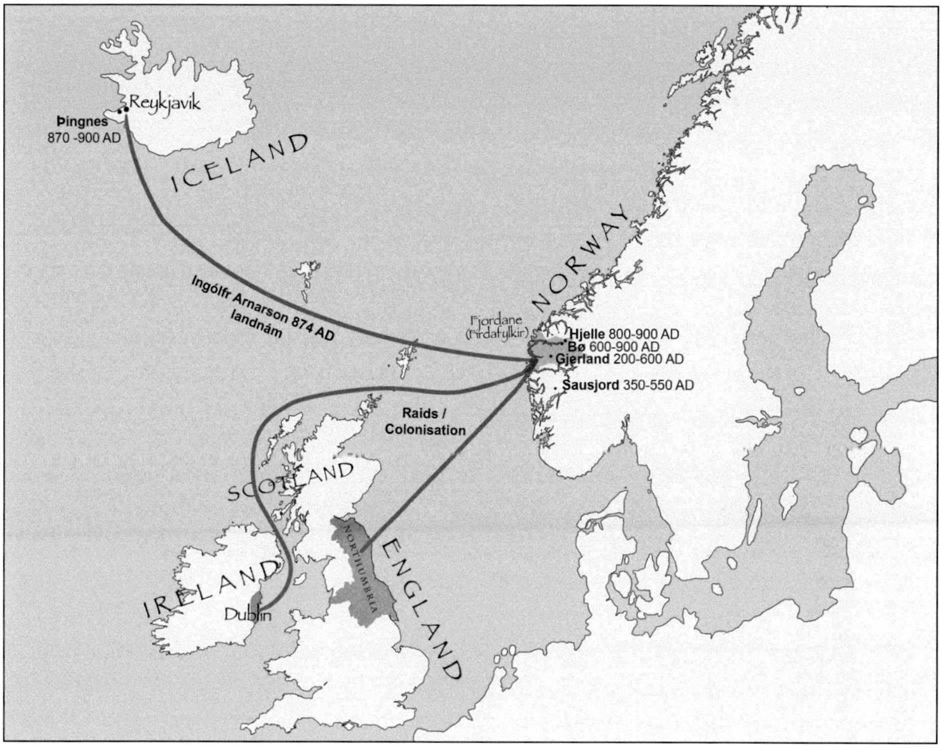


*Fig. 4.4. Map illustrating the possible historical connection between the western Norwegian courtyard sites and the early Icelandic thing. Illustration: © Asle Bruen Olsen.*

coins and other objects from the 9th century brought back through raids and colonization (Bakka 1963: 55). And, furthermore, this area is represented with the so far largest known Norwegian Viking ship buried under Rundehågjen in Eid (Magnus 1967: 61, 141). This ship certainly shows the ability of these local societies to equip vessels for raids and journeys across oceans.

More important in this context is that the Hjelle courtyard site, which according to several radiocarbon dates was abandoned around AD 880 (Olsen 2005: 327), probably existed when Ingolfr Arnarson lived in Fjaler, possibly also at the time of his final departure from Fjordane (Fig. 4.4). It is almost unlikely that he was not familiar with the courtyard assemblies in Stryn as well as other courtyard sites in the area. If this was the case, then he would have had knowledge of the institution and the system this represented. He may even have been an active participant in courtyard site assemblies. With this background it is reasonable to assume that he, as an influential person in the organization of the core settlements in the Reykjavik area, contributed to the establishment of the first thing assembly modelled after the assemblies in the society he left, like the ones in Stryn. Consequently, from this possible historical and chronological affinity between the two institutions, the *Western Norwegian courtyard sites should be interpreted and understood as thing assemblies.*

The position of Ingolfr and his family in the establishment of the thing assembly in the new land is supported by written sources. According to the book of Icelanders the oldest thing assembly was situated at Kjalarnes north of Reykjavik. This is supposed to have been founded by Þorstein, son of Ingolfr. The sources also point to Þorstein as the precursor of the national general assembly, the Althing, at *Þingvellír.* Kjalarnes is described as the most important local thing before the Althing, but it has not been identified archaeologically. One opinion is that it shortly after its establishment was moved to Krossnes, and that Þingnes in reality represents the Kjalarnes assembly referred to in the book of Icelanders (Þorlaksson 2007: 40).

The law practiced at the early Icelandic thing was recited at the assembly by a law speaker. This started before the Althing and the later Icelandic implementation of the Norwegian Gulating law code. According to Helgi Þorlaksson (2007: 40), the early Icelanders are presumed to have applied common and customary law and legal principles to which they were accustomed in their home countries. It is therefore likely that a West Norwegian courtyard site law code was brought to Iceland by Ingolfr and his followers, and formed an important part of the judicial practice at the early thing, probably with modifications applied to Icelandic circumstances.

## Concluding remarks

It is generally agreed that Ingolfr Arnarssons immigration to Iceland was motivated by his opposition to the new ruling forces that wanted to abolish the equality of tribal leaders, with the vision to contribute to the formation of a 'free' society based on old values, a society in which the local thing was a strong pillar (Þorlaksson 2007: 52). This implies that Ingolfr had the reproduction of the traditional pre-state tribal society as a political and ideological agenda.

From the story of Ingolfr Arnarsson and the strong possibility of him and his followers as a link between the early Icelandic thing and the late Norwegian courtyard sites, represented by the Hjelle and Bø sites, it is – in my opinion – more relevant than before to use the Icelandic analogy as a framework for discussion and analysis on social and political organization of the pre-state Iron-Age societies in Norway. The polycentric tribal structure indicated by the location of the courtyard sites and the social egalitarianism reflected in the physical construction of the sites seems to be in accordance with how the early Icelandic society can be described from written and archaeological sources. A premise for further research should therefore be that the early Icelandic tribal society in most aspects mirrors the western Norwegian pre-state society in the Iron Age.

Iceland had basically a tribal organization in the colonization period. However, this obviously does not mean that the social and political structure of the early Icelandic society was purely egalitarian, and that it reflects a Norwegian structure without any form of hierarchy and ranking. As mentioned above, the Icelandic leaders (*goðar*) were recruited mainly within a group of freeborn men with status linked to ancestry and wealth, thus forming a kind of aristocracy. In Norway, the existence of an aristocracy is expressed by a marked differentiation in the burial custom from the Late Roman period. This aristocracy probably built much of its power on the ability to control trade and to mobilize warrior followers, and over time conflicts within this aristocracy must have been an important factor in the development from tribal confederacy to early kingdom in West Norway as well as in other regions. Before the process of territorial unification and the formation of a more stratified society in Norway, the aristocracy was hardly a uniform class, but in the areas it held a strong position in, it is likely to have had a monopoly on the recruitment of leaders elected at the assemblies.

### *References*


Armstrong, Niall

2010. Early Iron Age courtyard sites in Norway as arenas for rites de passage. In *Socialisation. Recent research on childhood and children in the past. Proceedings from the 2nd International Conference of the Society for the Study of Childhood in the Past in Stavanger, Norway, 28–30th September 2008*, edited by Grete Lillehammer, pp. 115–124. AmS-skrifter, Vol. 23. Arkeologisk museum, Universitetet i Stavanger, Stavanger.

Bakka, Egil

1963. *Some English decorated metal objects found in Norwegian Viking graves.Contributions to the art history of the eight century AD.* Annual publication for the Univeristy of Bergen. Norwegian Universities Press, Bergen. Humanistisk serie pp. 1 – 66.

Berglund, Birgitta

1995. *Tjøtta-riket. En arkeologisk undersøkelse av maktforhold og sentrumsdannelser på Helgelandskysten fra Kr.f. til 1700 e.Kr.* Dr. philos. dissertation, University of Trondheim, UNIT. Electronic document, http://www.nb.no/nbsok/nb/746385a26d565b23fb38f19c28f1b340.nbdigital?lang=en#0

Brink, Stefan, Oliver Grimm, Frode Iversen, Halldis Hobæk, Ulf Näsman, Alexandra Sanmark, Przemyslaw Urbanczyk, Orri Vésteinsson, Marie Ødegaard and Inger Storli

2011. Comments on Inger Storli: 'Court Sites of Arctic Norway: Remains of Thing Sites and Representations of Political Consolidation Processes in the Northern Germanic World during the First Millenium AD?' *Norwegian Archaeological Review* 44(1): 89–117.

Byock, Jesse

2001. *Viking Age Iceland.* Penguin Books, London.

Diinhoff, Søren and Sigmund Bødal

2013. *Tingsted og naustmiljø. Resultater efter tre års udgravninger ved Bø på Stryn.* Year book for University Museum of Bergen. University of Bergen, Bergen.

Eínarsson, Bjarní

1995. *The Settlement of Iceland: A Critical Approach. Granastaðir and the Ecological Heritage.* Hið íslendska bókmenntafélag, Reykjavik.

Grimm, Oliver

2010. *Court Sites in Southwest Norway – A Social Organization in an International Perspective.* AmS-Skrifter, Vol. 22. Museum of Archaeology, University of Stavanger, Stavanger.

Grimm, Oliver and Frans-Arne Stylegar

2004. Court sites in southwest Norway. Reflection of a Roman period political organisation? *Norwegian Archaeological Review* 37(2): 111–133.

Gunnarsdóttir, Gudny Gerður

2007. The beginning of Reykjavik. In *Reykjavik 871±2. Landnámssýningin = The Settlement*

*Exhibition*, edited by Orri Vésteinsson, Helgi Þorláksson, Árni Einarsson and Brydís Sverrisdóttir, pp. 8–9. Reykjavik City Museum, Reykjavik.

Hatling, Stian and Asle Bruen Olsen.
2012. Arkeologiske undersøkelser av et eldre jernalders ringformet tunanlegg ved Sausjord gnr. 284, bnr. 3, Voss kommune, Hordaland. Unpublished report, University Museum of Bergen, Section for Cultural Heritage Management.

Johansen, Olav Sverre and Tom Søbstad
1977. De nordnorske tunanleggene fra jernalderen. *Viking* 41: 9–56.

Kallhovd, Karl
1994. *Den kulturhistoriske orden. En analyse med utgangspunkt i Leksaren.* Dissertation in Nordic archaeology, University of Oslo, Oslo.

Magnus, Bente
1967. *Studier i Nordfjords yngre jernalder.* Dissertation in Nordic archaeology, University of Bergen.

Myhre, Bjørn
1973. I en åker på Gjerland i Førde. *Arkeo* 1: 15–28.

Ólafsson, Guðmundur
1987. Þingnes by Elliðavatn: The first local assembly in Iceland? In *Proceedings of the Tenth Viking Congress. Larkollen, Norway, 1985,* edited by Charlotte Blindheim and James Knirk, pp. 343–349. Skrifter, Ny rekke Vol. 9. Universitetets Oldsakssamling, Oslo.

Olsen, Asle Bruen
2004. Arkeologiske undersøkelser av et vikingtids tunanlegg på Hjelle i Stryn. Hjelle gbnr 20/2, Stryn kommune, Sogn og Fjordane. Unpublished report, University Museum of Bergen, Section for Cultural Heritage Management.
2005. Et vikingtids tunanlegg på Hjelle i Stryn. En konservativ institusjon i et konservativt samfunn. In *Fra funn til samfunn. Jernalderstudier tilegnet Bergljot Solberg på 70-årsdagen,* edited by Knut Andreas Bergsvik and Asbjørn Engevik, pp. 319–354. UBAS Nordisk, Vol. 1. Arkeologisk institutt, Universitetet i Bergen, Bergen.
2013. Undersøkelsen av et eldre jernalders tunanlegg på Sausjord, Voss, Hordaland. Et nytt bidrag til kunnskapen om jernalderssamfunnets sosiale og politiske organisasjon. *Viking* 76: 87–112.

Olsen, Morten
2003. *Den sosio-politiske organiseringen av Jæren i eldre jernalder. Et tolkningsforsøk med utgangspunkt i skriftlige kilder og tunanleggene.* Hovedfag's thesis, University of Tromsø, Tromsø.

Pétursdóttir, þóra.
2007. *'Deyr fé, deyja frændr'. Re-animating mortuary remains from Viking Age Iceland.* Master's thesis in archaeology, University of Tromsø, Tromsø. Electronic document, http://munin.uit.no/handle/10037/1165.

Randers, Kjersti
1989. Et ringformet tun? på Gjerland. Unpublished report, Bergen Museum.

Stefánsson, Hjörleifur and Sigriður Þorgímsdóttir
2007. Rekjavik 871±2. In *Reykjavik 871±2. Landnámssýningin = The Settlement Exhibition*, edited by Orri Vésteinsson, Helgi Þorláksson, Árni Einarsson and Brydís Sverrisdóttir, pp. 132–133. Reykjavik City Museum, Reykjavik.

Stenvik, Lars
2001. *Skei. Et maktsenter fram fra skyggen.* Vitark, Vol. 2. Vitenskapsmuseet NTNU, Trondheim.
2005. Samfunnsorganisasjon. In *Landskapet blir landsdel: fram til 1350,* edited by Sigmund Alsaker, Kalle Sognnes, Lars Stenvik, Merete Røskaft and Olav Skevik, pp. 133–146. Trøndelags historie, Vol. 1. Tapir akademisk forlag, Trondheim.

Storli, Inger
2000. 'Barbarians' of the North. Reflections on the establishment of courtyard sites in north Norway. *Norwegian Archaeological Review* 33(2): 81–103.
2001. Tunanleggenes rolle i nordnorsk jernalder. *Viking* 64: 87–111.
2006. *Hålogaland før rikssamlingen. Politiske prosesser i perioden 200–900 e.Kr.* Instituttet for sammenlignende kulturforskning, Vol. 123. Novus forlag, Oslo.
2010. Court sites of Arctic Norway: remains of thing sites and representations of political consolidation processes in the northern Germanic world during the first millenium AD? *Norwegian Archaeological Review* 43(2): 128–144.

Strøm, Ingvild Onsøien
2007. *Tunanlegg i Midt-Norge. Med særlig vekt på Væremsanlegget i Namdalen.* Master's thesis, NTNU University Museum, Trondheim.

Þorlaksson, Helgi
2005. 'Historical background: Iceland 870–1400'. In *A Companion to Old Norse-Icelandic Literature and Culture*, edited by Rory McTurk, pp. 136–154. Blackwell, Oxford.
2007. Assembly sites: Þingnes and Guli. The first settler: Norwegian roots. The story of Ingólfr and justification of authority. In *Reykjavik 871±2. Landnámssýningin = The Settlement Exhibition*, edited by Orri Vésteinsson, Helgi Þorláksson, Árni Einarsson and Brydís Sverrisdóttir, pp. 40–53. Reykjavik City Museum, Reykjavik.

*Chapter 5*

# Place names and settlement development around an aristocratic residence. Thoughts from an on-going study of the hinterland of Tissø

*Sofie Laurine Albris*

*Abstract*

Through the 6th–11th centuries AD, people in western Zealand threw weapons and jewellery into Lake Tissø. Twenty years of excavations have revealed a Late Iron-Age and Viking-period magnate's farm with large feasting halls, market places and workshops. A residence of this size would have had power over a very large area. However, the place has not left traces in any written accounts. Here, another source is employed in an investigation of the landscape surrounding the magnate's residence. The place name *Tissø* contains a word *tī m., meaning 'god', or the equivalent name of the Old Norse god Tyr. Other ancient place names may reflect functions and a settlement structure inflicted by the central residence. This paper presents an on-going study that evaluates settlement patterns through comparative analyses of archaeological remains and place names. The aim is to improve our understanding of the social and ideological landscape throughout the Viking period, but the thoughts presented here should be considered preliminary.

## Introduction

Tissø is the second largest lake on the Danish island of Zealand and the surrounding landscape is rich in finds from the entire prehistoric period. Several weapons and other objects have been found in the lake itself. Some date to the Early Iron Age, but most were deposited in the Late Iron Age and Viking period. In 1977 a Viking-period gold ring weighing almost 2 kg was found in a field on the western bank of the lake. Subsequently, through 20 years of investigations, the Danish National Museum has unearthed a Late Iron-Age and Viking-period settlement. The large site consists of a magnate's residence with large feasting halls, market places and workshops (*cf.* Jørgensen 2002, 2009: 337–346). The first hall was built around AD 550 (Bican 2010), and in the late 7th century a new main hall was erected 500 m to the south. Here several phases of halls, of which the largest was

48 m long, were built on the same location. In total, the settlement covered *c.* 500,000 $m^2$ and is estimated to have housed at least 50 permanent residents. The excavations and surveys have documented 50 houses and 200 pit houses, and through magnetic surveys it is estimated that the total number of pit houses throughout the period was up to 600. Approximately 12,000 metal objects and 250 kg of animal bones have been found. The pit houses and finds indicate that occasional markets and gatherings were held here, with up to 1000 people attending. From around AD 1050, activities gradually ceased at the site. Its successor may be the early medieval manors at Lunden or Sæby on the southern and eastern banks of the lake. In spite of its size, the Tissø residence is not mentioned in any written accounts. We know of Tissø's contemporary and parallel site Lejre on central Zealand (Christensen 1991, 2007), but the few historical documents from the pre-Christian period do not mention Tissø.

Ancient place names may help the investigation of the landscape surrounding the magnate's residence. Although place names were written down in the Middle Ages, they reflect an older, oral tradition of naming places that is independent from the practices of historians. Thus, place names may reflect functions and settlement organisations from the times when the names were formed. Archaeological investigations constantly increase our knowledge of settlement development through the Iron Age and Viking period, offering new possibilities for evaluation of place name patterns in relation to archaeological material.

In this paper, some thoughts are presented from a comparative study of the place names and archaeological remains around Lake Tissø and its hinterland. The investigation is part of my ongoing PhD project and the material presented is to be considered preliminary. The aim of the comparative analyses is to elucidate the long-term settlement development of this part of north-western Zealand, and to discuss the role of the magnate's residence in the landscape from a new perspective.

## Defining the area or region of the 'central place'

In both place name research and archaeology, it is thought that aristocratic residences like Tissø had power over and effect on large surrounding areas (Helgesson 2008: 53). The definition of the region and its possible influence is however mainly a question of interpretation based on natural boundaries, historical borders and administrative units. In the present survey, I have defined an area consisting of the parishes around the lake and towards the sea, the Great Belt. I see the Tissø-settlement as the focal point in a network of sites within a surrounding region. This region may not have clear boundaries and the surveyed area does not cover its entire scope. It is a selection based on the communicative landscape, assumed to have been structured around the large lake, the main waterways, and oriented towards the sea.

The magnate's farm at Tissø is by far the dominating settlement within this area. A petty king like the one who may have resided at Tissø probably had power over a group of people, rather than over a defined territory (Sindbæk 2008: 76). Yet there are no significant traces of agricultural production on the site itself and a residence of this size would therefore have needed to obtain resources from a large hinterland. Important questions are: How were land-ownership, distribution of resources and agrarian strategies in the area affected by the residence? Did the site inflict some kind of structure on the settlements around it, and is this reflected in the different source categories, archaeology and place names?

## The name Tissø and place names as part of long-term social processes in the landscape

Place names are formed and disappear as part of social processes where people inhabit and move around in their landscape (Albris 2014b). The fact that the names are locally bound, make them a unique and valuable source of information about the cultural landscape. Another important quality of place names is that they are a product of communication, and their creation and survival rely on their continued use within a group of people (Strid 2011: 292). Place names are therefore very sensitive to social change and different kinds of discontinuity. Paradoxically, they can also survive through significant transformations, and I argue that when they do, they mark some kind of continuity or transfer of information. In a long-term perspective, the patterns of place names must therefore be understood in relation to processes of agrarian production, political power, administration, and demography.

The Tissø-site gives us a good example of the complicated relation between place names, the cultural landscape, and social change. Here, the issue of the spatial dimensions in religious practices and beliefs is illustrated through the relation between the place name and the archaeological finds. The name of the Lake *Tissø* and the Iron-Age/Viking-period settlement must somehow be connected. The specific of the place name is a word *tī m., meaning 'god", or the equivalent *Tī, the Old Danish name for the Norse god Tyr (Holmberg 1986: 115). The name of this deity is found in the name of the weekday *Tuesday* and in several place names from the Danish area. However, Tyr does not occur in Sweden and only once in Norway, revealing some regional differences in the pre-Christian Scandinavian religion (Brink 2007a: 121). Tyr was probably an old Germanic god, and his name is derived from Proto-Germanic *tiwaz, Indo-European *deiuos. It is related to the name of the Greek god Zeus, the Indian Dyaus, and the Roman Jupiter. The fundamental meaning of these names is 'god, the heavenly', and there has probably been an appellative which was identical with the name *Tyr*: Old Norse týr, Old Danish *tī, simply meaning 'god'.

The most probable interpretation of the name Tissø is that the generic is the Danish word *sø*, 'lake' and the specific is in the plural form. Tissø thus translates into 'lake of the gods". However, there is a formal possibility that the generic could be the word *ø*, 'island', also used for high ground in wet or boggy areas (Jørgensen 2008: 345). Early written versions of the Lake Tissø name (1452 Tisøe) do not reveal the original form of the generic element, and it is impossible to distinguish between *sø* and *ø* when they are preceded by a noun or name in the genitive masculine form. In the Viking period, the situation of the residence on the western bank was on a holm or peninsular between the lake and surrounding wetland (Fig 5.1). If the generic is the word ø, the specific must be genitive singular, meaning 'the island of Tyr/the god'. The name would have been transferred to the lake through metonymy at a later stage.

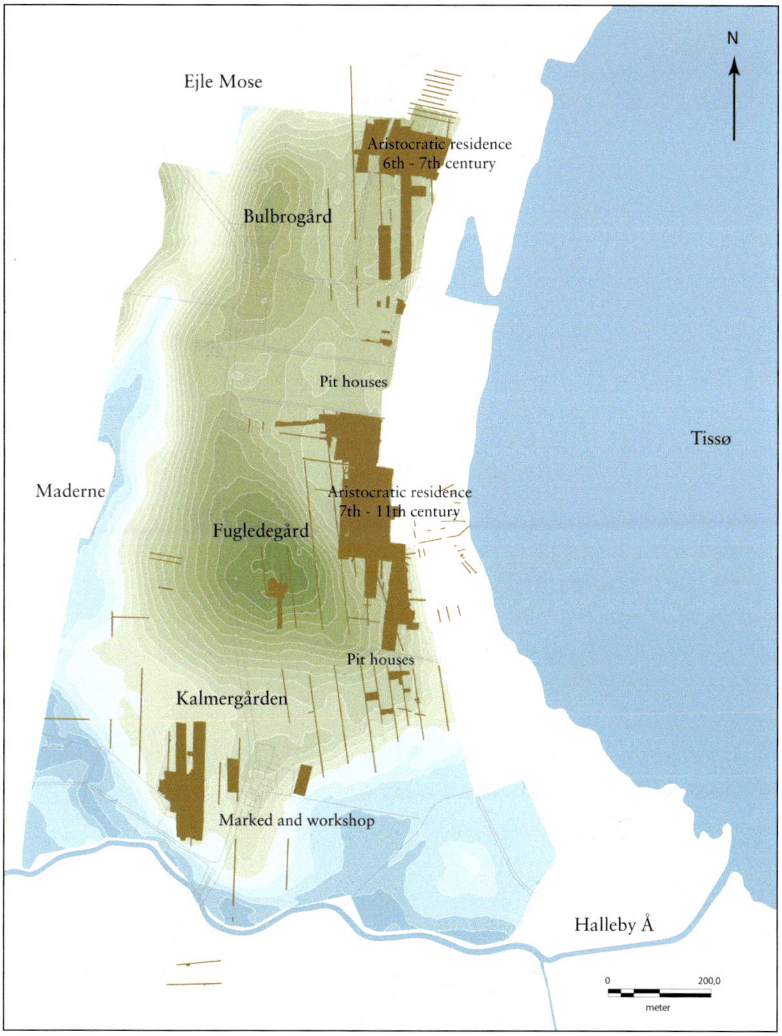


*Fig. 5.1. Overview of the manorial residence at Tissø with the Viking-period topography reconstructed. Map: Pia Brejnholt and Josefine Franck Bican, © Nationalmuseet.*

As shown, there are several possibilities for the interpretation of the name Tissø, even though it is almost certainly a sacral name (Jørgensen 2008: 297). Regardless of the exact interpretation of the name, the place had a religious importance before the conversion to Christianity. Some of the most significant Iron-Age central places can be linked to place names with a religious content. Besides Tissø, examples are Gudme on Funen (Kousgård Sørensen 1985) and Helgö in the Swedish Mälar Region (Zachrisson 2004). Some smaller sites that functioned as local centres also seem to have had sacral names (Grimm and Pesch 2011; Vikstrand 2001). The names imply that religious functions were tied to central places at different levels, and they have supported the interpretation of such sites as cult centres (*cf.* Andrén *et al.* 2006; Jørgensen 2009). The actual relation between these settlements and their names remains elusive, but both names and settlements are empirical facts. In contrast, it seems strange that no religious place names can be linked to the sacrificial bogs of the Iron Age, such as Illerup in Jutland or Vimose on Funen. Charlotte Fabech (1992: 144–148), who has pointed this out, has argued that the ritual use of the bogs ceased or changed during the 5th century AD. Fabech sees a shift happening in the beginning of the Late Iron Age, where cult involving votive deposits in 'natural' or open air offering sites is transferred to worship in constructed shrines, controlled by the elite (*cf.* Fabech 1999). It has been argued that deposits in wetlands continued into the Viking period (Henriksen 2010; Lund 2004; Vikstrand 2001: 410–417), yet apparently not in a way that ensured the survival of religious place names. Possibly sacral names were never given to the bog sites, but it is unlikely that their long-term use and varying practises did not result in any name giving. They must have played an important part in collective awareness through a long time (Ilkjær 2002: 205).

Lake Tissø cannot be classified as a site with large-scale weapon deposits, but the lake and its surrounding wetlands hold finds of spears, swords, axes, tools, jewellery, and figurines as well as animal and human bones from the Early Iron Age through to the Late Viking period (Lund 2006; Pedersen 2003). This shows that the religious significance of the lake dates back a long time. It is likely that the formation of the sacral name is connected with the establishment of the earliest magnate's farm by Bulbrogård, but it cannot be determined which of these came first. In my view, it is plausible that most of our pre-Christian religious place names were formed from the beginning of the Late Iron Age and into the Viking period. The spatial dimensions of the religious life were closely connected with other processes in society, and the motives in religious names seem parallel to other name types that date from the Late Roman Iron Age and onward. As religious activities and places were integral parts of the total social life and landscape, I argue here that the focus on sacred places should be more oriented towards a settlement historical context. With the increase of archaeological information, we get a more detailed picture of population density and settlement development through the Iron Age and Viking period, and a better foundation for a settlement historical approach.

### Religious life as part of the social environment

Among Scandinavian archaeologists, there has been a tradition for using the Romanian scholar Mircea Eliade and his ideas about cosmological symbolism when dealing with central places and their setting in the landscape (*cf.* Eliade 1959; Hedeager 2001, 2011: 148–149). In the future, I aim to employ a different perspective, using the French sociologist Emile Durkheim and his pupil and nephew Marcel Mauss' thinking on religious life as a social process and the description of social phenomena as *social morphology* (Durkheim 2001; Mauss 1979). In my view, it is necessary to examine the settlement patterns in general to draw a picture of the role of religion in the social landscape. In the following, I will take some initial steps towards a description of the Tissø region.

## Variations in naming and differences in settlement development

In recent years, Danish place name research has focused on identifying naming patterns using models from the Swedish area: Since the 1970s, Swedish researchers have uncovered an Iron-Age and Viking-period settlement organisation reflected in place names, particularly in central Sweden. This theory began with the scholar Lars Hellberg's ideas of reoccurring structures in place names in the Mälar area, so-called 'name environments' (Hellberg 1975). The heart of each of these name environments is an old name that includes the word *tuna* or *husa*, supposed to reflect administrative centres of the Roman or Germanic Iron Ages (Brink 2007b: 62). While Hellberg believed that the name environments were closely connected with the early Svea state, another Swedish scholar, Stefan Brink has noted how archaeology shows that the organisation reflected in the Mälar region place names also existed in the Danish area. Yet in southern Scandinavia it is hard to detect similar naming patterns (Brink 1998). This issue has been explored further by Lisbeth E. Christensen. Her study of areas around the place name element *sal* in Denmark confirmed that structures of the Swedish model do not appear in the Danish place name material (Christensen 2010). Brink has proposed that place names have disappeared because of later restructuring (Brink 1998: 301).

I think Brink is only partly right: Transformations in structures of settlement, cultivation strategies, and ownership have definitely been more extensive in the Old Danish area than in the rest of Scandinavia. However, despite significant restructuring, a substantial amount of early place names are preserved in Denmark and Scania. But naming patterns are different: here, the place name element *Tuna/tuna,* which makes the core of the Swedish name environments (Vikstrand 2010: 24), is very rare. On the other hand, a contemporary name type, *-lev/-löv*, is concentrated in South Scandinavia. We need to study the South Scandinavian areas on their own terms to see whether local naming structures may be identified. If not, it may be possible to detect the early restructuring that can have caused their disappearance.

## The survey

The foundation of the on-going investigation of place names and archaeology presented here is a mapping of the relevant source material in a GIS database. The landscape will be analysed in terms of spatial concepts as monumentality, access, and visibility (*cf.* Smith 2010). Archaeological material has initially been extracted from the Danish Cultural Agency's database of Sites and Monuments. This material will be divided into subcategories and supplied with data from excavation reports in the National Museum and Kalundborg Museum. Since this has not yet been carried out, the mapping must be considered to be preliminary. Most emphasis is placed on a review of place names from the area. Place names have been extracted through a thorough examination of the archives and digital material at the Department of Scandinavian Research, University of Copenhagen. Since the place names of the region have not yet been published in the series *Danmarks Stednavne*, the material has been interpreted and dated primarily on the basis of the name research tradition that is

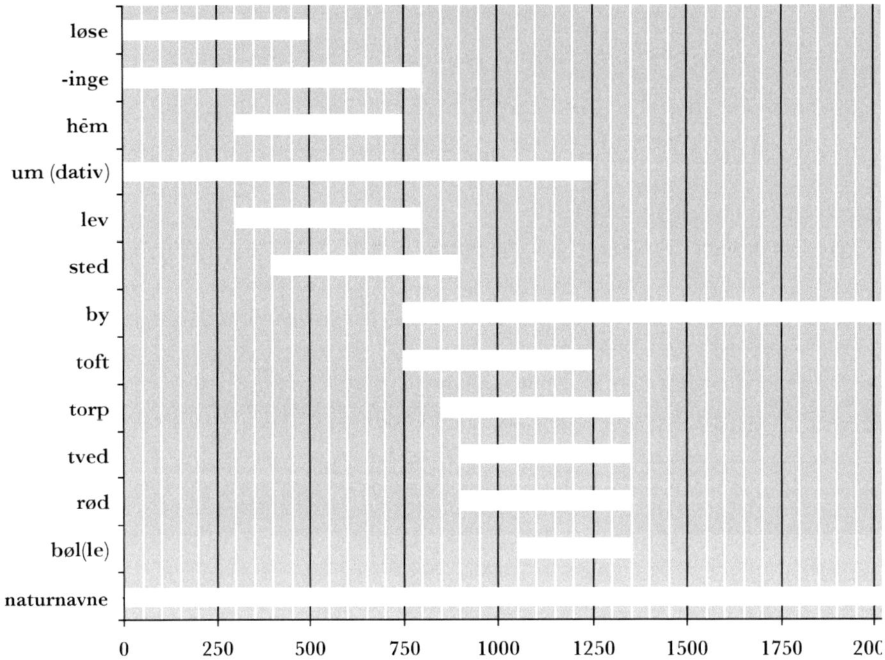


*Fig. 5.2. The relative chronology of Danish place name types. The term 'naturnavne' covers topographical names that have been in use for so long, that they cannot be placed within the sequence (developed by Gammeltoft and Nissen Knudsen 2010).*

practised in Copenhagen and publications. The names that have been mapped are those that are considered to be old (pre-Christian or early medieval). Also, names that possibly refer to functions of the central place or to pre-Christian religion have been selected (following Christensen 2010). Since the data has not yet been through a more critical selection, again the analyses of material presented here should be considered preliminary.

## Place name horizons and changes in settlement patterns around Lake Tissø

Place names are methodologically difficult to employ in archaeology, mainly because most name types are productive for a long time (*cf.* Christensen and Kousgård Sørensen 1972: 222–223; Grøngaard Jeppesen 1984). Furthermore, the views on interpretations and datings of some place name types can vary between the Scandinavian countries. The present survey focusses on the established Danish research tradition. Here, the oldest Scandinavian place names are divided into several types, and their formation can be fixed within certain time spans or horizons that are placed within a relative chronology (Fig. 5.2; Christensen og Kousgård Sørensen 1972: 166–194; Holmberg 1996: 56–57). These datings are mainly based on philological arguments, combined with historical information, such as Scandinavian place names on the British Isles.

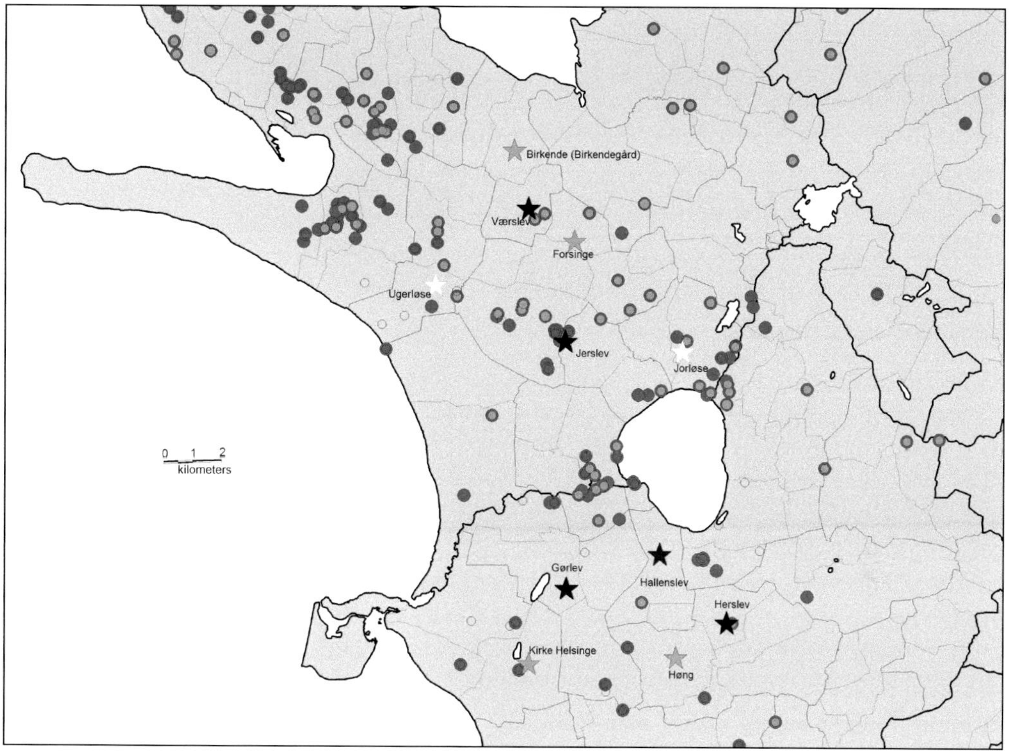


*Fig. 5.3. Older name types and finds from* c. *AD 1–500. Dots show archaeological finds: Dark grey = Pre- Roman and Early Roman Iron Age, Light grey = Late Roman Iron Age. Stars show place names. Grey = -inge, white = -løse, black = -lev. The background map shows boundaries from the Danish 17th century cadaster. Digitised: © Peder Dam.*

In the Tissø area, the oldest name types are *-inge* and *-løse*. Etymologically, these name types refer to qualities in topography or the natural environment. The *-inge* names are Birkinge (1363 Byrchinge), 'the place with birch trees', Forsinge (1271 Forsing) 'the place with the stream', and Helsinge (1370–1380 Helsinge), 'the narrow place'. The *-løse* names are Ugerløse (1333 Vgerlosæ), 'the clearing by *Wikur' ('the one who winds', probably an earlier name for a local stream), and Jorløse (1231 Jurløs) 'the clearing with wild boars'. Although *-inge* and *-løse* names were recorded in the Middle Ages as names for settlements, it is difficult to determine the exact type of location they have originally pointed out. They do not necessarily refer to settlements, and their content does not express ownership or other social structures. When looking at the distribution map (Fig. 5.3), the correlation between the oldest name types and archaeological finds from the Early Iron Age (including the Late Roman period) is not very strong. This can be due to many factors. First, both settlements and names can move around in the landscape. Most villages were not fixed in their present location until the end of the Viking period (*cf.* Grøngaard Jeppesen 1984). Secondly, we cannot be sure that the available archaeological material is sufficiently representative for the Iron-Age settlement pattern (Kristiansen 1985: 7–10). Formally, it should be possible to find traces from the Iron Age in the areas with old name types. In contrast, there are areas with several archaeological traces from the Early Iron Age, even though there are no old names. This is especially significant towards the sea in the north-western part of the map and on the north-eastern and western sides of the lake, along the stream Halleby Å. Although there may be undatable topographical names, it is likely that older names have disappeared in these areas.

### Functions and ownership reflected in *-lev*?

As mentioned, *-lev* is a name type that is typical for south Scandinavia. The name element is related to the English verb *leave* and denotes something that is *left* to someone. Therefore it is often interpreted as 'inheritance' (Bjerrum 1974: 1, 7; Søndergaard 1972: 133–140). Although the exact interpretation is widely discussed, the name type indicates an advanced social organisation in the Late Iron Age of South Scandinavia (Jørgensen 2008: 177). The name type is productive from the Late Roman Iron Age until the Early Viking Age, and it has a parallel type *-leben* in the Thüringen area in Germany. Although the lev-names are formed over a long period of time, they reflect a new way of structuring the landscape that is very different from the earlier name types. These names are not just descriptions of the characteristics of a location; they are a claim on a defined place. To underline this, their survival as place names shows that this claim was universally accepted as an important quality of this place. There has been much debate on lev-names in the context of rich graves from the Roman Iron Age (*cf.* Albrectsen 1970; Nielsen 1977). Some researchers have seen the lev-names as an indication of emerging land-ownership in the Late Iron Age (Hedeager 1990: 150–154, 187). However, as ownership is already marked with field boundaries, fences and monuments in the Early Iron Age, the lev-names must represent a new type of ownership. The Swedish name scholar Lena Peterson places emphasis on the meaning of the Old Danish word *kununglēf*, meaning 'property assigned to the king'. She proposes that the specifics with appellative meanings indicate that *-lev* in these cases should be read as 'official property' (Peterson 2010: 189–90). The appellative, she argues, can be the title of a subordinate or tenant, to whom the property was assigned, perhaps as a fief or a privilege. In this light, it is interesting to see the lev-names in relation to magnate's farms and central places.

To my mind, the formation of the lev-settlements in the Tissø area can be seen in context of the establishment of the aristocratic residence in the 6th century. This is underlined by the content of lev-names in the parishes around the lake. Lev-names with appellative specifics are not common (Søndergaard 1972: 117), and most of the lev-names in the region follow the traditional pattern: They contain masculine personal names such as **Fialin* in Føllenslev (1321–1323 Fyælenslef), *Rethar* in Reerslev, (1321–1323 Rethерslef), and *Øthar*, 'the destroyer' in Ørslev (1354 Ørslef). However, in the parishes within the surveyed area, the lev-names are slightly different. Whereas Hallenslev (1284 Halluænslef) may contain a lost personal name **Halin*, the only certain personal name is *Erik* in Jerslev (1199, Erixleffue). Being a

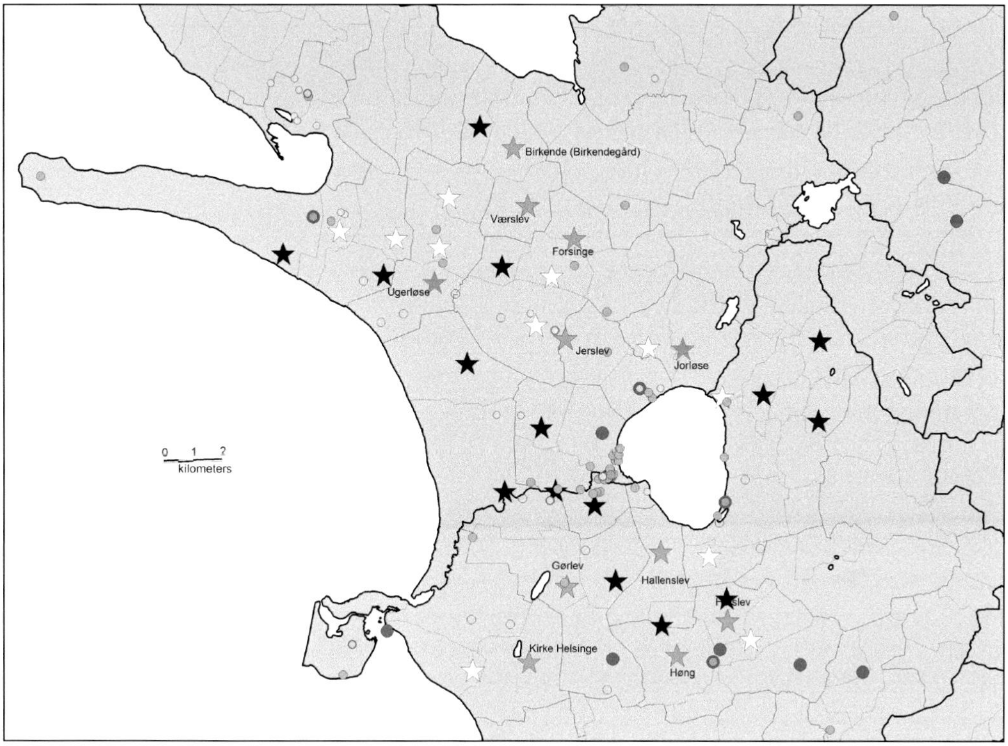


*Fig. 5.4. Finds from* c. *AD 500–1050 and name types that appear in the Viking Age. Dots show archaeological finds: dark grey = Germanic Iron Age, light grey = Viking Age. Stars show place names: grey = older name types, white = -by, black = -torp. The background map shows boundaries from the Danish 17th century cadaster. Digitised: © Peder Dam.*

royal name in Sweden, this name is noteworthy. The name Gørlev (geir, 'spear') seems to describe topography. Two specifics are appellatives that refer to functions and may be seen as official titles: Herslev (1202–1241 Hersleff) contains the word *hær* 'army, warrior', and Værslev (1321–1323 Weslef) contains the word *vi*, meaning 'sanctuary' or 'priest at a sanctuary'.

Looking at the distribution map, Early Iron-Age finds actually seem to cluster around Herslev, Jerslev and Værslev. This means that the names are given to already existing settlements, which implies a change or restructuring relating to the formation of the lev-names.

## Late Iron Age/Viking-Age place names and finds

The major changes that transformed the landscape during the transition to Christianity are clearly reflected in place name material around Tissø, especially in the name elements *-by*, 'town, settlement' (the meaning 'single farm' also occurs, but mainly in Western Jutland) and *-torp*, 'outlying settlement' (Fig. 5.4).

Torp-names mainly derive from the late Viking Age and early medieval period (*cf.* Lerche Nielsen 1997). The surveyed area around Lake Tissø contains 15 torp-names. Of these, nine are found within 5 km of the lake, and all follow the common scheme for torp-names: the specifics are either personal names like Tȳkir in Tystrup (1339 Thygestorp), animal names like owls in Uglerup (1483 Vglerøp), or they describe topography like a flint-rich ground in Flinterup (1312 Flintorp).

It has been observed that the formation of torp-names is particularly marked in the area around Uppåkra in Scania, which is interpreted as a fragmentation of the domain of the central place (Anglert 2003: 133; Lihammer 2003: 80–99). In a previous investigation, I have observed an intense torp-formation with 13 torps within a radius of 5 km around the smaller central place of Boeslunde in south-western Zealand (Albris 2011: 73–74). Something similar is seen around the central place Gudme on Funen (Jørgensen 2009: 332–333). Here we find 11 torp-names within 5 km in an area that is completely void of older name types (Holmberg 1996: 59–60).

Torp-names also show a significant fragmentation going on in the Tissø area, but here it does not seem as intense. The highest density is not found immediately around the central place: Most torp-names lie in a belt stretching from south of the lake towards the coast to the north-west. The restructuring in this region may have been a more gradual process, which is probably mirrored in the by-names that almost follow the distribution of torp-names. The by-element is probably active already in the 9th century and thus productive earlier than *-torp*.

Several of the *-bys* and *-torps* are placed in areas with many finds from the Early Iron Age. They may be seen as part of a re-settling of formerly cultivated areas. Although there have been several rounds of thorough excavation of the Tissø site, the settlements in the surroundings are not well known. In these years, detectorists have taken interest in the hinterland, and metal finds are emerging in many of the *-torp* and *-by* settlements such as Bakkendrup, Tystrup, Ubby, and Melby. Across the lake, at Sæby, 'the town by the lake', aerial photos reveal several pit houses, while gold finds as well as an early medieval church and magnate's farm belonging to the Danish noble family Hvide, suggest that some of the functions of the Tissø residence were transferred onto other structures in the area.

## Breaks or gradual transformations?

Through identification of continuity and breaks in settlement history, archaeology can help us understand what made place names change or disappear. In my previous survey of south-western Zealand, I was able to describe some general tendencies in settlement development that correspond well with results from eastern Zealand (Albris 2014a; Christensen and Tornbjerg 2009: 77–79):

1. 150 BC–2nd century AD. Settlements are numerous, but often small and short lasting, scattered on high ground. Within a resource area (the Danish 'ejerlav'), there is often one larger settlement of longer duration, occasionally with cultural layers and metal finds.

2. In the Late Roman and Early Germanic period, 3rd–6th century AD, settlements are difficult to identify in the field, but there seems to be a gradual reduction of the number of sites at the same time as the central settlement becomes larger and more complex.
3. In the Late Germanic and Early Viking period settlements stay generally in the same location. In the Late Germanic period, the settlements concentrate to one single main settlement per resource area.
4. In the Late Viking and early medieval period some settlement areas are abandoned, while activities occur in new places.

On this background, two periods can be described as crucial to the preserved body of place names in south-western Zealand:

1. 3rd–4th century AD: Centralisation and specialisation: Changing agrarian strategies and abandonment of old field systems. No breaks or depopulation, but transitions and transformations.
2. 10th–12th century AD: torp- and parish-formation, Christianisation.

As I see it, these transitions caused discrepancies between archaeology and the oldest place names. It is likely that a similar process can be applied to the Tissø region, but here the archaeological material is not yet sufficient for a detailed description of settlement development. Instead, I conclude with a tentative description of landscape development from regional pollen records extracted from the lake: In his recent doctoral research, Anthony Ruter has extracted and treated pollen data from Tissø. The sub-Atlantic pollen sequence here is problematic and the pollen from Tissø can only describe a very general development through the Iron Age (Ruter 2011: 35–37, 130–132). Changes in the depositional environment in the Iron Age could be due to a reduced sea water level in The Great Belt, but also human interference, maybe even dredging to facilitate navigation in the system of streams (Ruter 2011: 81–83). Generally, in the area there is a fall in different types of arboreal pollen in the Iron Age. These are replaced by a rise in beech and a two to fourfold increase in non-arboreal pollen, including a marked increase in cereal pollen (Ruter 2011: 127–128). The Late Iron-Age ecosystem was very diverse with about 50% forest coverage mixed with open meadows, wetlands and cultivated fields.

Rise and decline in beech pollen may reflect that settlement development around Tissø was similar to the process in other parts of Zealand outlined above. Whereas beech rises to 25% of the pollen in the early pre-Roman Iron Age, it declines to 10% between 200 BC and AD 200. It recovers again to 25% in the Germanic Iron Age and declines a second time around AD 900 (Ruter 2011: 127–128). This pattern fits well with the above mentioned settlement phases. The distribution maps indicate a Late Iron-Age abandonment or contraction of the apparently widely dispersed settlements from the Early Iron Age (Figs 5.3 and 5.4). The rise in beech pollen towards the Germanic Iron Age could be connected with these processes that probably caused the disappearance of some names. Meanwhile, this restructuring may also have started the coining of new types like the *-lev* names. Again, the second decline in beech pollen coincides with the period where we see formations of many new names ending in *-by* and *-torp*.

The changes in forest coverage cause increased non-arboreal pollen, but do not seem to affect the cereal pollen, which rises steadily through the period. Rye first appears in Tissø in the 5th century AD, and increases in the medieval period (Ruter 2011: 38, 128–129). It can be suggested that the introduction of rye and a peak in micro-charcoal around AD 500 could be related to the establishment of the magnate's farm at Tissø. However, it is still difficult to establish an exact relation between pollen and settlement development.

## Conclusion

This preliminary survey indicates that structural changes and social functions that may relate to the aristocratic residence can be identified through the place names around Lake Tissø. As the focal point in the inland water system, Lake Tissø worked as a natural gathering point in the physical landscape. The Tissø settlement is thought to have hosted seasonal assemblies such as markets and religious feasts, maybe even thing-gatherings (Nørgård Jørgensen *et al.* 2011). As such, the residence and market place worked as a *social* centre within the region as much as a centre of power and religion.

### *References*

Albris, Sofie L.

2011. When a place is not called a 'home of the gods'. A preliminary examination of archaeology and place names in Boeslunde, Zealand, in the light of the Gudme/Gudhem workshop. In *The Gudme/Gudhem phenomenon: papers presented at a workshop organized by the Centre for Baltic and Scandinavian Archaeology (ZBSA) Schleswig, April 26th and 27th, 2010*, edited by Oliver Grimm and Alexandra Pesch, pp. 207–230. Schriften des Archäologischen Landesmuseums. Ergänzungsreihe, Vol. 6.Wachholtz, Neumünster.

2014a. *At bo, at benævne. Arkæologi og stednavne i jernalderens og vikingetidens landskab. Eksempler fra Sydvestsjælland.* Navnestudier, Vol. 41. Dissertation published by the Name Research Section, Department of Scandinavian Research, University of Copenhagen. Museum Tusculanum Press, Copenhagen.

2014b. At skabe 'sted' – en ny teoretisk vinkel på arkæologi og stednavne i jernalderens og vikingetidens landskab. In *Att befolka det förflutna*, edited by Anne Carlie and Maria Petersson, pp. 8–31. Riksantikvarieämbetets Förlag, Stockholm.

Albrectsen, Erling

1970. Den ældre jernalders bebyggelse på Fyn. *Kuml* 1970: 123–144.

Andrén, Anders, Kristina Jennbert and Catharina Raudvere (editors)

2006. *Old Norse Religion in Long-term Perspectives. Origins, Changes, and Interactions.* Vägar till Midgård, Vol. 8. Nordic Academic Press, Lund.

Anglert, Mats

2003. Uppåkra bland högar, ortnamn och kyrkor. In *Landskapsarkeologi och tidig medeltid – några exempel från södra Sverige*, edited by Mats Anglert and Joakim Thomasson, pp. 115–144. Uppåkrastudier, Vol. 8 and Acta Archaeologica Lundensia Series in 8°, Vol. 41. Almqvist and Wiksell, Stockholm.

Bican, Josefine F.

2010. Bulbrogård, the first aristocratic complex at Tissø – and a new approach to the aristocratic sites. In *Herrenhöfe und die Hierarchie der Macht im Raum südlich und östlich der Nordsee von der Vorrömischen Eisenzeit bis zum frühen Mittelalter und zur Wikingerzeit. Gedächtnis-Kolloquium Werner Haarnagel (1907-1984)*, edited by Erwin Strahl pp. 147–154. Rahden/Westf. Siedlungs- und Küstenforschung im südlichen Nordseegebiet, Vol. 33. Marie Leidorf, Rahden.

Bjerrum, Anders

1974. Om betydningen af -lev. In *Festskrift til Kristian Hald på halvfjerdsårs-dagen 9.9. 1974. Navneforskning, dialektologi, sproghistorie*, edited by Poul Andersen, pp. 1–7. Navnestudier published by Institut for Navneforskning, Vol. 13. Akademisk Forlag, Copenhagen.

Brink, Stefan

1998. Land, bygd, distrikt och centralort i Sydsverige. Några bebyggelsehistoriska nedslag. In *Centrala Platser – Centrala Frågor. Samhällsstrukturen under Järnåldern. En Vänbok till Berta Stjernquist*, edited by Lars Larsson and Birgitta Hårdh, pp. 297–326. Uppåkrastudier, Vol. 1 and Acta archaeologica Lundensia. Series in 8°, Vol. 28. Almqvist and Wiksell, Stockholm.

2007a. How uniform was the Old Norse religion? In *Learning and Understanding in the Old Norse World. Essays in Honour of Margaret Clunies Ross*, edited by Judy Quinn, Kate Heslop and Tarrin Wills, pp. 105–136. Brepols, Turnhout.

2007b. Skiringssalr, Kaupang, Tjølling – the Toponymic evidence. In *Kaupang i Skiringssalr*, edited by Dagfinn Skre, pp. 53–64. Kaupang excavation project Publication Series, Vol. 1, and Norske Oldfunn, Vol. XXII. Aarhus University Press, Århus.

Christensen, Tom

1991. Lejre beyond legend – the archaeological evidence. *Journal of Danish Archaeology* 10(1): 163–185.

2007. A new round of excavations at Lejre (to 2005). In *Beowulf and Lejre*, edited by John D. Niles and Marijane Osborn, pp. 109–126. Arizona Center for Medieval and Renaissance Studies, Vol. 323. Arizona Center for Medieval and Renaissance Studies, Tempe, Arizona.

Christensen, Tom and Svend Å. Tornbjerg

2009. Jernalderbosættelsen i det gamle Roskilde Amt. In *Mellem fjord og bugt – Køge Museum, Roskilde Museum*, edited by Hans-Christian Eisen, pp. 25–86. Historisk Samfund for Roskilde Amt, Roskilde.

Christensen, Vibeke and John Kousgård Sørensen

1972. *Stednavneforskning. Afgrænsning, terminologi, metode, datering*, Akademisk Forlag, København.

Christensen, Lisbeth E.

2010. *Stednavne som kilde til yngre jernalders Centralpladser*. Ph.D. dissertation, Faculty of Humanities, University of Copenhagen, Copenhagen. Electronic document, http://nfi.ku.dk/publikationer/phd-afhandlinger/LEC-afh_tekst.pdf/

Durkheim, Emile

2001. *The Elementary Forms of Religious Life*. Translated by Carole Cosman. Oxford University Press, New York. Originally published in 1912, Les Formes élémentaires de la vie religieuse. Le Système totémique en Australie. Travaux de L'Année sociologique. Bibliothèque de philosophie contemporaine, Libraire Félix Alcan, Paris.

Eliade, Mircea

1959. *The Sacred and the Profane. The Nature of Religion.* Translated by Willard R. Trask. Harcourt Brace and World Inc, New York.

Fabech, Charlotte

1992. Sakrale pladser i sydskandinavisk jernalder. En evaluering. In *Sakrale navne. Rapport fra NORNAs sekstende symposium i Gilleleje 30.11.– 2.12.1990*, edited by Bente Holmberg and Gillian Fellows-Jensen, pp. 141–168. Norna-Förlaget, Uppsala.

1999. Centrality in sites and landscapes. In *Settlement and Landscape. Proceedings of a Conference in Århus, Denmark, May 4–7 1998*, edited by Charlotte Fabech and Jytte Ringtved, pp. 455–474. Jutland Archaeological Society, Højbjerg.

Gammeltoft, Peder and Bo Nissen Knudsen

2010. *Hvor gamle er stednavnene?* Electronic document, www.navn.ku.dk/stednavne/hvorgamle/, accessed 10 March 2013.

Grøngaard Jeppesen, Torben

1984. Landsbyens alder – arkæologisk belyst. In *Bebyggelsers og bebyggelsesnavnes alder. NORNAs niende symposium i København 25–27 oktober 1982*, edited by Vibeke Dalberg, Gillian Fellows-Jensen, Bent Jørgensen and John Kousgård Sørensen, pp. 158–168. Norna-Förlaget, Uppsala.

Grimm, Oliver and Alexandra Pesch (editors)

2011. *The Gudme/Gudhem Phenomenon: Papers Presented at a Workshop Organized by the Centre for Baltic and Scandinavian Archaeology (ZBSA) Schleswig, April 26th and 27th, 2010*. Schriften des Archäologischen Landesmuseums, Ergänzungsreihe, Vol. 6.Wachholtz, Neumünster.

Hedeager, Lotte

1990. *Danmarks jernalder mellem stamme og stat.* Aarhus Universitetsforlag, Århus.

2001. Asgård reconstructed? Gudme – a central place in the north. In *Topographies of Power in the Early Middle Ages*, edited by Mayke de Jong and Francis Theuws, pp. 467–507. Transformations of the Roman World, Vol. 6. Brill, Leiden.

2011. *Iron Age Myth and Materiality: an Archaeology of Scandinavia AD 400–1000.* Routledge, London.

Helgesson, Bertil

2008. Kan regionalitet påvisas genom arkeologiskt fyndmaterial? Några metodiska och källkritiska närmanden. *Hikuin* 35: 49–62.

Hellberg, Lars

1975. Ortnamnen och den forntida sveastaten (Presentation av ett Forskningsprojekt). In *Inledningar till NORNAs fjärde symposium Ortnamn och Samhälle på Hanaholmen den 25.–27.4.75. 1. Namngivning*, pp. 92–110.

Henriksen, Mogens B.

2010. Deposits of Gold in the Migration Period Landscape. Examples from the Island Fyn (Funen). In *Worlds Apart? Contacts Across the Baltic Sea in the Iron Age. Network Denmark–Poland, 2005–2008*, edited by Ulla L. Hansen and Anna Bitner-Wróblewska, pp. 389–432. Nordiske Fortidsminder, serie C, Vol. 7. Det Kongelige Nordiske Oldskriftselskab, Copenhagen.

Holmberg, Bente

1986. Den Hedenske Gud Tyr i Danske Stednavne. In *Mange Bække Små. Til John Kousgård Sørensen på Tresårsdagen 6. 12. 1985*, edited by Vibeke Dalberg and Gillian Fellows-Jensen, pp. 109–128. C. A. Reitzels Forlag, Copenhagen.

1996. Stednavne som historisk kilde. In *Atlas over Fyns kyst i jernalder, vikingetid og Middelalder*, edited by Ole Crumlin-Pedersen, Erland Porsmose and Henrik Thrane, pp. 53–60. Odense Universitetsforlag, Odense.

Ilkjær, Jørgen

2002. Den bevidste ødelæggelse i krigsbytteofringerne. In *Plats och praxis: studier av nordisk förkristen ritual*, edited by Kristina Jennbert, Anders Andrén and Catharina Raudvere, pp. 203–214. Vägar till midgård, Vol. 2. Nordic Academic Press, Lund.

Jørgensen, Bent

2008. *Danske Stednavne.* 3rd edition. Gyldendal, Copenhagen.

Jørgensen, Lars
2002. Kongsgård – kultsted – marked. Overvejelser omkring Tissøkompleksets. struktur og funktion In *Plats och praxis: studier av nordisk förkristen ritual*, edited by Kristina Jennbert, Anders Andrén and Catharina Raudvere, pp. 215–248. Vägar till Midgård, Vol. 2. Nordic Academic Press, Lund.
2009. Pre-Christian cult at aristocratic residences and settlement complexes in southern Scandinavia in the 3rd–10th centuries AD. In *Glaube, Kult und Herrschaft. Phänomene des Religiösen im 1. Jahrtausend n. Chr. in Mittel- und Nordeuropa*, edited by Uta von Freeden, Herwig Friesinger and Egon Wamers, pp. 329–354. Kolloquien zur Vor- und Frühgeschichte Band, Vol. 12. Habelt, Bonn.
Kousgård Sørensen, John
1985. Gudhem. *Frühmittelalterliche Studien* 19: 131–138.
Kristiansen, Kristian
1985. Post-depositional formation processes and the archaeological record. In *Archaeological Formation Processes. The Representativity of Archaeological Remains from Danish Prehistory. A Danish Perspective*, edited by Kristian Kristiansen, pp. 7–11. Nationalmuseet, København.
Lerche Nielsen, Michael
1997. *Vikingetidens personnavne i Danmark belyst gennem runeindskrifternes personnavne og stednavne på -torp sammensat med personnavneforled.* Unpublished Ph.D. dissertation, Faculty of Humanities, Institute for Name Research, Copenhagen University, Copenhagen.
Lihammer, Anna
2003. Kungen och landskapet. Funderingar kring förändringar i västra Skåne under sen vikingatid och tidig medeltid. In *Landskapsarkeologi och tidig medeltid – några exempel från södra Sverige*, edited by Mats Anglert and Joakim Thomasson, pp. 71–114. Uppåkrastudier 8. Acta Archaeologica Lundensia. Series in 8°, No. 41. Almqvist and Wiksell International, Stockholm.
Lund, Julie
2004. Våben i vand. Om deponeringer i vikingetiden. *Kuml* 2004: 197–220.
2006. Vikingetidens værktøjskister i landskab og mytologi. *Fornvännen* 101: 323–341.
Mauss, Marcel
1979. *Seasonal Variations of the Eskimo. A Study in Social Morphology. In Collaboration with Henri Beuchat.* Translated by James J. Fox. Routledge and Kegan Paul. London. Originally published in 1950, *Essai sur les variations saisonnières des sociétés eskimos. Étude de morphologie sociale.* l'Année Sociologique, tome IX, 1904-1905.
Nielsen, Helge
1977. En undersøgelse af jernalderfundenes udbredelse i Præstø Amt. In *Kontinuitet og bebyggelse: beretning fra et symposium d. 12.–14. maj 1977 afholdt af Odense universitet*, edited by Henrik Thrane, pp. 49–54. Skrifter fra institut for historie og samfundsvidenskab, Vol. 22. Odense University, Odense.
Nørgård Jørgensen, Anne, Lars Jørgensen and Lone Gebauer Thomsen
2011. Assembly sites for cult, markets, jurisdiction and social relations. Historic-ethnological analogy between north Scandinavian church towns, Old Norse assembly sites and pit house sites of the Late Iron Age and Viking Period. In *Archäologie in Schleswig – Arkaeologi i Slesvig: "Det 61. Internsationale Sachsensymposium 2010", Haderslev/ Danmark*, edited by Linda Boye and Sunhild Kleingärtner, pp. 95–112. Archäologie in Schleswig, Vol. 61. Wachholtz, Neumünster.
Pedersen, Lisbeth
2003. Tissø – offersø, vandreservoir og rekreativ ressource. Tissø og Åmosernes kulturhistorie og natur. *Fra Holbæk Amt Årbog for kulturhistorien i Holbæk Amt* 2003: 9–26.

Peterson, Lena
2010. Reconstructing lost words from old personal names – and the meaning of the place-name element -lev. In *Probleme der Rekonstruktion untergegangener Wörter aus alten Eigennamen. Akten eines internationalen Symposiums in Uppsala 7.–9. April 2010*, edited by Lennart Elmevik and Svante Strandberg, pp. 185–193. Acta Academiae regiae Gustavi Adolphi, Vol. 112. Kungl. Gustav Adolfs Akademien för svensk folkkultur, Uppsala.

Ruter, Anthony
2011. *The Holocene Paleolimnology of the Tissø and the Terrestrial Paleoecology of Western Zealand Recostructed from High-resolution Lacustrine Data*. Unpublished Ph.D. dissertation, Department of Geography and Geology, Faculty of Science, University of Denmark, Copenhagen.

Sindbæk, Søren M.
2008. Kulturelle forskelle, sociale netværk og regionalitet i vikingtidens arkæologi. *Hikuin* 35: 63–84

Smith, Michael E.
2010. Empirical urban theory for archaeologists. *Journal of Archaeological Method and Theory* 18: 167–192.

Stednavneudvalget, Institute for Name Research and Department of Name Research
1922. *Danmarks Stednavne*. Published from 1922. Vols 1–15 by Stednavneudvalget, Vols 16–24 by Institute for Name Research, and from Vol. 25 by Department for Name Research, Copenhagen.

Strid, Jan P.
2011. Ortnamn och kulturlandskap under den äldra järnåldern. In *Navnemiljøer og samfund i jernalder og vikingetid. Rapport fra NORNAS 38. symposium i Ryslinge 12.15. maj 2009*, edited by Lisbeth E. Christensen and Bent Jørgensen, pp. 275–300. NORNA-förlaget, Uppsala.

Søndergaard, Bent
1972. *Indledende studier over den nordiske stednavnetype lev (löv)*. Akademisk Forlag, Copenhagen.

Vikstrand, Per
2001. *Gudarnas Platser. Förkristna sakrala ortnamn i Mälarlandskapen*. Acta Academiae regiae Gustavi Adolphi, Vol. 77 and Studier till en svensk ortnamnsatlas, Vol. 17. Kungl. Gustav Adolfs Akademien för svensk folkkultur, Uppsala.
2010. Ortnamn och den äldre järnålderns högstatusmiljöer. In *Makt, kult och plats. Högstatusmiljöer under den äldre järnåldern. Två seminarier arrangerade av Stockholms läns museum under 2009 och 2010*, edited by Peter Bratt and Richard Grönwall, pp. 24–30. Arkeologi i Stockholms län, Vol. 5. Stockholms Läns Museum, Stockholm.

Zachrisson, Torunn
2004. The holiness of Helgö. *Excavations at Helgö XVI Exotic and Sacral Finds from Helgö*, pp. 143–176. Kungl. Vitterhets Historie och Antikvitets Akademien, Stockholm.

*Chapter 6*

# The powerful ring. Door rings, oath rings and the sacral place

*Marianne Hem Eriksen*

*Abstract*

This paper considers a connection between the Viking-Age door, judicial regulation, and the cult place. It is argued that the door constituted a meaningful boundary to sacral and domestic spaces in the Viking Age, a boundary with judicial and cultic implications. I focus particularly on ring-shaped door-handles, which in the Viking Age seem exclusively linked with cult buildings and aristocratic halls. In a few instances door rings have been intentionally deposited in sacral buildings. Furthermore, the ring is a powerful sacral symbol in Norse worlds, and neck and arm-rings are archaeologically interpreted as expressions of leadership and social rank. Rings are also connected with oaths – 'swearing a ring oath', associated with the god Ullr. Ultimately, the paper suggests that deposition of door rings in buildings with sacral qualities must be considered a practice holding a specific and powerful meaning, and that door rings and doors could have cultic-judicial connotations in the Viking Age.

## Introduction

Doors are everyday objects. We walk through doorways several times each day without much reflection. In Viking-Age longhouses, doors were functional architectural features, providing access control, light, and ventilation to the dwelling. However, doors are simultaneously near-universally understood as liminal architectural elements. The door can symbolise transition, transgression, and liminality; doors and thresholds are central in *rites de passage* in numerous cultures (*e.g.* Blier 1987: 27–29; Boivin 2008: 54–55; Bourdieu 1977: 130–132; Davidson 1993; Lefebvre 1991: 209–210; Trumbull 1896; Turner 1967: 94), including in Late Iron-Age Scandinavia (Eriksen 2013, 2015).

This paper explores one of the associations of the Viking-Age door: the door as a cultic and judicial boundary. The point of departure is ring-shaped door handles and their close association with cult and hall buildings. A qualitative investigation of archaeological and historic sources that illuminates the connotation of rings and particularly ring-shaped door handles is presented in the article. The ring was a powerful sacral symbol in Norse worlds, and neck- and arm-rings are archaeologically interpreted as expressions of leadership and social rank. Rings are also connected with oaths or pacts in the historical sources. Through a discussion of ring symbolism and amulet rings, a possible connection between door rings and oath rings is considered. Moreover, supplementary material is provided from written sources, as legal paragraphs concerning doors from the oldest Scandinavian laws are brought into the discussion.

Attempting to understand aspects of mentality in the past is difficult. The material discussed in the article is widespread in time and space. Particularly the use of written sources must be undertaken with a critical approach. Yet, the correlation between different archaeological material and later, written sources is telling and point in the same direction: certain doors, or doors at certain times, could in the Viking Age be experienced as cultic and judicial boundaries.

## Four door rings

Ring-shaped door handles are known from antiquity and onwards in Europe (Karlsson 1988: 352). In Scandinavia, ring-shaped door handles are above all associated with medieval church portals, where the rings typically have apotropaic animal heads, warding off evil spirits (Ödman 2003: 89). Door rings can be functional objects, used as knockers or as handles to pull the door with. Simultaneously – and possibly more importantly – they constitute ornamental and symbolic artefacts (Hahnloser 1959; Karlsson 1988: 347). It has been assumed that because of the association with medieval churches, door rings were introduced to Scandinavia with Christianity (Ödman 2003: 90), or else that there existed ring handles in Scandinavia, but that these must be different than Continental ones (Karlsson 1988: 352). Re-interpretations and recently excavated material questions this assumption.

### *The Forsa ring*

The Forsa ring is an enigmatic object with a complex social biography. The ring's original context is uncertain, but in 1599 it was recorded hanging on the door between the weaponry and the church in Forsa, Hälsingland, Sweden. According to tradition, it was moved to Forsa from the church portal in nearby Hög parish sometime in the Middle Ages (Ruthström 1990). The ring is intriguing for two reasons: first of all, it has a runic inscription containing the oldest law provision in Scandinavia (Brink 2008). Secondly, the Forsa ring establishes a connection between door rings and the pre-Christian sacral place.

A large ring *c.* 43 cm in diameter, the Forsa ring is made of iron, and has an inscribed runic text of nearly 250 runes (Fig. 6.1). On either side of the ring a smaller ring is forged, with a single and a double spiral respectively. The spirals – three in total – have been suggested to represent the three levels of punishment that the runic text prescribes (see below). There is also, depending on the interpretation, a small cross *or* a Thor's hammer decoration on either the bottom or top of the ring (Sundqvist 2007: 170). The artefact is

*Fig. 6.1. The Forsa ring from Forsa church in Hälsingland, Sweden. Photo: © Marianne Hem Eriksen.*

too large to be a functional door handle, but was presumably rather used for its ornamental and symbolic value.

The runic inscription on the Forsa ring was first recorded around 1700 by clergyman Olof Celsius. The runes are of the short-branched type typical of the 9th century. The ring was formerly interpreted as a medieval artefact with a puzzlingly archaic rune text, describing the ecclesiastic rules of paying tithes (Bugge 1877). However, new interpretations place the ring firmly within a Viking-Age, pagan context (Brink 2003, 2008; Liestøl 1979; Ruthström 1990; for a diverging opinion see Löfving 2010 and rebuttal by Brink 2010 and Källström 2010).

Stefan Brink (2008: 29) has provided one of the newest translations:

> One ox and to *aura* [in fine] [to?] *staf* [or] *aura staf* [in fine] for the restoration of a cult site (*vi*) in a valid state for the first time; two oxen and four *aura* for the second time; but for the third time four oxen and eight *aura*; and all property in suspension if he doesn't make right. That, the people are entitled to demand, according to the law of the people that was decreed and ratified before. But they made [the ring, the statement or?], Anund from Tåsta and Ofeg from Hjortsta. But Vibjörn carved.

According to Brink, the inscription regulates the required behaviour of visiting the *vi*, the sacral place or sacral building. The text stipulates the fines one had to pay if one destroyed or desecrated (?) the *vi*, measured in cattle and *aura*, an economic unit of value (Brøgger 1921; Kilger 2008). It is unclear precisely what kind of sacral place is meant by the term *vi*, as this could refer to a multiplicity of sacral places including cult buildings and open-air sanctuaries (Nordberg 2011), but as we shall see, finds of other door rings may shed light on this question.

The reinterpretations of the runic inscription on the Forsa ring have several implications. First of all, the new readings place the inscription, the content, and thereby the artefact, in the 9th (or 10th) centuries. Secondly, Brink (2008: 29) points out the implication of the phrase 'the law of the people'. This turn of phrase indicates that the medieval institution of *landscape laws* – laws valid in a certain geographical area, *land* – was introduced already in the Viking Age, which from a perspective of legal history is of high importance.

The most central point in this context is that in the Viking Age, an individual or group chose to inscribe *a door ring* with a text regulating the punishment of someone desecrating the cult place. It should be mentioned that some scholars consider that the Forsa ring was not originally a door ring (Brink 1996; Sundqvist 2007). It has been questioned if the iron cramp attached to the ring is original or secondary. However, the ring's first known position was on a door; there are contemporary depictions of large, accentuated door rings on sacral buildings (Fig. 6.4, below); and there are other door rings associated with sacral buildings (discussed below). I therefore assume that the Forsa ring was originally associated with a door – hung with the iron cramp or by other means. The question is: Is it a coincidence that a door ring was chosen as a medium for this specific legal statement? Furthermore, which door did the Forsa ring originally belong to?

### *The Uppåkra rings*

The Uppåkra cult building – a timbered building constructed in an utterly monumental manner – is famous for its intense cluster of ritualised, valuable, and exotic objects: among them figural gold foils, imported glassware, a bronze and silver beaker, and a golden bracteate. The cult building was rebuilt seven times from the Migration Period to the early Viking Age, and with a life span of six centuries, it constituted a focal point of pre-Christian cult in its vicinity (Larsson 2007, 2011; Larsson and Lenntorp 2004). A handful of interpreted sacral buildings (*hov*) are known from Scandinavia (Andersson *et al.* 2003; Jørgensen 1998; Lidén 1969; Nielsen 2006; Rønne 2011; Söderberg 2006), and they are often connected with the upper strata of society, the king, and the warrior-band.

Intriguingly, two ring handles were excavated at Uppåkra (Ödman 2003). The first was identified by the use of metal detector, *c.* 10 m from the cult building. The iron ring has a diameter of 23.8 cm, and has a broken cramp iron that would be used to fasten the ring in the door. A hole would be drilled in the door, and when the cramp was inserted the two iron ends would be bent, one upwards and one downwards, to fasten the ring properly (Ödman 2003: 94). Four knobs have been distributed evenly on the ring. The door ring, as a stray find without context, was expected to be medieval and belonging to the Uppåkra church.

*Fig. 6.2. The door ring at Uppåkra during excavation, deposited standing vertically in one of the postholes from the cult building. Photo: © Lars Larsson/the Uppåkra Project.*

The second door ring, however, had a very specific archaeological context, which also influenced the interpretation of the first ring. This ring was found in the north-west posthole of the cult building. The archaeological context allows us to reconstruct the following chain of events: In the later phase of the *hov* building, the small cult house was deconstructed, and the four massive posts supporting the weight of the roof were pulled down. Within the now open posthole, the people of Uppåkra deposited an ox skull and a door ring into the ground. Not only was the door ring deposited, but it was placed vertically, on edge, in the posthole (Fig. 6.2; Ödman 2003).

The diameter of the ring is 14.7 cm. This ring likewise has a cramp iron to be used for fastening the handle on the door (Fig. 6.3). Based on the length of the cramp, the thickness of the door where it once hung can be estimated to be about 6.5 cm, which would be a substantially built door, and underlines the monumentality of the construction (Ödman 2003). The two rings are very similar, and their likeness has prompted the investigators to suggest that both rings are associated with the cult building (Larsson 2007: 17). The door rings were in all probability hanging on the portal of the cult building at Uppåkra before being, at least in the case of the second ring, intentionally deposited. This placed deposit seems to be one of the last rituals of Uppåkra, and the act of depositing the door ring may be understood as a concluding act – or symbolic burial – of the *hov* itself. Such concluding acts have also been observed in the royal hall complexes of Iron-Age Scandinavia – which

*Fig. 6.3. The Uppåkra ring after excavation. Photo: © Lund University Historical Museum.*

are likewise buildings with ritual connotations (*e.g.* Eriksen 2010; Herschend 1993, 1997, 1998; Söderberg 2005).

### *The Järrestad Ring*

The deposited door ring of Uppåkra is not the only ring-handle that has been intentionally deposited at a *hov*. A parallel may be found at the central place of Järrestad, Scania, southern Sweden, where a sequence of three monumental hall buildings were erected between *c.* AD 500 and 1050 (Söderberg 2003, 2005). The site included many rich and valuable artefacts, and there are traces of gold production taking place at the site. Connected with the hall buildings was a large enclosure with a small structure interpreted as a sacral building. And in one of the postholes of the *hov* building at Järrestad – much like at Uppåkra – a placed deposit was found, including an axe, an anvil, and a broken iron ring interpreted as a door ring (Söderberg 2005: 233).

Similar to the Uppåkra case, the deposit is understood as a *rite de passage* of the cult building, and perhaps of the entire central place. This means that at two *hov* sites, one certain and one probable door ring are among the artefacts chosen as to represent the building in its concluding deposition – the 'burial' of the building.

## Door rings and the sacral space

So far, three artefacts point to a connection between the door ring and the sacral place. First, there is the inscription on the large ring from Forsa, describing the penalties for destroying the cult site; secondly, the vertically placed door ring in the posthole at the *hov* at Uppåkra; and thirdly, the deposit of smith's tools and a possible door ring in the *hov* at Järrestad. And there are even further indications of a link between cult buildings or halls and door rings.

The Sparlösa rune stone, from Västergötland, Sweden, is dated to *c.* 800 (Nordén 1961). The runic inscription carved on the stone is debated amongst runologists and will not be

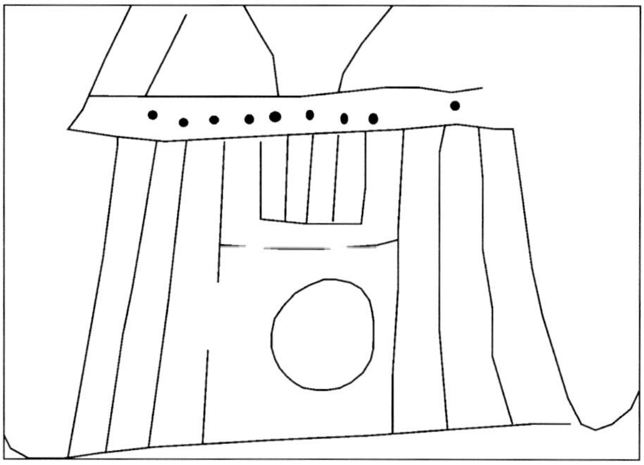

*Fig. 6.4. The building depicted on the Sparlösa rune stone, with an accentuated door ring hanging on the portal of a possible hov building. Tracing done by the author from a Wikimedia Commons image.*

discussed here. In addition to the runes, the Sparlösa stone includes a rich iconography. In the upper part of one side of the stone, there is a depiction of a building. It is difficult to say for certain if the depiction is of a king's hall or a *hov* (although the possible mention of a *vi* in the runic text could be an indication), but the building has a large, accentuated door ring placed on a rectangular portal (Fig. 6.4). The size of the door ring is intriguing, when considering the size of the Forsa door ring.

The connection between door rings and the sacral space is furthermore supported by the written sources. In the poem *Rigsþula* from the Poetic (Elder) Edda, the god Rig walks from house to house and founds the social classes: thralls, farmers, and the aristocracy. The thrall-house is described as an ON *hús* (house) with an open door; the people inside are dirty and poor. The farmer's house is named an ON *hǫll* (hall), also with an open door. The aristocratic house is termed an ON *salr*, its door is open towards the south (towards the warmth of the sun?) and 'the door ring is against the doorpost'. Thus, the only dwelling that would have a door ring is the aristocratic *salr* (see Carstens in this volume on terminology of hall buildings). Research from the last two decades has underlined the ritual and sacral qualities of the aristocratic hall buildings, indicating that they had a central role in pagan cult (Callmer and Rosengren 1997; Hedeager 2002; Herschend 1993; Nordberg 2003).

Moreover, in the *Saga of Olaf Tryggvason,* King Olaf wishes to marry Queen Sigrid. When proposing to her, he sends her a ring, supposedly of gold, that he had taken off the hov at Lade: 'King Olaf sent Queen Sigrid the great ring of gold which he had taken from *off the door of the temple at Ladir*, and it was deemed a most noble gift' (author's emphasis). However, it turns out that the ring is fake and made of copper. Nevertheless, in this text it is explicitly made clear that the ring hung on the door of the 'pagan temple'. Combined with the image of the Sparlösa stone, we can safely assume that door rings did hang on the portals of cult buildings and halls of the Viking Age. This was probably also the case for the Forsa ring; instead of being deposited at a *hov* site when the cult site was abandoned, this particular ring was transferred to a new cult building – the church.

## The power of the ring

Using a door ring as the object of law provisions regulating the sacral space was hardly done by coincidence. Rings have been powerful and magical objects in much of European prehistory, especially in Iron-Age Scandinavia (Hedeager 2011: 12–13; Karlsson 1988: 354–355; Vierck 1981). Neck and arm-rings have been interpreted as expressions of leadership and social rank (*e.g.* Hedeager 2011: 204–205). The ring-swords of the Migration and Merovingian periods are widely interpreted as material expressions of a judicial and social pact between the king and his retainers (*e.g.* Davidson 1962: 75–76; Steuer 1989). The ring is likewise a potent symbol in Norse mythology, expressed in the *Völsunga Saga*; in Odinn's ring Draupnir, which reproduces itself every night; and in Midgardsormen, the circular snake that engulfs the world.

The 'oath rings' known from several written sources are particularly relevant to the topic at hand. *Eyrbyggja saga* states that in the *hov* there stood a stall in the middle of the floor, and 'thereon lay a ring [...] on that men must swear all oaths'. According to *The Anglo-Saxon Chronicle*, when King Alfred made peace with the Great Danish Army at Wareham in 876, the Vikings swore him oaths on the 'sacred ring', sometimes translated as 'the sacred bracelet' – indicating an arm-ring. Oath rings are connected to pacts, swearing oaths, and loyalty. Incidentally, we still use rings in one particular judicial ritual with connotations of swearing loyalty: when entering marriage.

The Norse god Ullr appears to be particularly associated with oath rings (*e.g.* Näsström 2001: 124–126; Ringstad 2005; Steinsland 2005: 245). Ullr is a god we know little of, possibly because he was especially popular in eastern Scandinavia, whilst the written sources are biased towards western Scandinavia. His name is preserved in place names around Oslo in Norway and Uppsala in Sweden, indicating that his cult was practiced in a belt across central Scandinavia (Steinsland 2005: 245). Ullr is an old deity and had possibly withdrawn to the background of the Viking-Age pantheon. In *Atlakviða*, Ullr is associated with swearing oaths, when Gudrun talks of oaths sworn by '[...] the southward verging sun, and by Sigty's hill, the secluded bed of rest, and *by Ullr's ring*' (author's emphasis). According to *Hávamál* 108, Odinn has also sworn a 'ring-oath'. Miniature amulet rings have been found at excavated central places and cult sites (Arrhenius 1961; Nielsen 2006; Zachrisson 2004). These enigmatic artefacts have been connected to oath rings and Ullr, but also to fertility rituals and the cult of Freya (Arrhenius 1961).

The amulet rings were probably multi-vocal and powerful symbols. The amulet rings of the cult site Lilla Ullevi in southern Sweden, literally meaning the 'little cult site of Ullr', may be particularly significant when discussing door rings and ring magic. The cult site was mainly used in the Merovingian period. Around a stone setting, possibly made to evoke the shape of the gable-end of a house, numerous miniature iron amulets were found. Among them were miniature Thor's hammers, a common amulet type in pre-Christian Scandinavia, and 67 miniature rings – only befitting a cult site of Ullr. Intriguingly, four of the small iron rings have cramps attached to them – making them resemble miniature door rings. The excavators hypothesise if these miniature rings may have been fixed to posts or other wooden constructions at the site (Bäck *et al.* 2008: 43–45).

The magical properties of the ring in Iron- and Viking-Age Scandinavia have been pointed out by the excavators of Lilla Ullevi (Bäck *et al.* 2008) and of Uppåkra (Ödman 2003). The archaeological context of the miniature rings and the associations of rings in the written sources point to the rings being powerful objects associated with Ullr, possibly used as oath rings. In Christianity, ring-handles on church portals have strong judicial connotations. According to tradition, if a person in the Middle Ages wanted to seek asylum in the church, he or she was safe from persecution as long as he was able to touch the door ring, sometimes referred to as a *sanctuary ring* (Geddes 1982: 357–359; Gjærder 1952: 226–227; Hahnloser 1959; Karlsson 1988: 357).

However, the fact that door rings belong on *doors* is scarcely debated. Was it only the circular form of the door rings that was important? What about the rings' spatial context – hanging on the door, the boundary between spaces?

## 'If only a splint of wood comes with...' Law texts and the door

The earliest law text of Norway, the *Gulating Law*, includes a section describing the measures a serf or tenant has to take when returning a farm to the rightful owner. The very beginning of the legal paragraph reads (author's translation):

> Now the doors shall be left behind, three entrances, and that, even if none were there when he came: *stove*-door [door to the living room] and *burs*-door [storage/pantry] and *eldhus*-door [kitchen]. Now if he takes one of these doors and lead it away, then he shall return it and pay the *landnåm* penalty. But if any of the threshold comes with, or the doorframe on the side or over; if only a splint of wood comes with; then it is *húsbrot*, and he shall pay three marks (*Gulating Law*, *landsleigebolk* 4).

In the text following this quote it is also underlined that the tenant should not take benches or other fittings of the house. Yet, the doors are mentioned first, and it is strongly emphasised that they should be kept in place; doors should be kept whole and undamaged. Not even a splint of the threshold or doorframe can he take with him, because that would classify as *húsbrot* – literally 'breaking the house', damaging the house. I argue that in the Gulating law the doors are given special provenance and are in some way regarded as representatives of the farmhouse.

In the Gulating Law there is additionally mention of a custom called *duradómr* – 'door-court' or 'door-trial': in household disputes, people on the farm can hold a trial by the main door of the house. In *Eyrbyggja saga*, haunting ghosts are tormenting the people of the farm of Fróda, and in the end a door-court is the only solution to the problem. All ghosts are summoned to the main door of the house, and one by one they are vanquished, expelled through *another door* than the one they entered, and are denied to return inside. If *duradómr* constituted a real practice, it clearly points to the domestic door also being a judicial arena at certain times or in certain (ritualised?) contexts.

## Conclusions: Entering sacral and domestic spaces

The examination of the Late Iron-Age door rings and their spatial contexts; ring-magic and judicial associations of rings; and law texts concerning doorways in domestic space has provided new insight of the social meaning of these objects. There was clearly a connection between door rings and sacral and/or aristocratic buildings in the pre-Christian Viking Age. Door rings were associated with a particular type of Late Iron-Age architecture: cult buildings and hall buildings, which are both ritualised spaces. Rings were fastened on the door with iron cramps or by other means: constituting ornamental, meaningful, and functional objects. As door rings were used in ritualised, aristocratic architecture, the artefacts may have had a communicative value of denoting the boundary to sacral and élite spaces. Concurrently – because of the connection with élite spaces and practices revealed in the written sources – the rings might have communicated status and power to onlookers and visitors.

In light of this connection, the deposition of door rings in buildings with sacral qualities must be considered a practice holding a specific and powerful meaning. The careful selection of the deposited artefacts could imply that door rings were among the artefacts buried as secondary agents of the *hov*. Could the ring, as a symbol of magic and power in much of European prehistory – act as a representative of the *hov* building? In other words, when the door ring at Uppåkra was buried with a cow skull, the door ring *was* the *hov*, buried with an animal sacrifice? And when the ring and smithing tools were deposited as a concluding act at Järrestad, the tools terminated the ritualised activities on site, whilst the ring was a representative of the building itself?

An understanding of the ritualised role of the door rings opens for a discussion on the judicial connotations of the door, and artefacts associated with the door. The fact that the oldest law text of Scandinavia was inscribed on a door ring is most unlikely a coincidence – choosing a medium of inscribing a law paragraph that explains the penalty of desecrating the sacral space, is hardly done by chance. Rings are powerful objects in this time period, connected to swearing oaths. I find it relevant that at the cult site of Ullr – the god with an oath ring – a great number of miniature amulet rings were deposited; including rings with cramp irons, made to be fastened on wooden structures, artefacts looking very similar to miniature door rings.

The door rings were not purely functional objects. They were made to be *seen*. The large size of the Forsa ring makes is an impractical, but highly striking artefact to hang on the door of the cult house or the hall. Possibly, the door rings were also created to be sensory engaged with, not only to be visible symbols of the ritualised space, but perhaps to be touched. I suggest that in the case of the Forsa ring, but possibly also at Uppåkra and Järrestad, it is conceivable that upon entering the sacral space, the door and door ring would function as *embodied reminders* of the accepted behaviour inside. Perhaps people would swear an oath on the door ring when entering the cult building or the aristocratic hall. This could be an oath of loyalty to the King, oaths of protecting the sacral space, and not to destroy or desecrate the cult place. This was certainly the case on the Continent: sources from the 9th to the 14th century tell tales of people taking oaths on the church ring handle (Karlsson

1988: 356–357). Upon crossing the threshold to the cult house and entering the ritualised space, a door ring could possibly work as a mnemonic, sensory experienced manifestation of the social rules accepted within the space.

Judicial associations of the domestic doorways are also indicated in the earliest law texts and some Icelandic sagas. The fact that the serf would be penalised if only a splint of wood from the door, doorframe, or threshold was taken from the house may indicate that the door functioned as a judicial representative of the entire house. The sagas and law texts describing a custom of holding court by the door, *duradómr*, support this suggestion. The main door of the house is used as a judicial arena where cases could be tried and solved.

The door is a bodily experienced boundary between the outside and the inside, between ordered and untamed spheres, and between differentiated social spaces. Doors and thresholds frequently have connotations of being borders in a ritualised, cosmological sense. I argue that in Viking-Age Scandinavia, the door was an everyday feature that at certain times or in given contexts had ritual and judicial connotations. This was particularly valid for the doors to the cult place – just as church portals were particularly ritualised in the medieval period. Yet, the law texts and the saga episodes suggest that domestic doors could also, in certain situations, have cultic-judicial implications. Portals and doors are literally *between*-spaces, spaces that communicate a sensation of being on the verge, under transformation. It is likely that the door, particularly the portal leading into the sacral space of the cult building, was experienced as a powerful boundary to cross.

*Acknowledgements*

I wish to thank Lars Larsson who took the time to procure the image of the Uppåkra ring during excavation, and Erika Rosengren at the Lund University Historical Museum who kindly granted permission to reproduce the image of the same ring after conservation. I am also very grateful to Lotte Hedeager and Elise Neumann for their insightful comments on this paper. Most of all, I would like to express my gratitude to all contributors to the *Viking Worlds* conference and this subsequent volume, for their enthusiastic support of a new and open forum for Viking studies.

*Abbreviations*

ON = Old Norse

*References*

Andersson, Gunnar, Lena Beronuis Jörpeland and Jan Dunér
2003. Gudarnas gård. Tre fallosfiguriner från Lunda i Strängnäs socken, Södermanland. *Fornvännen* 98: 124–126.

*The Anglo-Saxon Chronicle*
[1823] Translated to English by J. Ingram. Electronic Edition. Project Guthenberg, Champaign, Ill.

Arrhenius, Birgit
1961. Vikingtidiga miniatyrer. *Tor* 7: 139–164.

Atlakviða
[1985] In *Eddadikt*, translated to Norwegian by Ludvig Holm-Olsen. Cappelen, Oslo.

Bäck, Mathias, Ann-Mari Hållans Stenholm and Jan-Åke Ljung
2008. Lilla Ullevi. Historien om det fridlysta rummet. Vendeltida helgedom, medeltida by och 1600-talsgård. In *UV Mitt, Rapport 2008: 39*. Riksantikvarieämbetet, Stockholm.

Blier, Suzanne Preston
1987. *The Anatomy of Architecture. Ontology and Metaphor in Batammaliba Architectural Expression*. Cambridge University Press, Cambridge.

Boivin, Nicole
2008. *Material Cultures, Material Minds: The Impact of Things on Human Thought, Society, and Evolution*. Cambridge University Press, Cambridge.

Bourdieu, Pierre
1977. *Outline of a Theory of Practice*. Cambridge University Press, Cambridge.

Brink, Stefan
1996. Forsaringen – Nordens äldsta lagbud. In *Beretning fra femtende tværfaglige vikingsymposium*, edited by Else Roesdahl and Preben Meulengracht Sørensen, pp. 27–55. Hikuin/Dept of Medieval Archaeology, Højbjerg.
2003. Law and legal customs in Viking Age Scandinavia. In *The Scandinavians from the Vendel Period to the Tenth Century. An Ethnographic Perspective*, edited by Judith Jesch, pp. 87–128. Centre for Interdisciplinary Research on Social Stress/Boydell Press, San Marino.
2008. Law and society. In *The Viking World*, edited by Stefan Brink and Neil S. Price, pp. 23–31. Routledge, London.
2010. Är Forsaringen medeltida? *Hälsingerunor*: 109–117.

Brøgger, A.W.
1921. *Ertog og øre: den gamle norske vegt*. Skrifter (Videnskabsselskapet i Kristiania), 2 Historisk-filosofisk klasse, Vol. 1921: 3. Dybwad, Kristiania.

Bugge, Sophus
1877. Runeinskriften paa Ringen i Forsa kirke i nordre Helsingland. In *Festskrift til det Kgl. Universitet i Upsala ved dets Jubilæum i September 1877 fra Det Kgl. Fredriks Universitet i Christiania*, vol. I. Christiania.

Callmer, Johan and Erik Rosengren
1997. *"...gick Grendel att söka det höga huset..." Arkeologiska källor till aristokratiska miljöer i Skandinavien under yngre järnålder. Rapport från ett seminarium i Falkenberg 16–17 november 1995*. GOTARC, series C, Vol. 17. Hallands länsmuseer, Halmstad.

Davidson, H. R. E.
1962. *The Sword in Anglo-Saxon England: its Archaeology and Literature*. Clarendon Press, Oxford.
1993. *Boundaries and Thresholds. Papers from a Colloquium of the Katharine Briggs Club*. Thimble Press, Stroud.

Eriksen, Marianne Hem
2010. *Between the Real and Ideal. Ordering, Controlling and Utilising Space in Power Negotiations. Hall Buildings in Scandinavia, 250–1050 CE*. Master's thesis, University of Oslo. Electronic document, http://urn.nb.no/URN:NBN:no-24932.
2013. Doors to the dead: The power of doorways and thresholds in Viking-Age Scandinavia. *Archaeological Dialogues* 20(2): 187–214.
2015. *Doors. Thresholds in Space, Ritual, and Mentality in Late Iron Age Scandinavia* (Working title). Forthcoming Ph.D. dissertation, Dept. of Archaeology, Conservation and History, University of Oslo.

Eyrbyggja saga
[1989] Translated to English with an introduction and notes by H. Pálsson and P. Edwards. Penguin, London.
Geddes, Jane
1982. IV. The Sanctuary Ring of Durham Cathedral. *Archaeologia (Second Series)* 107: 125–129.
Gjærder, Per
1952. *Norske pryd-dører fra middelalderen.* Universitetet i Bergen Skrifter, Vol. 24. University of Bergen, Bergen.
*Gulating Law*
[1981] Published as *Gulatingslovi*, translated to Norwegian by K. Robberstad. Norrøne Bokverk, Vol. 33. Samlaget, Oslo.
Hahnloser, Hans R.
1959. Urkunden zur Bedeutung des Türrings. In *Festschrift für Erich Meyer zum sechzigsten Geburtstag 29. Oktober 1957. Studien zu Werken in den Sammlungen des Museums für Kunst und Gewerbe Hamburg*, edited by Erich Meyer, pp. 125–146. Hamburg.
Hedeager, Lotte
2002. Scandinavian 'Central Places' in a cosmological setting. In *Central Places in the Migration and Merovingian Periods. Papers from the 52nd Sachsensymposium, Lund, August 2001*, edited by Lars Larsson and Birgitta Hårdh, pp. 3–18. Acta archaeologica Lundensia. Series in 8°, Vol. 39. Almqvist and Wiksell, Stockholm.
2011. *Iron Age Myth and Materiality. An Archaeology of Scandinavia AD 400–1000.* Routledge, London.
Herschend, Frands
1993. The origin of the hall in southern Scandinavia. *Tor* 25: 175–199.
1997. *Livet i hallen. Tre fallstudier i den yngre järnålderns aristokrati.* Occasional Papers in Archaeology, Vol. 14. Institutionen för arkeologi och antik historia, Uppsala universitet, Uppsala.
1998. *The Idea of the Good in Late Iron Age Society.* Occasional Papers in Archaeology, Vol. 15. Department of Archaeology and Ancient History, Uppsala University, Uppsala.
Jørgensen, Lars
1998. En storgård fra vikingetid ved Tissø, Sjælland. In *Centrala platser, centrala frågor: samhällsstrukturen under Järnåldern: en vänbok till Berta Stjernquist*, edited by Lars Larsson and Birgitta Hårdh. Acta Archaeologica Lundensia series in 8°, Vol. 28. Almqvist and Wiksell, Lund.
Källström, Magnus
2010. Forsaringen er vikingtida. *Fornvännen* 105: 228–232.
Karlsson, Lennart
1988. *Medieval Ironwork in Sweden*, Vol. 1. Almqvist and Wiksell, Stockholm.
Kilger, Christoph
2008. Wholeness and holiness: Counting, weighing and valuing silver in the early Viking Period. In *Means of Exchange. Dealing with Silver in the Viking Age*, edited by Dagfinn Skre, pp. 253–326. Kaupang Excavation Project Publication Series, Vol. 2. Aarhus University Press, Aarhus.
Larsson, Lars
2007. The Iron Age ritual building at Uppåkra, southern Sweden. *Antiquity* 81: 11–25.
2011. A ceremonial building as a 'home of the gods'? Central buildings in the central place of Uppåkra. In *The Gudme-Gudhem phenomenon. Papers Presented at a Workshop Organized by the Centre for Baltic and Scandinavian Archaeology (ZBSA), Schleswig, April 26th and 27th,*

*2010*, edited by Oliver Grim and Alexandra Pesch, pp. 189–206 Schriften des Archäologischen Landesmuseums. Wachholtz, Neumünster.

Larsson, Lars and Karl-Magnus Lenntorp

2004. The enigmatic house. In *Continuity for Centuries. A Ceremonial Building and its Context at Uppåkra, Southern Sweden*, edited by Lars Larsson, pp. 3–48. Almqvist and Wiksell, Stockholm.

Lefebvre, Henri

1991. *The Production of Space*. Blackwell, Oxford.

Lidén, Hans-Emil

1969. From pagan sanctuary to Christian church: The excavation of Mære church in Trøndelag. *Norwegian Archaeological Review* 2(1): 3–21.

Liestøl, Aslak

1979. Runeringen i Forsa. Kva er han, og når vart han smidd? *Saga och sed*: 12–27.

Löfving, Carl

2010. Forsaringen är medeltida. *Fornvännen* 105: 48–53.

Nielsen, Ann-Lill

2006. Rituals and power. About a small building and animal bones from the late Iron Age. In *Old Norse Religion in Long-term Perspectives. Origins, Changes, and Interactions. An International Conference in Lund, Sweden, June 3–7, 2004*, edited by Anders Andrén, Kristina Jennbert and Catharina Raudvere, pp. 243–247. Vägar till Midgård, Vol. 8. Nordic Academic Press, Lund.

Nordberg, Andreas

2003. *Krigarna i Odins sal: dödsföreställningar och krigarkult i fornnordisk religion*. Fil. Dr. dissertation, Stockholms universitet, Religionshistoriska institutionen, Stockholm.

2011. Vad är en kultplats? *Fornvännen* 106: 215–231.

Nordén, Arthur

1961. 'Sparlösa' och 'Kälvesten': Våra äldsta historiska runinskrifter. *Fornvännen* 56: 256–270.

Näsström, Britt-Mari

2001. *Fornskandinavisk religion: en grundbok*. Studentlitteratur, Lund.

Rigsþula

[1985] In *Eddadikt*, translated to Norwegian by Ludvig Holm-Olsen. Cappelen, Oslo.

Ringstad, Bjørn

2005. Gildehallen på Aure. In *Fra funn til samfunn: Jernalderstudier tilegnet Bergljot Solberg på 70-årsdagen*, edited by Knut Andreas Bergsvik, pp. 259–278. UBAS Nordisk, Vol. 1. Arkeologisk institutt, Universitetet i Bergen, Bergen.

Rønne, Preben

2011. Horg, hov og ve – et førkristent kultanlæg på Ranheim i Sør-Trøndelag. *Årbok – Ranheim Bydels Museums Historielag*.

Ruthström, Bo

1990. Forsa-ristningen: vikingtida vi-rätt? *Arkiv for nordisk filologi* 105: 41–55.

Saga of Olaf Tryggvason

[1911] Published as *The Sagas of Olaf Tryggvason and of Harald the Tyrant*, translated to English by E. H. Hearn and G. Storm. Williams and Norgate, London.

Söderberg, Bengt

2003. Järnålderns Järrestad. Bebyggelse, kronologi, tolkningspersektiv. In *Järrestad. Huvudgård i centralbygd*, edited by Bengt Söderberg, pp. 109–174. Riksantikvarieämbetet, Stockholm.

2005. *Aristokratiskt rum och gränsöverskridande. Järrestad och sydöstra Skåne mellan region och rike 600–1100*. Riksantikvarieämbetet, Stockholm.

2006. Några perspektiver på kulten i en härskarmiljö. Järrestad under yngre järnålder. In *Kulthus and dödshus. Det ritualiserade rummets teori och praktik*, edited by Mats Anglert, Magnus Artursson and Fredrik Svanberg, pp. 153–166. Riksantikvarieämbetet, Stockholm.

Steinsland, Gro
2005. *Norrøn religion. Myter, riter, samfunn.* Pax, Oslo.

Steuer, Heiko
1989. Archaeology and History: Proposals on the social structure of the Merovingian Kingdom. In *The Birth of Europe: Archaeology and Social Development in the First Millenium A.D.*, edited by Klavs Randsborg, pp. 100–121. Analectala Romana Instituti Danici, Roma.

Sundqvist, Olaf
2007. *Kultledare i fornskandinavisk religion.* Occasional Papers in Archaeology, Vol. 41. Institutionen för arkeologi och antik historia, Uppsala universitet, Uppsala.

Trumbull, H. Clay
1896. *The Threshold Covenant or the Beginning of Religious Rites.* Clark, Edinburgh.

Turner, Victor W.
1967. Betwixt and between. The liminal period in rites de passage. In *The Forest of Symbols.* Cornell University Press, Ithaca, NY.

Vierck, Hayo
1981. *Imitatio imperii* und *interpretatio Germanica* vor der Wikingerzeit. In *Les pays du Nord et Byzance. Actes du collocue nordique et international de byzantologie, tenu à Upsal 20–22 avril 1979*, edited by Rudolf Zeitler, pp. 64–113. Acta Universitatis Upsaliensis Figura Nova Series, Vol. 19. Almqvist and Wiksell, Stockholm.

Zachrisson, Torun
2004. Det heliga på Helgö och dess kosmiska referenser. In *Ordning mot kaos. Studier av nordisk förkristen kosmologi*, edited by Anders Andrén, Kristina Jennbert and Catharina Raudvere, pp. 343–388. Vägar till Midgård, Vol. 4. Nordic Academic Press, Lund.

Ödman, Anders
2003. Tankar kring två ringhandtag från Uppåkra. In *Fler fynd i centrum. Materialstudier i och kring Uppåkra*, edited by Birgitta Hårdh, pp. 89–96. Uppåkrastudier, Vol. 9. Almqvist and Wiksell, Stockholm.

PART II

# GENDERED THINGS, GENDERED SPACES?

*Chapter 7*

# She came from another place. On the burial of a young girl in Birka

*Charlotte Hedenstierna-Jonson*

*Abstract*

In the mid-10th century a young girl of high social standing was buried in one of the more distinguished grave fields in Birka. She was placed in a coffin together with a few personal objects. Her dress was of high quality, as was the jewellery worn with it. The burial at first seems like nothing out of the ordinary. The different elements all occur at this period in time. But when deconstructing the grave it becomes more of an enigma. Though commonly called the 'Birka girl', this 5-year-old most likely did not come from Birka or the surrounding region at all, but from another place altogether. What can modern research learn from the skeleton of a child from the 10th century and what do the results from one individual alone tell us about a place like Birka?

## Birka – an emerging urban centre

Situated on a small island in Lake Mälaren, not far from present-day Stockholm, Birka was a major trading and craft-working centre for the eastern region of Viking-Age Scandinavia. The settlement was a cultural melting pot whose material culture reflects a far-reaching network of contacts. This urban-like settlement operated as a hub in the trade of prestigious objects and advanced crafts.

Birka changed over time, both in its physical make-up and in its role in and involvement with its surrounding region. The town-like structure was founded in the mid- to late 8th century as a centre for trade and crafts (Ambrosiani 2013: 57–70; Hedenstierna-Jonson 2012: 214). During this initial phase, Birka was part of a trade network operating round the coastline of the Baltic, with links to other trading networks from Friesland in north-western Europe all the way down to the Mediterranean. Birka quickly developed into a place of importance for both its region and beyond. In its first century it was already considered important enough for the church of Hamburg-Bremen to send out a missionary and representative, Ansgar, who reached the island in AD 829 (Ambrosiani 2012, 2013; Hedenstierna-Jonson 2012; *Rimbert*).

A decisive change took place towards the end of the 9th century when Birka became the westernmost centre for trade with the network operating with the East (Ambrosiani 2001; Hedenstierna-Jonson 2009; Hedenstierna-Jonson and Holmquist Olausson 2006; Jansson 1987). Trade was conducted on a different level than before. Trading expeditions had become ventures of high economical risk, involving complicated merchandise that included slaves, silver and other valuable commodities. There was a transfer of power as local or even regional rulers, chieftains or kings would have had limited control over the extensive geographical areas covered, and the amounts of moveable wealth ministered by trading families and workshops. Only those who travelled the route would have had actual authority. During the 10th century, the inhabitants of Birka would have become truly urban, being the second or even third generation of 'town-dwellers'. The inhabitants of 10th century Birka considered themselves to be part of an urban culture set apart from the surrounding way of life of the Lake Mälaren region (Hedenstierna-Jonson 2009, 2012). This urban culture was polyethnic, formed by the assimilation of different people drawn together by common enterprises in trade, crafts and warfare.

## The individual in focus

When Birka was established it was without precedent, at least in the region of the eastern Viking World. The first generation of inhabitants left their traditional rural lifestyle behind and formed a new existence. The ensuing generations became the first truly urban people. The inhabitants of this early urban centre and their interaction with their surrounding region constitute two main questions in the research project 'Birka, Rus' and Nordic Gentes – identity, self-image and cultural expression in Viking-Age Sweden'. The particular circumstances surrounding the life, death and burial of one of these urban individuals, the so-called 'Birka girl', is the focus of this paper.

But how much can a single individual convey in terms of knowledge of a prehistoric society? Ian Hodder (2000) claims that the identification of individuals, and individual events, is not of much value or interest in the understanding of the pre-historic processes. Hodder emphasises the need to make a distinction between unique events and long-term structures. A burial represents such a single event and can only describe that particular moment in time.

Nina Nordström (2007), on the other hand, states in her research on prehistoric individuals in science and media that they represent more than just themselves. They carry a 'luggage of business' with them that in different ways affects our understanding of them and the time in which they lived (Nordström 2007: 79). This is in concordance with Lynn Meskell (1999: 9–10) who states that the 'single identity is made up of a multiplicity of social variables – age, sex, class, status, religion, ethnicity, *etc.* – embedded within a matrix of social relation.' If we can discern some of these different variables we can learn more about the period in which the individual lived. The individual opens up tiny windows into prehistory – making the past slightly more personal to us.

## Hjalmar Stolpe and grave Bj 463

The prehistoric individual is first and foremost found in graves, as other contexts generally comprise a mix of people and actions making the individual difficult to separate from the group. The knowledge gained, and research made into Birka is to a large extent derived from, or connected to, graves. Approximately 3000 graves have been identified, clustered together in a number of different grave fields. Out of these a little more than 1100 have been excavated, mainly by Hjalmar Stolpe during the second half of the 19th century. The burial practice is extremely varied with cremations, inhumations, coffins and chamber-graves. The cremations could possibly be seen as continuing the regional burial rite traditions (*cf.* Andersson 2005), even though the grave fields in which they lie constitute a break in convention, as they are not visibly connected to the family's home. But the burial practice would become even more disparate. Although already present during the first phase, 10th century Birka saw an increase in various forms of inhumation (*cf.* Gräslund 1980).

The grave containing the Birka girl was excavated by Stolpe during his campaign in 1876 (numbered Bj 463). Stolpe had regarded this grave with particular interest during the excavation. Undoubtedly touched by the finely preserved skeleton of a young child he decided to keep the grave intact and remove the remains along with the earth in which they rested. Stolpe stated in his excavation notes that initial preparations had been made to remove the skeleton, together with adornments and coffin nails in situ, resting on a thick layer of the underlying soil. '[…] *upptaga skelettet jemte prydnader och kistspikar i orubbadt skick, hvilande på en tillräckligt tjock skifva af underlaget* […]' ('… take up the skeleton together with adornments and coffin nails in an undisturbed state, resting on a sufficiently thick part of the underlay …') (Stolpe 1876: 18). The burial was transported to Stockholm and put on display in the prehistory exhibition in the National Museum. Stolpe never found the time to publish the results of his Birka excavations. The task was left to his successor Holger Arbman who compiled Stolpe's notes and meticulous drawings of the individual burials into the well-known volumes of *Birka: Untersuchungen und Studien 1, Die Gräber. Text und Tafeln,* published in 1940 and 1943. As grave Bj 463 was placed unmarked in the exhibition and Stolpe's notes were quite brief in this particular case, it took Arbman some time to identify it. He refers to this in the burial's entry in *Die Gräber*: 'Mit grösster Wahrscheinlichkeit ist das Grab mit einem im Museum in situ auf bewahrten Kinderskelett ohne Grabnummer von Björkö identisch' (Arbman 1943: 132).

## Burial practice and grave gifts

Burial Bj 463 was placed in one of the best locations in Birka, on a terrace just outside the hill fort and overlooking the town area. This burial ground, known as 'the grave field north of Borg', contained a group of burials, predominantly inhumations, many with coffins. In this particular area numerous graves were disturbed by later burials, as if there were a limited space to hold them. These graves lacked the mound superstructure typical for traditional cremation burials in the region. Stolpe noted a string of stones surrounding these burials providing an enclosed area and it has been suggested that this could be a Christian burial ground or cemetery (Arbman 1943: plan iii; Gräslund 1980: 74).

The girl was placed in a rectangular coffin measuring 1.35 × 0.4 m (Arbman 1943: 131–132). The exact orientation of the coffin is not stated by Arbman but found in the plans drawn up by surveyor J. J. Nordstrand in 1888–1889, and later included in his publication of the burials (Arbman 1943: plans i–v), in which Bj 463 is depicted with an east–west direction. In Nordstrand's maps all inhumation graves are recorded to scale and with the exact orientation given by Stolpe (*cf.* Gräslund 1980: 11).

Stolpe and later Arbman documented the archaeological data as it could be studied without disturbing the bones. These studies resulted in a grave plan with a detailed drawing of the skeleton and a list of grave goods. The latter encompassed a small knife, a needle-case made of bone, a round brooch of gilded copper alloy and a number of blue, yellow and gold- and silver-foil glass beads (21 according to Arbman 1943: 132).

The brooch is decorated in Borre-style displaying three animal heads linked together with ribbon-like interlace. This round brooch-type is not uncommon; a number are also known from other burials in Birka (*cf.* Arbman 1940, 1943). In the Lake Mälaren region the use of a single brooch is less frequent than that of the three-piece arrangement with two oval brooches complemented with an equal-armed brooch (*cf.* Jansson 1985: 11–12). A single-brooch style of dress accompanied by a knife is more consistent with the burials of Denmark and Northern Germany where Christianity at this time was already established and inhumation burials had become customary (*cf.* Arents and Eisenschmidt 2010). The round brooch and beads, together with the burial practice of inhumation within a coffin, dates the burial to the mid-10th century (Gräslund 1980: 15, 17–18; Jansson 1985: 200–201).

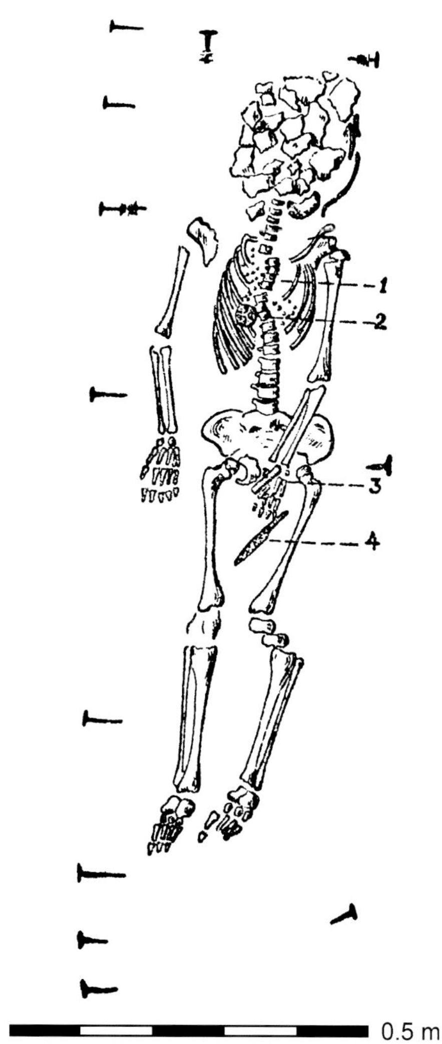


*Fig. 7.1. Hjalmar Stolpe's drawing of grave Bj463 from 1876 (published in Arbman 1943: Abb. 74).*

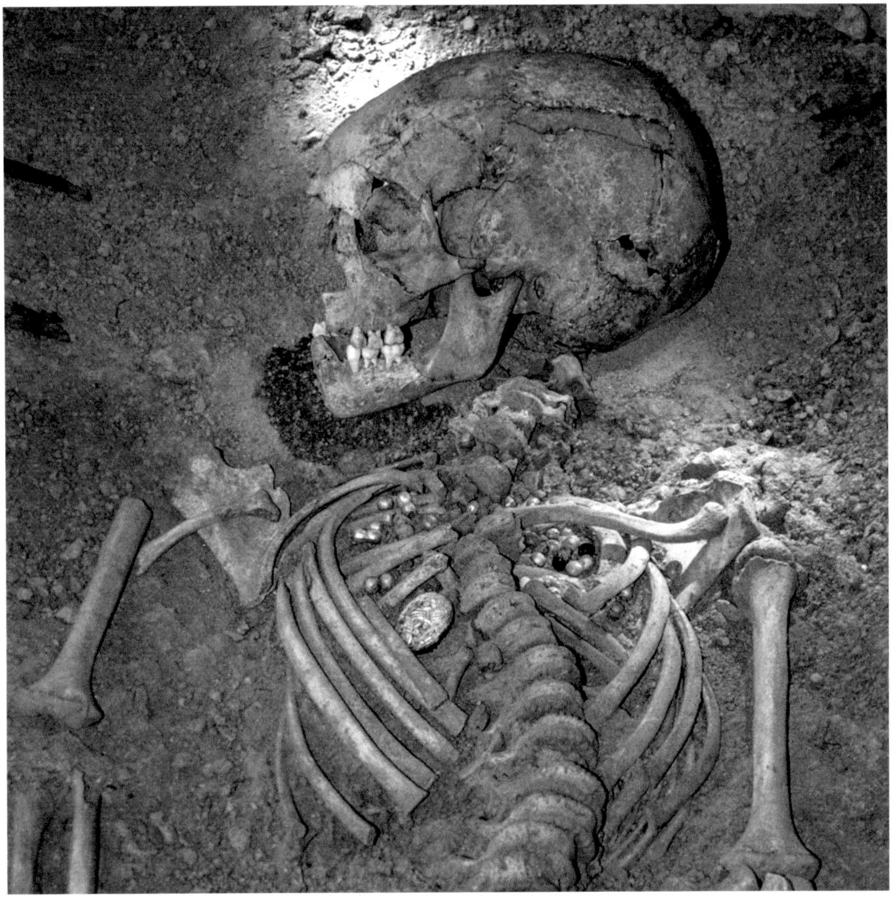

*Fig. 7.2. The child in grave Bj463 after the skull was pieced together. The chest area contained the round brooch and most of the 47 glass beads. Photo: © Gabriel Hildebrand, SHM.*

## Age, health and cause of death

The high-status character and somewhat unusual nature of the burial and grave gifts, together with the crushed state of the skull had evoked questions relating to the child's status, age, health and cause of death. In many discussions the girl was presented as a 10–12-year-old despite the obvious slightness of her body. In 2011 the Swedish History Museum initiated a teaching project as part of a children's activity program aimed at reconstructing the girl from Birka. As the skull of the child had been crushed post-mortem, possibly due to the collapsing lid of the coffin, one important task was to retrieve as many pieces of the cranium as possible. A specialised excavation was performed, limited to the head-end of the coffin. Apart from enabling the conservator and osteologist to piece together most of the skull, a further 26 glass beads were found conforming to the shapes and colours of those already documented.

*Fig. 7.3. During 2011, a public excavation of grave Bj463 was performed as part of a teaching project at the Swedish History Museum. The excavation was limited to the head-end of the grave and aimed at retrieving as many parts of the damaged skull as possible. Photo: © Gabriel Hildebrand, SHM.*

The excavation and the teaching-project also enabled further examination of the grave material, involving osteology and biochemistry. Analyses made by osteologists Anna Kjellström and Elin Ahlin Sundman from the Osteoarchaeological Research Laboratory at Stockholm University resulted in new and improved knowledge of the girl. Based on her teeth, her age could be determined to between 5–6 years. Sex was not possible to determine by osteology but the gender indicated by the grave goods is female.

The skeletal material shows few or no signs of malnutrition, and the child's general state of health seems to have been good. There is no osteological evidence as to the cause of death. Ahlin Sundman (2012) has studied the sinuses of Viking-Age people as sinusitis leaves traces in the bone structure. Chronic sinusitis can cause severe health problems that eventually can contribute to an early death. But even though this particular child shows traces of sinusitis these are very slight and could not be considered a health problem (Ahlin Sundman 2012).

### Diet and possible place of origin

The potential given by bone chemistry, in this case the stable isotopes of sulphur ($^{34}S$), carbon ($^{13}C$) and nitrogen ($^{15}N$) have made it possible to pose questions concerning diet and migration patterns. Nitrogen levels show an individual's place in the food chain – a vegetarian would thus have lower levels than a carnivore. Carbon levels distinguish between a marine or terrestrial diet, and sulphur levels derive from the geographical prerequisites of the region from where the food came. This analysis was conducted by Markus Fjellström (2012) at the Archaeological Research Laboratory at Stockholm University where samples were taken from the teeth and jawbone to catch possible changes in diet and location over time. Due to the tender age of the girl these results to some extent reflect the diet and place of origin of her mother.

As a control, the outcomes from these samples were compared to a previous study by Anna Linderholm, Charlotte Hedenstierna-Jonson, Olle Svensk and Kerstin Lidén (2008) which included 20 individuals from different grave fields at Birka as well as animal bones from the settlement. The results show that the girl from Bj 463 had a predominantly meat-based diet deriving from terrestrial animals; maybe not what you would expect for a young girl living on a small island surrounded by brackish water with a plentiful supply of fish. The girl corresponds in terms of diet to the other individuals that have been analysed. Her sulphur levels are also comparative to theirs and separate her from the animals judged to be local to the island. She is therefore, like these others, most likely not of local origin (Fjellström 2012; *cf.* Linderholm *et al.* 2008).

Anna Kjellström (2012) in her extensive project 'People in Transition' has mapped the health, age and dietary patterns of individuals in the Lake Mälaren region during the transition between the Viking Age and medieval times. The outcome of this project makes it possible to set the Birka girl into a wider context.

Kjellström's results are based on 250 inhumation burials in Birka. They give a restricted image of the population as they only represent a minor portion of the approximately 3000 burials. The analysed bones all derive from inhumations, as isotope analysis cannot be performed on cremated bones. As such they represent a minority deviating from the widespread practice of cremation. According to Kjellström's study there are significant differences between men and women in Birka with regard to age and health but not concerning diet (Kjellström 2012; Kjellström *et al.* 2013). In comparison to the men buried in Birka the women buried there were younger, which indicates either that women died at a younger age or that women moved out of Birka when older, living there only during a particular period in their youth. The health differences are even more interesting. The women in Birka show higher levels of physical stress than both their male cohabitants and women from neighbouring rural contexts. The women's health was inferior, as regards both nutrition and infection. As these recordable traces derive from the time of their upbringing, the results actually show gender-related differences. In terms of the dietary evidence there are no differences between the male and female diet in Birka (Kjellström 2005, 2012; Kjellström *et al.* 2013).

### Children in society and in burials

The death rate of children in Viking-Age society was relatively high, as might be expected. The proportion of children's graves in grave fields generally amount to approximately 25–30% of the total (Gräslund 1980: 82). The actual number of child burials in Birka is not known as the osteological material from the cremation burials has yet to be analysed. Out of the excavated burials, 45 have been identified as children based on osteology and the size of the burial (Arbman 1943). In addition to these, Anne-Sofie Gräslund (1973) has proposed another 39 burials that could have contained children but where the skeletal remains are not preserved. Gräslund's (1973) assessment is instead based on particular finds that she links to the presence of children in burials. But even including these uncertain burials the proportion of children's graves in Birka amounts to a mere 17%. This raises questions on the character and composition of the population in this urban settlement. The scarcity of buried children also means that each child grave makes a statement about the society and not just the individual.

It has been suggested that Viking-Age burial practices should be seen as selective representations of the living population (*e.g.* Herschend 2009: 33–34, 120–121; Mejsholm 2009: 152, 255; Wikborg 2007: 198–200). The mortuary ideology distinguished the individuals who were thought to be most suited for such a manifestation and only in exceptional cases were children considered to fit these social qualifications (*cf.* Mejsholm 2009: 255). The structure and contents of child burials indicate that society did not differentiate between children and adults in terms of status and formal representation (*cf.* Stoodley 2000: 469). It is however reasonable to believe that the responsibilities of an adult in practice differed from those of a young child. Formally these responsibilities may very well have been the same. Thus the grave does not reflect aspects of eventual childhood or the activities of a child, but rather the position in society that the interred individual represents. This does not exclude the possibility of childhood in terms of how children were considered and treated in daily life, only that these parameters were inadequate in mortuary ideology (*cf.* Lillehammer 2010: 12–13).

Returning to the Birka girl we know of many particulars concerning her health, status, age and type of burial, but how can we interpret what she represents? In accordance with the above-mentioned criticism by Hodder (2000), the study of burial Bj 463 only gives us an image of what actually took place at the time of this child's death. Yet there are a number of features in the style of burial and contents of her grave that convey a perception of 10th century Birka society and its worldview. What can thus be said of the Christian or Christian-influenced style of burial, and how are we to interpret the grave gifts in relation to the girl's age? Was she in death seen as a child or as a representative of adult society?

In her studies on Anglo-Saxon society Sally Crawford (1999, 2007) states that in ritual terms 'any body assigned an age of ten years or above at the time of death could have been perceived as an adult' (Crawford 2007: 84). Other researchers have defined childhood as the period between 7 and 15 years of age (Kanvall 1995: 10–11; Mejsholm 2009: 25). According to this, the girl in Bj 463 was on the verge of childhood when she died, leaving infancy behind her, but with many years to go before becoming an adult. The manner of her burial and the wealth of her necklace nonetheless give an impression of a person with a position and role in society.

Nick Stoodley (2000) has discussed the transference between ages as seen through grave gifts in early Anglo-Saxon burial rites. Even though there are a number of differences between Anglo-Saxon and Scandinavian Viking-Age burial practices, Stoodley's results make an interesting comparison. Stoodley (2000: 462–463) suggests that an age-threshold occurred at about five, marking an age from which a feminine identity could be conferred. According to Stoodley, beads played an important role in signalling age difference. The second stage of the feminine lifecycle reached its threshold at the age of 10–12 years. At this time the grave gifts became plentiful and more complex. Women would pass through another three stages during their lifecycle. Placing the girl from Birka into Stoodley's scheme she would chronologically be considered a young child, practically an infant. But her complex set of grave gifts and the sheer number of beads would instead place her in the childhood/young adult category. This indicates that there was a discrepancy between the chronological age and the social age of the girl and that she in death represented more than herself. Her tender age makes it highly unlikely that she was in possession of status and wealth holding the position of a widow. She should rather be seen as a representative of a family, its function and household, *etc.* As a child representing a family, her burial could in all respects resemble or be equivalent to that of an adult.

The significance of the needle-case has yet to be considered. There are 64 known examples from burial contexts in Birka. A survey made by Lena Klintberg in 1995 shows that needle-cases are rarely found outside urban contexts (*cf.* Mälarstedt 1984). Generally found in burials of wealthy females of high social standing their presence could be interpreted as symbols of some kind of leadership. Klintberg (1995) suggests that these women were involved in the production and trade of textiles. There may even be an element of hereditary status as two of the needle-cases in Birka were found in children's graves (Bj 463 and Bj 846).

## A young girl from another place – conclusions

At first the burial containing the so-called Birka girl may seem like nothing out of the ordinary. The various elements all occur at this period. But when deconstructing the grave the different features become more of an enigma. The tender age of the buried girl, the presence of a needle-case, the brooch and numerous beads and the practice of inhumation burial in coffins, all together raise the question of origin and affinity. How was it that she came to be buried in such a distinguished manner in a place far from home?

She represented something more in her grave than a mere child. The status and position of the family was possibly of more importance in the funeral rite than that of the buried individual. In terms of affiliation she can be seen as a representative of the urban life of 10th century Birka. The burial practice and the particulars of the grave field in which she was set to rest indicate possible Christian connotations. The needle-case is perhaps the most interesting single object in this complex picture. It could place the girl within a particular group of merchants and workshops involved in textile production and trade.

Finally, the isotope values place her somewhere outside the urban settlement of Birka in terms of origin while her meat-based diet recalls that of a warrior rather than a small child. So despite her tender age this little girl who came from elsewhere to Birka, in death possibly represents the circumstances that brought her there.

### *Acknowledgements*

Warm thanks to Leena Drenzel, Ulrik Skans, Li Kolker and Oscar Nilsson with whom I worked on the "Birka girl" project at the Swedish History Museum. I would also like to express my gratitude to Anna Kjellström at the Osteoarchaeological Research Laboratory for her generous collaboration. This study forms part of the research project 'Birka, Rus' and Nordic Gentes', funded by Riksbankens jubileumsfond.

### *References*

Ahlin Sundman, Elin

2012. Bihåleinflammation på Björkö. Om hälsorisker i urban miljö. In *Birka nu. Pågående forskning kring världsarvet Birka och Hovgården,* edited by Charlotte Hedenstierna-Jonson, pp. 111–119. Historiska museet, Studies, Vol. 22. The National Historical Museum, Stockholm.

Ambrosiani, Björn

2001. The Birka Falcon. In *Eastern Connections. Excavations in the Black Earth 1990–1995. Pt. 1 The Falcon Motif,* edited by Björn Ambrosiani, pp. 11–27. Birka Studies, Vol. V. Riksantikvarieämbetet, Stockholm.

2012. Birkaforskning i perspektiv av grävningarna 1990–1995. In *Birka nu. Pågående forskning kring världsarvet Birka och Hovgården,* edited by Charlotte Hedenstierna-Jonson, pp. 9–18. Historiska museet, Studies, Vol. 22. The National Historical Museum, Stockholm.

2013. *Stratigraphy Vol. 1 Part One: The Site and the Shore. Part Two: The Bronze Caster's Workshop.* Birka Studies, Vol. 9. Riksantikvarieämbetet, Stockholm.

Andersson, Gunnar

2005. *Gravspråk som religiös strategi.* Arkeologiska undersökningar, Vol. 61. Riksantikvarieämbetet, Stockholm.

Arbman, Holger

1940. *Tafeln. Die Gräber,* Vol. 1. Birka, Untersuchungen und Studien, Kungl. vitterhets historie och antikvitets akademien, Vol. 1. Almqvist and Wiksell, Stockholm.

1943. *Text.* Die Gräber, Vol. 2. Birka, Untersuchungen und Studien, Kungl. vitterhets historie och antikvitets akademien, Vol. 1. Almqvist andWiksell, Stockholm.

Arents, Ute and Silke Eisenschmidt

2010. *Die Gräber von Haithabu,* Vol. 1–2. Die Ausgrabungen in Haithabu. Wachholtz Verlag, Neumünster.

Crawford, Sally

1999. *Childhood in Anglo-Saxon England.* Sutton Publishing, Stroud.

2007. Companions, co-incidents or chattels? Children in the Early Anglo-Saxon multiple burial ritual. In *Children, Childhood and Society,* edited by Sally Crawford and Gillian Shepherd, pp. 83–92. BAR International Series, Vol. 1696. British Archaeological Reports, Oxford.

Fjellström, Markus

2012. Isotopanalyser av Birkaflickan, Adelsö, Uppland. Uppdragsrapport nr. 208. Manuscript on file, Archaeological Research Laboratory, Stockholm University.

Gräslund, Anne-Sofie

1973. Barn i Birka. *TOR* 1972–1973: 161–179.

1980. *The Burial Customs. A Study of the Graves on Björkö.* Birka, Untersuchungen und Studien, Vol. IV. Almqvist and Wiksell, Stockholm.

Hedenstierna-Jonson, Charlotte

2009. Rus', Varangiand and Birka warriors. In *The Martial Society. Aspects of Warriors, Fortifications and Social Change in Scandinavia,* edited by Lena Holmquist Olausson and Michael Olausson, pp. 159–178. Thesis and Papers in Archaeology, Series B, Vol. 11. Archaeological Research Laboratory, Stockholm University, Stockholm.

2012. Birkafolket. In *Birka nu. Pågående forskning kring världsarvet Birka och Hovgården,* edited by Charlotte Hedenstierna-Jonson, pp. 213–226. Historiska museet. Studies 22. Stockholm.

Hedenstierna-Jonson, Charlotte and Lena Holmquist Olausson

2006. *The Oriental Mounts from Birka's Garrison. An Expression of Warrior Rank and Status.* Antikvariskt arkiv, Vol. 81. Kungl.Vitterhetshistorie och antikvitets akademien, Stockholm.

Herschend, Frans

2009. *The Early Iron Age in South Scandinavia. Social Order in Settlement and Landscape.* Occasional Papers in Archaeology, Vol. 46. Uppsala universitet, Uppsala.

Hodder, Ian

2000. Agency and individuals in long-term processes. In *Agency in Archaeology,* edited by Marcia-Anne Dobres and John E. Robb, pp. 21–33. Routledge, London.

Jansson, Ingmar

1985. *Ovala spännbucklor. En studie av vikingatida standardsmycken med utgångspunkt från Björköfynden.* Aun, archaeological studies Vol. 7. Uppsala.

1987. Communications between Scandinavia and Eastern Europe in the Viking Age. In *Der Handel der Karolinger- und Wikingerzeit: Bericht über die Kolloquien der Kommission für die Altertumskunde Mittel- und Nordeuropas in den Jahren 1980 bis 1983,* edited by Klaus Düwel, Herbert Jankuhn, Harald Siems and Dieter Timpe, pp. 773–807. Untersuchungen zu Handel und Verkehr der vor- und frühge-schichtlichen Zeit in Mittel- und Nordeuropa, Vol. IV. Vandenhoeck and Ruprecht, Göttingen.

Kanvall, Petra

1995. Barn i förhistorisk tid. En teoretisk diskussion kring begreppet "barn". In *Arkeologi om barn,* edited by Barbro Johnsen and Stig Welinder, pp. 7–12. Occasional papers in archaeology, Vol. 10. Societas archaeologica Upsaliensis, Uppsala.

Kjellström, Anna

2005. *The Urban Farmer: Osteoarchaeological Analysis of Skeletons from Medieval Sigtuna Interpreted in a Socioeconomic Perspective.* Theses and papers in osteoarchaeology, Vol. 2. Osteoarchaeological Research Laboratory, Stockholm University, Stockholm.

2012. Projektet människor i brytningstid. Skelettgravar i Birka och dess nära omland. In *Birka nu. Pågående forskning kring världsarvet Birka och Hovgården,* edited by Charlotte Hedenstierna-

Jonson, pp. 69–80. Historiska museet, Studies, Vol. 22, The National Historical Museum, Stockholm.

Kjellström, Anna, Anna Linderholm, Charlotte Hedenstierna-Jonson and Kerstin Lidén
2013. Stable Isotope Analysis of Viking-early medieval sites in the Mälaren valley. Manuscript on file, Stockholm University, Durham University, Swedish History Museum.

Klintberg, Lena
1995. *Nålhus – kvinnliga attribut?* Master's thesis, Department of Archaeology and Classical Studies, Stockholm University, Stockholm.

Lillehammer, Grete
2010. Introduction. In *Socialisation. Recent Research on Childhood and Children in the Past*, edited by Grete Lillehammer, pp. 9–19. AmS-skrifter, Vol. 23. University of Stavanger, Stavanger.

Linderholm, Anna, Charlotte Hedenstierna-Jonson, Olle Svensk and Kerstin Lidén
2008. Diet and status in Birka: stable isotopes and grave goods compared. *Antiquity* 82: 446–461.

Mejsholm, Lotta
2009. *Gränsland. Konstruktion av tidig barndom och begravningsritual vid tiden för kristnandet i Skandinavien.* Occasional Papers in Archaeology, Vol. 44. Uppsala universitet, Uppsala.

Meskell, Lynn
1999. *Archaeologies of Social Life: Age, Sex, Class Etcetra in Ancient Egypt.* Blackwell, Oxford.

Mälarstedt, Hilkka
1984. Nadelbuchsen. In *Systematische Analysen der Gräberfunde,* edited by Greta Arwidsson, pp. 191–194. Birka, Untersuchungen und Studien, Kungl. vitterhets historie och antikvitets akademien, Vol. II. Almqvist and Wiksell, Stockholm.

Nordström, Nina
2007. *De odödliga. Förhistoriska individer i vetenskap och media.* Vägar till Midgård, Vol. 10. Nordic Academic Press, Falun.

*Rimbert*
[1986] *Boken om Ansgar. Ansgars liv.* Translated by E. Odelman. Samfundet Pro fide et christianismo, Vol. 10. Proprius, Stockholm

Stolpe, Hjalmar
1876. *Grafundersökningar på Björkö.* Aftryck ur Tidskrift för Antropologi och Kulturhistoria. Vol. 1. Nr. 10. 1876.

Stoodley Nick
2000. From the cradle to the grave: age organization and the early Anglo-Saxon burial rite. *World Archaeology* 31(3): 456–472.

Wikborg, Jonas
2007. De levande och de döda. Gravfältens kontinuitet och relation till bebyggelsen. *Att nå den andra sidan. Om begravningar och ritual i Uppland,* edited by Michel Notelid, pp. 173–200. Arkeologi E4 Uppland, Vol. 2. Societas Archaeologica Upsaliensis, Riksantikvarieämbetet and Upplandsmuseet, Uppsala.

*Chapter 8*

# Roles and perceptions of shielings and the mediation of gender identities in Viking and medieval Iceland

*Patrycja Kupiec and Karen Milek*

*Abstract*

This paper examines archaeological and written sources for shieling activities, the extent to which these may have had a role in the enactment of different genders, and possible attitudes towards shielings in Viking-Age and medieval Iceland. By comparing the archaeological, legal, and saga evidence for the separation of infield from outfield, the distances between shielings and farms, and gendered activities, a new picture of summer pasture sites emerges. Archaeological investigations of boundary walls and medieval laws support the notion of the homefield as a demarcated social space separated from the outfield. However, the estimates for average distances between shielings and farms suggest that contact could have been maintained between the two, which stands in contrast to the saga narratives that tend to depict shielings as secluded and dangerous. While the sagas portray shielings as predominantly female domains, the archaeological evidence suggests that some shieling sites were associated with a wide range of activities and genders. The paper concludes with a suggestion that the ambiguous status of shielings may have been only partly due to their physical isolation; even more important may have been the shifting roles and gender identities of the people who used them.

## Introduction

Transhumance is believed to have been a common economic practice from at least the Iron Age in parts of the British Isles, Ireland, and Scandinavia (Gardiner 2011; Mahler 2007; Skrede 2005). The seasonal movement of livestock from the main farm to summer pastures played a particularly important role in the subsistence economics of small farms in Scandinavia and the North Atlantic islands settled by Scandinavians in the Viking Age. While interdisciplinary research has been conducted on shielings in Scandinavia (*e.g.* Karlsson *et al.* 2010; Skrede 2005), very little is known about how the shieling system operated in Iceland, where a particularly harsh climate and short growing season were unfavourable for barley agriculture, especially in the north of the country (Simpson *et al.* 2002), creating a strong dependence on animal husbandry.

The recent excavation of Viking-Age and medieval shielings in Iceland presents an opportunity to examine the physical evidence for shieling locations, the activities that took place at these sites, and their social roles. While shielings were undoubtedly an important feature of the Icelandic pastoral economy, this paper will focus on the perception of summer pastures in the Viking and medieval periods and on the concepts of identity that might have been mediated through shielings. It has been suggested that shielings might have had a somewhat ambiguous status due to their marginal locations and the distances that separated them from home farms (Hastrup 1989: 81). Such models, while opening the debate about possible attitudes towards shieling sites, are based on a presumed binary opposition between the safe and socialised space of *innangarðs* ('within the enclosure/inside the fence') and the unknown and dangerous space of *útangarðs* ('outside the enclosure/fence'). This model of a binary contrast between *innangarðs* and *útangarðs,* however, has been criticised as being too simplistic, and based on terminology that seems to have been a relatively late innovation in medieval Icelandic (Vikstrand 2006: 354–356).

We readdress the question of this ambiguous status of Icelandic shielings by examining archaeological evidence from assumed Viking–medieval period shielings and by reviewing surveyed putative shieling sites, focusing on boundary walls to explore whether shielings were considered discrete entities or extensions of the farm, and on shielings' locations to explore whether their isolation was real or perceived. The status attributed to shielings was probably closely interwoven with the identities of those who spent their summers at these sites. Historically Icelandic shielings have been predominantly female spheres of activity, with women being responsible for milking the animals, and making non-perishable dairy products for winter consumption (Hitzler 1979). Shielings might have therefore played an important role in shaping female identity, and, *vice versa*, the way in which these places were perceived could have been affected by their association with women. The evidence for female- and male-related activities at Viking and medieval shielings will be examined to shed light on Icelandic shielings as gendered spaces in these earlier periods.

While there is a relative paucity of excavated shieling sites in Iceland, the review of archaeological evidence will be contextualised against a review of the rich medieval written sources: Icelandic law books, *Grágás* and *Jónsbok*, as well as saga literature. The documentary record attesting to the importance of summer pastures for the Icelandic economy is considerable, and the laws concerning proper use of shielings are common entries in the twelfth century *Grágás*, and the 13th century *Jónsbok*.

Shielings are also frequently mentioned in the medieval sagas of Icelanders (*Íslendingasögur*, or 'Family Sagas'). Íslendingasögur are believed to have been first written in the thirteenth and fourteenth centuries, but they describe events which happened in the period AD 850–1050. The debate about the origin of the sagas as either repositories of oral tradition that accurately preserved knowledge about previous centuries, or literary inventions of medieval authors that had no basis in fact, has dominated saga scholarship for the last two centuries (for a summary see Firth 2012). Today, most historians and literary scholars agree that the Family Sagas differ greatly in their historicity and are generally not a reliable source of information about major developments in the Viking Age, such as the conversion to Christianity, or the conquest of England (Cormack 2007; Sigurðsson 2004). The ways in which the sagas describe these events tends to be imbued with artistic license, idealisations, exaggerations and distortions of facts. However, it can be argued that if they are used critically and sensitively, Íslendingasögur may be rather good sources for developing a more nuanced understanding of mentalities, social practices, farm life, subsistence strategies, and everyday customs in Viking and medieval Iceland. Archaeological remains and later historical sources suggest that subsistence practices and the organisation of household production did not change very much between the Viking Age and the Sturlunga Age, when the sagas were written. On the other hand, pre-Christian mentalities and political relationships depicted in some Family Sagas are significantly different from those portrayed in the Contemporary Sagas of the mid-13th century (Callow 2006), suggesting that they may give us a view of a more distant past and may therefore be used as a source to supplement our understanding of shieling system and its role in shaping gender identities as far back as the Viking Age.

## Innangarðs or útangarðs: materiality and meanings of boundaries

> 'Boundaries link a series of meanings and social practices such as in and out, excluded and included, bounded and unbounded, and centre and periphery.' (Aldred 2008: 318)

### *Archaeology*

The practice of enclosing a farm's homefield with a semi-circular or sub-rectangular boundary wall, which separated it from the outfield grazing areas where shielings were located, is thought to have been a norm in Iceland from the settlement period in the 9th to the 19th century, with evidence for the early enclosures growing as the number of excavated and dated examples increases (Aldred 2008). The boundary wall around the Vatnsfjörður farm has been tentatively dated to the Viking Age based on the use of podzolised turf in the early phases of its construction – a soil type that developed prior to human settlement in the region and that is otherwise only found in the construction of the Viking-Age buildings at the site (Milek 2011: 65). At other sites, tephrochronology has permitted more precise dating of homefield enclosures. The earliest phases of the enclosure walls at Hofðagerði, Hrærekksstaðir, Ingiríðarstaðir and Oddstaðir were dated to pre-1300 (Aldred 2004, 2008; Roberts 2009; Pálsdóttir 2008). Earlier tephras have made it possible to date the homefield enclosure walls at Brenna and Steinbogi to pre-1158, and Neðri-Ás, and Granastaðir to pre-1104 (Aldred 2008; Einarsson 1995: 87; Vésteinsson 1998, 2003). Therefore, the archaeological evidence so far suggests that the practice of enclosing the homefields and separating these 'infield' areas from 'outfield' areas in Iceland goes back to the Viking Age.

The sections excavated through these boundary walls offer interesting insights into their construction and maintenance. At Vatnsfjörður, Granastaðir, and other sites, the boundary walls consisted of multiple phases of stone and/or turf construction and repair, suggesting that they were carefully maintained and built up over centuries, presumably to retain a certain height and visibility in the landscape. In some parts of Iceland homefield boundaries were nested within much larger systems of earthworks pre-dating AD 1477, which were constructed as property divisions between farms, and as additional fences to manage outfield pastures, similar to the so-called 'hill dykes' (ON *utgarðr*) that characterised pre-improvement western Norway and the Northern Isles of Scotland (Stylegar 2004). In north-east Iceland, where extensive systems of these earthworks have been surveyed, they are 330–630 cm wide and survive to a height of 40–100 cm, with 200–700 cm wide trenches on either side, from which the turves were taken to build and maintain the wall (Aldred 2008; Aldred *et al.* 2007; Einarsson *et al.* 2002). While it is not possible to know for certain how high either type of wall stood in the Viking or medieval period (though see *Laws*, below, for the suggestion that 150 cm was the ideal), their imposing physicality suggests that they served an important function for the management of livestock on the farm: to keep free-ranging animals from grazing on the grass in the homefield, which was vitally important for winter fodder (Amorosi *et al.* 1998).

It is also important to consider the likely symbolic importance of farm boundaries as visual markers of land claims in what were sometimes contested landscapes. The materiality and visibility of farm boundary walls probably also made them agents – potentially quite powerful ones – in perceptions of what and where 'home' was. As a physical demarcation of place, a farm boundary almost certainly made people feel differently when they were inside of it and outside of it. The psychological impact of crossing that boundary in order to enter the outfield cannot be quantified, and it would undoubtedly have varied between individuals and households, but it could have been significant. While the heavily used, modified, and managed Icelandic Viking-Age landscape does not support Hastrup's (1989) suggestion that the space outside of the farm boundary wall was wild, untamed, and dangerous (*e.g.* Aldred 2008; Dugmore *et al.* 2000; Mooney 2013), the perception of shielings and those who stayed at them *is* likely to have been affected by their physical location outside the homefield boundary wall. At the same time, the breaks or gates in these walls, which allowed movement of people and animals across them, were physical and no doubt perceptual links between the infield and outfield activity areas, including shielings. We should be open to the possibility that when people crossed through the boundary wall in order to journey to and engage in outfield activities, some aspects of their identity may have altered in the process, for the roles they had in the outfield areas probably affected how they perceived themselves and how they were perceived by others.

### *Laws*

The social and economic importance of boundary walls for Icelandic farmers is attested by the numerous clauses in *Grágás* that regulated their making. To be legally accepted, the boundary walls had to be built of stone and turf; they had to be 5 ft (*c.* 150 cm) at the ground and 3 ft (*c.* 90 cm) at the top, and not less than 5 ft (*c.* 150 cm) in height, and they should contain gates at the crossing of roads (*Grágás II*: K 181). The precise instructions for the construction of boundary walls were also included in the later *Jónsbok* laws, suggesting that it was considered important for famers to comply with these regulations. The construction and maintenance of large earthworks would have been a labour-intensive task requiring community involvement, with neighbours deciding on the location of the boundaries between farms and the allocation of tasks related to their maintenance (Aldred 2008: 317). The walls had to be regularly straightened and built up to maintain a 'legal' height. A period of 2 months in the spring and 1 month in the summer was set aside each year for the construction or repair of enclosures: the so-called 'fence season' (*garðǫnn*). The second part of *garðǫnn* took place after haymaking, and it overlapped with *selmánuðr*, 'shieling month' (Björnsson 1995: 6–8; Hastrup 1985: 29). Although they should probably be viewed as guidelines for good practice, and it is not impossible that on some farms the same people were engaged with both fence repair and transhumance, it is also possible that these laws regulating the timing of outfield activities preserve evidence for a seasonal gendered division of labour, in which men repaired boundary walls around homefields, while women were away at shielings.

These medieval laws contain very limited references to boundaries around shielings, stating that shielings could only be built within the holding of the mother settlement, and that their boundary markers should 'be where they were of old', and not moved, unless it was possible to relocate them with minimal damage (*Jónsbok*: VII, 43). Their maintenance is not discussed in the laws, and it appears that there were no strict legal requirements regulating their appearance, dimension, or construction methods. These limited entries suggest that shieling boundaries were somewhat more flexible and ephemeral than homefield boundaries, maybe even consisting of more symbolic and moveable markers rather than large earthworks. It is not inconceivable that the presence of a shieling in a more marginal setting, and the track that would have connected the shieling to the home farm, were in themselves enough to make a statement about the ownership of that land.

The medieval documentary sources complement the archaeological evidence for the existence of substantial turf- and stone-built boundary walls that separated the infield and outfield in the Viking and medieval periods, and add much to our understanding of the materiality of these structures. The fact that the laws preserve regulations about the size, state, and routine maintenance of boundary walls suggests that they were physically, visually, and cognitively significant monuments in the Icelandic landscape – simultaneously practical and meaningful. There must have been an intrinsic value in these earthworks, calculated on the basis of the many days and weeks of labour it cost households every year to build and repair them. However, we should also consider that these structures, observed, mended, and traversed on a routine basis since childhood, undoubtedly had a role in the development of the *habitus* (*cf.* Bourdieu 1977) of Viking-Age and medieval Icelanders, and were an important part of the mental map of what was expected and perceived as 'appropriate' for a mature working farmstead. The routine practice of crossing through these structures while travelling to and from outfield activity areas such as shielings must have had implications for how the seasonal move to shielings was perceived by those engaged in transhumance.

The psychological impact of crossing a very visible boundary enclosing the homefield and moving away from it towards a social space that was less clearly demarcated could have resulted in the perception of the shieling as being a 'not at home' place: lonely, isolated, and unprotected. As will be elaborated below, this perception of shielings as being somewhat unsafe is what clearly resonates in the narratives written down in Íslendingasögur.

## Real or perceived isolation: the distance from the home farm

> '[...] there is a great distance separating the beds of Þord and Guðrún these days, since she is in the shieling while he is working feverishly at building a hall.'(Laxdæla saga)

The location of the shieling influenced the degree of contact that could be maintained with the home farm during the shieling season. If the distance between the shieling and the home farm was significant, the opportunities for frequent contact were probably limited, separating those who participated in summer transhumance both physically and psychologically from the daily rhythms of the farm and its inhabitants. This in turn would have had an impact on how shieling life was perceived both by those who spend their summers in the upland pastures and by those who stayed behind. However, if the distance that had to be travelled to reach the summer pastures was short, and especially if the shieling and farm were intervisible, shielings could have been in real terms and in the minds of those who stayed at them an extension of the farm.

### *Archaeology*

Previous archaeological work on shielings in Iceland that has considered their spatial relationship with the home farm has tended to focus on field survey data, place name evidence and later documentary sources that mention the ownership of upland pastures. Guðrún Sveinbjarnardóttir's study of shielings in Berufjörður and Eyjafjallasveit in eastern Iceland and Skagafjörður in northern Iceland (Sveinbjarnardóttir 1991), and her research on farm abandonment in medieval and post-medieval Iceland (1992) established that in most cases shielings were located relatively close to the main farm, with an average distance of less than 5 km separating the two, which would have allowed easy access and frequent contact. She also noted interesting regional and chronological differences, with the earlier shielings in the south of Iceland clustering closer to farms and at lower elevations, while later shieling sites in the same region were generally found at higher and more inland locations. A study of the spatial distribution of shielings, and independent and dependent farms in the Saurbæjarhreppur region in the north, showed a different bimodal pattern for the distance between farm and shieling, with a large group lying on average 1.5 km from the farm and a smaller group at 3 km (Gunnarsdóttir 2002: 55–58). This pattern did not seem to relate to the age of the site (based on documentary sources), but to the wealth of the farm, with the wealthier farms owning more distant shielings, presumably because they owned more land. A study carried out in Dýrafjörður in the Western peninsula revealed a similar average distance between shielings and home farms, 2.6 km (Guðmundsson 2008). A review of archaeological surveys in all regions of Iceland showed that shieling sites were typically located *c.* 2 km from their home farms, or 0.5–3 hour walk, depending on the elevation and terrain (Pálsdóttir 2005). The only fully excavated shieling in Iceland, the Viking-Age site of Pálstóftir, in the highlands of east Iceland, is located 15 km from the nearest known settlement, although it is possible that it belonged to a closer unrecorded farm (Lucas 2008). The partially excavated putative medieval shieling at Faxadalur, in the west, was located 8.5 km from the farm of Reykholt, to which it belonged from at least the sixteenth century (Vickers and Sveinbjarnardóttir 2013).

The average shieling–farm distances proposed by these studies would definitely not prevent communication, and perhaps even daily travel between the upland pastures and mother settlements, for example for provisioning those living at shielings and for bringing milk and other products back to the home farm. Bearing in mind these estimates, it is unlikely that shielings would have been considered excessively secluded or isolated, although the vitally important issue of intervisibility between the farm and the shieling has not yet been explored. However, due to the limitations of the survey data there are numerous problems with using these estimates to make inferences about transhumance patterns, especially in earlier periods. The dating and identification of the shieling sites in the studies outlined above is largely based on documentary sources, such as the 1703 land register (Magnússon and Vídalín 1924–1947 [1703]), and place names. Without further excavation these sites can only be securely dated to the modern, or at best the post-medieval period, offering little information about the developments or changes in the shieling tradition since the settlement of Iceland. Complex occupation histories are recorded for historically known shielings, with phases of disuse, abandonment, or reuse as permanently occupied farms or winter sheep houses without significant changes in the layout of the site (Sveinbjarnardóttir *et al.* 2011). For example, the site of Þorvaldsstaðasel, in north-east Iceland, had a complex occupation history, with a clear change of the building's function from a periodically occupied shieling to permanently occupied dwelling. This shift was not detected during the excavation of this site, and only became apparent during microscopic investigation of the soil micromorphology samples taken from its floor deposits (Kupiec *et al.* in press). Therefore, although the archaeological evidence so far suggests that shielings were typically *c.* 2 km from their home farms, with distances of up to 15 km possible in regions where farms owned very large tracts of upland, and where useable summer pastures were highly dispersed, these inferences must be treated with caution because the survey work on which they are based has yet to be followed up with more extensive excavation and scientific analyses.

### *Sagas and laws*

Like the archaeological field survey evidence, the stories recounted in Íslendingasögur paint a diverse picture of the possible locations of shielings and their spatial relationships with home farms. For example, the shieling owned by Auðunn in *Grettis saga* was within a day's walk of the main farm and he was able to regularly fetch dairy products from it, while in *Laxdæla saga*, the shieling belonging to Bolli Þorleiksson's farm in Sælingsdalr was located within a walkable distance to the main farm. The shieling belonging to Þorstein in *Heiðarvíga saga* was also located within a day's walk from the main farm, and Þorstein's wife and daughters brought clean laundry from the shieling to the farm on Sundays. Shielings could also be located further away from the home farm, in the next valley, or in the highlands between two valleys. When Einarr Þorbjarnarson travelled for many kilometres in search of lost sheep in *Hrafnkels saga Freysgoða*, he stopped at several shielings along the way, suggesting that the shielings were located a considerable distance from the farms in the valley. The shieling that belonged to Guðrún and Þord in *Laxdæla saga* was also located at a significant distance from their farm, and as a consequence the couple spent their summers apart.

Although there is no explicit mention of the intervisibility or lack of intervisibility between farms and shielings, Íslendingasögur also imply a certain seclusion that characterized shielings, which made them attractive for illicit activities and encounters. For example, shielings are depicted as perfect meeting places for a love-struck man to secretly visit his beloved while she was away from the prying eyes of male members of her family. In *Hænsna-Þóris saga*, Þórodd meets with Jófrið at a shieling site to the displeasure of her father Gunnar. These illicit encounters sometimes also ended in violence, as for example in *Hallfreðar saga vandræðaskálds*, in which the main character visits his old love Kolfinna at a shieling site and subsequently rapes her. Due to their secluded location, shielings were also described as places where a woman could give birth to a child born out of wedlock, such as Þórdís' child in *Bárðar saga Snæfellsáss*.

Íslendingasögur often portray shielings as dangerous places. Violence at shieling sites is usually associated with feuding men, for example, the murders of Bolli and Helgi in *Laxdæla saga*, the disagreement between Gunnar and Þórodd in *Hænsna-Þóris saga*, the unsuccessful attack on Bjarni by Þorkell in *Vopnfirðinga saga*, the murder of Einarr in *Hrafnkels saga Freysgoða*, and the killing of Þorstein's brothers, son, and two farmhands in *Þorsteins saga hvíta*. In most cases the male presence at the shieling is reported as unusual, and connected to a crime or other illicit activities. However, it is important to note that the sagas also occasionally describe men haymaking close to the shieling, or tending the livestock (for example, Einar in *Hrafnkels saga Freysgoða*). The saga evidence does not specify whether these men would have spent the night at the shieling, or whether they would return to the home farm at the end of a working day. The ambiguous status of shielings is also supported by their association with the men who existed outside of the society, outlaws. After being sentenced to lesser outlawry, the main character of *Grettis saga* had to seek temporary shelter with his relatives and supporters, and when that support began to falter he was forced to progressively move deeper into marginal spaces, starting with a shieling site, and then moving between woodlands, caves, and marshlands, and sometimes returning to shielings.

In contrast to the Family Sagas, medieval Icelandic laws do not directly mention the distances between shielings and home farms, but one notable exception hints at possible shieling locations. Two Icelandic law codices stipulate that paths to shielings could cut through private land, and anyone who obstructed them was to be fined for the damage caused to the farmer by the delay in reaching pastures (*Grágás* K 182; *Jónsbok*: VII, 42). These laws indirectly suggest that shielings could have been located a considerable distance away from the farms to which they belonged. The later, 15th century household law, *Búalög*, stipulated that the milkmaids working at the shieling were to return to work on the main farm after daily milking was finished, while only the shieling-housekeeper stayed behind to keep the site in good order (*Búalög* 1915: 22, 34, 61). This law attests to a short distance that separated shielings and farms in the early post-medieval period.

Comparing the archaeological and written evidence suggests that the distances between farms and shielings alone probably did not contribute to their perception as isolated, marginal places. The distances that separated them were not significant and contact between the two could have been easily maintained, with the shieling being simply conceived as an extension of the farm in the summertime. However, due to the topographical settings of shielings (usually in upland areas), even a distance of a few kilometres could sometimes have affected the intervisibility with the home farms, making them physically secluded from the protective eyes of the men on the farm. While archaeological survey work has yet to include a detailed study of shieling–farm intervisibility, mainly because of the difficulty of linking Viking-Age and medieval shieling sites with the farms that owned them, the evidence in the sagas suggests that in the 13th and 14th centuries shielings were perceived as remote and isolated, making them attractive shelters to those who broke the established social norms: outlaws, murderers, and adulterers. While the saga stories that take place at shielings are highly dramatised, and shielings were undoubtedly *selected* by saga writers to be the settings of anti-social and sometimes violent events (which may or may not have happened), it is very likely that shielings could be used in this way because in the medieval period they were thought of places that were isolated, unprotected, and potentially vulnerable.

## Objects, activities, and the mediation of gender identities

'Þórdís, the housewife, was always at the shieling.' (Bárðar saga Snæfellsáss)

### *Archaeology*

In historic periods, shielings had variable functions, depending on their location and their distance from the main farm. These functions could include tending livestock, milking, preparing dairy products, gathering hay, or doing other upland activities, such as charcoal making, iron extraction, hunting, or gathering of wild plants (Borchgrevink 1977). Investigations into the history of the shieling tradition across the North Atlantic usually rely on Reinton's (1969) model created for Norwegian shielings, which classifies them into three main types. The 'full shieling' is characterized by the residence of people and animals throughout the summer, for the purpose of processing milk into non-perishable dairy products. According to this model, the 'full shieling' is usually located at a significant distance from the main farm, and it includes a large number of structures, including animal pens, living quarters, and storage spaces for dairy products and hay, *etc*. The 'dairy shieling' is characterized by shorter occupation periods and a closer proximity to the main settlement, with milk transported to the farm on a daily basis. The structures at 'dairy shielings' are limited to simple dwellings and animal pens. The third type, the 'haymaking' shieling, is centred on haymaking, and is only occupied in the late summer. The structures at the 'haymaking' shieling are usually limited to living quarters and a hay barn.

The wider applicability of the model has been called into question when applied to Icelandic shielings (Sveinbjarnardóttir 1991). In the 19th and early 20th centuries, shielings in Iceland could be used flexibly, and a single site could combine all of the dairying, haymaking, and residential functions outlined in Reinton's (1969) model, though with different functions emphasised at different times of the year. In Skagafjarðarsýslu in north Iceland, for example, early 20th century shielings that were used for summer grazing and milking of both sheep and cows had multi-roomed, turf-built structures that were used as sleeping quarters, kitchens, and pantries during the summer, and as sheephouses and hay fodder storage rooms during the winter (Jónasson 2010: 62–63). Sometimes minor physical alterations were even made to these structures on a seasonal basis – particular doors between rooms either opened up or blocked up with temporary turf walls – to adapt them to these different functions. In the 19th and early 20th centuries, Icelandic shielings were mainly female domains, with milking and the preparation of dairy products being the focal activities (Hitzler 1979). Sometimes a male shepherd, who tended the animals and occasionally helped with the butter churning, was present but he often slept some distance away from the shieling – at least officially (Bjarnason 1955; Jónasson 2010: 62). This type of ethnographic information provides us with ideas about how older Icelandic shieling sites might have been used, and by whom, but without further archaeological investigation it cannot be assumed that Norwegian models or early historic Icelandic models can be applied to the Viking and medieval periods. Recent excavations of possible Viking-Age and medieval shieling sites have enabled new studies of the types and distributions of artefacts, bones, and insect remains, and the microscopic analysis of organic, chemical, and mineralogical residues in the occupation deposits, all of which can shed light on the sorts of activities that were conducted at these sites.

To date eight putative Viking or medieval-period shielings have been the subject of archaeological investigations in Iceland: the Viking-Age site of Kot in southern Iceland (Hallmundsdóttir 2009), the Viking-Age site of Pálstóftir in eastern Iceland (Lucas 2008), the medieval sites of Faxadalur, Norðtungusel, Reykholtssel, Þórsárdalssel, and Gautsstaðagrófarsel in western Iceland (Ellertsson Csillag and Hermannsdóttir 2013; Sveinbjarnardóttir *et al.* 2011), and the late medieval site of Þorvaldsstaðasel, in north-east Iceland (Gísladóttir *et al.* 2011; Kupiec *et al.* in press). Of these, only Pálstóftir and Kot have been subjected to more than preliminary test pitting. Since the post-excavation analysis of the Kot site is still ongoing, this review of the archaeological evidence on shieling activities will focus mainly on Pálstóftir, which was identified as a shieling based on its relatively small size, marginal location, and the geoarchaeological and insect evidence for periodic (non-permanent) occupation (Lucas 2008).

Absolute dating from the tephra sequence at the site and a series of radiocarbon dates placed the occupation of Pálstóftir between *c.* AD 950 and 1070. During the excavation four structures were uncovered: two dwellings with hearths, one small storage room, and one enclosure interpreted by the excavators as an animal pen (Lucas 2007, 2008). The microscopic analysis of the floor surfaces supported the interpretation of the site's function as a periodically occupied shieling, with soil micromorphology samples recording multiple thin floor layers, each separated by 'abandonment' phases characterised by clean wind-blown silt and fine sand (Kupiec 2010; Milek 2007). Micromorphological analysis also confirmed that one of the structures was used for hay storage. The occupation surfaces in two dwellings were less compacted and had lower quantities of anthropogenic inclusions than are typical of floor deposits in the residential buildings of Viking-Age farms (*e.g.* Milek 2012; Milek and Roberts 2013). The unroofed enclosure interpreted by the excavators of Pálstóftir as an animal pen showed no evidence for animal dung in the soil thin section from its occupation deposits, and it seems unlikely that the animals were kept there for long periods of time. The enclosure could have been mucked out at the end of the shieling season; however, no sharp boundaries between the layers were observed during the microscopic analysis to attest to this maintenance practice. It is possible that at Pálstóftir, like in some Icelandic ethnographic examples (*e.g.* Bjarnason 1955), animals were only brought to the shieling for milking, and the open enclosure at Pálstóftir could have been used for this purpose.

In addition to the soil micromorphological evidence for the collection and storage of hay (Kupiec 2010; Milek 2007), artefactual and faunal assemblages at Pálstóftir suggest that a range of other activities also took place at this shieling. Chert and quartzite flakes were the most abundant type of find, with the majority probably representing strike-a-lights, but with two pieces showing microwear traces compatible with working soft stone or shell (Chabot 2007), suggesting that small-scale craft activities might have taken place at the site. This notion was supported by the finds of a fragment of a crucible and copper alloy spillage, both attesting to small-scale copper working (Lucas 2008). The finds assemblage also contained an iron punch, which could have been used for a variety of craft purposes, such as punching leather or copper. Neither hammerscale nor metallurgical slag were observed in the field or in thin section, which suggests that metalworking at the site was limited to copper (Kupiec 2010; Milek 2007). Four dress items were also found: a copper alloy stud, a fitting, a pair of perforated coins dating to the 11th century, and a Viking-Age polychrome glass bead, which might represent personal adornment of the site's inhabitants. Beads in Viking-Age Iceland have been found in both male and female graves, so these ornaments are non-gender specific (Eldjárn 2000). In one of the residential spaces five sheep astragali were found in a cluster, suggesting they had been held in a bag (Lucas 2008). They probably represent gaming pieces and provide evidence for the leisure time of Pálstóftir's inhabitants.

The faunal assemblage at Pálstóftir suggests that the hunting of wild fowl (greylag goose, pink-footed goose, and whooper swan) also took place in the vicinity (Rosenlund 2007). However, due to the limited nature of this assemblage, it is not possible to speculate whether it was undertaken solely for subsistence on the shieling or for the main farm. Greylag geese and pink-footed geese migrate to Iceland in April (Boyd *et al.* 2000). Both species of goose, as well as the whooper swan, leave Iceland for wintering grounds in Britain in mid-

September to mid-November (Bell *et al.* 1988; Garðarsson 1991), indicating that these birds must have been hunted in Iceland in the spring-summer, or early autumn. Both species of goose also undergo a flightless moulting period in June–July, which enables them to build up body reserves for autumn migration (Loonen *et al.* 1991). During the moult, which usually lasts for 25–30 days, geese are an easy target for human predation, and it is most likely that the birds were caught close to the site in July, during *selmánuðr*, and were not brought as provisions from the main farm.

No equipment for milking or milk processing was found at Pálstóftir, and this situation was mirrored at Kot, where the artefactual assemblage consisted only of iron nails associated with the collapse of the buildings (Hallmundsdóttir 2009), and at Þorvaldsstaðasel, where the small assemblage included a thimble and a clay pipe, rivets, and nails (Gísladóttir *et al.* 2011). A thimble from Þorvaldsstaðasel attests to sewing, but it was recovered from late post-medieval deposits. Ethnographic accounts suggest that a range of equipment necessary for milk processing was brought to shielings: *skyr* barrels, *sýra* barrels, *skyr* rusts, *skyr* screens, a barrel of calf rennet, troughs, churns, milk pails, cheese moulds, pots, and milk strainers (Jónsson 2010: 62–63; Pálsdóttir 1979: 266). All of these would have been transported back to the home farm, however, as they were needed to store the dairy products, and since they were made from organic materials they are not usually preserved in the archaeological record. As pointed out by Lucas (2008: 96), 'evidence for dairying is harder to corroborate on any of the sites, but it is difficult to see why a seasonal settlement should exist unless this was part of it'. Although few shieling sites in Iceland have so far been subjected to large-scale excavations, the evidence from Pálstóftir attests to the very wide range of activities that could take place at the same shieling, including the gathering of hay, the working of soft stone, small-scale non-ferrous metalworking, the working of leather, wild fowl hunting, cooking, sleeping, and – as evening entertainment – gaming.

The gender constructs potentially associated with the activities that took place at Pálstóftir are highly ambiguous. Interpretations of activities and material culture typically implicated in the construction Viking-Age male, female, and 'third' genders, a term that may apply to 'womanly men', 'manly women', transgendered individuals, or the type of 'queerness' often associated with shamen or *seiðr*-workers, tend to be based on literary references, runic inscriptions, depictions in applied art, and the objects found in biologically sexed male and female burials, though it is widely acknowledged that objects in burials can have a multitude of meanings, and may not simply have been the personal belongings of the deceased (*e.g.* Jesch 1991; Jochens 1995; Price 2002; Solli 1999). Metalworking and its associated material culture, for example, tends to be associated in the construction of the male gender in the Viking world, since all of the smiths referred to in the Icelandic sagas and mythological poetry are men (*e.g.* Skallagrímur in *Egils saga*). In Iceland, where over 700 artefacts have been found in just over 300 Viking-Age burials, of which around 110 have been sexed (Friðriksson 2000), neither smithing tools nor objects associated with non-ferrous metalworking, such as crucibles, have been found in a burial context. Therefore, while it is not unlikely that ferrous metalworking was a male activity, there is currently no evidence to suggest that non-ferrous metalworking and its associated material culture played a role in the construction of any gender in Viking-Age Iceland. The same can be said for other crafts evident at Pálstóftir: using an iron punch to work leather or other material, and using chert flakes for soft stone working. Iron punches are so far absent from Viking-Age burials in Iceland, and there is no intrinsic reason why leather working and soft stone working should be associated with one gender construct more than another. We should probably consider these tasks to be gender neutral – conducted by either men or women, or, at the most, by women doing slightly more 'manly' tasks. Considering the total absence of textile implements at Pálstóftir, one artefact category that can reliably be associated with women's roles and the construction of female identities in the Viking Age (for a summary of the evidence see Milek 2012), it is possible that any women at the shieling opted for more portable crafts than those that would have required the transportation of bulky or heavy materials, such as raw wool and looms.

Concerning the hunting of wild fowl, documentary evidence suggests that hunting was a man's task (notably *Grágás*: K14, K18; *Grágás II*: 374, 375), and in the Old Norse poem *Rígsþula*, bird hunting is specifically practiced by high-ranking men. It is quite possible, therefore, that men were present at Pálstóftir for at least a period of time during the spring, summer, or early autumn, during the goose moulting season. However, we should make a distinction between legal and literary references, which probably portray stylized medieval ideals, and the activities that were actually practiced as part of everyday life in Viking-Age and medieval Iceland. There is no intrinsic reason why wild fowl could not have been netted by women who adopted this more 'manly' role while at the shieling during the summer months.

The interpretation of the cluster of sheep astragali, if they were indeed gaming pieces, is equally difficult. Scholars of the Viking Age tend to consider gaming to be a man's leisure pursuit because gaming pieces are commonly found in male burials in Scandinavia and Scandinavian Scotland (Greig 1947; Owen and Dalland 1999: 127–132). In Iceland, gaming pieces have only been found in three Viking-Age burials, none of which have been biologically sexed, but one of which also contained a sword, spear-head, axe, and shield-boss, which are almost universally found in male graves (there are a few exceptions; Eldjárn 2000: 580). In the sagas, where gaming is normally a high-class male activity, women are never depicted playing board games together, but they occasionally do play with men (*e.g. Gunnlaugs saga Ormstungu*; Jochens 1995: 104). While it is difficult to know how far to interpret this, given that saga authors used the scenario of mixed-gender gaming to further their particular plot lines (*e.g.* it was a context in which a couple could spend a lot of time together and fall in love), it is possible that gaming at Pálstóftir was a male pursuit, a mixed-gender pursuit, or the pursuit of women who chose to engage in a leisure activity that, according to Jochens (1995: 100), they rarely had time for back on the home farm.

Concerning the soil micromorphological evidence for grass harvesting and storage at Pálstóftir, all literary and archaeological evidence indicates that this task was shared by men and women. There are references to both men and women harvesting hay in *Erbyggja saga* and *Sturlunga saga*, for example, in the latter of which a mother multi-tasks, nursing her child at the same time as raking. In Iceland, sickles have been found in four Viking-Age burials, one of which is of indeterminate gender, one of which was in a biologically sexed female grave, one of which was in a grave containing oval brooches, a trefoil brooch, and spindle whorls, and was probably that of a woman, and one of which was found in a grave that also contained a sword and was probably that of a man (Friðriksson 2000: 558, 582, 589). At shielings, therefore, it is equally likely for men and women to have been engaged in harvesting grass for fodder.

The evidence for gendered activities among the Pálstóftir artefacts is equivocal, and it is equally likely that men, women, both genders or 'third genders' were present at this shieling during the summer months. However, the very ambiguity of the Pálstóftir artefactual evidence also raises the interesting question of whether shielings in Viking-Age and medieval Iceland could have been places where people took on different roles from those on the home farm, and, therefore, whether these were sometimes places where different gender identities could emerge. Distanced from the home farm and the rest of the household, both men and women could have felt at liberty to engage in activities that were typically associated with the performance of the other gender – in the case of men, milking and dairy production, and, in the case of women, leather and stone working, hunting, gaming, and non-ferrous metalworking. As will be seen below, the diverse and mutable picture of *seljalíf* (shieling life) that is gained from the archaeological evidence to date is in stark contrast to literary sources such as the Íslendingasögur.

### *Sagas*

In the world of the medieval Íslendingasögur, it is usually women who are present at shieling sites. According to the Family Sagas, girls were socialized into their role as shieling 'keepers' and boys as farm owners early in their lives (Jochens 1995: 122); for example, in *Heiðarvíga saga*, the wife and her two young daughters spend summers at the shieling, while her husband and two sons work at the farm. In *Bárðar saga Snæfellsáss*, a 15-year-old Þórdís stays at a shieling in the summer and early autumn, a habit that continued throughout her adult life. In special circumstances and in affluent households, the women might be accompanied by a shepherd (*smalamaðr*), whose job it was to herd the ewes into milking pens, but the sagas always depict women as the primary shieling keepers. Sagas provide us with descriptions of the activities women carried out on a daily basis at shielings: milking ewes and cows, separating milk into curds (*skyr*) and whey (*sýra*), cooking, cleaning, supervising servants gathering hay and wood, mending clothing, washing linen, and bathing in the rivers and lakes (*e.g. Bárðar saga, Laxdæla saga*; *Hrafnkels saga Freysgoða*; *Heiðarvíga saga*).

In Íslendingasögur, animal herding, milking, and milk processing were the primary foci of shieling life. *Hænsna-Þóris saga* suggests the change of pasture was thought of as beneficial for the animals that yielded little milk. Milking was done at least once every 24 hours and, according to *Grettis saga*, it was often the first task that women performed each morning. Raw milk was stored in a shed on site, and at some shielings dairy products were also prepared. For example, the shieling described in *Laxdæla saga* had facilities for preparing *skyr* (Icelandic soft cheese) and whey, but hard cheese and butter were produced at the home farm. Food produced at shieling sites was brought to the farm at the end of each shieling season or whenever it was needed to supplement the summer diet. For example, Auðunn in *Grettis saga* went to a shieling to get food and returned with *skyr*. Taken as a whole, these 13th and 14th century literary sources are so consistent in their association of shielings with milking, dairy production, and women, that it is very unlikely that women would not have been present at shielings during this period.

## Conclusion

The archaeological evidence, viewed alongside near-contemporary written sources such as laws and the Family Sagas, offers interesting insights into how Icelanders may have used and perceived shielings in the Viking and medieval periods, and how shielings might have played a role in the mediation of gender identities. The archaeological investigations of turf-built boundary walls dating to these periods, contextualized against a review of medieval laws regulating their construction, attest to the clear separation of the infield and outfield, with a substantial effort put into the annual maintenance of the homefield boundary wall. As this boundary would have been very visible in the surrounding landscape, its crossing during the journey to the shieling could have had a psychological impact on the people engaged in transhumance, physically marking their seasonal separation from the affairs of the farm. The laws did not strictly regulate the enclosure walls around shielings, perhaps adding to their perception as different from the clearly demarcated and controlled social space of the farm. However, the estimates for the average distances between shielings and home farms, based on both archaeological survey data and written evidence, do not support the notion of summer pastures as marginal spaces isolated at a great distance from farms. The distances that separated shielings and mother settlements were usually not significant and contact between the two could have been easily maintained on a daily basis, with the shieling being simply an extension of the farm in the summertime. Rather, it is more likely that there have been a lack of intervisibility between the farm and the shieling due to the local topography, combined with the fact that shielings were outside of the homefield boundary walls, which could have propagated the perception of shielings as isolated and unprotected places.

The evidence that can be drawn from the Sagas of Icelanders certainly suggests that shielings *were* perceived as secluded and isolated in the medieval period. Sagas portray them as places where women stayed during the summer months to carry out the relatively mundane tasks of looking after and milking herds of sheep and cattle, and processing milk products, but in the saga narratives shielings also attracted and facilitated socially unaccepted behaviours. Violence at shielings is a common thread in Íslendingasögur, and those who broke the law often sought shelter at upland pastures. These physical attacks were sometimes directed at women who were working at shielings away from the protection of the male members of their families. Illicit encounters, love affairs, and secret illegitimate births are also common themes in saga narratives about shielings. It is clear that shielings were viewed by the saga writers as good settings for high drama, because their relative seclusion gave people an opportunity to temporarily escape the watchful eyes of neighbours, relatives and social superiors.

It is this perceived isolation from the home farm and the rest of the household, fostered partly by the act of crossing through the homefield boundary wall into an outer liminal space, partly by the distance, and in many cases the lack of intervisibility with the home farm, that could have made shielings places where people felt free to engage in activities and take on roles that were different from those on the home farm. At the Pálstóftir shieling, the ambiguity of how the material culture found on the site contributed to the construction of gender identities suggests three possible interpretations, all of which differ significantly from the portrayal of shielings in Old Norse-Icelandic literature: (1) *both* men and women were resident during the summer months, carrying out all the necessary tasks associated with milking and dairying, but also hunting and doing a wide range of other craft activities, including non-ferrous metalworking, leather working, and soft stone working; (2) men and women used shielings at slightly different times in the spring, summer, and early autumn, and the functions of the shieling site essentially changed as its residents changed; (3) one or both of these genders engaged in activities and took on roles that transcended the normative bounds of gender stereotypes as we have constructed them based on medieval literary and legal sources. If men alone were shieling keepers at Pálstóftir, for example, they would have had to do the milking, an activity that the written sources suggest was a designated female task, and which would under normal circumstances (on the home farm) almost certainly have been considered 'unmanly' (*e.g.* the insult directed at Loki in *Lokasenna*; Jochens 1995, 1996). If women alone were shieling keepers at Pálstóftir, they also engaged in a variety of other tasks, including metal, stone and leather crafts, and hunting, which go unrecorded for this gender in the saga literature. It is possible that we should be considering these activities to be gender neutral, conducted by both genders in outfield areas, similar to the harvesting of hay fodder. However, if these activities *were* generally men's tasks, as they are usually interpreted, the perceived isolation and privacy of shieling sites may have freed the women who stayed at them to engage in these 'manly' tasks and negotiate different gender identities without risk of insult or reproach.

Studies of transgendered and 'third' gender identities in the Viking world have tended to focus on the dramatic examples in Old Norse–Icelandic literature of women who appropriated men's roles and stepped out onto the public stage as warriors or maiden-kings (*e.g.* Friðriksdóttir 2013), men who performed *seiðr* (*e.g.* Price 2002), and Old Norse gods and giants who operated outside of social and sexual norms (*e.g.* Solli 1999). These literary examples, which have been debated for over a decade, are now supported by archaeological evidence from graves that non-typical gender identity construction was current in the Viking Age, with biologically sexed males and females occasionally being buried with jewellery, weapons and tools – generally assumed to be gender signatures – that are more typically buried with the opposite gender (Lauritsen and Hansen 2003). However, the evidence from Pálstóftir highlights the possibility that alternative gender identities could also have been mediated on a daily basis through the choice to carry out particular tasks and use objects that were normally used to enact another gender (see Sørensen 2009 for a review of the malleable and performative aspects of gender identities). Old Norse–Icelandic literary and legal sources do not record such choices, and alternative interpretations are available for the archaeological evidence at Pálstóftir. Nevertheless, it is possible that Viking-Age and medieval Icelandic shieling sites, which were outside of a physical and cognitive 'home' boundary, required a short journey to reach, and were often out of sight of the home farm, were perceived as being isolated and private places where individuals were free to cross the boundaries of normative gender roles and identities.

The three interpretations proposed for the Pálstóftir artefactual evidence are not mutually exclusive, and it is possible that in Viking-Age Iceland shieling functions, the timing of their use, and the genders that used them on a seasonal basis were much more flexible and mutable than has hitherto been understood from the literary evidence alone. It is also possible that this flexibility changed between the Viking Age, when Pálstóftir was occupied, and the 13th–14th centuries, when the sagas were written. The only way to test these ideas is to excavate and date more shielings. It is to be hoped that the evidence from future excavations of early shieling sites, with interpretations well integrated with documentary and literary sources, will continue to provide a clearer picture of gendered seasonal activities in Viking and medieval Iceland.

*Acknowledgments*

This research was funded by the Carnegie Trust for the Universities of Scotland. The authors would like to thank Gavin Lucas, Guðrún Sveinbjarnardóttir, Guðrún Alda Gísladóttir, James Wollett and Margrét Hrönn Hallmundsdóttir for their support for this research. Gratitude is also extended to the editors and an anonymous reviewer for comments and suggestions that helped to improve this paper.

*References*

Aldred, Oscar

2004. *Archaeological investigations, Höfðagerði, Núpar 2003. Framvinduskýrsla/Interim report.* Fornleifastofnun Íslands, Reykjavik.

2008. Unfamiliar landscapes: infields, outfields, boundaries and landscapes in Iceland. In *Recent Approaches to the Archaeology of Land Allotment*, edited by Adrian M. Chadwick, pp. 299–321. Archaeopress, Oxford.

Aldred, Oscar, Árni Einarsson, Elín Ósk Hreiðarsdóttir and Birna Lárusdóttir

2007. *Forn garðlög í Suður-Þingeyjarsýslu. A system of earthworks in north-east Iceland.* Fornleifastofnun Íslands, Reykjavik.

Amorosi, Tom, Paul C. Buckland, Kevin J. Edwards, Ingrid Mainland, Tom H. McGovern, Jon P. Sadler and Peter Skidmore

1998. They did not live by grass alone: the politics and palaeoecology of animal fodder in the North Atlantic Region. *Environmental Archaeology* 1: 41–54.

*Bárðar saga Snæfellsáss* [Bard's Saga]

[1997] Translated by S. M. Anderson. In *The Complete Sagas of Icelanders,* edited by Viðar Hreinsson, pp. 237–267. Leifur Eiríksson Publishing, Reykjavik.

Bell, Michael V., J. Dunbar and J. Parkin

1988. Numbers of wintering Pink-footed and Greylag Geese in north-east Scotland 1950–1986. *Wildfowl Trust Annual Report* 10: 43–58.

Boyd, Hugh, Michael V. Bell and Donald Watson
2000. Spring weather and the migration of geese from Scotland to Iceland. *Ringing and Migration* 20(2): 153–165
Bjarnason, Jónas B.
1955. Um fráfærur og pössun á ám, þegar ég var smali fyrir 80 árum. In *Búsæld og barningur: Svipir og sagnir*, edited by Jón Jóhannesson, pp. 53–62. Húnvetningafélagið, Reykjavik.
Björnsson, Arni
1995. *High days and holidays in Iceland.* Mál og menning, Reykjavik.
Borchgrevink, Anne-Berit
1977. The 'seter'-areas of rural Norway; a traditional multipurpose resource. *Northern Studies* 9: 2–24.
Bourdieu, Pierre
1977. *Outline of a Theory of Practice.* Cambridge University Press, Cambridge.
*Búalög*
1915–22. Reykjavik, Sögufélagið.
Callow, Chris
2006. Reconstructing the past in medieval Iceland. *Early Medieval Europe* 14(3): 297–324.
Chabot, Jacques
2007. Micro-wear. In Fornleifauppgröftur á Pálstòftirum við Kárahnjúka 2005, edited by Gavin Lucas, pp.81. Unpublished Report, Landsvirkjun, Iceland.
Cormack, Margaret
2007. Fact and fiction in the Icelandic Sagas. *History Compass* 5(1): 201–217.
Dugmore, Andrew J., Anthony J. Newton, Guðrún Larsen and Gordon T. Cook
2000. Tephrochronology, environmental change and the Norse settlement of Iceland. *Environmental Archaeology* 5: 21–34.
Egils saga
[1975] Translated and edited by Christine Fell. Dent, London.
Einarsson, Bjarni F.
1995. *The Settlement of Iceland: a Critical Approach. Granastaðir and the Ecological Heritage.* Hið íslenska bókmenntafélag, Reykjavik.
Einarsson, Árni
2002. An extensive system of medieval earthworks in northeast Iceland. *Archaeologia Islandica* 2: 61–73.
Eldjárn, Kristján
2000. *Kuml og haugfé*, edited by Adolf Friðriksson. Mál og menning, Reykjavik.
Ellertsson Csillag, Sindri and Ásta Hermannsdóttir
2013. *Seljabúskapur á norðanverðu Snæfellsnesi.* Skýrsla II. Fornleifafræðistofan, Reykjavík.
Firth, Hugh
2012. Coercion, vengeance, feud and accommodation: homicide in medieval Iceland. *Early Medieval Europe* 20(2): 139–175.
Erbyggja saga
[1989] Translated by Hermann Pálsson and Paul Edwards. Penguin Books, London.
Friðriksdóttir, Jóhanna Katrín
2013. *Women in Old Norse Literature: Bodies, Words and Power.* Palgrave Macmillan, New York.
Friðriksson, Adolf
2000. Viking burial practices in Iceland. In *Kuml og haugfé*, by Kristján Eldjárn, edited by Adolf Friðriksson, pp. 549–610. Mál og menning, Reykjavik.

Gardiner, Mark
2011. Time regained: booley huts and seasonal settlement in the Mourne mountains, Co. Down, Ireland. In *Life in Medieval Landscapes: People and Places in Medieval Britain: papers in memory of H. S. A. Fox*, edited by Sam Turner and Robert Silvester, pp. 106–124. Oxbow Books, Oxford.
Garðarsson, Arnþór
1991. Movements of Whooper Swans *Cygnus Cygnus* neck-banded in Iceland. *Wildfowl Special Issue No. 1*: 189–194.
Gísladóttir, Guðrún Alda, Uggi Ævarsson, and James Wollett
2011. *Interim Report of Archaeological Fieldwork on Svalbarð in summer of 2010 and winter 2011.* Fornleifastofnun Íslands, Reykjavik.
*Grágás. Laws of early Iceland: Grágás I, the Codex Regius of Grágás, with material from other manuscripts.*
[2006] Translated by A. Dennis, P. Foote and R. Perkins. University of Manitoba Press, Winnipeg.
*Grágás II.Laws of early Iceland: Grágás II, the Codex Regius of Grágás, with material from other manuscripts.*
[2000] Translated by A. Dennis, P. Foote and R. Perkins. University of Manitoba Press, Winnipeg.
*Grettis saga*
[1974] Translated by D. Fox and H. Pálsson. University of Toronto Press, Toronto.
Guðmundsson, B.
2008. Sel og selstöður við Dýrafjörð. Unpublished manuscript. University of Iceland.
*Hallfreðar saga vandræðaskálds* [The saga of Hallfred the Troublesome Poet]
[1997] Translated by D. Whaley. In *The Complete Sagas of Icelanders,* edited by Viðar Hreinsson, pp. 225–255. Leifur Eiríksson Publishing, Reykjavik.
Gunnarsdóttir, Sædís
2002. *The Transhumant Landscape of Saurbæjarhreppur. A Study of Shielings, Dependent Farms and their Locations in Connection to the Mother Settlements.* Unpublished master's thesis. School of Archaeological Studies, University of Leicester.
Greig, Sigurd
1947. *Gjermundbufunnet: en høvdingegrav fra 900-årene fra Ringerike.* Norske Oldfunn VIII, Oslo.
*Gunnlaugs saga Ormstungu* [The Story of Gunnlaug Serpent-Tongue]
[1957] Translated by Rory Quirk. Thomas Nelson and Sons, London.
Hallmundsdóttir, Margrét Hrönn
2009. *Upphaf og þróun byggðar við Heklurætur: Fornleifarannsókn á rúst í landi Kots í Rangárvallasýslu.* Unpublished report.
Hastrup, Kirsten
1985. *Culture and History in Medieval Iceland: An Anthropological Analysis of Structure and Change.* Clarendon Press, Oxford.
1989. Saeters in Iceland 900–1600. An anthropological analysis of economy and cosmology. *Acta Borealia* 6: 72–85.
Hænsna-Þóris saga
[1975] Translated by H. Pálsson. Southside, Edinburgh.
*Heiðarvíga saga* [The Saga of Slayings on the Heath]
[1997] Translated by K. Kunz. In *The Complete Sagas of Icelanders*, edited by Viðar Hreinsson, pp. 67–131. Leifur Eiríksson Publishing, Reykjavik.

Hitzler, Egon.
1979. *Sel-Untersuchnungen zur Geshicte des isländischen Sennwesens seit der Landnahmezeit.* Universitetsforlaget, Oslo.

*Hrafnkels Saga Freysgoða*
[2001] Translated by T. Gunnel. In *The Sagas of the Icelanders,* edited by Örnólfur Thorsson, pp. 436–463. Penguin Books, New York.

Jesch, Judith
1991. *Women in the Viking Age.* Boydell Press, Woodbridge.

Jochens, Jenny
1995. *Women in Old Norse Society.* Cornell University Press, Ithaca, New York.
1996. *Old Norse Images of Women.* University of Philadelphia Press, Philadelphia.

*Jónsbók*
[2010] The laws of later Iceland: the Icelandic text according to MS AM 351 fol.Skalholtsbok eldri. Translated by J. K. Schulman. AQ-Verlag, Saarbrücken.

Jónasson, Jónas
2010. *Íslenzkir þjóðhættir,* edited by Einar Sveinsson. Bókaútgáfan Opna, Reykjavik.

Karlsson, Hanna, Marie Emanuelsson and Ulf Segerström
2010. The history of a farm–shieling system in the central Swedish forest region. *Vegetation History and Archaeobotany* 19: 103–119.

Kupiec, Patrycja
2010. *Viking Age Shielings: Finding Evidence for Seasonal Occupation.* Unpublished undergraduate dissertation. Department of Archaeology, University of Aberdeen.

Kupiec, Patrycja, Karen Milek, Guðrún Alda Gísladóttir and James Wollett
In press. Elusive sel sites: the geoarchaeological quest for Icelandic shielings and the case of Þorvaldsstaðasel, in northeast Iceland. In *Seasonal Exploitation of Uplands from Prehistory to the Modern Day,* edited by John Collis, Mark Pearce, and Heidi Robin. J. R. Collis Publications, Sheffield.

Lauritsen, Tina and Ole Thirup Kastholm Hansen
2003. Transvestite Vikings? Electronic document, http://www.idavallen.org/artiklar/transvikings.html, accessed 19 January 2014.

*Laxdæla saga*
[2001] Translated by K. Kunz. In *The Sagas of the Icelanders,* edited by Örnólfur Thorsson, pp. 270–422. Penguin Books, New York.

Lokasenna
[1996] Edited and translated by Caroline Larrington, in *The Poetic Edda,* pp. 84–101. Oxford University Press, Oxford.

Loonen, Maarten, J. J. E. Menno Zijlstra and Mennobart R. Van Eerden
1991. Timing of wing moult in Greylag Geese *Anser anser* in relation to the availability of their food plants. *Ardea* 79: 253–259.

Lucas, Gavin
2007. Fornleifauppgröftur á Pálstòftirum við Kárahnjúka 2005. Unpublished Report, Landsvirkjun, Iceland.
2008. Pálstóftir: a Viking Age shieling in Iceland. *Norwegian Archaeological review* 41(1): 85–101.

Magnússon, Árni and Pál Vídalín
1924–1947. *Manntal á Íslandi Árið 1703 Tekið að Tilhlutun Árna Magnússonar og Páls Vídalín Ásamt Manntali 1729 í Þrem Sýslum (Jarðabók 1703).* Hagstofu Íslands, Reykjavik.

Mahler, Ditlev
2007. *Sæteren ved Argisbrekka. Økonomiske forandringer på Færøerne I Vikingetid og Tidlig Middelalder.* Faroe University Press, Tórshavn, Fróðskapur.
Milek, Karen
2007. Micromorphological analysis of the floor sediments from Pálstóftir: evidence for seasonal activity and the functions of the buildings. In Fornleifauppgröftur á Pálstóftum við Kárahnjúka, edited by Gavin Lucas, pp. 83–92. Unpublished Report, Landsvirkjun, Iceland.
2011. Sections through the Homefield Boundary. In *Vatnsfjörður 2010: Framvinduskýrslur/Interim Reports*, edited by Karen Milek, pp. 64–68. Fornleifastofnun Íslands, Reykjavik.
2012. The roles of pit houses and gendered spaces on Viking-Age farmsteads in Iceland. *Medieval Archaeology* 56: 85–130.
Milek, Karen and Howell Roberts
2013. Integrated geoarchaeological methods for the determination of site activity areas: a study of a Viking Age house in Reykjavik, Iceland. *Journal of Archaeological Science* 40(4): 1845–1865.
Mooney, Dawn Elise
2013. *The Use and Control of Wood Resources in Viking Age and Medieval Iceland.* Unpublished Ph.D. dissertation, University of Aberdeen.
Owen, Olwyn and Magnar Dalland
1999. *Scar: A Viking Boat Burial on Sanday.* East Linton, Scotland.
Pálsdóttir, Albína H.
2005. *Segðu mér sögu af seli. Fornleifafræðileg úttekt á íslenskum seljum.* Unpublished BA thesis, University of Iceland.
Pálsdóttir, Helga
1979. Sennwirtschaft auf Teigur (transcript of an interview recorded in 1967). In *Sel-Untersuchnungen zur Geshicte des isländischen Sennwesens seit der Landnahmezeit.* Translated by E. Hitzler, pp. 264–270. Universitetsforlaget, Oslo.
Pálsdóttir, Lilja Björk
2008. *Fornleifakönnun á framkvæmdasvæði fyrirhugaðs Dettifossvegar: Töveggjarstekkur, Hrærsstaðir og Maríugerði.* Fornleifastofnun Íslands, Reykjavik.
Price, Neil
2002. *The Viking Way: Religion and War in Late Iron Age Scandinavia.* Department of Archaeology and Ancient History, Uppsala.
Reinton, Lars
1969. *Til seters.* Samlaget, Oslo.
Rigsþula
[1996] Edited and translated by Caroline Larrington, in *The Poetic Edda*, pp. 246–252. Oxford University Press, Oxford.
Roberts, Howell
2009. *Archaeological Excavations in Þegjandadalur 2007–2008.* Fornleifastofnun Íslands, Reykjavik.
Rosenlund, Knud
2007. The animal bones. In Fornleifauppgröftur á Pálstòftirum við Kárahnjúka 2005, edited by Gavin Lucas, pp. 47–51. Unpublished Report, Landsvirkjun, Iceland.
Sigurðsson, Gisli
2004. *The Medieval Icelandic Saga and Oral Tradition: A Discourse on Method.* Milman Parry Collection of Oral Literature, Cambridge.

Simpson, Ian, W. Paul Adderley, Garðar Guðmundsson, Margrét Hallsdóttir, Magnús Sigurgeirsson, and Mjöll Snæsdóttir

2002. Soil limitations to agrarian land production in pre-modern Iceland. *Human Ecology* 30: 423–443.

Skrede, Marit Anita

2005. Shielings and landscape in western Norway – Research traditions and recent traditions. In *Utmark: the Outfield as Industry and Ideology in the Iron Age and the Middle Age,* edited by Ingunn Holm, Sonja Innselset and Ingvild Øye, pp. 31–43. University of Bergen, Bergen. Solli, Britt.

1999. Odin – the *queer*? Om det skeive i norrøn mytologi. In *Et hus med mange rom: vennebok til Bjørn Myhre på 60-årsdagen*, AmS-Rapport 11B, edited by Ingrid Fuglestvedt, Terry Gansum and Arnfrid Opedal, pp. 393–427. Stavanger Archaeological Museum, Stavanger.

Sørensen, Marie Louise Stig

2009. Gender, material culture, and identity in the Viking diaspora. *Viking and Medieval Scandinavia* 5: 253–269.

Sturlunga saga

[1970–1974] Translated by Julia H. McGrew and R. George Thomas. Twayne and American-Scandinavian Foundation, New York.

Stylegar, Frans-Arne

2004. Some notes on earthworks and dykes in Iceland and in the North Atlantic. *Archaeologia Islandica* 3: 48–60.

Sveinbjarnardóttir, Guðrún

1991. Shielings in Iceland: an archaeological and historical survey. *Acta Archaeologica* 61: 76–91.

1992. *Farm Abandonment in Medieval and Post-Medieval Iceland: an Interdisciplinary Study.* Oxbow Books, Oxford.

Sveinbjarnardóttir, Guðrún, Kristoffer Dahle, Egill Erlendsson, Guðrún Alda Gísladóttir and Kim Vickers

2011. The Reykholt shieling project: some preliminary results. In *Viking Settlements and Viking Society*, edited by Svarar Sigmundsson, pp. 162–175. Hið íslenzka fornleifafélag and University of Iceland Press, Reykjavik.

*Þorsteins Saga Hvíta*

[1997] Translated by A. Maxwell. In *The Complete Sagas of* Icelanders, edited by Viðar Hreinsson. Leifur Eiríksson Publishing, Reykjavik.

Vésteinsson, Orri

1998. *Fornleifarannsókn á Neðra Ási í Hjaltadal 1998.* Fornleifastofnun Íslands, Reykjavik.

2003. *Fornleifarannsókn á Steinboga í Mývatnssveit 2002.* Fornleifastofnun Íslands, Reykjavik.

Vickers, Kim and Guðrún Sveinbjarnardóttir

2013. Insect invaders, seasonality and transhumant pastoralism in the Icelandic shieling economy. *Environmental Archaeology* 18(2): 165–177.

Vikstrand, Per

2006. Ásgarðr, Miðgarðr, and Útgarðr. A linguistic approach to a classical problem. In *Old Norse religion in long-term perspectives. Origins, changes, and interactions*, edited by Anders Andrén, Kristina Jennbert and Catharina Raudvere, pp. 354–357. Nordic Academic Press, Lund.

*Vopnfirðinga saga*

[1997] Translated by J. Tucker. In *The Complete Sagas of* Icelanders, edited by Viðar Hreinsson, pp. 313–335. Leifur Eiríksson Publishing, Reykjavik.

Ólason, Vésteinn

1998. *Dialogues with the Viking Age: Narration and Representation in the Sagas of the Icelanders.* Heimskringla, Reykjavik.

*Chapter 9*

# 'Truth' and reproduction of knowledge. Critical thoughts on the interpretation and understanding of Iron-Age Keys

*Heidi Lund Berg*

*Abstract*

Despite the lack of larger empirical and theoretically informed studies, interpretations of Iron-Age keys appear to be firmly established and are reproduced in discussions on gender, power and social stratigraphy to such a degree that they form potential truisms. Keys are described as primarily female artefacts, attributes of the 'housewife', symbols of material fortune and cultic-religious icons. However, these interpretations mainly stem from a dominantly historical point of view and do not correlate with archaeological sources. Based on a study of keys from Eastern Norway, this article presents a critical review of the current understandings of Iron-Age keys that dominate research literature. Important aspects to this discussion are the processes behind reproduction of knowledge and the nature of scientific discourse – traces of which are observable in the creation of the 'truth' about Iron-Age keys.

## Introduction

A key is a locking device. Its main purpose is to open or close – a door, a casket or similar items. Still, in Scandinavian Iron-Age research tradition, the practical abilities of keys as technical objects are rarely given emphasis in discussions on their social significance. In such cases, they are mainly understood as symbolic objects, related especially to women and their social roles. The latter form of understanding is, however, only to a small extent grounded in studies of archaeological material (Aannestad 2004: 69–70). Instead, medieval literary evidence from the 11th to 14th centuries has strongly influenced the academic understanding of prehistoric keys. As I will argue, interpretations portraying the key as a female attribute during the Iron Age, in one way or another, are founded on retrospective use of historical evidence – eddic poetry and medieval law codes, in particular – the source value of which

I find questionable. Also, traditional perceptions of gender representations in graves have played a part in this process as well, where the notion of the key as a female gender-specific artefact mirrors now outdated ideas of Iron-Age gender relations.

Archaeologists' tendency to interpret a predominantly technical (as opposed to 'functional') object as symbolically gendered is problematic, for several reasons. Firstly, it holds the inherent (and perhaps subconscious) presumption that symbolic meanings are more academically interesting and 'valuable' than technological and practical perspectives, resulting in a separation of the symbolic from the practical. This attitude may prevent broader understandings of past phenomena (in this case Iron-Age locking technology) as narrow and specific interpretations may exclude perceptions of the past as diverse and multifaceted. Secondly, the perception of keys as gendered objects has caused researchers to disregard archaeological sources that contradict the established interpretations of keys as female symbols. Thirdly, the notion upholds a stereotypic picture of keys as well as of Iron-Age women (and men). As I will illustrate, there is a clear exclusion of male perspectives in discussions of keys, where the contents of Old Norse written sources have been used selectively, creating biased generalisations that affect our perceptions of Iron-Age societal gender relations and of keys as object category and past social phenomenon.

I will argue that the currently dominating perception of Iron-Age keys has been reproduced in research literature for over a century, to such an extent that it may be considered a truism. A few singular voices against this truth have been raised in the later years (see Arwill-Nordbladh 1990; Pantmann 2006), but have not sparked a larger critical debate on the subject. On the basis of a study of Iron-Age keys from Eastern Norway (Berg 2013), this article aims at presenting an empirically based revision of the past and current understandings of keys. Through a critical discussion on the processes of knowledge reproduction and scientific discourse, it will illustrate how the truisms are results of historically and politically situated scientific practice.

## A short history of keys: things and thoughts

Keys make up an artefact group characterised by material and technological diversity and complexity. They represent a continued practice of implementing security measures in material form for nearly 6000 years, the earliest ones dating back to Ancient Mesopotamia (Bonomi 1853: 149; de Vries *et al.* 1993: 32), followed by technological advances made in Egypt, Greece and the Roman Empire (Edgren 1997: 43; Eras 1957: 33; Pitt-Rivers 1883: 19). The first keys in Scandinavia appear in archaeological contexts during the Roman Iron Age, in the 2nd–3rd centuries AD (Kristoffersen 2000: 116, 136; Tomtlund 1972: 7). Mainly made of metals such as iron and copper alloys, these early keys make up a very limited artefact group in this period, but increase in numbers and complexity in the Viking and Middle Ages (Fig. 9.1). Throughout the Iron Age, keys are predominantly found in graves, but are also well known from settlement and urban contexts, single depositions and as single finds (*e.g.* Andrén and Nilsson 1976; Crabb 1971; Kristoffersen 2000; Lund 2006; Pantmann 2006; Petersen 1951; Roesdahl 1993; Westphalen 2002).

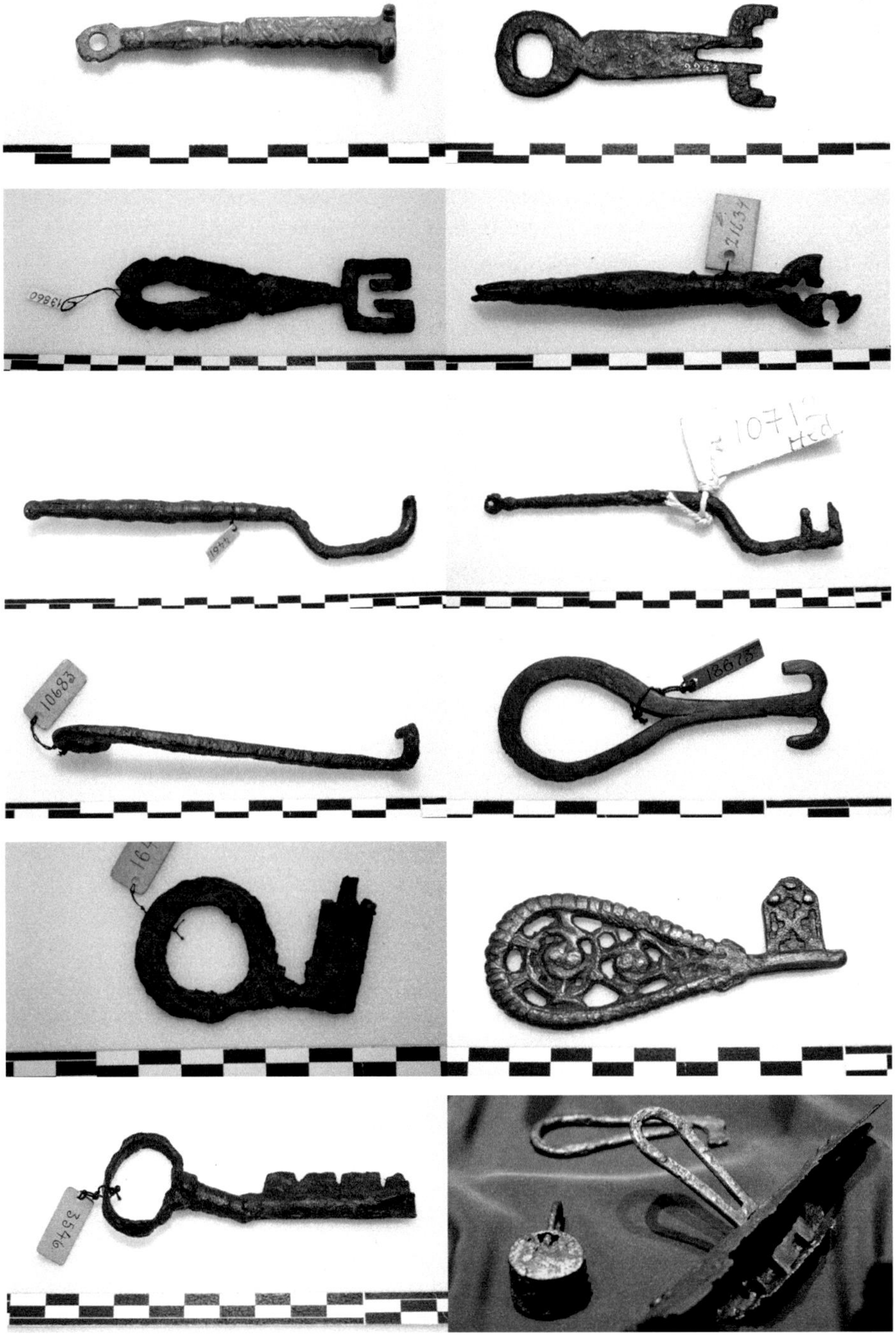

*Fig. 9.1. Examples of Iron-Age keys from Eastern Norway. They all represent different locking principles, materials and forms of decoration. Photos: © Heidi Lund Berg.*

Scandinavian archaeologists have concerned themselves with keys since the late 1800s. They were given place in the large reference works of the time (*e.g.* Müller 1888–1895; Rygh 1885; Worsaae 1854), which laid out the foundations for the later typological classifications of the artefact group (see Almgren 1955; Petersen 1951). With the exception of a few early publications (*e.g.* Almgren 1942; Carlsson 1942), most of the research on keys before 1975 concerned itself with discussing animal style or describing recently excavated archaeological material (Crabb 1971; Martens 1956; Olsén 1952; Tomtlund 1970, 1972, 1978). From around 1975 and onwards, researchers turned their focus on presenting interpretations of the keys themselves. Although related, the interpretations can be divided into four main themes. Common traits are the reliance on written source material and retrospective use of their contents, selective use of archaeological material in support of said sources and emphasis of the symbolic meanings of keys often related to women.

The first theme is the key as a symbol of power, material wealth and responsibility. Based on Scandinavian medieval law codes, the key is portrayed as a signifier for the key-bearer, sometimes described as a woman or housewife (as in *Borgartingslova*, dated to the 12th and 13th centuries, Olavsson 1914). In this context, the key is believed to have symbolised the social status, judicial rights and obligations the person held, often in terms of the wife's position and rights within the marriage (*e.g.* Aannestad 2004: 76–77; Frimannslund 1967: 386; Kristoffersen 2000; Roesdahl 1993: 218). The second theme is closely related to the previous. It concerns what I have termed the 'keys of the housewife theory', which is the most commonly encountered interpretation in writings on keys. Inspired by the contents of certain law codes, eddic poetry (mainly *Þrymskviða* and *Rigsþula*, Holm-Olsen 1993) and some saga literature, the key is believed to represent the married woman or 'housewife', her social and economic position, and her power within the household (*e.g.* Aannestad 2004; Andrén and Nilsson 1976; Kristoffersen 2000; Reinsnos 2006; Roesdahl 1993; Steinsland 2005; see also Hildebrand 1883: 128–129; Hyltén-Cavallius 1863–1868: 191; Steuer 1982). Inspired by such written sources, keys found in equipped female graves from the Viking Age and all the way back into the Migration Period have been used as grounds for defining the buried women as housewifes and, in some cases, keys have been considered a gender-specific artefact in grave contexts (Arwill-Nordbladh 1990: 256; Jesch 1994: 25; Kristoffersen 2000).

The third and fourth themes portray the keys as cultic and/or religious icons, again with female connotations. One presents the key as a symbol of Freya and, by association, of female leadership, childbirth and the afterlife. Portrayed in eddic literature such as *Þrymskviða,* and being a part of Roman and medieval European belief, the key was tied to symbolising Freya as a divine female leader, ruler of the hall Folkvang, keeper of the dead in the afterlife and helper of women in labour (Arwill-Nordbladh 1990: 257; Steuer 1982: 205, see also Holbæk 1966: 368; Näsström 1998: 184). Concerning the latter, the key was thought to be the tool that ensured a successful birth by 'unlocking' the woman's loins. The other theme emphasises the key's position as symbol of Christian faith, or, more specifically, of Christian influence in Scandinavia in the Merovingian and Viking periods (*e.g.* Aannestad 2004; Almgren 1942; Gellein 2007; Nancke-Krogh 1992; Steuer 1982). The most commonly referred source in this respect is the biblical verse Matthew 16:19, where Jesus gives Peter

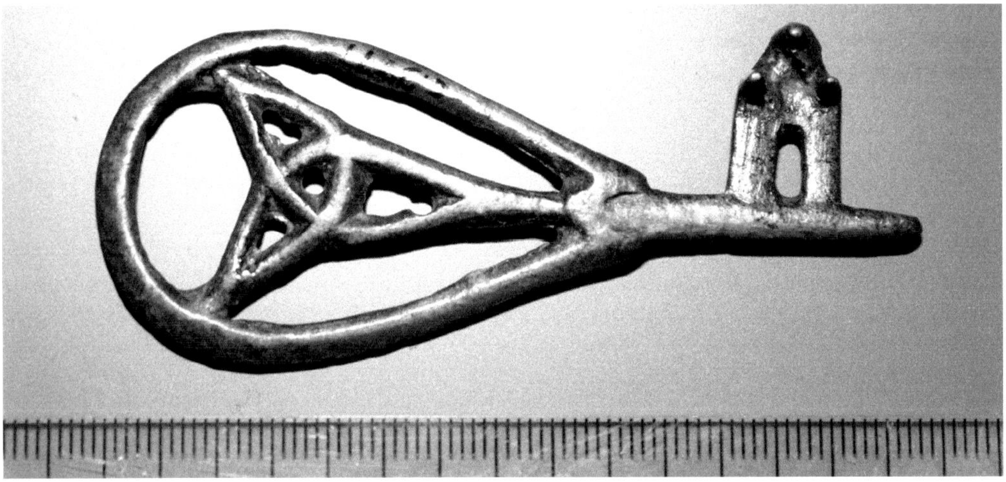

*Fig. 9.2. Key of copper alloy with a triquetra inside the handle, dated to the Viking Age, displayed at the Museum of Cultural History, Oslo. Photo: © Heidi Lund Berg.*

the keys to Heaven. The verse has been used to support the notion that Iron-Age keys were not meant for ordinary locks, but for opening the Heavenly Gates (Ulfhielm 1986: 1). Christian symbols on the handles of keys have been seen as evidence for this view; yet, some have also a connection to women. For example is the so-called triquetra found on one Norwegian Viking-Age key (Fig. 9.2). The symbol is traditionally understood as a sign of the Holy Trinity, but is also interpreted as a pre-Christian sign of the woman, symbolising fertility and motherhood (Aannestad 2004: 75–76; Kostveit 1997: 74).

These are the main themes of interpretation concerning keys. Apart from their dependence on written source material and symbolic elements, they are also quite specific, in my opinion. Considering keys and locks have existed for thousands of years, the promoted understandings of the Iron-Age phenomenon are narrow and inflexible in terms of human action and significance. They leave little room for variation and relativity in the role of keys, which implies a static, simplified, and (highly) generalising view of society in prehistoric Scandinavia. Selectively using archaeological material in supporting the 'meaning' of keys, they fail to sufficiently explain why the key was significant and in what way. Seemingly, the information from the written sources is considered enough to explain keys and locks as past phenomena. This is curious, as when observing the body of archaeological material, I find that there are several aspects that do not correlate with current understandings/ interpretations.

## The archaeological evidence

In the winter of 2012, looking into the topic of Iron-Age keys, the contrast between the views portrayed in research literature and the archaeological material became evident to me.

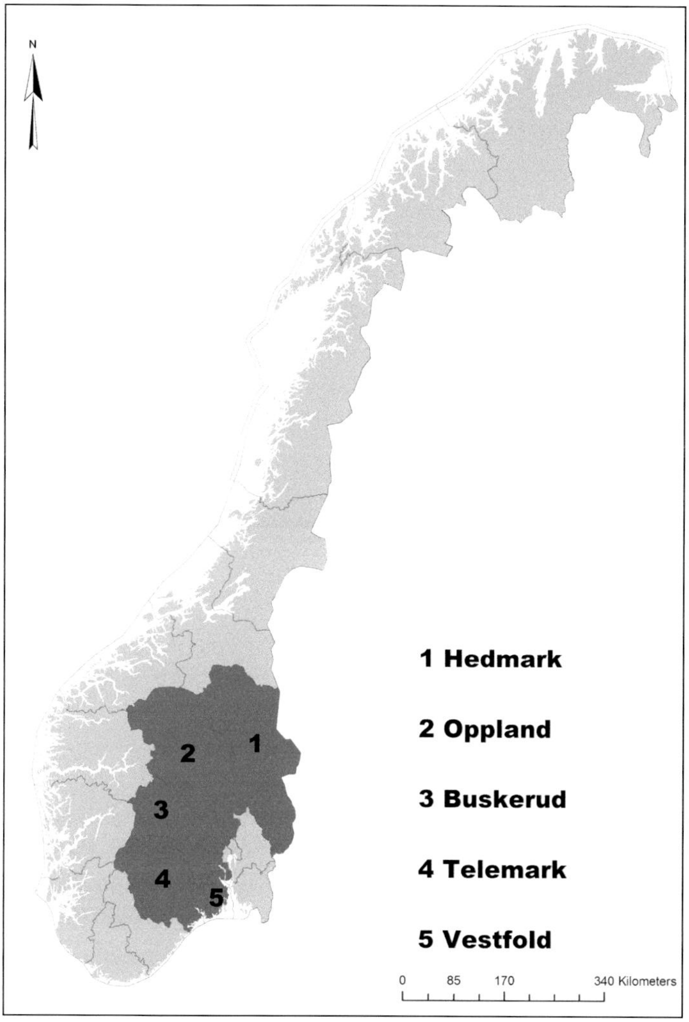


*Fig. 9.3. Map of Norway marking the five selected counties included in the study. Illustration: © Heidi Lund Berg.*

The most obvious aspect was the emphasis on women, that keys were symbols of feminine power – when the archaeology clearly showed that men were also related to keys (and much in the same manner). Some researchers acknowledged this fact (*e.g.* Aannestad 2004; Kristoffersen 2000; Reinsnos 2006), but refrained from taking it into their interpretations, not accepting how the inclusion of men would affect understandings of the phenomenon. Curious and inspired by the many contradictions, I made keys the topic of my master's thesis, performing an analysis of Iron-Age keys from five selected counties of Eastern Norway (Fig. 9.3). My main concern was to gain insight into the relation between humans and keys in prehistory: How were keys used? What determined their shape and function? Why were they deposited in different contexts throughout this nearly thousand year long period? Was there a 'key practice' of the Iron Age? Seeking the answers to these questions

| Period | Female | Male | Female & male double | Non-gendered |
|---|---|---|---|---|
| EIA | 5 (7) | 3 | 1 | 7 |
| LIA | 37 (43) | 30 (36) | 7 | 23 |

*Table 9.1. Graves with keys from Eastern Norway. Graves with two or more individuals of the same gender are included in the total of that gender. Number in paretheses include graves with uncertain gender.*

| Period | Female graves | | | Male graves | | | Female & male double graves | | |
|---|---|---|---|---|---|---|---|---|---|
| | *type 1* | *type 2* | *type 3* | *type 1* | *type 2* | *type 3* | *type 1* | *type 2* | *type 3* |
| EIA | 12 | 0 | 0 | 6 | 2 | 0 | 2 | 0 | 0 |
| LIA | 42 | 11 | 1 | 32 | 9 | 3 | 6 | 2 | 1 |

*Table 9.2. Key types in gendered graves from eastern Norway. The graves with uncertain gender are included.*

| Period | Female graves | | Male graves | | Female & male double graves | |
|---|---|---|---|---|---|---|
| | *Iron* | *Copper alloy* | *Iron* | *Copper alloy* | *Iron* | *Copper alloy* |
| EIA | 9 | 3 | 8 | 0 | 2 | 0 |
| LIA | 48 | 6 | 41 | 3 | 8 | 1 |

*Table 9.3. Keys of iron and copper alloy in gendered graves from eastern Norway. The graves with uncertain gender are included.*

involved a critical re-evaluation of the previous understandings in correlation with a broad study of archaeological material. To a significant extent, it resulted in a rejection of their validity (Berg 2013), the grounds for which I will give a short summary here.

Starting with the most common perspective; the key representing women generally and the housewife specifically is a view which builds on two premises: 1) that keys are predominantly found in women's graves and 2) that keys in male graves have completely different meanings. In the case of Eastern Norway, observations show that there are in fact no grounds on which to differentiate between the significance of keys for men and women. With regard to several source critical issues, there are no clear indications that keys occur more often in male versus female graves (Table 9.1). Neither is there any apparent relation between key types and gender (Table 9.2), not when it comes to decoration and material (copper alloy versus iron, Table 9.3), nor the occurrence of caskets (Table 9.4), or potential key chains indicated by multiple key finds in single graves (Table 9.5).

The housewife is portrayed as a strong female character governing the domestic sphere. Still, researchers tend to vary in their criteria for what characterises/constitutes a housewife. Is it a term describing the average free Iron-Age woman or is it an elite figure? What is clear is that keys in general were not a common occurrence in graves – neither female, nor male. As an example: the Viking Age is the period with the most key finds from graves, and in the area of study, 143 keys are found in 117 graves from this period. This is a very small number considering there has been registered approximately 6000–8000 Viking-Age graves in Norway (Solberg 1985, 2003: 222; Stylegar 2010: 71). Although simplified, this

| Period | Total no. graves | Female graves | Male graves | Female & male double graves | Non-gendered graves |
|---|---|---|---|---|---|
| EIA | 7 | 3 | 2 | 1 | 1 |
| LIA | 31 | 9 | 14 | 4 | 4 |

*Table 9.4. Graves with locks or caskets in gendered graves from eastern Norway. The graves with uncertain gender is included.*

| Period | % graves with multiple keys | No. keys deposited in pairs | | No. keys deposited in threes | | Female graves with multiple keys | | Male graves with multiple keys | | Non-gendered (or both sex) graves with multiple keys | |
|---|---|---|---|---|---|---|---|---|---|---|---|
| | | *Keys* | *Graves* | *Keys* | *Graves* | *Two keys* | *Three keys* | *Two keys* | *Three keys* | *Two keys* | *Three keys* |
| EIA | 58.6 | 14 | 7 | 3 | 1 | 3 | 1 | 2 | 0 | 1 (1) | 0 (0) |
| LIA | 26.6 | 40 | 20 | 18 | 6 | 4 | 3 | 9 | 1 | 5 (2) | 2 (0) |

*Table 9.5. Graves with potential key chains indicated by keys being found together in the same grave. The graves with uncertain gender are included.*

relation shows that the women (and men) who were buried with keys were quite few. This is also reflected in the Viking towns Birka and Kaupang, where graves with keys make up only 7% and 2.4% respectively, out of the studied graves (Berg 2013: 99; *cf.* Stylegar 2007; Ulfhielm 1989: 122–123).

Compared to the housewife as a gender ideal, this fits poorly with the image of the key being her attribute – for the Viking Age as well as the preceding periods. If every woman buried with grave goods was a woman of housewife status, one should think that keys deposited in such graves were a more frequently recurring phenomenon. Exempting the possibilities that keys were rarely laid down in burials or that wooden keys is a missing class of evidence, there are clear indications that women and men were buried with keys for other reasons than symbolising general gender roles.

### *Keys and truths: a short discussion*

For the interpretations arguing for cultic and religious symbolism related to keys, there is little archaeological evidence supporting these notions, as has been pointed out (*e.g.* Gellein 2007; Kristoffersen 2000: 139). With the exception of a few cooking spits, by some argued to be the staff of the sorceress (*e.g.* Price 2004, with references), there is nothing indicating a ritual connection between keys and Freya, fertility and childbirth, or shamanism in general. And exempt from some singular keys carrying Christian symbols, it seems that a Christian understanding of keys is poorly supported as well. These finds only illustrate that Christian as well as pre-Christian ideas existed side by side in the material expression of keys, as in many other artefact groups, resulting from contact between different areas in Europe from the 8th century and onwards.

There is, however, one interpretation that has more going for it, archaeologically speaking: the understanding of the key as a symbol of power and wealth. Here, the keys themselves, surviving locks and remnants of caskets, chests and doors are all tangible evidence that people had the technical knowledge and a real need to regulate the access to rooms and things, to material as well as immaterial resources and valuables, by the help of locking technology. The archaeological contexts that have produced keys are often related to material wealth, in the form of objects of high quality and access to and exploitation of valuable resources. In graves, keys are often found alongside objects of exclusive materials and quality, indicating a relation to higher social strata. At central places and towns, keys are related to activities involving the working of precious materials, the production and distribution of goods on a larger scale, where people and things interact in a network of trade and exchange (Kaupang is a good example in Norwegian context, see Pedersen 2010; Skre 2007). In such contexts, keys have probably had functions related to the storage and protection of portable resources and the closing of specific houses, rooms or areas. At the same time, they may have symbolised the key-bearer's access to these places. In this way, they may have been useful both as tools and as markers of ownership and responsibility. In single depositions, whether sacrificed or lost, keys – along with weapons, tools and other equipment – represent a sense of influence and power related to the person who deposited the objects. The objects reflect upon the owner/giver, showing that he or she is one who owns and can spare valuable things, and at the same time can affect his or her surroundings through ritual action (*cf.* Mauss 1954; Weiner 1992). In all cases, keys exist archaeologically in relation to places, persons, actions, and things which indicate a close connection to power and wealth.

Based on archaeological finds, the study of keys from Eastern Norway has shown the interpretations of keys to rest on poor evidence. Despite the fact that researchers have presented a broader basis for interpretation, ideals about the housewife and the feminine stand in the foreground of our perceptions of this Iron-Age phenomenon. So why have the notion of keys being gendered and primarily symbolic become a truism in archaeological discourse? There are most likely several factors at play, one of which concerns interpretive methodology.

## Retrospection and source criticism

Using historical evidence to shed light on archaeological material is an approach with long traditions within the discipline, one which rests on inference through retrospective method. Retrospection is based on the principle that by starting from something known and projecting it backwards in time, one can infer or explain aspects that are unknown (*e.g.* Lyman and O'Brien 2001: 308–310). This is a well established method of interpretation within archaeology, but is not without problems (*cf.* Holmsen 1940: 32; 1976: 4; Myhre 2002: 14; Pilø 2005: 8). As discussed by R. Lee Lyman and Michael J. O'Brien (2001) on the issue of analogical reasoning in Americanist archaeology, one of the main problems with what they term the 'direct historical approach' is that the analogy works progressively less well the larger the temporal distance is between the historical evidence and the archaeological manifestation. This aspect of time touches upon much of the criticism concerning the use of medieval written material in Scandinavian Iron-Age archaeology. Whether or not it is scientifically sound to infer aspects of gender relations, religious beliefs, societal power structures, family life *etc.* from sources that are several centuries younger than the period in question, has been much debated, and the answers vary. The hardest critics contest that the Old Norse writings should only be used to shed light on the period in which they were written down and thereby have little relevance for the pre-Christian period (Andrén 2004: 389; Lund 2009: 18; Steinsland 2005: 36). Dating sources such as the eddic poems are another source critical issue which has separated philologists from archaeologists, literature researchers and historians of religion (Axelsen 2012: 9; Lund 2009: 19).

A discussion about the specific historical sources involved in the study of keys lies outside the scope of this paper. I will, however, state that I find the sources on keys to be understood too simplistically in most cases, and as objects of considerable source criticism (such as their age), I consider them to be unsound sources for such generalising interpretations of this Iron-Age phenomenon (for a further discussion see Berg 2013). The case of the keys illustrates the often difficult relationship between *things* and *texts* and how this tension keeps affecting archaeological reasoning. The existence of medieval written sources is unique and precious, providing information that many different scientific fields may benefit from. There is, however, a need for being critical towards what kind of information they actually provide. As Julie Lund (2009: 23) has attested, it is through archaeological analysis that Old Norse sources can be seen as something more than literature, but I uphold that the manner in which this is done demands attention. The latent consequence in using written source material is that archaeologists stop studying the past, but simply *answer* it on the basis of stereotypical perceptions. In this relation it is worth mentioning a thought brought forth by Irmelin Axelsen (2012: 74, my translation):

> The meeting between thing and text refers to two different events: The meeting that occurs in all historical archaeology where the material and the written culture must be weighed against each other; and the meeting between archaeological practice and the written. [...] When text becomes more important than things, can the [archaeological interpretation] still be described as archaeological?

The domination of text over thing in the case of the keys cannot be seen in isolation as solely a methodological question. For some reason, the contents of the texts have been preferred over alternative views. The key as a female attribute, as symbol of the housewife, has dominated our perception of these objects for more than a century. How did it gain such a position in our views of the past? Where does it come from? The answers to these questions involve discussing two other factors influencing the creation of truisms: 1) how researchers produce and *reproduce* knowledge through academic discourse, and 2) the historical and political situatedness of such knowledge (re)production.

## Power, language and knowledge

How we as researchers create and recreate knowledge within scientific discourse has gained attention in the field of archaeology and related disciplines during the last decades (*e.g.* Axelsen 2012; Chilidis 2012 with references; di Leonard 1991; Olsen 1991; Skandfer 2005). The processes that underlie what archaeologists count as 'fact' have to a greater degree become topic of critical discussion within different fields of specialisation, including Scandinavian Iron-Age research.

Two researchers who have sparked such discussions are French philosopher Michel Foucault (1972) and British linguist Norman Fairclough (2001, 2003), and their work on critical discourse analysis. As discussed by Bjørnar Olsen (1991: 67–68), Foucault's perspective is that the past presented as 'pre-history' and 'history' is not solely a result of archaeological science, but a construction in itself that has been created under certain historical conditions. Belonging to this construction is a long line of rules that determine 'who is allowed to say what, which statements are serious archaeological statements, what is sensible, reasonable and true [...]' (Olsen 1991: 67, my translation). Foucault's discursive analysis is thereby a description of what can be said at any given time; which statements that survive, disappear, are reused, suppressed or censored; which terms are perceived as durable, dubious or untenable; which individuals, groups or classes that have access to say certain things (Olsen 1991: 68). Fairclough has summed these up in his interpretation of the term *power*, and its relation to language and knowledge. The term power is understood by the reception a statement or representation can get, and how this can lead to a truth being reproduced (Axelsen 2012: 15; Fairclough 2001: 32). Power is active in the form of rhetoric and jargon (how a statement is phrased and received), and position (the influence the one making the statement has on the discourse). Thereby, the statement's effect in the discourse is determined by *who* is making it and *how* it is made (cf. Axelsen 2012: 18–19; Neumann 2001: 116–117).

On the basis of these aspects, different statements are reproduced differently within research. Some texts will be referred to and quoted by other researchers, thereby becoming dominating within research literature – what Iver B. Neumann (2001: 52) describes as *canonical texts*, as they have broad reception (*cf.* Axelsen 2012: 17). Such canonical texts are based on so-called *monumental texts*, textual sources on which the statements are based. By studying the canonical and monumental texts one can reach those representations that characterise the discourse. These are what Neumann terms 'socially reproducing facts', which are 'things and phenomena *as they appear to us*', and which have to be continuously be 're-presented' to retain validity (Axelsen 2012: 17–18; Neumann 2001: 33, my translation). In other words, the truths or facts that characterise the discourse must be repeated regularly in order to be valid and effective within research.

Summed up, scientific 'truths' are arguments (power, language and knowledge) which have been repeated and consolidated in research and become perceptions of 'that's how it is'. In the discussion on the key, its role as housewife symbol appears as a 'that's how it is'-case. From the beginnings of the discipline up until today the connection between the female role and keys can be identified. Other interpretations have been presented, still the housewife theory forms the most dominating perspective – *i.e.* it has power within the discourse. The 'housewife with the keys' appears as a socially reproducing fact; a notion or explanation of a *thing* and a *phenomenon* as it appears to us. The notion has been 're-presented' regularly throughout research history, and thereby retains its validity.

Within the Scandinavian discourse, it is not easy to identify any definite works that have set standards for the interpretation of keys. The term housewife is referred to several places without direct reference to specific publications, and there are indications that discussions within gender research and historical studies have inspired archaeology on this area (Arwill-Nordbladh 1991: 63, see also Enright 1996). However, by analysing the literature on keys the last 50 years one can identify the possibly monumental texts on which the researchers' statements rest: the Old Norse written sources, *Rigsþula* and *Þtrymskviða* in particular, alongside some law texts (for example *Borgartingslova*, Olavsson 1914). It is mainly these sources who are used as interpretive frameworks for the archaeological finds. The question then is why these sources have been given such significance. How and why certain notions or perceptions take hold cannot be explained solely on the academic authority and rhetorical skills of researchers. A statement's impact is most likely related to its ability to be recognised – that one can relate to it. It is apparent that the image of the housewife with the keys seems familiar and comfortable to the ones reproducing it, and this actualises the aspects of knowledge reproduction concerning historical and political situatedness.

### *National romanticism and gender ideals*

As discussed by Olsen (1991: 66–67), Hans-Georg Gadamer's term 'effective history' ([1975] 2004) describes how science is always historically situated. Following it, interpretation and understanding are not ahistorical qualities, but 'effects' of history. It entails that as archaeologists trying to understand a (pre)historical phenomenon, we are already affected by history, including the 'history of our people, research history and our personal biography' (Olsen 1991: 67). This historical embeddedness of our scientific perspectives helps decide what is considered worth studying, what objects should be studied, and how they are portrayed in research literature. Importantly, it also affects the production and reproduction of knowledge, as what is termed 'truth' to a significant degree corresponds with the current socio-political climate in which research is performed. The case of the keys is one illustrating example of this, as it mirrors the developments within political discussion on gender relations in late 19th and 20th centuries.

Acknowledging the problems concerning the housewife gender role, archaeologist Elisabeth Arwill-Nordbladh (1991, 1998) has revisited the topic of Viking-Age female ideals. By studying the notions of gender in Viking-Age research, she presents what she perceives as the socio-political foundation for the concept of the housewife. Arwill-Nordbladh illustrates how Viking-Age gender roles are strongly influenced by changes in Scandinavian gender roles around the mid-1800s, alongside an increasing interest in Old Norse ideals. The mid-19th century was a socio-political period in Scandinavia characterised by the neo-Gothicism and national romanticism. Archaeology was given a central place in establishing a sense of nationhood, where the Old Norse became an ideal for family life and women's position in society. Old Norse symbolism communicated in the written sources was an important element in the idealisation of the bourgeois family. The image of the prehistoric housewife as the head of the household, ruling the indoors, her position subordinate to the husband who reigned the outdoors, became firmly rooted in this family ideal, strengthening the current gender ideology.

By ordering material culture according to 19th century gender ideology, archaeologists contributed to further strengthen the idea of separate areas of activities for men and women – supporting the binary dichotomies male/female, public/private, community/family (Hjørungdal 1994a: 54–55, 1994b: 142). Incorporating the current ideas of gender relations, archaeology helped legitimise and bring authority to bourgeois ideology by providing prehistoric roots to the gender divide (Hjørungdal 1994a: 55). This traditional binary interpretation of gender is still firmly established in archaeological practice, especially concerning classification of graves, despite the increasing criticism brought on by feminist views the past thirty years (*e.g.* Engelstad 1991; Hjørungdal 1994a, 1994, 1995; Lundø 2004; Widerberg 1992).

However, despite the growing political and ideological struggle for women's rights in the early 1900s, the housewife ideal persisted, becoming a stereotype repeated in archaeological literature. Slowly, by the 1980s and 90s, the image changed somewhat with the development of feminist notions in archaeology, describing a stronger, more powerful and influential housewife-role than before. Still, the housewife with the keys as a domestic ideal has only to a small degree changed from its 19th century form, and has to a large degree stood unopposed (Arwill-Nordbladh 1991: 63).

The key, as a consequence, has become a part of this stereotypical package, which has manifested itself as a distinct view of the past. Arwill-Nordbladh's studies show how statements presented in research literature separated by a century can be nearly identical – they are results of a female ideal which is rooted in socio-political ideas and reproduced in scientific perceptions of the past.

Although new and critical studies have been presented, the stereotype still lives on, much likely resulting from what anthropologist Micaela di Leonardo (1991: 34) terms '[…] the politically constituted nature of knowledge production, and its historical embeddedness […]'. In other words, the creation of the truism 'the keys of the housewife' is not simply a product of an exaggerated faith in written sources, but of reproduced notions with roots in political and societal undercurrents at the beginnings of archaeology and modern Scandinavia.

### In conclusion: what is true?

'Truth', as we have seen, is something we create and recreate within scientific practice. This practice is, however, never fully objective and ahistorical, but relies hugely on power relations within as well as outside of academia. Keys have for nearly 150 years been regarded as female attributes, signifiers of the housewife and highly symbolic objects. Yet, a review of the archaeology of eastern Norway strongly suggest such views to be constructions inspired by national romantic ideas of gender in early modern Scandinavia. Notably, I do not contest that keys have had symbolic roles to men and women of the Viking Age. On the contrary, I consider their symbolic potential to be significant in several ways, especially concerning expressions of belonging and social status (for a further discussion see Berg 2013). I am, however, critical to the manner in which interpretations of the key are so clearly separated from the technical aspects of the device, and thereby, from the premises for the development of Viking-Age locking technology in general. Reliance on medieval texts has to a significant degree caused the key to be understood derived from the origins of its development, where symbolism goes before and is separated from technical function.

On a general level, the case of the keys provides a reminder of just how embedded we as archaeologists are in our contemporary society when we do research – and, more specifically, it provides a good example of the meeting between things and texts in archaeological scientific practice.

The discussion presented here also illustrates a curious consequence of knowledge reproduction and power structures within academia: it is not necessarily the reasonable or the true which make up understandings of what is 'fact'. As observed by Foucault, in the words of Olsen (1991: 68): that which acquires status as 'true' or 'sensible' is result of a historical process where power and knowledge works together. Following this, truth is always what authority and reason make it to be, and our perceptions of the past will continue to be questioned, re-evaluated, and tested against the ever-growing spectre of source materials.

*Acknowledgements*

I would like to thank Per Ditlef Fredriksen for proof reading as well as for much good advice and inspiration. I am also very grateful to the Museum of Cultural History in Oslo, for allowing me to photograph their collection of keys as part of my master's project. I would also like to express my gratitude to my colleagues in the conference arrangement committee and editorial group, for the enthusiasm and dedication. And most importantly, a great thank you to the contributors to this volume and the Viking Worlds conference.

*References*

Aannestad, Hanne Lovise
2004. En nøkkel til kunnskap – om kvinneroller i jernalder. *Viking* 65: 69–82.

Almgren, Bertil
1942. 'Thors märke' och himmelrikets nycklar. *Årsboken Uppland.* Upplands fornminnesförening och hembygdsförbund.
1955. *Bronsnycklar och djurornamentik.* Appelberg.

Andrén, Anders and Thorvald Nilsson
1976. Lås och nycklar. In *Uppgrävt forflutet för PKbanken i Lund,* edited by A. W. Mårtensson, pp. 399–406. Archaeologica Lundensia. Investigationes de antiqvitatibus urbis lundae VII. Museum of Cultural History, Lund.

Arwill-Nordbladh, Elisabeth

1990. Nyckelsymbolik i järnålderns kvinnogravar. *Fornvännen* 85: 254–259.

1991. The Swedish image of Viking Age women: stereotype, generalisation, and beyond. In *Social Approaches to Viking Age Studies*, edited by R. Samson, pp. 53–64. Cruithne Press, Glasgow.

1998. *Genuskonstruktioner i nordisk vikingatid: førr och nu.* GOTARC. Series B, Gothenburg archaeological theses, No. 9. University of Gothenburg, Gothenburg.

Axelsen, Irmelin

2012. *Kristendommen drepte hesten: en analyse av hesten som arkeologisk forskningsobjekt.* Master's thesis. Institute of Archaeology, Conservation and History, University of Oslo. Electronic document, http://urn.nb.no/URN:NBN:no-32274.

Berg, Heidi Lund

2013. *"Nøkkelpraksis". Østnorske jernaldernøkler som symbol og teknologi.* Master's thesis. Institute of Archaeology, Conservation and History, University of Oslo. Electronic document, http://urn.nb.no/URN:NBN:no-36964.

Bonomi, Joseph

1853. *Nineveh and its palaces: the discoveries of Botta and Layard, applied to the elucidation of holy writ.* 227 Strand, London.

Carlsson, Lizzie

1942. Nyckeln som rättslig symbol. *RIG* 25: 6–99

Chilidis, Konstantinos

2012. *The Construction of Knowledge in Archaeology – the Case of "Philip's Tomb" at Vergina in Northern Greece.* Ph.D. dissertation at the Faculty of Humanities. Institute of Archaeology, Conservation and History, University of Oslo, Oslo.

Crabb, Peter J.

1971. Låse og nøgler. In *Århus Søndervold: en byarkæologisk undersøgelse*, edited by H. Hellmuth Andersen, P. J. Crabb and H. J. Madsen, pp. 183–196. Jysk Arkeologisk Selskabs Skrifter, Bind IX. Gyldendalske Boghandel, Nordisk Forlag, Copenhagen.

de Vries, Marc, Nigel Cross and Donald. P. Grant

1993. *Design methodology and relationships with science.* NATO ASI series. Series D, Behavioural and social sciences, Vol. 71. Kluwer, Dordrecht.

di Leonardo, Michaela

1991. Introduction: gender, culture, and political economy: feminist anthropology in historical perspective. In *Gender at the Crossroads of Knowlegde. Feminist Approaches in the Postmodern Era*, edited by M. di Leonardo, pp. 1–48. University of California Press, Berkeley.

Edgren, Torsten

1997. Bakom lås och bom. Kring en vikingatida nyckeltyp. In *Ord och några cisor tillägnade Kurt Zilliacus*, edited by M. Blomqvist, pp. 43–49. Meddelande från Institutionen för Nordiska språk och nordisk litteratur vid Helsingfors Universitet, Serie B, 18. Institutionen för nordiske språk och nordisk litteratur, University of Helsinki, Helsinki.

Engelstad, Ericka

1991. Images of power and contradiction: feminist theory and post-processual archaeology. *Antiquity* 65: 502–514

Enright, Michael J.

1996. *Lady with a Mead Cup: Ritual, Prophecy and Lordship in the European Warband from La Téne to the Viking Age.* Four Courts Press, Dublin.

Eras, Vincent. J. M.

1957. *Locks and Keys Throughout the Ages.* H. H. Fronczek, Amsterdam.

Fairclough, Norman
2001. *Language and Power*, 2nd edn. Longman, Harlow.
2003. *Analysing Discourse. Textual Analysis for Social Research.* Routledge, London.
Foucault, Michel
1972. *The Archaeology of Knowledge.* Translated by A. M. Sheridan Smith. Routledge, Cornwall.
Frimannslund, Rigmor
1967. Nyckelbärare (Norge). In *Kulturhistorisk leksikon for nordisk middelalder: fra vikingtid til reformasjonstid*, edited by F. Hødnebø, pp. 386–387. Bind XII Mottaker-Orlogsskib. Gyldendal Norsk Forlag, Oslo.
Gadamer, Hans-Georg
[1975] 2004. *Truth and Method.* 2nd revised edn, translation revised by J. Weinsheimer and D. G. Marshall. Sheed and Ward, Continuum Publishing Group, London.
Gellein, Kristin
2007. *Kristen innflytelse i hedensk tid? En analyse med utgangspunkt i graver fra yngre jernalder i Hordaland*, edited by J. Zehetner, pp. 9–113. Universitetet i Bergen Arkeologiske Skrifter: Hovedfag/Master 2, Institute of Archaeology, University of Bergen.
Hildebrand, Hans
1883. *The Industrial Arts of Scandinavia: in the Pagan Time.* London.
Hjørungdal, Tove
1994a. Materiell kultur og kjønn i arkeologien: Kjønnsbestemmelse av forhistoriske graver på 800-tallet. *K.A.N. Kvinner i arkeologi i Norge* 17–18: 52–56
1994b. Poles apart. have there been any male and female graves? *Current Swedish Archaeology* 2: 141–149.
1995. Gender-critical archaeology in Sweden. A review. *Current Swedish Archaeology* 3: 105–119.
Holbæk, Bengt
1966. Maria i folketradisjonen. In *Kulturhistorisk leksikon for nordisk middelalder: fra vikingtid til reformasjon*, edited by F. Hødnebø, pp. 367–373. Bind XI. Luft-Motståndsrätt. Gyldendal Norsk Forlag, Oslo.
Holm-Olsen, Ludvig
1993. *Edda-dikt.* 2nd revised edn. Translated by L. Holm-Olsen. J. W. Cappelens Forlag, Lillehammer.
Holmsen, Andreas
1940. Nye metoder innen en særskilt gren av norsk historieforskning. *Historisk Tidsskrift* 32: 27–45. Den Norske Historiske Forening, Oslo.
1976. Om å gå bakover i historien. *Heimen* XVII: 3–12.
Hyltén-Cavallius, Gunnar Olof
1863–1868. *Wärend och Wirdarne: ett försök i svensk ethnologi.* Norstedt, Stockholm.
Jesch, Judith
1994. *Women in the Viking Age.* Boydell Press, Woodbridge.
Kostveit, Åsta Østmoe
1997. *Kors i kake, skurd i tre. Tegn och symboler i folkekulturen.* Landbruksforlaget, Oslo.
Kristoffersen, Siv
2000. *Sverd og spenne. Dyreornamentikk og sosial kontekst.* Studia Humanitatis Bergensia, No. 13. Høyskoleforlaget, Kristiansand.
Lund, Julie
2006. Vikingetidens værtøjkister i landskab og mytologi. *Fornvännen* 101: 323–341.
2009. *Åsted og vadested: Deponeringer, genstandsbiografier og rumlig strukturering som kilde til*

*vikingetidens kognitive landskaber*. Acta Humaniora, Vol. 389. Doctoral thesis at the Faculty of Humanities. Institute of Archaeology, Conservation and History, University of Oslo, Oslo.

Lundø, Siv Anita
2004. Representasjon av kjønn i populærvitenskapelig formidling. *Primitive Tider* 7: 115–124.

Lyman, R. Lee and Michael J. O'Brien
2001. The direct historical approach, analogical reasoning, and theory in Americanist archaeology. *Journal of Archaeological Method and Theory* 8(4): 303–342.

Martens, Irmelin
1956. En bronsenøkkel fra Ommang i Løten. In *Universitetets Oldsaksamling Årbok* 1954–1955, pp. 64–66. J. Petlitz Boktrykkeri, Oslo.

Mauss, Marcel
1954. *The Gift: Forms and Functions of Exchange in Archaic Societies.*Translated by I. Cunnison. Choen and West, London.

Müller, Sophus
1888–1895. *Ordning af Danmarks Oldsager*. II. Jernalderen. C. A. Reitzel, København.

Myhre, Bjørn
2002. Del 1. Landbruk, landskap og samfunn 4000 f.Kr.–800 e.Kr. I *Norges landbrukshistorie I: 4000 f.Kr.–1350 e.Kr. Jorda blir levevei*, edited by B. Myhre and I. Øye, pp. 12–213. Det Norske Samlaget, Oslo.

Nancke-Krogh, Søren
1992. *Shamanens hest: tro og magt hos vikingerne.* Nyt Nordisk Forlag, Arnold Busck, Copenhagen.

Neumann, Iver B.
2001. *Mening, materialitet, makt: En innføring i diskursanalyse.* Fagbokforlaget, Bergen.

Näsström, Britt-Mari
1998. *Frøya: den store gudinnen i Norden.* Pax, Oslo.

Olavsson, Torleiv
1914. *Ældre Borgartingslov: Vikens kristenret, tillikemed endel ældre lovregler om ekteskapsstiftelse og trolovelse m.m., som er indført deri fra Eidsivalovens eller Borgartingslovens verdslige del*, translated by T. Olavsson, Kristiania.

Olsen, Bjørnar
1991. Kjelmøyfunnenes (virknings)historie og arkeologi. *Viking* 54: 65–87.

Olsén, Pär
1952. Et vendeltida nyckelskaft. *TOR* 1949–1952: 116–124.

Pantmann, Pernille
2006. Ej blot til pynt – Dualismen i gravfundne nøgler fra vikingetid. Et studie af gravfundne nøgler og deres symbolik samt deres betydning for revurdering af kvinderoller i vikingetid. Magister's conference. Saxo Insitute, Prehistoric Archaeology, University of Copenhagen, Copenhagen.

Pedersen, Unn
2010. *I smeltedigelen: Finsmedene i vikingtidsbyen Kaupang.* Ph.D. dissertation at the Faculty of Humanities. Institute of Archaeology, Conservation and History, University of Oslo, Oslo.

Petersen, Jan
1951. *Vikingetidens redskaper.* Skrifter utgitt av Det norske videnskaps-akademi i Oslo. II. Hist.-filos. klasse 1951:4. Dybwad, Oslo.

Pilø, Lars
2005. *Bosted – urgård – enkeltgård: en analyse av premissene i den norske bosetningshistoriske*

*forskningstradisjon på bakgrunn av bebyggelsesarkeologisk feltarbeid på Hedemarken*. Oslo Archaeological Series vol. 3. Institute of Archaeology, Art History and Conservation, University of Oslo, Oslo.

Pitt-Rivers, Augustus Henry Lane-Fox

1883. *On the Development and Distribution of Primitive Locks and Keys*. Chatto and Windus, London.

Price, N.

2004. The archaeology of Seiðr: Circumpolar traditions in Viking pre-Christian religion. *Brathair* 4 (2): 109–126

Reinsnos, Ambjørg

2006. *Bak lås og slå. Ein arkeologisk analyse av nøklar og låsar i Hordaland frå rundt 800 til 1700 e.Kr.* Master's thesis in Archaeology. University of Bergen, Bergen.

Roesdahl, Else

1993. On keys. In *Twenty-eight papers presented to Hans Bekker-Nielsen on the occasion of his sixtieth birthday 28 April 1993*, edited by H. Bekker-Nielsen, pp. 217–224. Odense University Press, Odense.

Rygh, Oluf

1885. *Norske Oldsager*. Cammermeyer, Christiania.

Skandfer, Marianne

2005. Fra eldre til yngre steinalder? Kronologiske og begrepsmessige utfordringer sett fra Nord-Norge. *Primitive Tider* 8: 97–106.

Solberg, Bergljot

1985. Social status in the Merovingian and Viking periods in Norway from archaeological and historical sources. *Norwegian Archaeological Review* 18(1–2): 61–76.

2003 *Jernalderen i Norge. Ca. 500 f.Kr.–1030 e.Kr.* 2nd edition. Cappelen Akademisk Forlag, Oslo.

Steinsland, Gro

2005. *Norrøn religion: myter, riter, samfunn*. Pax, Oslo.

Steuer, Heiko

1982. Schlüsselpaare in frühgeschichtlichen Gräbern. Zur Deutung einer Amulett-Beigabe. Studien zur Sachsenforschung. In *Studien zur Sachsenforschung* 3, pp. 185–274. Vol. 27. Lax, Hildesheim.

Stylegar, Frans-Arne

2010. Hvorfor er det færre kvinne- enn mannsgraver fra vikingtiden i Norge? *Primitive Tider* 12: 71–79.

Tomtlund, Jan-Erik.

1970. Hänglåsen på Helgö. *Fornvännen* 65: 238–247.

1972. *De förhistoriske hänglåsen: en delstudie.* Uppsats för tre betyg, Nordisk och jamförande Fornkunskap. Uppsala universitet, Uppsala.

1978. Lock and keys. In *Excavations at Helgö V: 1. Workshop part II*, edited by K. Lamm, A. Lundström and H. Clarke, pp. 3–14. Kungl. Vitterhets Historie och Antikvitets Akademien, Almqvist and Wiksell International, Stockholm.

Ulfhielm, Anna

1986. Vikingatida nycklar från Gotland. Unpublished thesis in Northern European Archaeology, University of Stockholm, Stockholm.

1989. Schlüssel. In *Birka II:3 Systematische Analysen der Gräberfunde*, edited by G. Arwidsson, pp. 122–132. Kungl. Vitterhets Historie och Antikvitets Akademien, Uddevalla.

Weiner, Annette B.
1992. *Inalienable Possessions: The Paradox of Keeping-While-Giving*. University of California Press, Berkeley.
Westphalen, Petra
2002. *Die Eisenfunde von Haithabu*. Die Ausgrabungen in Haithabu, Zenhnter Band, Neumünster.
Widerberg, Karin
1992. Vi behöver en diskussion om könsbegreppet. *Kvinnovetenskaplig tidsskrift* 4: 27–31.
Worsaae, Jens Jacob Asmussen
1854. *Afbildninger fra Det Kongelige Museum for nordiske Oldsager i Kjøbenhavn*. Copenhagen.

PART III

# PRODUCTION, EXCHANGE AND MOVEMENT

*Chapter 10*

# Manors and markets. Continental perspectives on Viking-Age trade and exchange

*Bjarne Gaut*

*Abstract*

This paper explores the importance of the Continental polynuclear estate for the development of trade and urbanization in the North Sea region. It emphasizes the integration of rural and market economy in the Carolingian period, where market towns were both outlets for surplus production and import channels for goods the rural estates did not produce themselves.

Ports and emporia along the North Sea coast served an important role in taxation and control of foreign traders and artisans. However, they also funneled the estates' mercantile agents and their goods into the North Sea and beyond. The paper will in particular focus on the links between religious institutions, missionary activity and 'free' traders visiting overseas market towns, like Kaupang. The way economic networks shaped social and mercantile interaction between different groups in the new urban markets is rarely considered in Viking-Age archaeology.

## Introduction

Among the excavated structures within the market town of Kaupang is the so-called *Frisian Merchant's house* (Skre 2011: 431–434). This is the remains of a mid-9th century building with an exclusive selection of small finds; Rhenish pottery, vessel glass, alien dress accessories – in short what looks like the material remains of a Frisian household. Pieces of hacksilver and coins suggest that the household members were involved in trade, perhaps interacting with their homeland or with Frisian settlements in other Viking-Age towns.

Who were these people? What social group did they belong to and why did they visit south-east Norway? Within what production framework and exchange network did the goods they traded originate? Although vital to understand the framework of exchange, Scandinavian archaeologists struggle to address these questions properly. Inhabitants and visitors to Kaupang and other urban sites are unconsciously categorised as merchants or artisans. Their origin and relations are mapped through the archaeological material they brought with them (Ambrosiani and Bäck 2007; Callmer 1998; Jankuhn 1986 [1956]; Steuer 1987 to mention but a few examples). However, little progress is made to understand the social networks these people embodied.

One important reason for this is the tendency within much of Anglo-Scandinavian archaeology to study wics and emporia in isolation from wider society. Specialist studies tend to focus on artefact description, craft specialisation and group dynamics within the community of mercantile entrepreneurs and free artisans (Callmer 2002; Gaut 2011). Although these are valuable aspects, they fail to explain the wider social and economic rationale for the development of these sites (for a critique see Moreland 2000; Perring and Whyman 2002). Focusing on urban exchange, rather than its links to production and consumption, it is easy to regard emporia as economic anomalies operating on different principles from society at large.

This text focusses on one element largely absent in Scandinavian studies of Viking-Age urbanism; the role of the Carolingian rural economy, and particularly the large ecclesiastical estates in the development of the North Sea trade. I will outline some relevant aspects of the Carolingian economy. I hope to illustrate how production and consumption structured the flow of goods within a wider geographical orbit, and that religious institutions were active partners in this network. The point I want to make is that the Continental mode of production contributed to shape the framework of exchange – even in overseas towns, like Kaupang.

### A short historiography

Henri Pirenne (1956 [1925]) famously argued that the 7th and 8th century Arab incursions in the Mediterranean reduced the volume of trade and isolated North-west Europe. To most early 20th century historians and archaeologists, urban life and market trade was intimately linked (*e.g.* Arbman 1937; Jankuhn 1986 [1956]). Long distance trade was carried out by a dwindling number of urban merchants. Meanwhile, the social elites isolated themselves in economically self-sufficient rural manors. Significantly, the low volume of trade and the isolation of merchants from the rural economy led to urban decline and prevented any economic expansion (*e.g.* Duby 1962; Grierson 1959). This bleak outlook on the early medieval economy coloured the historical narrative for decades (Hodges 2000: 16–33; Verhulst 2002: 2–8).

Archaeology and history have since countered Pirenne's grand thesis on several points (summarised by McCormick 2001). Apart from questioning the effect of Arab naval activity on trade in the Mediterranean region, excavations have revealed the continuous presence of large-scale trade and urban-like settlements in parts of North-west Europe throughout the early medieval period. Not least the documentation of North Sea trade has been important in this respect. Economic decline has been replaced with specialised sites for production and trade, a prolific silver economy and wide distribution of non-perishable commodities in the North Sea zone (Grierson and Blackburn 1986; Hill and Cowie 2001; Hodges 2000; Steuer 1987; more cautiously Wickham 2005: 794–818).

The relationship between town and countryside has also been reviewed. George Despy's (1968) seminal study illustrated how urban and rural economies in the Maas valley were integrated at a much earlier stage than previously believed. The basis of this and later re-evaluations has been a close re-reading of individual pieces of written evidence; charters, property lists, letters and hagiographic texts. As a result, our understanding of the late Merovingian and Carolingian economy is comprehensively altered (for general introductions see Toubert 1990; Verhulst 2002).

## The estate-driven economy

Around 810, Abbot Irminon of Saint-Germain-des-Prés drew up a detailed list of all the monastery's properties where the landholders owed rent and/or other tenurial services. The register provides insight into the economy of some 25 villas and their dependent farms. In addition to the cultivated crops and the land rent, it lists fiscal tax, the name of the tenant farmer, his family and their social status.

Abbot Irminon's cadastre belongs to a group of texts – *polyptychs* – that were drawn up and preserved in increasing numbers during the 8th and 9th centuries. The trend seems connected to the development of large estate systems at this time, and the purpose was most likely to determine and fix the obligations of the tenants and to standardise and optimise the management of the estates (Davies 1987; Morimoto 2001: 607; Verhulst 2002: 40). At the same time, the importance of written records when settling land disputes increased. There are some indications that the documents were drawn up on requests from the court or church leaders. The Survey of Fontanelle refers explicitly to Charlemagne and a number of letters by Abbot Lupus of Ferrière-en-Gâtinais point to audits of monastic property throughout the realm in the mid-9th century (Loyn and Parcival, no. 23; Lupus: Letters nos 40–43).

Although the terminology of the polyptychs can be challenging, and some redactions abbreviated or truncated, the best examples provide a detailed and vivid picture of the material and human resources allocated to individual manors. Other documents (*e.g.* those pertaining to the monastery of Fontanelle) only provide a list of the total number and size of controlled farms. However, for the majority of estates, no inventories are known at all. It is further difficult to use the polyptychs as a source to economic change because they, by nature, provide a static picture of the estate structure (Morimoto 2001: 605–606). Only in a few fortunate exceptions, like the polyptych of Bobbio with records from both 862 *and* 883, is it possible to study landholding through time. It therefore becomes a subjective interpretation how typical the structures reconstructed from charters or polyptychs were for the Carolingian economy, and how early and why they originated unless unequivocally stated. Treated with pragmatic caution, these documents nevertheless provide the best insight into the organisation of the Carolingian economy.

The sources reveal how rural manors in the Frankish heartlands grew in size, intensified production and increased their surplus during the late Merovingian and Carolingian period. Written evidence suggests that this was achieved through technological investment, but also through new social obligations and tenurial duties which tied the population closer to the land

and their landlord (Verhulst 2002). Archaeological evidence corroborating this development is sparse – although there are some indications of restructuring and concentration of settlement during this period (Loveluck 2005; Steuer 1989; Theuws 1990: 60–65).

Ecclesiastical landowners took very much part in this development. Through a widespread system of donations and land grants, monastic and episcopal institutions quickly became dominating landowners (*e.g.* Balzaretti 2000; Lebecq 2000; Toubert 1990). These ecclesiastical estate systems could be of considerable size (Verhulst 2002: 32–39). As we have already seen, the Paris monastery of Saint-Germain-des-Prés controlled a minimum of 25 villas, comprising 1700 *mansi* (30,000 hectares) of arable land and woods. For the monastery of Fontanelle, the corresponding figures (from 787) are 1400 mansi and 39 mills for own use and provision, and more than 2400 additional mansi temporarily granted as *precaria* to other landholders against an annual rent. Smaller monasteries tended to have 10–20 villas attached, each cultivating some hundred hectares of land.

It is more difficult to obtain a clear understanding of the extent of aristocratic landholdings, due to the very different source situation for ecclesiastical and lay property. *Capitulare de Villis* and *Brevium Exempla* (Loyn and Parcival 1975, nos 15 and 23) suggest that attempts were made to organise fiscal properties, but if lay polyptychs ever existed none have been preserved. It is generally assumed that lay holdings were regional, smaller and more prone to division through inheritance or religious donations. Only the holdings of the so-called *Reichsadel*, the foremost nobility of the realm, were dispersed throughout the kingdom (Balzaretti 2000: 246–252; Verhulst 2002: 33).

Where several manors belonged to a single fiscal, ecclesiastic, or aristocratic landowner the land was interconnected and administered *en-bloc* – known as *grands domaines*. To ease administration and increase self-sufficiency, the holdings were rearranged through purchase or exchange to create continuous blocks of land. Such estate networks often developed a *polynuclear* structure. An important part of the peasant tenure was their obligation to transport agrarian surplus and other commodities between different parts of the estate, to where consumption took place. Beyond the propensity to concentrate landholdings around already existing properties, two basic principles seem to have guided the development toward large ecclesiastical estates; 1) a wish on behalf of the landowner to get *access to crucial natural resources*; and 2) a wish to get *access to markets*, where goods not available within the estate network could be procured and surplus production could be sold off (Toubert 1990).

There is good evidence that the large landowners actively spread their holdings to provide access to the range of resources they required – for example wine, olives, salt, fisheries, wool, metal ore, stone products and pottery (Toubert 1990: 76–78). One of the best illustrations of this situation is the blossoming salt industry of the Early Middle Ages (Bruand 2002: 185–202; Kuchenbuch 1978: 293–298; Verhulst 2002: 80–82; for the Anglo-Saxon material see Blair 1997: 84–87; Foot 1999: 48, n. 60). The Italian monastery of Bobbio acquired for example parts in the salt springs at Piancasale through an 8th century royal donation. However, the source was insufficient to supply a holding the size of Bobbio's. Towards the end of the 9th century the monastery is also recorded as one of many estates extracting salt at Comacchio in the Po estuary. In a similar manner, the monastery of Fulda was one of many ecclesiastical institutions with interests in the resources of the Frisian saline coast, in addition to salt mines in the Hessian mountains.

Small-scale involvement of secular landowners and individual farmers can be traced where the sources permit detailed investigation. However, the ability of the Church to mobilise investment capital that far outperformed most freeholders, combined with long-term investment strategies, go some way to explain why ecclesiastical estates were instrumental in the establishment of salt pans and quarrying at springs throughout 8th and 9th century Europe. Although the source material is limited, Toubert (1990: 76–78) suggests that large landowners must have dominated high-investment crafts, like the extraction and smelting of mineral ore or the manufacture of glass. While systematic organisation of the extensive landholdings made room for specialisation of individual manors, redistribution of the surplus within the polynuclear estate system secured provisioning throughout.

### The integration of estate- and market economy

Contrary to the beliefs of Gorge Duby (1962) and Henry Pirenne (1956 [1925]), the polynuclear estate-systems did however *not* form closed and self-sufficient economies. Throughout the 8th and 9th centuries, the evidence suggests that an ever-increasing part of the surplus production from the estate complexes was sold off at the nearest market (see *e.g.* Lebecq 1993, 2000; Steuer 1999; Verhulst 2002). The so-called Statutes of Abbot Adalhard of Corbie, from 822, specifies for example that manors further than 30 km away from the monastery should sell their grain surplus at nearby markets rather than transporting it to the estate centre (Verhulst and Semmler 1962). This contributed to the local grain trade and provided a silver surplus that the monks of Corbie could use to procure other extra-manorial necessities.

Most frequently mentioned among the commercialised products are wine, salt, oil, grain or flour and textiles. It is for example well attested and studied how large monastic estates like Saint-Germain-des-Prés, or Prüm in the Eiffel district, would mobilise their surplus of wine for sale. In a famous study, Jean-Pierre Devroey (1984: 577–579; *contra* Durliat 1968) argued that Saint-Germain-des-Prés not only sold its own surplus production, but also consciously purchased wine outside their estate in Angers, Orléans and Blésois for resale. In total, the monastery handled 600,000 litres of wine annually, while their own consumption hardly exceeded 100,000. This left Saint-Germain with 500,000 litres of wine to sell or exchange in other ways. The majority of this was probably disposed of through the annual fair of Saint-Denis, near Paris.

The history of the Saint-Denis market is well known, and shall not be rehearsed here (McCormick 2001: 648–653; Theuws 2004 with references). Suffice it to say that 8th century sources record the presence of Anglo-Saxons, Frisians and merchants of numerous other nations at the market, while a spurious 7th century diploma – probably reflecting the situation in the 9th century – specifies the large number of merchants from Quentowic, Rouen and Anglo-Saxon areas that travel to Paris from the seaboard. According to the same source the fair was greatly extended to accommodate also merchants from Northern Italy,

Spain and the Provence. Scandinavians may well also have been among the peoples visiting the market (Lebecq 1983: no. lxxix).

From the *Life of St. Samson of Dol-en-Bretagne* it can be discerned that the market also provided a framework for administrative exchanges between large monastic institutions. The vita, known to us from a mid-9th century redaction, describes how Samson during a journey to Paris encountered St. Germain in the vineyards surrounding his monastery. The ensuing conversation revealed that the subsistence basis of the two houses were very different. While the monastery of Dol-en-Bretagne had a large surplus production of honey and beeswax they were in short supply of wine. A reciprocal exchange between Saint-Germain and Dol would be of mutual benefit, and the saints agreed on an annual barter of one tenth of the Breton harvest of honey (and presumably wax) against one tenth of the Parisian wine.

Although the text is set in the saints' lifetime, the scene fits more comfortably the economic structures of the 8th or 9th centuries (Devroey 1984: 578–579). It is likely that the story served to explain the origin of an exchange relation between Dol-en-Bretagne and Saint-Germain, still extant around 850 but initiated some time previously. The vita indicates that the exchange took place in Paris during the annual market and that it was the Breton monks who organised the transport of the goods. Other contemporary sources indicate that also *neguntiantes* – professional merchants or transporters – could act on behalf of religious institutions on similar occasions (below).

More permanent economic links to market towns were often formalised through the presence of a small annexe (*cellae, xenodochia, mansions* or *stationes*) close to the site, or a plot of land (*sedillia)* within the urban site itself. Here, representatives of the estates could reside and buildings serve as storehouses for goods. Particularly well studied is Quentowic, situated close to the Canche estuary in Northern France (Lebecq 1993, with text references). Despite sparse archaeological knowledge of this site, unusually rich textual evidence makes it clear that a number of manorial institutions were present in the *vicus* or established in the near vicinity, and that they took advantage of the available market and port facilities.

The earliest source is a privilege from 765 revealing that the monastery of Saint-Vaast possessed a property at Campigneulles, a village some kilometres from the site now identified as Quentowic. Another diploma issued by Charles the Bold in 845 states explicitly that the monastery of Saint-Riquier controlled two plots in the port. Saint-Bertin, a third regional monastery acquired, through donation from a certain Gundbertus in 857, substantial properties in the town in addition to what the house already possessed in Tubersent nearby. Among other proprietors in Quentowic, with holdings mainly in more remote geographical areas, were the monasteries of Fontanelle and Ferrière-en-Gâtinais. Ferrière was granted the cella of Saint-Josse just outside the town by Louis the Pious, while Fontanelle controlled both the church of Saint Pierre without the town as well as plots in the vicus itself.

A closer look at the source material indicates that the economic structures found in Quentowic were replicated in several similar market towns and ports. One remarkable source – *Notitia de areis* – specifies no less than 34 tracts of land within Paris owned and rented out by the Monastery of Saint-Pierre de Fosse (later Saint-Maur) in AD 867/9. The list sets out in great formulaic detail the tenant, the location and size of the plot and its access to public streets or markets. Some of the plots were built and used for small-scale industries or storage, and the tenants were involved in trade and craft production. Together, the rent paying occupants contributed 36 solidi and 11 denari to Saint-Pierre's annual income. This is by itself an illustration of the growing importance of the monetary economy by the 9th century. However, Saint-Pierre also received rent in kind (*eulogiae)* from some tenants. This practice indicates that many of the tenants had close rural ties, and suggests that a number of the townsmen were present in Paris as representatives of rural estates from where these commodities originated.

The text also refers to 11 *other* ecclesiastical institutions and three aristocrats with property rights in the same part of Paris. The fact that neither of these possessions is known from other documents, even those of Saint-Germain-des-Prés from where extensive archives and inventories are preserved, illustrates the problematic source situation when trying to reconstruct urban property rights in the early medieval period. In the case of Saint-Pierre's Paris properties, the plots provided an annual rent and the extent of the ownership was therefore meticulously recorded. However, as Dieter Hägermann (1991: 358) has pointed out, this would not have happened if the plots were used by the owners themselves for access to the market. In most such cases, the presence of town ownership will inevitably be beyond reach of the modern historian, although some can be inferred from references in diplomas or narrative sources.

This way it can for example be deduced that that both the monasteries of Fulda and Hersfeld had properties in Mainz during the 9th century (Hägermann 1991, n. 14 with references) and that Saint-Remi de Reims controlled plots of land in Chalôns-sur-Marne and Vroil-sur-la-Chée. Saint-Amand-les-Eaux rented out two similar plots in Tournai to the abbey of Lobbes and a group of independent textile workers, in addition to controlling further areas in Dinant and Namur (Hägermann 1991: 363–364). Another chance survival reveals that the abbey of Remiremont in the early 9th century obtained assurances from Empress Judith that the lands bordering onto their houses in Chalon-sur-Saône would remain unoccupied, because the open space was essential to their trading activity (MGH Formulae Merowingici et Karolini, Formularum Epistolarum Collectiones Minores III, no. 3).

If one should generalise from these scraps of contemporary evidence I would argue that direct ecclesiastical and, to a lesser extent, lay ownership of urban properties must have been a general feature of Carolingian economy. This conclusion stands in contrast to arguments often made about royal property and toll rights, particularly in new towns like the 7th and 8th century ports in the North Sea region. The element of royal control within Scandinavian Viking-Age towns will be discussed elsewhere (Gaut in prep.). With regard to the Carolingian situation, the plots must in many cases have originated as royal property but later been abstained through political favours and acts of piety. A minority of sources illustrates that such plots could be owned by members of the aristocracy. But while the landholdings of this group frequently were subject to shifting ownership and partition, church land tended to remain under ecclesiastical control. It is therefore likely that the early medieval period saw a continuous growth of church ownership in towns, like the countryside. However, this did not necessarily imply a monopolisation of market access, as this was not in the interest of the religious institutions! Rather, they would let plots of land to aristocrats and independent entrepreneurs against an annual land rent and/or a tax on exchange that took place there.

This development is clearly observed in the property list of the episcopal *Saint-Martin's* church in Utrecht – the core of which records properties controlled by the church prior to AD 860 (Henderikx 1986: 544–546). In addition to a list of individual donations, one finds here a general reference to the right of one tenth of all royal taxes and incomes in the area – the *decima regalis.* The privilege originated at the time of Peppin III (753) but was confirmed at intervals by Charlemagne (769), Louis the Pious (815), king Zwentibold of Lotharingia (896) and Henry I (927/30). According to the diploma of Louis the Pious (Lebecq 1983: no. lxxx), the decimal-rights within Dorestad was administered through actual church ownership of one tenth of the plots in the settlement on which merchants and craftsmen – known as Saint-Martin's men – settled and paid rent. A similar arrangement is also proposed by Jan Besteman (1990: 7–9) for the subsidiary toll station of Medemblik on the coast of the Almere.

The examples serve to illustrate the significant presence of ecclesiastical landowners, and to a lesser extent secular aristocracy, within markets and ports bordering onto the North Sea region. These connections linked the rural exchange system to urban economies, and ensured that surplus production from the (largely) ecclesiastical estate networks could be sold off (Lebecq 2000; Marazzi 2003; Steuer 1999; Theuws 2004). They also created opportunities for permanently settled or visiting agents – neguntiantes – to purchase necessities for cash payment or in exchange of kind. It has been argued that this dependable availability of a rural surplus became decisive for urban growth and the development of market economy during the 8th and 9th century (Devroey 1985, 1993; Toubert 1990; Verhulst 1999).

Also narrative sources, like the letters of Abbot Lupus of Ferrière-en-Gâtinais, underline the importance of the monastic links to the urban economy. During Lupus' abbacy, in 840/42, Louis the Pious' original grant of the monastery's cella at Saint-Josse in Quentowic was revoked by Lothair I, probably as a direct result of the civil wars and partition of the empire. Until Saint-Josse was restored to Ferrières in 852, the difficult economic situation caused by the loss of resources and access to the market is a frequent topic in Lupus' writing. Among the commodities specifically mentioned procured through Saint-Josse's agency, are candle wax, clothes, fish, cheese and also vegetables. As a result of the deprivation, Lupus (in slightly argumentative terms) describes how the monks and their servants are reduced to wearing rags, rarely eating fish or cheese and being unable to provide hospitality for the many pilgrims arriving through Quentowic (Lupus: Letters nos 42, 43, 47, 48).

### Overseas trade

Another important point to make is that this market integration – especially in places like Quentowic – provided access to markets *beyond* the limits of the Carolingian realm. Too much have been written about the exclusive economic role of the emporia of the 8th and 9th centuries. It is important to keep in mind that they were not the only towns of the Viking world – not even the largest ones. They did not represent an exclusive topographical layout, nor did they serve as proto-industrial craft centres or secular alternatives to religious trade systems, although they are at times presented in all these guises (Hodges 2000: 69–118; Theuws 2004; *cf.* Verhaeghe *et al.* 2005: 267–269; Verhulst 1999, Wickham 2005: 681–692).

What was truly exceptional about the emporia was the fact that they were part of an external border control system: Merchants were liable to pay *decima* – a 10% toll – on all goods that were moved through these sites. The emporia also served as entry points for alien travellers, who underwent rigorous control to be allowed into the kingdom (Matthews 1999; Whitelock 1955: no. 197).

Many harbours and border posts also contained regulated sale- and visitation zones for foreign merchants. Studies have revealed how trade and communication was organised in a similar way throughout much of North-western Europe, and the Mediterranean world (Middleton 2005, with references). Evidence suggests that the system was based on reciprocal diplomatic agreements between regents, and that this provided stable conditions for commerce and communication. There is no room to pursue this argument, but I believe the Scandinavian Viking-Age towns primarily were established to emulate this system (Gaut in prep.). Early medieval royal prestige was tied to military force and diplomacy, but also to an ability to regulate trade and travellers.

Several diplomas indicate that also religious houses participated in trade outside the Frankish realm. In 831, Louis the Pious exempted the Church of Strasbourg of all tolls on land and waterways throughout the realm, except for in Quentowic, Dorestad and across the alpine passes (*ad clusas*) where a 10 percent toll was due (Regesta Imperii I, no. 980). Other communities were exempt customs even at the border. Charlemagne granted in 779 immunities to the community of Saint-Germain-des-Prés from all tolls throughout the realm, north and south of the Loire. The exemption included specifically the harbours of Rouen, Quentowic and Dorestad, in addition to locations in the local hinterland of the estate centre (MGH Dipl. Karol. I, no. 122; Lebecq 1983: no. lxxxi). A final example is the 753 charter of Peppin III that grants the monastery of Saint-Denis freedom from all dues and tolls throughout the realms of Frankia and Italy, whether concerning the estates of the said church or the men who live on its lands or those who are known to be engaged on its business (Lebecq 1983: no. lxxix).

Unless the monasteries actually participated in the North Sea trade, these privileges make little sense. Trade could be carried out by monks or frequently by other agents; professional merchants, dependent tenants, slaves or lay-brethren. One such character was the Frisian merchant Ibbo, who carried out trade expeditions across the sea on behalf of the abbey of St Maximin in Trier, during the late 8th century (Lebecq 1983: no. xxvii; McCormick 2001: 656).

Looking at the Anglo-Saxon charter evidence, we find that Saint-Denis also acquired land in Rotherfield, Hastings and Pevensey in Sussex in 790, and was granted privileges for land in Lundenwic (Sawyer 1968, nos 1186 and 133). The latter charter is admittedly not an original, but it is confirmed in 857 and 960 (Sawyer 1968, nos 318 and 686), and I have not seen any convincing reason for why the early charter should have been forged. An educated guess is that the charters refer to the presence in London of agents involved in trade on behalf of the Paris monastery. A lively cross-Channel exchange is well attested elsewhere (McCormick 2001: 639–663; Wickham 2005: 794–819).

Also Anglo-Saxon bishops and religious houses – like Minster-in-Thanet – must have traded under similar privileges (Blair 2005: 251–263; Kelly 1992). The rights were typically specified for a certain number of boats; whether manned by monks and lay-brothers, or dependant merchants trading on their behalf. Sarah Foot (1999: 47–48) lists the involvement of the Church in salt industry and iron- and lead-working. The Bishop of Worcester, whose estates lay largely in the West Midlands, traded for example with two ships on London; presumably bringing produce from his properties to the Continental markets (Sawyer 1968, no. 98). It is assumed that other rich minsters had similar interests in (overseas) trade. The Anglo-Saxon evidence is however more limited than the Frankish, because only a minority of ecclesiastical archives have been preserved.

### A Scandinavian connection?

The question is to what extent similar exchange structures influenced trade and urbanisation in Scandinavia? This is difficult to answer with confidence, because there are few contemporary descriptions of the region. It is nevertheless clear that Kaupang and other urban settlements around the North Sea flourished through the distribution of Continental goods and that ecclesiastical landowners partook in the production of these.

The early Scandinavian mission clearly focussed on urban markets, where many Continental merchants resided. According to the 9th century *Life of Ansgar*, missionaries representing both the Bishop of Reims and the monastery of Corvey visited Birka, Haithabu and Ribe and settled there. The construction of a church in Haithabu is said to have increased the population and trading activity greatly. Although the religious gloss is difficult to accept for a modern reader, the importance of pastoral care and the physical presence of the Church should not be underestimated. To the early medieval mind, Scandinavia was situated at the end of the world, and localised pastoral care would be an important element in the spiritual battle for the territory and the merchants' souls (Wood 1987).

Judging from Rimbert's text, both the missionaries and the foreign inhabitants maintained close contact with their home communities. The text also provides a picture of a mission that depended on continuous donations and resources from their Continental landholdings to finance their presence. Although the vita is preoccupied with religious books and vestments, these supplies could well have comprised food and commodities for daily upkeep. Possibly, missionaries and mercantile agents also took advantage of their long-distance liaisons to make dividends on trade, like we have seen agents from other ecclesiastical institutions do in Carolingian and Anglo-Saxon towns. It is thus not unlikely that envoys from Reims, Corvey or other religious houses participated in the supply of raw materials and other commodities to Haithabu, Birka and Kaupang.

Isotope analyses reveal for example that lead found at Kaupang is likely to originate in England (Pedersen 2010: 272–284) – possibly the Peak-District where Repton Abbey and Hanbury Minster had mining interests (Sawyer 1968, nos 190, 1624). Similarly, the monastery of Prüm and the Archbishop of Cologne controlled land in pottery and glass producing regions (Verhulst 2002: 79–83, with references). Such products were distributed throughout Scandinavia and could well originate from ecclesiastical estates, but it is currently impossible to correlate information about property structure, specific kilns or mines and individual products.

The purchase and release (or fostering) of slaves was an important element of pastoral care and missionary work of the period. Ansgar is said to have given up his cloak to free a slave and Rimbert forfeited both his horse and several liturgical vessels to the same end (*Vita Rimberti,* Chapters 17 and 18). A reference in the contemporary *Life of Filibert* indicates that the required resources also could come directly from trade within the estate system:

> When, through royal munificence and the gifts of the faithful, a large amount of silver had come to him [Abbot Filibert], he carefully selected a tenth of the goods as an offering. But at the end of every year, he always found that the goods added up to more than before he had taken a tenth:
>
> *He therefore used that tenth to pay for the release of prisoners and as alms for the poor, so much so that he sent his monks across the sea in fully loaded boats, and flocks of captives redeemed by him praised the power of Christ.* (Life of Filibert, Chapter 23, translation by John Clay, emphasis added)

Although, the source is not concerned with Scandinavian conditions, it illustrates a practice where missionary activity and trade could exist side by side.

There is a longstanding Scandinavian tradition to study the influence of the tithe and ecclesiastical landholdings on the late medieval urban economy (*e.g.* Bull 1931). I have pointed out that polynuclear estate-systems directed commodities toward the emerging urban centres already in the Viking Age. Large religious institutions were involved in craft production and exchange both within and without the Carolingian realm. Agents, and to a lesser extent monks, partook in commercial voyages and settled overseas as representatives of their institutions. These envoys would depend on supplies for upkeep and valuables to invest in commercial goods that their estate centres required.

Any Scandinavian mercantile activities on behalf of ecclesiastical institutions are obscured by the later conversion history. Although there are no indications that Continental religious houses established estates in Scandinavia as early as the 9th or 10th centuries (Hybel 2011), it is possible to substantiate that their representatives established themselves in market towns. This introduction of a new social group must have implications for our interpretation of mercantile and social dynamics in the market towns. Representatives of religious houses had potentially very different agendas to independent merchants and artisans, and they were tied by other social obligations.

## *References*

Ambrosiani, Björn and Mathias Bäck
2007. "Our Man in Pskov" – Birka's Baltic connection in the 9th and 10th centuries: pottery as a source for tracing cultural interaction. In *Cultural Interaction between East and West. Archaeology, Artefacts and Human Contacts in Northern Europe*, edited by Ulf Fransson, Marie Svedin, Sofie Bergerbrant and Fadir Androshchuk, pp. 180–184. Stockholm studies in Archaeology, Vol. 44. Stockholm University, Stockholm.

Arbman, Holger

1937. *Sweden und das Karolingische Reich. Studien zu den Handelsverbindung des 9. Jahrhunderts.* Wahlström and Widstrand, Stockholm.

Balzaretti, Ross

2000. Monasteries, towns and the Countryside: reciprocal Relationships in the Archdiocese of Milan, 614–814. In *Towns and their Territories in Late Antiquity and the Early Middle Ages*, edited by Gian Pietro Brogiolo, Nancy Gauthier, Neil Christie, pp. 235–257. The Transformation of the Roman World: a scientific programme of the European Science Foundation, Vol. 9. Brill, Leiden.

Besteman, Jan

1989. The pre-urban development of Medemblik: From an early medieval trading centre to a medieval town. In *Medemblik and Monnickendam: Aspects of medieval urbanization in northern Holland*, edited by H. A. Heidinga and H. H. van Regteren Altena, pp. 1–30. Cingula, Vol. 11. Universiteit van Amsterdam, Albert Egges van Giffen Instituut voor Prae- en Protohistorie, Amsterdam.

Blair, John

1997. *Anglo-Saxon Oxfordshire.* Alan Sutton, Stroud.

2005. *The Church in Anglo-Saxon Society.* Oxford University Press, Oxford.

Bruand, Olivier

2002. *Voyageurs et marchandises aux temps carolingiens. Les réseaux de communication entre Loire et Meusse aux VIIIe et IXe siècles.* Bibliotheque du moyen âge 20, Brussels.

Bull, Edvard

1931. *Fra omkring 1000 til 1280.* Det norske folks liv og historie gjennem tidene, Vol. 2. Aschehoug, Oslo.

Callmer, Johan

1998. Archaeological sources for the presence of Frisian agents of trade in northern Europe *c.* AD 700–900. In *Studien zur Archäologie des Ostseeraumes. Von der Eisenzeit zum Mittelalter. Festschrift für Michael Müller-Wille*, edited by Anke Wesse and Michael Müller-Wille, pp. 469–481. Wachholtz, Neumünster.

2002. North-European trading centres and the early medieval craftsman. Craftsmen at Åhus, north-eastern Scania, Sweden *c.* AD 750–850+. In *Central Places in the Migration and the Merovingian Periods. Papers from the 52 Sachsensymposium, Lund, August 2001*, edited by Birgitta Hårdt and Lars Larsson, pp. 125–157. Uppåkrastudier, Vol. 6 and Acta archaeologica Lundensia series in 8°, Vol. 39. Almqvist and Wiksell, Stockholm.

Davies, R. H. C.

1987. Domesday Book: continental parallels. In *Domesday Studies: Papers read at the Novocentenary Conference of the Royal Historical Society*, edited by James Carl Holt, pp. 15–39. Boydell Press, Woodbridge.

Despy, George

1968. Villes et campagnes aux IXe et Xe siecles. L'exemple du pays mosan. *Revue du Nord* 50: 145–168.

Devroey, Jean-Pierre

1984. Un monastère dans l'économie d'échanges: les services de transport à l'abbaye de St Germain-des-Prés au IXème siècle. *Annales. Economies Société Civilisation* 39: 570–589.

1985. Réflexion sur les premiers temps carolingiens (768–877): Grands domaines et action politique entre Seine et Rhin. *Beihefte der Francia* 13: 475–488.

1993. "Ad utilitatem monasterii": Mobiles et préoccupations de gestion dans l'économie monastique du monde franc. *Revue Bénédictine* 103: 224–240.

Duby, George
1962. *L'économie rurale et la vie des campagnes dans l'Occidentale médiéval.* Paris.
Durliat, Jean
1968. La vigne et le vin dans la région parisienne au début du IXe siècle d'apres le polyptyque d'Irminon. *Le Moyen Age* 74: 387–419.
Flobert, P. (editor)
1897. *La vie ancienne de saint Samson de Dol.* Paris.
Foot, Sarah
1999. The Role of the Minster in Earlier Anglo-Saxon Society. In *Monasteries and Society in Medieval Britain. Proceedings of the 1994 Harlaxton Symposium*, edited by Benjamin Thompson, pp. 35–58. Paul Watkins, Stamford.
Gaut, Bjarne
2011. Vessel glass and Evidence of Beadmaking. In *Things from the Town: Artefacts and Inhabitants in Viking-Age Kaupang*, edited by Dagfinn Skre, pp. 169–279. Kaupang Excavation Project Publication Series, Vol. 3 and Norske Oldfunn, Vol. 24. Aarhus University Press, Århus.
in prep *Manors, Missionaries and Markets: Continental perspectives on Viking Age trade and exchange.* Ph.D. dissertation, University of Oslo.
Grierson, Philip
1959. Commerce in the Dark Ages: A critique of the evidence. *Transactions of the Royal Historical Society* 9: 123–140.
Grierson, Philip and Mark Blackburn
1986. *The Early Middle Ages: 5th–10th Centuries.* Medieval European Coinage, Vol. 1. Cambridge University Press, Cambridge.
Hägermann, Dieter
1991. Grundherrschaft und städtischer Besitz in urbarialen Quellen des 9. Jahrhunderts (Saint-Maur-des-Fossés, Saint-Remi de Reims und Saint-Amand-les-Eaux). In *Villes et campagnes au Moyen-Age. Mélanges G. Despy*, edited by Jean-Marie Duvosquel and Alain Dierkens, pp. 355–365. Éditions du Perron, Liège.
Hägermann, Dieter, Konrad Elmshäuser and Andreas Hedwig (editors)
1993. *Das Polyptychon von Saint-Germain des-Prés.* Böhlau, Köln.
Hägermann, Dieter and Andreas Hedwig (editors)
1989. *Das Polyptychon und die Notitia de Areis von Saint-Maur-des-Fossés.* Sigmaringen.
Henderikx, P. A.
1986. The Lower Delta of the Rhine and teh Maas: Landscape and habitation from the Roman Period to *c.* 1000. *Berichten ROB* 36: 447–599.
Hill, David and Robert Cowie (editors)
2001. *Wics: The Early Medieval Trading Centres of Northern Europe.* Sheffield Archaeological Monographs, Vol. 14. Sheffield Academic Press, Sheffield.
Hodges, Richard
2000. *Towns and Trade in the Age of Charlemagne.* Duckworth debates in archaeology. Duckworth, London.
Hybel, Nils
2011. The Roman Catholic Institutions and the Creation of Large Landed Estates in Denmark. In *Settlement and Lordship in Viking and Early Medieval Scandinavia*, edited by Bjørn Poulsen and Søren M. Sindbæk, pp. 223–238. The Medieval Countryside, Vol. 9. Brepols, Turnhout.
Herbert Jankuhn
1986 [1956] *Haithabu: Ein Handelsplatz der Wikingerzeit.* 8th edn. Karl Wachholtz Verlag, Neumünster.

Kelly, Susan

1992. Trading privileges from eight-century England. *Early Medieval Europe* 1: 3–28.

Kuchenbuch, Ludolf

1978. *Bäuerliche Gesellschaft und Kloseterrherschaft im 9. Jahrhundert. Studien zur Sozialstruktur der familia der Abtei Prüm.* Vierteljahrschriften für Sozial- und Wirtschafsgeschichte. Beihefte, Vol. 66. Franz Steiner, Wiesbaden.

Lebecq, Stéphane

1983. *Marchands et navigateurs frisons du haute moyen âge.* 2 vols. Lille.

1993. Quentovic: Un état de la question. In *Studien zur Sachsenforschung 8. Beiträge vom 39. Sachsensymposion in Caen, Normandie 12. bis 16. September 1988*, pp. 73–82. Hildesheim.

2000. The role of the monasteries in the systems of production and exchange of the Frankish world between the seventh and the beginning of the ninth centuries. In *The Long Eighth Century (Production Distribution and Demand)*, edited by Inge Lyse Hansen and Chris Wickham, pp. 121–148. Transformation of the Roman World, Vol. 11. Brill, Leiden.

Levison, William (editor).

1910. *Vita Filiberti abbatis gemeticensis et heriensis.* MGH SS rer. Merov. 5, pp. 583–604, Hannover.

Lohier, F. and R. P. J. Laporte (editors)

1936. *Gesta Sanctorum Fontanellensis coenobii.* Paris.

Loveluck, Chris

2005. Rural settlement hierarchy in the age of Charlemagne. In *Charlemagne: Empire and Society*, edited by Joanna Story, pp. 230–258. Manchester University Press, Manchester.

Loyn, Henry and Parcival, John

1975. *The Reign of Charlemagne: Documents on Carolingian Government and Administration.* Documents of Medieval History, Vol. 2. St. Martins, London.

Marazzi, Frederico

2003. The early medieval alternative: monasteries as centres of non city-based economic systems in Italy between eighth and ninth century A.D. In *Nourrir les cites de Méditerranée: Antiquité – Temps Modernes*, edited by Birgitte Marin and Caterine Virlouvet, pp. 739–767. L'atelier méditerranéen. Maison méditerranéenne des sciences de l'homme. Aix-en-Provence.

Matthews, Stephen

1999. Frontier Controls and Evasion in Early Medieval Europe. *Medieval Life* 12: 7–12.

McCormick, Michael

2001. *Origins of the European Economy. Communications and Commerce, AD 300–900.* Cam-bridge University Press, Cambridge.

Middleton, Neil

2005. Early medieval port customs, tolls and controls on foreign trade. *Early Medieval Europe* 13: 313–358.

Moreland, John

2000. Concepts of the Early Medieval economy. In *The Long Eighth Century (Production Distribution and Demand)*, edited by Inge Lyse Hansen and Chris Wickham, pp. 1–34. The Transformation of the Roman World, Vol. 11. Brill, Leiden.

Morimoto, Yoshiki

2001. Aspects of the Early Medieval peasant economy as revealed in the polyptych of Prüm. In *The Medieval World*, edited by Peter Linehan and Janet L. Nelson, pp. 605–620. Routledge, London.

Pedersen, Unn

2010. *I smeltedigelen: Finsmedene i vikingtidsbyen Kaupang.* Ph.D. dissertation, University of Oslo.

Perring, Dominic and Mark Whyman
2002. *Town and Country in England: Frameworks for Archaeological Research.* CBA Research Report 134. Council for British Archaeology, York.
Pirenne, Henry
1956. [1925] *Medieval Cities. Their Origins and the Revival of Trade.* Translated by F. D. Halsey. Revised edn. Doubleday Anchor Books, New York.
Rimbert: Ansgars liv
1986. In *Boken om Ansgar. Ansgars liv,* translated by Eva Odelman, with comments by Anders Ekenberg. Skrifter, Samfundet Pro fide et christianismo, Vol. 10. Stockholm.
Sawyer, P. H.
1968. *Anglo-Saxon Charters: an annotated list and bibliography.* Handbook of the Royal Historical Society, Vol. 8. Royal Historical Society, London.
Skre, Dagfinn
2011. The Inhabitants: Origins and Trading connections. In *Things from the Town: Artefacts and inhabitants in Viking-Age Kaupang,* edited by Dagfinn Skre, pp. 417–441. Kaupang Excavation Project Publications Series, Vol. 3. Norske Oldfunn 24. Aarhus University Press, Århus.
Steuer, Heiko
1987. Der Handel zwischen Nord- und Westeuropa aufgrund archäologische Zeugnisse. In *Der Handel der Karolinger- und Wikingerzeit,* edited by Klaus Düwel, Herbert Jankuhn, Harald Siems und Dieter Timpe, pp. 113–197. Untersuchungen zu Handel und Verkehr der vor- und frühgeschichlichen Zeit in Mittel- und Nord-Europa, Vol. 4 and Abhandlungen der Akademie der Wissenschaften, Phil.-Hist. Klasse, 3. series, Vol. 156. Göttingen.
1989. Archaeology and history: proposals on the social structure of the Merovingian Kingdom. In *The Birth of Europe; Archaeology and Social Development in the First Millennium AD,* edited by Klaus Randsborg, pp. 100–122. Analecta Romana Instituti Danici Supplementum 16, Vol. L'Erma di Bretschneider, Roma.
1999. Handel und Wirtschaft in der Karolingerzeit. In *Beiträge zum Katalog der Ausstellung,* edited by C. Stiegemann and M. Wemhoff, pp. 406–416. 799: Kunst und Kultur der Karolingerzeit. Karl der Große und Papst Leo III. in Paderborn, Vol. 3. Philip von Zabern Verlag, Mainz.
The Letters of Lupus of Ferrières
[1966] Translated with an introduction and notes by Regenos, Graydon W. Hague.
Theuws, Frans
1990. Centre and periphery in Northern Austrasia (6th–8th centuries). An archaeological perspective. In *Medieval Archaeology in the Netherlands: Studies Presented to H. H. van Regteren Altena,* edited by J. C. Besteman, J. M. Bos, H. A. Heidinga, pp. 41–69. Universiteit van Amsterdam, Assen.
2004. Exchange, religion, identity and central places in the early Middle Ages. *Archaeological Dialogues* 10: 121–138.
Toubert, Pierre
1990. La part du grand domaine dans le décollage économique de l'Occident (8–10e siècles). *La croissance agricole au moyen-âge: Chronologie, modalités, géographie,* pp. 53–86. Abbaye de Flaran, Vol. 10. Editions Bière.
Verhaeghe, Frans with Chris Loveluck and Joanna Story
2005. Urban developments in the age of Charlemagne. In *Charlemagne: Empire and Society,* edited by Joanna Story, pp. 259–287. Manchester University Press, Manchester.
Verhulst, Adriaan
1999. *The Rise of Cities in North-West Europe.* Themes in International Urban History, Vol. 4. Cambridge University Press, Cambridge.

2002. *The Carolingian Economy.* Cambridge Medieval Textbooks. Cambridge University Press, Cambridge.
Verhulst, Adrian and Josef Semmler
1962. Les statuts d'Adalhard de Corbie de l'an 822. *Le Moyen Age* 68: 91–123, 233–269.
Waitz, Georg (editor)
1884. *Vita Ankarii Auctore Rimberto. Accedit Vita Rimberti.* MGH SS rer. Germ. 55. Hannover.
Whitelock, Dorothy
1955. *English Historical Documents I, c. 500–1042.* Methuen, London.
Wickham, Chris
2005. *Framing the early Middle Ages: Europe and the Mediterranean, 400–800.* Oxford University Press.
Wood, Ian
1987. Christians and pagans in ninth-century Scandinavia. In *The Christianization of Scandinavia. Report of a Symposium held at Kungälv, Sweden 4–9 August 1985*, edited by Birgit Sawyer, Peter Sawyer and Ian Wood, pp. 36–67. Viktoria Bokförlag, Alingsås.

*Chapter 11*

# Making the cloth that binds us. The role of textile production in producing Viking-Age identities

*Ben Cartwright*

*Abstract*

It is difficult to overstate the importance of textile production to a Viking-Age way of life. From sails, to sacking, cloth as a tradable asset, and the clothes that allowed individuals to go out into land and seascapes, textiles were central to a specific way of being in the world. But what of those who were responsible for this never ending production, how did this demand shape and facilitate their experience of being of that age? Using the example of the Merovingian to Viking-Age site of Bjørkum, Lærdal, Norway, this paper will investigate how the processes of spinning and weaving were connected to a (non-static) sense of landscape, community and self. If spinning and weaving, and the seasonal rhythms of climbing to upland shielings and meeting points were features of an interconnected pre-'Viking World'-view, how significant might a potential Viking-Age change in production have been?

## Textile production and the Viking Age

The Viking Age seems to have been a period of textile revolution. From heavy weather gear to elite garments, textiles were at the heart of daily life. The exploitation of the sea-routes, so central to the Viking-Age economy (*e.g.* Skre 2011), were bound up in textile demands, for example, sailcloth (a technological pre-requisite for the Viking Age) and shaggy ocean-going pile cloaks. The cloaks have been found in Viking graves beside the west way from western Norway across the top of Scotland and down into the Irish Sea, and are known to have been manufactured in sites across the Viking world, such as in Birka, York and Iceland (Bender Jørgensen 2012; Geijer 1938; Guðjónsson 1962; Henshall 1952; Pritchard 1992; Walton 1989).

The warp-weighted loom was the primary tool for textile production in the Viking Age. The study of the loom and habits of weaving, are therefore, important factors in the reconstruction of 'society as a whole' (*e.g.* Brink 2008: 4). The weaving of warp and weft threads represents more than a knot in a fabric. They are symbolic of a series of processes based in loom and textile demands that spread out like paths across the landscape. This rhythm of particular activities and exposure to particular places at certain time of the year, by certain people, has been termed the 'performance of rurality' (Wood 2010).

Producing textiles at the loom created, in part, the habits of locality. Agricultural cycles were intimately linked to cloth demands, from clothing lists, and furnishings, through to the more mundane items to aid lifting and transport of produce not to mention the sheep themselves. This combination of fabric types allowed inhabitants to go out into land/seascapes, and attach meanings to the natural features they came into contact with, that then re-emerged in the stories that created a sense of 'home' (*e.g.* Hastrup 2008).

It has been argued that the demands for new types of cloth in Merovingian and Viking-Age Norway, may have irreversibly altered how people performed rurality. For example, the potential expansion of heathland for coastal grazing in Norway, based on pollen data, may well be linked to the need to produce larger amounts of specific fabric types (Bender Jørgensen 2012: 173, 179). Less known is the effect on upland areas where shieling systems created a bi-annual social world, transporting families and livestock from more isolated winter farmsteads to the outdoor social freedom of summer grazing sites in the hills (Lucas 2008; Magnus 2002; Stewart 2005). Central to these social worlds were activities related to the production of textiles (*e.g.* Larson 2001).

The case study of Bjørkum, Lærdal, Norway, provides a chance to study two ubiquitous skill sets – spinning and weaving, in a specific locality. The site occupied a valley floor during summertime, in the Lærdal valley, Sogn og Fjordane. It was surrounded by upland shielings (*e.g.* Bjørgo *et al.* 1992). The site was made up of several pit-house and three-aisled structures. It was probably occupied by a transient craft population, based on finds of slag, comb-making debris, beads and other artefacts including those for textile production (Ramstad 2011; see also Cartwright 2012).

Chronologically, Bjørkum spans the birth of the Viking Age, from the late Merovingian period, through to the early 11th century AD. As such, it adds to the regional picture of continuity and change as suggested in several recent studies on 'farming systems' (*e.g.* Øye 2003), and textile production (*e.g.* Bender Jørgensen 1986), not to mention changes in trade and landscape use during the establishment of the proto-urban sites further to the south (Sindbæk 2009; Skre 2007). By assessing the socio-historical shifts in demand for particular products, I hope to add a more human element by focusing on what these shifts in demand may have meant for their producers, both physically, and also as part of a community.

## Crafting: What we make makes us

It is often stated that crafting crafts the practitioner, that what we make, makes us (*e.g.* Heidegger 2010: 404; see also Miller 2009: 13; Sennet 2008). Much of what people think about the world around them, their emotional attachments, comes from what they learn in social interactions, the stories, little rituals and conversations that shape their way of seeing a place. In this case, crafting, as a social experience, shapes the crafters – what they make, makes them.

The crafts of spinning and weaving were no exception to this. By investigating skill sets, as learnt histories of body movement, handed down over the generations, we can study how people were both influenced by and, at the same time, influencing the social and material worlds they lived in (Cartwright in prep. a). Continuities and changes in traditions of practice have ramifications for the creation of systems of value. And as such, the study of craft over time is a study of community and self.

From its emergence in the Migration period, the warp-weighted loom (and by association, spindle whorls) seems to represent a more than physical 'manufacture'. A variety of evidence suggests an association between women, spinning and weaving with the production of fate (*e.g.* Magnusson and Pálsson 1960). From the loomweights included in the elite female grave at Vorbasse, Denmark in the 3rd century AD (Andersson Strand and Mannering 2011), through to Viking-Age similarities between distaffs and sorceresses' staves (Gardeła 2008; Heide 2006; Price 2007) and later eddic and saga narratives, textile production seems to have been a context where Viking world-views were rewoven. This evidence as well as ethno-historic parallels, suggest that the working groups or 'communities of practice' (Wenger 1998) involved with the loom are likely to have been gendered (*e.g.* Magnusson and Pálsson 1960: 349–351; see also Hoffmann 1964; Larson 2001; Milek 2012; Naji 2009). Early Viking-Age burials where textile equipment is placed alongside the female deceased, and later written sources suggest that textile production was a key element in essentialised notions of being female.

A group of practitioners, rather than an individual, is suggested by the size of the looms. This can be observed roughly in the length of loom-weights when found *in situ*. Or by the parts, for example, the warp beam from the Farm Beneath the Sand is 195 cm in length (Østergård 2009: 59). It is also suggested by the evidence for related tasks in the same context (*e.g.* Milek 2012). Related tasks, such as warping, often required more than one set of hands (in historic sources, ethnographic and ethnohistoric research, *e.g.*, Hoffmann 1964; Magnusson and Pálsson 1960; Naji 2009).

Learning the skill sets would have been done by apprenticeship starting in early childhood. The hours spent honing particular actions, learnt from older hands, meant that by the time practitioners reached adulthood many of the skills probably had become second nature. Historic accounts from Norway state that children as young as six years were involved in related tasks, such as dye plant gathering and material sorting (Larson 2001). Their education would have incorporated the social values of the weaving groups.

Textile production is intimately involved in the habit of locality. Craft brings people together; certain people in certain contexts. Traditionally, this was important in the dispersed communities of the rural Atlantic North where seasonal demands meant that people spent a lot of time working on their own. In textile production the harvesting and carding of the wool are examples of activities that were often turned into social events. For example, in Shetland it was an old joke that these might be the only times you would see husband and wife together in public (Mylne 2011: 104).

These task-specific gatherings acted as nodal points (*e.g.* Sindbæk 2007: 64) in the spread of information between peers. So while the production of cloth at the loom was a gendered task, textile production at large functioned within and contributed to the reproduction of wider cosmologies, setting up contexts where knowledge could be modified and transferred. These craft-related contexts would have valued, and given weight to, knowledge that was acquired and reborn in the practice of weaving and spinning. For example, spinners could apply and communicate a specific knowledge set in the often more communal tasks of rooing (essentially plucking the wool) or shearing. Certain types of fibre, from different ages of animal, are required for certain textiles. In every fleece there are several different grades of wool. Depending on which part of the animal it is gathered from, and whether it is guard or underhair, the properties of any given spun yarn can vary enormously (Christiansen 2004).

The planning ahead for certain textile demands was intimately linked to these tasks. For example, reconstructions have suggested that the yarn used in shiny mittens used by Lofoten fishermen in historic periods were best when from a ewe lamb of 3 years with no pregnancies (Bender Jørgensen 2012: 175). This hints at a very intimate knowledge of annual cycles in the landscape by those producing textiles. In historic periods, the female head of an inland rural household was also expected to plan ahead for the following years concerning warp and weft needs (Larson 2001). In the 19th and 20th century, farmers' wives kept lists for that year's textile output. They recorded a full range of clothing from work outfits to undergarments, to daughter's wedding dresses, clothing for the hired help, bedding, and, if there was time, ornamental coverlets (Larson 2001).

Textile production in Viking-Age Norway displays many characteristics that indicate similar levels of organisation. The range of textiles requiring different yarn types and preparation, from sacking to sail cloth, not to mention the fine cloth found in elite burials, suggests a multi-faceted economy that would have had to be planned for. Specific localities would have had to deal with these demands in conjunction with the landscape conditions they functioned within.

The case study of Bjørkum, Lærdal, Norway, provides a unique chance to study the role of cloth production at a seasonal production site in the uplands where east met west. Of interest is its relation to many of the social shifts involved in upland use as a practicing of rurality that seems to be intimately implicated in the birth of the Viking Age (Kaland 1987: Magnus 2002; Øye 2003).

### Bjørkum, Lærdal, Norway

Bjørkum was discovered in 2009 by the University Museum of Bergen Archaeology Unit (Ramstad 2011). The site itself is located half way down the Lærdal valley, which links the Atlantic fjordal network of Sognefjorden with the mountainous interior of eastern Norway (Fig. 11.1). The site was unexpected; what was thought to be a routine survey before the expansion of the valley floor road, yielded 15 pit-houses and two or three three-aisled structures dating from the Merovingian period into the Viking Age. The post-excavation analyses are ongoing (Cartwright in prep. b; Ramstad in prep.). The interpretation presented here is therefore a work in progress.

Based on radiocarbon dating, the site would appear to have two main periods of use: a primary phase AD 700–850, and subsequent and less substantial reuse of one of the three-

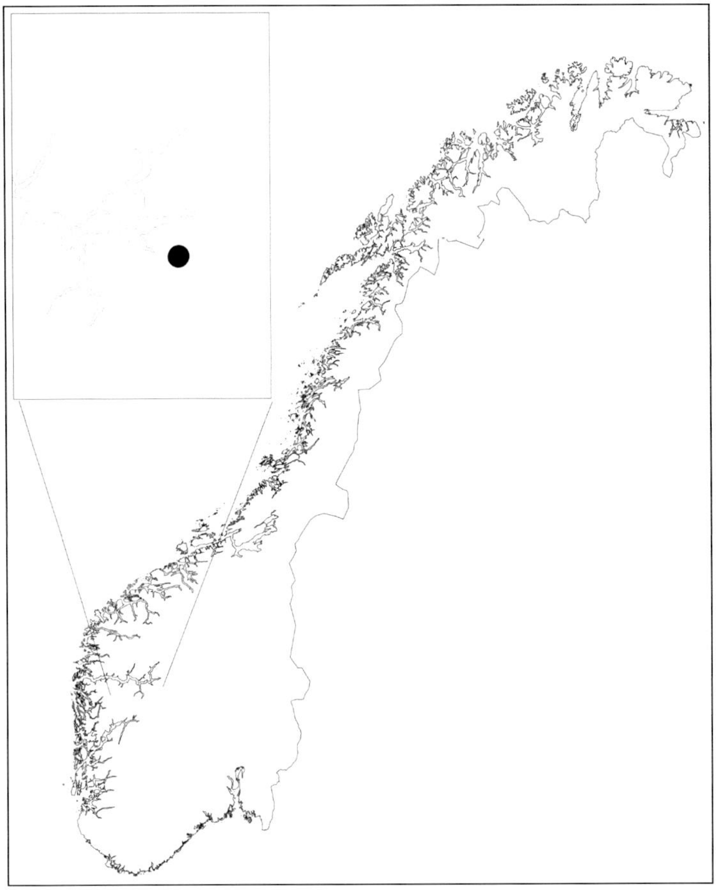

*Fig. 11.1. Map with Bjørkum. Illustration: © Ben Cartwright.*

aisled structures, Structure 1, in AD 950–1050. The pit-houses were shallow tented structures with no evidence for walling, and were surrounded by outdoor cooking pits. They have more in common with similar temporary constructions at sites such as Tissø, Denmark, where they are also thought to have been used during seasonal meetings in the summer, focused on the cultic centre of the hall (Nørgård Jørgensen *et al.* 2011). It seems unlikely, given the winter conditions, that this was a permanently occupied site (Ramstad in prep.). Historic records suggest rough winters, and for much of the excavation, shadows from the surrounding hills meant the ground was frozen solid (Nørgård Jørgensen *et al.* 2011).

The three-aisled structures and pit-houses were not built in the style of permanent dwellings. The pit-houses at Bjørkum are unlike the more substantial and permanent pit-houses with walling and roofs known from numerous Viking-Age sites. At Stedje, Sogndal, which is in relative proximity to Bjørkum, the pit-houses had internal hearths and were clustered around a three-aisled hall (Mortensen 1997, 1998: 187, 192–193). There are also examples of the use of more substantial pit-houses in Ribe, Denmark (Bender Jørgensen 1991), Iceland (Milek 2012), and Anglo-Saxon England (Walton Rogers 2007).

Artefacts from the site included faunal remains and numerous fish bones from the adjacent Lærdal River. So plentifully stocked is this river that the Crown traditionally held the fishing rights (Ramstad, pers. comm.). There was also evidence for manufacture: comb making debris, slag and a wealth of textile related equipment, including 27 loomweights, 20 spindle whorls, needles, a bone distaff, and beads of glass, amber and rock crystal, including a roughout, some of which were gold foiled – that could have been used as separate accessories and/or to adorn textiles (*e.g.*, Geijer 1979: 215–217; see also Heckett 1990: 95; Wincott Heckett 2003).

The site is surrounded by upland shieling sites (Bjørgo *et al.* 1992). This might suggest that it functioned within a seasonal movement from farmstead to upland pasture. Bjørkum also lies close to a potential thing site and a *skeid* (Ramstad 2011). Both sites were sites of meeting for dispersed rural communities. The *skeid* was a carnivalesque celebration. Events traditionally included stallion fighting, and strange inversions of social relationships (Stylegar 2010). Likewise, a possible thing site close by would also suggest a link between the valley floor site of Bjørkum and a summer rhythm of movement and meeting in the valley and adjacent hills. In the early phase clientele from seasonal assembly sites may have offered a clientele for the weavers at Bjørkum.

It would appear that this pattern of seasonality changed at some stage in the later Viking Age. A large farm appears to have been established in the later Viking Age outside the periphery of the excavation. An associated late Viking-Age/medieval smithy was excavated around 15–20 m to the west of the settlement site. The farm was probably associated with a medieval market (Ramstad 2011). This would seem to suggest that changes in landscape use at Bjørkum might mirror those from upland Norway where new house sites, tenancy and land management strategies were a feature of the Late Viking Age to early medieval period (Øye 2003: 408).

## Textile history

Sogn og Fjordane has a rich archaeological textile history with ten finely furnished so-called male 'warrior burials' from the Migration period. Perhaps the best known of which, Evebø/Eide contained a variety of cloth types synonymous with the age: polychrome dyed fabrics, tablet woven bands displaying animal motifs, and a cloak of dog tooth check (Bender Jørgensen 1986: 309–310). The predominant cloth type of the period is Haraldskjær twill, a 2/2 twill, where the weft threads go over then under two warp threads (Fig. 11.2). The warp and weft are spun z/z, where z and s refer to the spin directions, clockwise and anti-clockwise. The fabric has thread counts concentrated around 10–13 threads per cm (Bender Jørgensen 1986: 309–310, 1992: 138).

At Evebø/Eide these twills were finer, along with two tunics, trousers and a cloak having thread counts of 14–16 to 18–20 threads per cm (Halvorsen 2012: 286). Tablet weaving, especially brocaded bands, is a speciality of the period, the bands often being used as cuffs

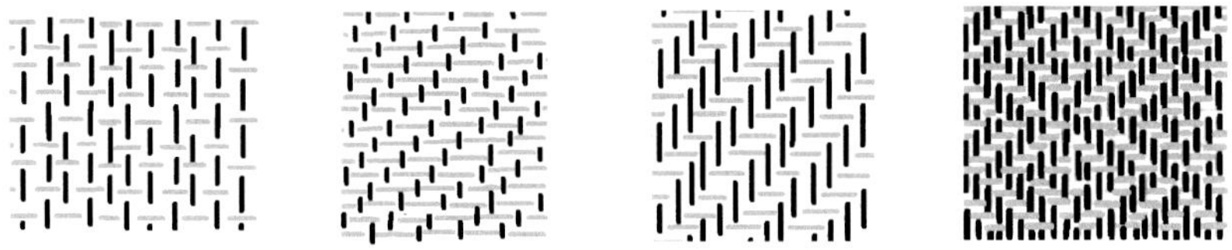

*Fig. 11.2. From left to right: Schematic drawings of tabby, 2/1 twill, and 2/2 twill. Drawing: Ben Cartwright (after Hoffmann 1964).*

finished in bronze clasps. The finds from Ugulen, Luster, Sogn og Fjordane include such a band that would have required 80 tablets for its construction (Halvorsen 2012: 286). There were no finds of tablets at Bjørkum. They are, however, very rare finds from settlement sites of the period.

Although the evidence is smaller in the Merovingian period, textiles appear to change dramatically in this period, with a greater variety of cloth types. Most notable is the increase in tabby weave, where the weft weaves over one under one warp thread, in z/z, and 2/2 twills in z/s (Bender Jørgensen 1986: 315). The ways textiles were being produced had changed, yarn was being spun differently, looms were being set up to weave in tabby and a new 2/2 twill (see below), and many of the fabrics had higher thread counts. While some thread counts overlap with previous concentrations around 10–13 threads per cm, there is a new preference for fabrics with between 18–30 and 35–40 threads per cm (Bender Jørgensen 1986: 309–310, 315).

The production of the 2/2 twills in z/z spun yarn, so resonant with the Migration Age, also changes. Its production in other Scandinavian countries declines in favour of other cloth types such as linen tabby (Bender Jørgensen 1992: 138). But in Norway it evolves into a new type. The warp for the 2/2 twill is spun hard and the weft spun soft and spinners were selecting different grades of wool for each, the cloth having the quality of tweed. Lise Bender Jørgensen has named this the Veka type, noting that the warp was often dyed blue, creating a diagonal contrast with the natural weft (Bender Jørgensen 1986: 321–324, 1992: 138). The range of textile demands and fibre sourcing would suggest a significant amount of organisation, as seen in later historic records (see above).

The Veka type would suggest that sheep breeding and production techniques were specialised and specifically 'Norwegian' by this period (Bender Jørgensen 1986: 321–324, 1992: 138). There are, however, some potential regional differences. The South-East being different to the West (including Sogn og Fjordane) in having a larger number of tabbies, and corresponding proportions of different weave types that better corresponds with Denmark, while the Veka type seems to be more common in the West (Bender Jørgensen 1986: 321).

## Textile tools from Bjørkum

For the purposes of this paper I will be examining spindle whorls and loomweights to gain a picture of textile production at Bjørkum across the chronology. The finds come from both the primary use of the site, an earlier phase spanning the 7th–late 9th centuries, and a late phase of use in the late 10th–early 11th centuries. The finds from earlier periods are concentrated in a number of pit-houses, while those from the later are concentrated in the re-use of a single three-aisled house, Structure 1.

*Spindle whorls*

There were 19 complete whorls (Fig. 11.3) and a single roughout from the site, ten from the early period and seven from the late. They were predominantly made of soapstone, with only three in other materials, two of fired clay and a single example in stone. The use of soapstone fits culturally with its chronological and geographic location (Baug 2011). The form of the whorls also fits well with those from an early Viking Scandinavian context (Øye 2011: 342).

Four, possibly five of the whorls are decorated. Four of these, from the early phase, have incised ornament. This ranges from lines and a cross incised along the rim, to complex segmenting and freehand symbols. Only one decorated example comes from the late phase, and it resembles known Viking-Age examples. It is a knife carved steatite whorl in a 'beehive' pattern. This style can be found in the Kaupang grave assemblage (C4287–88, Blindheim and Heyerdahl-Larsen 1995). There are also examples from a later date in the Western Isles of Scotland, and at Bryggen, Bergen, in different media (Cartwright 2012, in prep. b; Øye 1988: figure II.11, II.12). Two of the later soapstone whorls from the reused three-aisled structure were lathe-turned. This may hint at a greater degree of standardisation.

The measurement of weight and diameter of spindle whorls are important functional parameters (Andersson 2003). The weight applies gravitational force to the fibres a spinner has drawn out, while the diameter applies rotational twist, a greater diameter being easier to spin more. The weight of the whorl is to a large extent responsible for the type of yarn produced. It has been argued that any spinner can produce a range of yarn with any spindle whorl (*e.g.* Walton Rogers 2007), but experimental tests suggest that whorls up to 15 g would have been used to produce fine yarn, whorls from 15–30 g were suitable for a range of yarn types, and whorls weighing 30 g or more were specialist whorls for producing coarser yarn types (Andersson Strand in prep.).

Experimental research also strongly suggests that spinners using equivalent whorl types spin yarns with far fewer degrees of difference between them. The number of metres spun from the same amount of wool, and yarn weight are far closer in such cases (Andersson Strand 2012: 208–210; see also Andersson 2003). Given the large amount of yarn that would have been needed to sustain Viking culture, and the range of different yarn types required for different textiles, it is highly likely that spinners would have chosen whorls to aid their tasks.

If one is trying to spin fine fibres with a heavy whorl, too much pressure (g) results in the breakage of the yarn. Conversely, a very light whorl will not apply enough force (g) to coarser fibres resulting in an uneven spin (Andersson Strand in prep.). In Viking-Age Atlantic Scotland, for example, new Viking-Age textile demands meant whorl types changed drastically from previous examples. The new whorls fit three task-defined weight bands (Cartwright in prep. b).

At Bjørkum, there seems to be a wider variety of whorl weights from 7–34 g in the early phase, perhaps hinting at a greater variety of thread productions across the ranges. Of the ten whorls, three are fine (7–13 g), six are multipurpose (16–28 g), and one heavy (34 g). These whorls would have been used for producing a variety of different yarn qualities. That different weights of whorl are often found alongside one another in the same pit-house would suggest that spinners had different skill sets and could employ them for the task at hand, rather than a 'one whorl fits all' scenario.

Whorls from the late phase at Bjørkum adhere to this pattern, suggesting similar ranges of thread production at the site. Of the seven spindle whorls, there are two fine whorls (5–14 g) and four middle range whorls (16–25 g) as well as one single heavier whorl (33 g). The pair of lathe-turned soapstone whorls from the same context in a reused three-aisled structure may hint at a greater control of thread production, as standardised production resulted in particular types resembling each other. They both weigh 21 g, and are 33/34 mm in diam., 15 mm high, and have holes of 8 mm minimum diam.

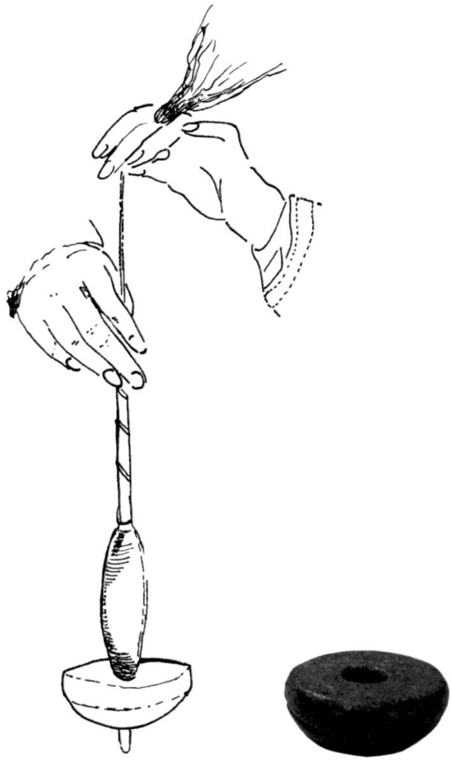

*Fig. 11.3. Spindle and spindlewhorl, with whorl from Bjørkum. Photo: © Ben Cartwright.*

*Loomweights*

As many as 27 complete loomweights were recovered from the site, 20 from the early phase in the pit-houses and six from the later reuse of Structure 1. Like the spindle whorls, it is possible to divide the functionality of the loomweights by measuring weight (g) and the thickness (mm) of the weight as seen from the side on edge (Mårtensson *et al.* 2009). The weights would have been hung front to back in rows. This is supported by archaeological finds where whole sets of loomweights are found together (*e.g.* those from Sorte Muld II, Bornholm, Denmark Hoffmann 1964: 312, fig. 131). It is important to select loomweights with the right weight and thickness for the desired textile being woven.

For example, tabby weave requires two sheds. This means that there are two rows of warp threads attached alternately to two different rows of loomweights; one in front and one behind (Fig. 11.4). The alternate weaving of a weft thread in front of these groups of

*Fig. 11.4. Warp-weighted loom with a loomweight from Bjørkum. Photo: © Ben Cartwright.*

threads (referred to as a shed) creates the grid like pattern. 2/1 twill requires three rows of loomweights, 2/2 twill requires four.

Studies conducted by the Danish National Research Foundation's Centre for Textile Research have created the possibility to investigate the optimal range of fabrics that an individual loomweight could have been used to produce (Andersson Strand 2012, in prep.; Mårtensson *et al.* 2009). The weight and the thickness of the loomweight are key determining factors. A light loomweight could only carry a few coarse warp yarns to keep them taut, which is important to ensure they remain in position in the cloth, while a heavy weight could only carry a high number of light yarns without them breaking (Mårtensson *et al.* 2009: 390). The weight delineates what range of yarn can be used per loomweight. Weaving tests suggest that numbers of warp-threads outside of a 5–30 threads per loomweight are increasingly unworkable (Mårtensson *et al.* 2009: 392). More than 30 threads and the weaving process becomes very difficult, fewer than five requires a very large number of loomweights placing extra emphasis on their thickness.

Broadly speaking, light and thin loomweights produce closed (less gap between the yarns) fine cloth, light and thick weights a more open (more gap between the yarns) and fine cloth. While heavy and thin weights produce a coarser, closed cloth, heavy and thick weights produce an open, coarser cloth (Mårtensson *et al.* 2009: 390). Weights of around 300 g and 30 mm thickness can produce a greater range of different fabric types with different thread patterns (open, closed, *etc.*) than weights that are significantly heavier or lighter (Anderson Strand in prep.).

The thickness of a loomweight affects the evenness of the fabric (Andersson Strand 2012: 210–213). If the total thickness of the loomweights exceeds the width of the fabric's starting border then the warp threads hang outwards. The warp threads on the edge are therefore more open and it is not possible to weave an even fabric (Mårtensson *et al.* 2009: 385). If the weights are narrower than the starting border, the fabric narrows, and it makes it extremely difficult to change shed (Mårtensson *et al.* 2009: 386). These are faults that affect the cloth and cannot be rectified in the weaving process. For an optimal weave the total width of the weights should be the same as or only marginally wider than the width of the starting border (Mårtensson *et al.* 2009: 389). This, and the regulation of tension, is a strong argument for the use of matching sets of loomweights.

Depending on the textile being woven there will be different rows of loomweights. This affects the number of threads per cm in the weave. If a weight weighs 300 g, and the weaver wants to weave in yarn of 30 g woven thread tension, ten threads can be attached to it. Woven thread tension (g) (hereafter w.t.t.) is the tension needed for a particular yarn to be taut in the weave. Coarser yarns have a heavier w.t.t. than lighter finer yarns. A difference of 10 g w.t.t. has a profound influence on weaving and fabric (Mårtensson *et al.* 2009: 396).

The thickness of the weight (mm) determines how many threads there are per cm attached to that weight. If the 300 g weight was 30 mm thick, in 30 g (w.t.t.) yarn there would be around seven threads per cm in a tabby weave (two rows of weights), ten threads per cm in 2/1 twill (three rows of weights), and 13 threads per cm in 2/2 twill (four rows of weights) (Andersson Strandin prep.; Hoffmann 1964: 183–187). 2/1 twill is incredibly rare in the periods under study (Bender Jørgensen 1982, 1996)

Taken together these functional parameters suggest that a loom, for optimal fabric production, should be set up using loomweights that match each other in weight and thickness. One archaeological loomweight can therefore represent a potential archaeological loom set up. Using the above methodology it is then possible to look for the optimal fabric production choices related to that object. An assemblage of loomweights can then tell us something of a range of skill sets being enacted at a site and how they may change over time.

At Bjørkum, the 27 loomweights can be phased to an early and a late usage of the site. They were made predominantly from soapstone with a few examples of other types of stone. Of the 20 weights found in a variety of pit-house structures, 19 weigh between 200–400 g. The six weights from the later phase were all found in the same reused structure as the spindle whorls from the late phase. They display a different range of dimensions to the earlier loomweights. Three in particular range from 489 g to 873 g. The heavier weights are also thin: 26–32 mm.

The majority of the weights come from the early phases, and show a trend for producing a range of fabrics, that supports the early spindle whorl evidence. The weights could have been used to produce a range of very fine fabrics. These closed tabbies and twills, with thread counts of 19–26 threads per cm, could have been woven with yarn as fine as 10 g (w.t.t.). This fine yarn could have been spun at the site with some of the excavated spindle whorls.

Notably, 2/2 twill textiles could have been woven in 10 g yarn up to 40 threads per cm, and 18–26 threads per cm in 20 g (w.t.t.). The first is an incredibly fine textile, and the second a fine textile that is right on the ranges known from Merovingian-period grave textiles (Bender Jørgensen 1986: 315). Based on radiocarbon dates, a new cloth type was introduced roughly half way through the early phase. The range of finer fabrics was complimented by a slightly heavier cloth, a coarser closed twill in yarns of 30–40 g (w.t.t.) of 9–13 threads per cm, that match known specifications for sailcloth production (Cooke *et al.* 2002).

The loomweights from the late phase suggest a break in production with a new range of cloth types being woven. There is a slight overlap with earlier productions with cloth being woven in yarn of 30–40 g (w.t.t.), but overall there is an opening of 20–30 g (w.t.t.) woven fabrics with lower thread counts per cm and a new variety of heavier cloth up to 70 g (w.t.t.). This is a considerable change in the need to weave and prepare yarn for new fabrics, for example spinning different thread types. At first glance this contrasts with the overall similarity in early and late spindle whorl measurements. But in both phases the spindle whorls could have produced the yarn required for the potential textiles suggested by the loomweights from that period, and the middle range lathe-turned spindle whorls of 21 g from the late phase may hint at a new standardisation of medium weight yarn that could have been used in some the cloth (Andersson Strand 2012, in prep; Mårtensson *et al.* 2009).

The majority of the potential textiles from the late phase were more likely in tabby weave, and in heavier yarns. The increase in tabby use is a known feature of Viking-Age Scandinavia (Bender Jørgensen 1986: 321). The changes suggest weavers at Bjørkum were producing cloth that would, despite its seemingly good quality, have been more suited to the internal demands of farm management than elite garments.

## Discussion: Making the cloth that binds us

In the early phase at Bjørkum, a river floor hub surrounded by shielings and upland, the weavers at the site seem to have produced very fine textiles comparable to those from the Merovingian-period burials in the region (*e.g.* Bender Jørgensen 1986: 315). The pit-houses contain debris suggesting various textile activities that would have been used to produce cloth that suggests a highly skilled workforce. This is dramatically different from the upland shieling sites of the mountain pasture that surround Bjørkum (Bjørgo *et al.* 1992).

The site did, however, most likely work within the bounds of this seasonal movement when flocks were driven up into the hills. This supports the argument for the site's role as a known component in the annual trips to the upland pasture as part of a wider social-economic landscape process. The location of a *skeid* and thing site in close proximity to Bjørkum may indicate that this landscape use was part of social processes concerning the negotiation of regional identities. Comparison with other seasonal pit-house sites such as Tissø, Denmark (Nørgård Jørgensen *et al.* 2011; see also Sindbæk 2009: 99), would suggest that Bjørkum's role may have been one of more than physical manufacture. Weaving was not just a materially functional activity (Heide 2006), but was also involved in the reweaving of a set of beliefs – beliefs that would have been disseminated and reaffirmed in childhood education and other community encounters.

It is difficult to state with certainty whether the individuals who worked at Bjørkum in its early phase were 'specialist' crafts people. Whole families occupied the structures, which were briefly home to a variety of practices, none of which seem to have been on a scale that suggests 'mass' manufacture. The artefacts at the site suggest a variety of genders and age groups congregated here. Finds such as slag, metal, and comb making debris alongside focal points such as the cooking pits, might suggest male and female craft practitioners operated and socialised at the site. A piece of chewed birch tar gum, a form of early chewing gum, imprinted with a child's teeth suggests that children were also present (Ramstad 2011).

What cannot be doubted is the quality of production. However, given the lack of 'workshops', and in comparison to later archaeological and historical data, this too could have been performed at a 'household' level by highly skilled practitioners. This does not preclude the production from fulfilling a unique niche within the locality as well as within the region, given its strategic location.

It would appear that in its early use, Bjørkum functioned as a social node (*cf.* Sindbæk 2007: 64) for people from across the region. The production of elite quality cloth, alongside other items of production, the market naming element, and the proximity to regional sites of assembly, may all suggest that Bjørkum could have functioned as pre-urban market site (Brink 2011; Ramstad 2011). In an age when it was important to look 'every inch a warrior', to be known at 'first sight' (Magnusson and Pálsson 1960: 248), the assembly sites may have offered a clientele after the latest Merovingian era fashions. This would represent an insight into the social patterns of pre-Viking landscape use, prior to the 'first wave of urbanism' in Scandinavia with the establishment of sites such as Kaupang (Skre 2008: 84).

In the Merovingian to Viking periods, coastal heathland management changed drastically, and potentially to accommodate sailcloth production (Bender Jørgensen 2010: 179; Kaland 1987: 174). The Merovingian period seems to display changes in landscape processes and farming systems, including the establishment of more upland shieling sites (Øye 2003: 408). It is interesting to note that the loomweights at Bjørkum change halfway through the early phase, to allow for the production of sailcloth-comparable fabrics. It seems as if the site reflects parts of the processes by which new social worlds were integrated with the landscape. It was a focal point (probably one of several) in a network of meeting places and seasonal cycles that saw communities coming together at certain places at certain times of the year.

At some point between the mid-9th and mid-10th centuries the 'practicing of rurality' (Wood 2010) seems to have shifted. The change into the late phase at Bjørkum, with new structures potentially associated with a larger magnate's farm, suggests that this regional 'coming together' no longer happened in the same way. The change in cloth types hints at possible changes in the seasonal social patterns at the site – or that they may even have disappeared for good. This clearly would have had a knock-on effect on several levels. Regional identities would then have had to be made in other places, and necessarily would have felt different, and involved different participants in new ways.

These new cloth types have more in common with working fabrics. A few of the heavier tabbies for example, are similar to some of the Anglo-Scandinavian cloth from York, which has been suggested to function as sacking (Walton 1989: 319). This is in part based on the irregularity in spinning of the yarn, for which there is no record at Bjørkum, and in part on the openness of the fabric (Walton 1989: 319). While some of the predicted later heavier textiles at Bjørkum would have been open, many would have been thick, and closed. Could these have been similar to the production of clothing and coarser, more hard-wearing cloth that is so visible in the later taxation records (Hoffmann 1964: 213, 214)?

This does at least seem more in line with the practicing of later land ownership at the site. The establishment of a farm unit represented by a late Viking-Age/medieval smithy just beyond the periphery of the Bjørkum settlement site, is in line with known changes in the structuring of tenancy, land management and the creation of new upland housing sites in the Late Viking Age to early medieval period (Øye 2003: 408).

## Conclusion

It is of course difficult to answer questions on the social impact of changes in landscape processes based on one site. However, the evidence for Bjørkum, in line with known regional shifts, might suggest that these changes might have been experienced differently, yet equally profoundly, across the variety of regional landscapes in pre-state Norway. The establishment of the site in the Merovingian period hints at a new feature in the regional rhythm of socio-political identity. Whether the later changes represent a hierarchical attempt to forge a Viking World from more diverse regional practices of rurality (Wood 2010) remains to be seen. There does, however, seem to be a concerted attempt to change products from the warp-weighted loom away from a more diverse range of fabric, with the potential for fine fabric that fits with known finds from the Merovingian period (Bender Jørgensen 1986, 1992). In the late phase, heavier textiles more reminiscent of working cloth, from sacking through to thicker twills, were woven. These may have been similar to the recorded taxable cloth items from later periods, which were exported and used to clothe farm-hands (Hoffmann 1964: 213, 214).

A study of textile production provides a measure of learnt body-techniques, and the superstitions and moral values that accompanied them as they were handed down, taught and learnt, between the generations. The break in production, and usage of the site, seems to suggest a change in the social cycles which Bjørkum was a part of. As a site where east meets west, with high quality goods and proximity to one, if not two, other meeting points in the landscape, it is possible to imagine a considerable pull factor to the site, perhaps one that had regional ramifications. What then happened in the late 10th–early 11th centuries AD to the dispersed family groups, who lost this venue for the exchanging of gossip and stories that shaped their social worlds in the summer shieling months? Was this shift part of the tying down of inhabitants to new patterns of tenancy and landholding that eventually saw a later farm established at Bjørkum?

*References*


Andersson, Eva

2003. *Tools for Textile Production from Birka and Hedeby. Excavations in the Black Earth 1990–1995.* Birka Studies, Vol. 8. Birka Project for Riksantikvarieämbetet, Stockholm.

Andersson Strand, Eva

2012. From spindle whorls and loomweights to fabrics in the Bronze Age Aegean and eastern Mediterranean. In *KOSMOS Jewellery, Adornment and Textiles in the Aegean Bronze Age. Proceedings of the 13th International Aegean Conference. University of Copenhagen, Danish National Research Foundation's Centre for Textile Research, 21–26 April 2010*, edited by Marie-Louise Nosch and Robert Laffineur, pp. 207–214. Aegaeum (Annales d'archéologie égéenne de l'Université de Liège et UT-PASP), Vol. 33. Peeters, Leuven, Liege.

In prep. From tools to textiles, concluding remarks. In *Tools, Textiles and Context: Textile Production in the Aegean and Eastern Mediterranean Bronze Age,* edited by Eva Andersson Strand and Marie-Louise Nosch. Oxbow Books, Oxford.

Andersson Stand, Eva and Ulla Mannering

2011. Textile production in the Late Roman Iron Age – a case study of textile production in Vorbasse, Denmark. In *Arkæologi i Slesvig. Sonderband "Det 61. Internationale Sachsensymposion 2010*, edited by Linda Boye, pp. 77–84. Wachholtz, Neumünster.

Baug, Irene

2011. Soapstone finds. In *Things from the Town: Artefacts and Inhabitants in Viking-Age Kaupang*, edited by Dagfinn Skre, pp. 311–337. Kaupang Excavation Project publication series, Vol. 3 and Norske Oldfunn, Vol. 24. Aarhus University Press, Aarhus.

Bender Jørgensen, Lise

1986. *Forhistoriske Textiler i Skandinavien.* Nordiske fortidsminder. Serie B, Vol. b. 9. Det Kongelige Nordiske Oldskriftselskab. Det Kongelige Nordiske Oldskriftselskab, København.

1991. Textiles and textile implements. In *Ribe Excavations 1970–76*, Vol. 3, edited by Mogens Bencard, Lise Bender Jørgensen, HelgeBrinch Madsen, pp. 59–78. Sydjysk Universitetsforlag, Esbjerg.

1992. *Northern European Textiles until AD 1000.* Aarhus University Press, Aarhus.

2012. The introduction of sails to Scandinavia: raw materials, labour and land. In *N-TAG TEN: Proceedings of the 10th Nordic TAG Conference at Stiklestad, Norway 2009*, edited by Ragnhild Berge, Marek E. Jasinski and Kalle Sognnes, pp. 173–181. Archaeopress, Oxford.

Blindheim, Charlotte and Birgit Heyerdahl-Larsen

1995. *Del A: Gravskikk.* Gravplassene i Bikjholbergene/Lamøya: undersøkelsene 1950–1957, Vol. 2 and Norske Oldfunn, Vol. 16. Universitetets kulturhistoriske museer, Oldsaksamlingen, Oslo.

Bjørgo, Tore, Siv Kristoffersen, Christopher Prescott and Rolf W. Lie

1992. *Arkeologiske Undersøkelser i Nyset-Steggjevassdragene* 1981–87. Arkeologiske rapporter, Vol. 16. Historisk museum, Universitetet i Bergen, Bergen.

Brink, Stefan

2008. Who were the Vikings? In *The Viking World*, edited by Stefan Brink and Neil S. Price, pp. 4–8. Routledge, Abingdon.

2011. Comments on Inger Storli: 'court sites of Arctic Norway: remains of thing sites and representations of political consolidation processes in the northern Germanic world during the first millennium AD?' *Norwegian Archaeological Review* 43(2): 89–117.

Cartwright, Ben

2012. Shimmering cloth, like the river by this path: Bjørkum, Lærdal, and the role of an inland production site in the Viking Age. *Archaeological Textile Review* 54: 39–43.

In prep. a *Weaving the World: The Role of Textile Production (Spinning and Weaving) in Producing the Viking Age Identities of Atlantic Scotland.* Ph.D. dissertation, University of Cambridge.
In prep. b Making cloth beneath the slopes: spinning and weaving at Bjørkum, Lærdal, Norway. In *Bjørkum – Utgravinger av en Vikingtidsplass i Lærdal. Bjørkum: The Excavations of a Viking Age Site in Lærdal, Western Norway*, edited by Morten Ramstad. University of Bergen Press, Bergen.

Christiansen, Carol
2004. A reanalysis of fleece evolution studies. In *Priceless Invention of Humanity – Textiles.* Report from *the 8th NESAT symposium 8 10 May 2002 in Lodz, Poland, 5th–7th May 1999*, edited by Jerzy Maik, pp. 11–18. *Acta Archaeologica Lodziensia* Vol. 50/1 and (NESAT) monograph, Vol. 8. Lodskie Towarzystwo Naukowe, Lodz.

Cooke, Bill, Carol Christiansen and Lene Hammarlund
2002. Viking woollen square-sails and fabric cover factor. *International Journal of Nautical Archaeology* 32(2): 202–210.

Gardeła, Leszek
2008. Into Viking Minds: Reinterpreting the staffs of sorcery and unravelling *Seiðr*. *Viking and Medieval Scandinavia* 4: 45–85.

Geijer, Agnes
1938. *Die Textilfunde aus den Gräbern.* Birka: Untersuchungen und Studien, Vol. III. Akademien, Uppsala. Sweden.
1979. The textile finds from Birka. *Acta Archaeologica* 50(14): 209–222.

Guðjónsson, Elsa
1962. *"Forn röggvarvefnaður," Árbók hins Izlenska Fornleifafélags.* Ísafoldarprentsja H.F, Reykjavík.

Halvorsen, Sunniva
2012. Norway. In *Textiles and Textile Production in Europe from Prehistory to AD 400.* Margarita Gleba and Ulla Mannering, pp. 274–290. Oxbow Books, Oxford.

Hastrup, Kirsten
2008. Icelandic topography and a sense of identity. In *Nordic Landscapes: Region and Belonging on the Edge of Europe*, edited by Michael Jones. and Kenneth Olwig, pp. 77–105. University of Minnesota Press, Minnesota.

Heckett, Elizabeth
1990. Some silk and wool head-coverings from Viking Age Dublin: uses and origins – an enquiry. In *Textiles in Northern Archaeology: NESAT 3: Textile Symposium in York, 6–9 May 1987*, edited by John-Peter Wild and Penelope Walton, pp. 85–96. Monograph (NESAT), Vol. 3. Archetype Productions, London.

Heide, Eldar
2006. Spinning seiðr. In *Old Norse Religion in Long-term Perspectives. Origins, Changes, and Interactions*, edited by Anders Andrén, Kristina Jennbert andCatharina Raudvere, pp. 164–170. Vägar till Midgård, Vol. 8. Nordic Academic Press, Lund.

Heidegger, Martin
2010. The thing. In *The Craft Reader*, edited by Glenn Adamson, pp. 404–408. Berg, Oxford.

Henshall, Audrey
1952. Early textiles found in Scotland. *Proceedings of the Society of Antiquaries of Scotland* 86: 1–28.

Hoffmann, Marta
1964. *The Warp Weighted Loom: Studies in the History and Technology of an Ancient Implement.* Universitetsforlaget, Bergen.

Kaland, Sigrid
1987. Viking/medieval settlement in the heathland area of Nordhordland. In *Proceedings of the Tenth Viking Congress, Larkollen, Norway, 1985*, edited by James E. Knirk, pp. 171–190. Universitetets oldsaksamlings skrifter, Ny rekke, Vol. 9. Oslo University Press, Oslo

Larson, Katherine
2001. *The Woven Coverlets of Norway*. University of Washington Press, Seattle.

Lucas, G.
2008. Pálstóftir: A Viking Age Shieling in Iceland. *Norwegian Archaeological Review* 41(1): 87–100.

Mårtensson, Linda, Marie-Louise Nosch and Eva Andersson-Strand
2009. The shape of things: understanding a loomweight. *Oxford Journal of Archaeology* 28(4): 373–398.

Magnus, Bente
2002. Dwellings and settlements: structure and characteristics. In *The Scandinavians from the Vendel Period to the Tenth Century. An Ethnographic Perspective*, edited by Judith Jesch, pp. 5–32. Boydell Press, Woodbridge.

Magnusson, Magnus and Hermann Pálsson
1960. *Njal's Saga*. Pengiun Classics, Harmondsworth.

Milek, Karen
2012. The roles of pithouses and gendered spaces on Viking Age farmsteads in Iceland. *Medieval Archaeology* 56: 85–130.

Miller, Daniel
2009. *Stuff*. Polity Press, Cambridge.

Mortensen, Mona
1997. For women only? Reflections on a Viking Age settlement at Stedje, Sogndal in western Norway. *Studien zur Sachenforschung* 10: 195–206.
1998. 'When they speed the shuttle' The role of textile production in Viking Age society, as reflected in a pit house from Western Norway. In *Textiles in European Archaeology: Report from the 6th Nesat Symposium 7th–11th May 1996 Borås*, edited by Lise Bender-Jørgensen and Christina Rinaldo. GOTARC, Series A, Vol. 1 and Monograph (NESAT), Vol. 6. Gothenborg University, Department of Archaeology, Gothenborg.

Mylne, Chris
2011. *Foula: The Time of My Life*. Islands Book Trust, Lewis.

Naji, Myriem
2009. Gender and materiality in-the-making: the manufacture of Sirwan femininities through weaving in southern Morocco. *Journal of Material Culture* 14(1): 47–73.

Nørgård Jørgensen, Anne Nørgård, Lars Jørgensen and Lone Gebauer Thomsen
2011. Assembly Sites for cult, markets, and social relations: historic-ethnological analogy between north Scandinavian church Toens, Old Norse assembly sites and pit house sites of the late age and Viking Period. In *Arkæologi i Slesvig: Sonderband "Det 61. Internationale Sachsensymposion 2010" Haderslev, Danmark*, edited by Linda Boye, pp. 187–195. Wachholtz, Neumünster.

Price, Neil
2007. *The Viking Way: Religion and War in Late Iron Age Scandinavia.* Oxbow Books, Oxford.

Pritchard, Frances
1992. Aspects of the Wool Textiles from Viking Age Dublin. In Archaeological Textiles in Northern Europe: Report from the 4th NESAT Symposium 1.–5.May 1990 in Copenhagen, edited by Lise Bender Jørgensen and Elisabeth Munksgaard, pp. 93–104. Konservatorskolen, Copenhagen.

Ramstad, Morten
2011. *Bjørkum: An Insight into the New Economic and Social Structures in the Early Viking Age.* Division of Cultural Heritage, Bergen Museum, Bergen.
In prep. *Bjørkum- Utgravinger av en Vikitgtidsplass I Lærdal. Bjørkum: The Excavations of a Viking Age Site in Lærdal, Western Norway.* Bergen University of Bergen Press, Bergen.
Sennet, Richard.
2008. *The Craftsman.* Penguin, London.
Sindbæk, Søren
2007. The small world of the Vikings: networks in early medieval communication and exchange. *Norwegian Archaeological Review.* 40(1): 59–74.
2009. Open access, nodal points, and central places: maritime communication and locational principles for coastal sites in south Scandinavia, *c.* AD 400–1200. *Estonian Journal of Archaeology* 13(2): 96–109.
Skre, Dagfinn
2008. The development of urbanism in Scandinavia. In *The Viking World*, edited by S. Brink and N. Price, pp. 83–93. Routledge, Abingdon.
Skre, Dagfinn (editor)
2007. *Kaupang in Skiringssal.* Kaupang Excavation Project Publication Series, Vol. 1, and Norske Oldfunn, Vol. XXII. Aarhus University Press, Aarhus.
2011. *Things from the town: artefacts and inhabitants in Viking Age Kaupang.* Kaupang Excavation Project publication series, Vol. 3 and Norske Oldfunn, Vol. 24. Aarhus University Press, Aarhus.
Stewart, Katharine.
2005. *Crofts and Crofting: Past, Present and Future.* Mercat Press, Edinburgh.
Stylegar, Frans-Arne
2010. *Horse Fights and Cow Fights in Norwegian Folk Tradition.* Electronic document, http://arkeologi.blogspot.co.uk/2010/10/horse-fights-and-cow-fights-in.html, accessed 15 August, 2013.
Walton, Penelope
1989. *Textiles, Cordage and Raw Fibre from 16-22 Coppergate.* The Archaeology of York: The Small Finds, Vol. 5 and the Archaeology of York, Vol. 17. Council for British Archaeology, London.
Walton Rogers, Penelope
2007. *Cloth and Clothing in Early Anglo Saxon England, AD 450–700.* Council for British Archaeology, York.
Wenger, Etienne
1998. *Communities of Practice: Learning, Meaning and Identity.* Cambridge University Press, Cambridge.
Wincott Heckett, Elizabeth
2003. *Viking Age Headcoverings from Dublin.* Royal Irish Academy, Dublin.
Wood, M.
2010. Performing rurality and practising rural geography. *Progress in Human Geography* 34(6): 835–846.
Østergård, Else
2009. *Woven into the Earth: Textiles from Norse Greenland.* Aarhus University Press, Aarhus.
Øye, Ingvild
1988. *Textile Equipment and its Working Environment, Bryggen in Bergen c 1150–1500.* Bryggen Papers, Main Series, Vol. 2. Norwegian University Press, Oslo.
2003. Outfields as part of the medieval farm: four archaeological case studies from western

Norway. In *Scandinavian Archaeological Practice – in Theory: Proceedings from the 6th Nordic TAG, Oslo 2001,* edited by Jostein Bergstøl, pp. 400–411. OAS, Vol. 1. University of Oslo Press, Oslo.
2011. Textile-production equipment. In *Things from the town: artefacts and inhabitants in Viking-Age Kaupang,* edited by Daginn Skre, pp. 339–372. Kaupang Excavation Project publication series, Vol. 3 and Norske Oldfunn, Vol. 24. Aarhus University Press, Aarhus.

*Chapter 12*

# Leadworking in Viking-Age Norway

*Unn Pedersen*

*Abstract*

Leadworking in Viking-Age Norway was hardly discussed until the Kaupang excavations demonstrated that lead was extensively used by the craftspeople in the small town by the outlet of the Oslo fjord. The non-ferrous metalworkers applied the metal in several processes, had access to ingots of different types and made tools, jewellery and adornments of lead. The use of lead formed an integral part of their craft activities, along with the working of silver, gold and copper alloys. In the last decade, more sites in the Oslofjord area have provided evidence of leadworking. Against this background, a collection of lead mounts from nearby graves are reinvestigated, in particular finds from the ship burial at Gokstad. A comparison of the workshop assemblage at Kaupang and the lead mounts from the graves provides new perspectives on Viking-Age craftspeople, and their use of raw materials and motifs.

## Introduction

Leadworking in Viking-Age Norway was hardly discussed until the Kaupang excavations revealed evidence of extensive use of lead in the small town by the outlet of the Oslo fjord (Pedersen 2010). Lead was integral in various non-ferrous metalworking techniques and an affordable and easily available raw material for the production of tools and adornments.

The many lead finds from Kaupang were surprising in light of earlier research; bronze casting has been a key topic, while the working of lead is rarely discussed. This article demonstrates that the leadworking at Kaupang is far from unique. Rather the use of lead seems to characterize several newly discovered sites in the Oslofjord area. Nearby graves are reinvestigated against this background, the ship burial from Gokstad in particular. It is also suggested that the neglected lead mounts in these graves might have been produced by non-ferrous metalworkers operating in the Oslofjord area.

### Leadworking at Kaupang

A large and heterogeneous assemblage of lead objects and waste was collected during excavations and metal-detecting campaigns at Kaupang 1998–2003. Lead makes up the clearly largest group among the non-ferrous metals, and includes 4.7 kg of spillage from casting and 6 kg of ingots (Pedersen 2010: 226, table 4.26). The majority of the lead was found in modern and late medieval plough layers, but a high number of stylistically datable artefacts speak strongly in favour of a Viking-Age date for most, if not all the finds.

The high percentage of lead artefacts, compared to the other finds of non-ferrous metals, primarily reflects that different metals were treated differently by the craftspeople. By comparing metal residues in crucibles and moulds with metal finds, it is obvious that gold and silver were handled with great care, while lead was treated rather carelessly (Pedersen in press a). Still, this does not change the fact that lead was used extensively.

Kaupang was established *c.* AD 800 as a seasonally visited costal site characterized by craft activities and trade, and developed into a town a few decades later (Pedersen and Pilø 2007; Skre 2008, 2011). Non-ferrous metalworkers were among the first to arrive, and lead was worked from the earliest days, throughout the 9th century, and possibly into the 10th, when the activity in general seems to decrease (Pedersen 2010, in press b; Pedersen and Pilø 2007; Skre 2008). While the preserved cultural deposits from the first half of the 9th century provide excellent potential for ascertaining the whereabouts of craftspeople at Kaupang, it is more challenging to track the activities in the later phases, which are heavily disturbed by ploughing. Distribution maps from the metal-detecting campaign, nevertheless, demonstrate that lead was worked over larger parts of the town from the early 9th century onwards (Pedersen 2010: fig. 4.97).

Raw materials, manufacturing waste and finished products provide much information on the metalworkers' use of lead at Kaupang. It demonstrates that they had access to lead in different forms: regular ingots of different shapes, fragments of lead containers and more irregular ingots. Lead containers are known from Britain (Brooks *et al.* 2004; Loveluck 1998), and some are found in hoards that relate to Viking activities (Graham-Campbell 2011: 130; Williams and Ager 2010: 13). Scientific analyses of selected objects from Kaupang demonstrate that the available raw material was pure lead with only naturally occurring trace elements. Locally cast objects and spillage from casting are of pure lead, with one exception, suggesting that the non-ferrous metalworkers preferred to use the raw material as it was (Pedersen 2010: 308).

The lead was worked into simple adornments and different tools, including weights, spindle whorls and line sinkers (Pedersen 2008, 2010: 258–271; Tansøy 2001; Øye 2011). The production of these objects did not demand great skills: as lead melts at low temperatures it could be melted over a fireplace in any container of pottery, iron or soapstone. Three soapstone moulds demonstrate exactly how the weights were cast, and prove that carving the mould and pouring in the melted metal was easy. This kind of leadworking could have been carried out by anyone, in theory, but the finished weights seem to point towards more skilled workers. The weights are adjusted to weight standards, demanding a set of weights and a balance, which would hardly have been available for everyone at Kaupang (Pedersen 2008). Furthermore, a large proportion of the weights have stamped-dot decoration, made by a punch – a specialist tool used by the non-ferrous metalworkers in the town (Pedersen 2008: fig. 6.22).

Turning to the workshop assemblage, there is no doubt that highly skilled and trained non-ferrous metalworkers used lead. Lead was utilized as raw material when making highly specialized tools for the production of dress accessories, fittings and decorative tools, as demonstrated by a unique collection of lead models and a lead mould (Pedersen 2010: 88–93). These lead tools reveal the types of objects being produced; the majority are typical Scandinavian dress accessories, made of copper alloys, silver or gold. Lead was also used by the non-ferrous metalworkers when cleaning silver and gold, as demonstrated by a specific type of pottery used for metalworking. The so-called heating trays used in such processes have shown traces of lead, detected through scientific examination (with a scanning electron microscope with EDX; Jouttijärvi 2007; Pedersen 2010: table 4.19). Lead was consequently used in many different ways by craftspeople who mastered a wide range of non-ferrous metals, and leadworking formed an integral part of the non-ferrous metalworking at Kaupang.

### More sites emerging

During the last decade, more evidence of leadworking has come to light in the Oslofjord area as a result of metal-detecting and the identification of new sites. Heimdaljordet is the most noteworthy. Geomagnetic surveys and systematic metal-detecting unveiled a site with plot division ditches and evidence of trade and craft activities (Bill and Rødsrud 2013; Pedersen and Rødsrud 2013). Excavations 2012–2013 confirmed that the site was divided into plots, but gave no firm evidence of buildings on the plots. The artefact material comprises dirhems, weights, ingots and waste from non-ferrous metalworking, including leadworking. Interpretations of the site and its artefact material are in progress, but there is no doubt that the leadworking at Kaupang and at Heimdaljordet is at least partly contemporary. The artefact material from Heimdaljordet seems to suggest a date range from *c.* AD 850–950 (Bill and Rødsrud 2013), overlapping with the dates from Kaupang. Thus, craftspeople were working lead at two coastal sites less than 15 km apart. Moreover, they were operating at two sites that had much in common, both with links to the uppermost elite. Kaupang was an integrated part of the Skiringssal complex, comprising an aristocratic hall and several cemeteries, including elite graves (Skre 2007), while Heimdaljordet is located right in front of the mound where the famous ship burial from Gokstad was found (Nicolaysen 1882). The discovery of Heimdaljordet challenges established interpretations of the socio-political milieu in the Oslofjord area, but seems to further underline that there were several local rulers in the early Viking Age (*cf.* Brøgger 1916, 1922; Gansum 1997; Myhre 2003, 2013; Skre 2007).

The knowledge of settlement structure around the Oslofjord area relies heavily on graves, due to few identified settlement sites or other types of sites from the Viking Age. However, increased metal-detecting activity provides a few glimpses into additional sites with evidence of leadworking. At Huseby, Rygge, Østfold, the discovery of dirhems, a weight and hacksilver

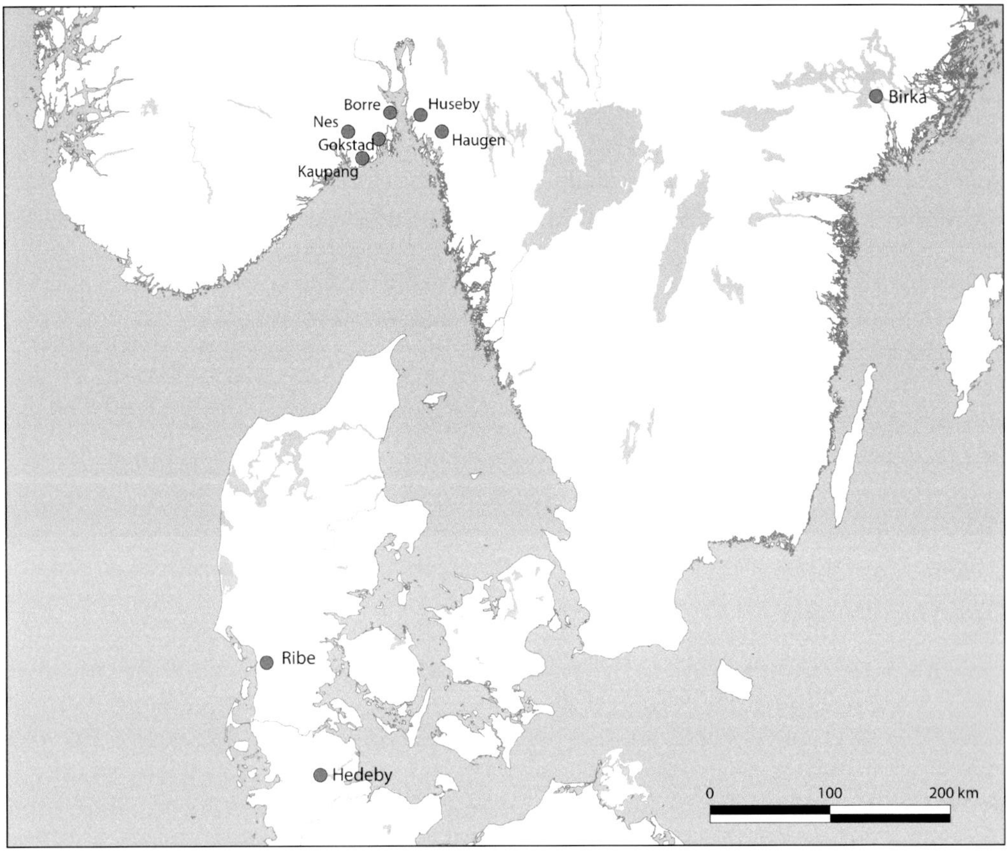


*Fig. 12.1. Scandinavian Viking-Age towns and sites in the Oslo fjord area with lead adornments or waste from leadworking. Illustration: © Kaupang Excavation Project, University of Oslo.*

initiated a small-scale investigation by the Museum of Cultural History, University of Oslo (Khazaei and Haugan 2013). A date in the late 9th century has been suggested, based on the coins (Khazaei and Haugan 2013), and the site is located further north and across the fjord from Gokstad (Fig. 12.1). Consequently, leadworking was carried out in the second half of the 9th century on at least three different sites within a restricted area. Reports of other, yet undated lead ingots (Stylegar and Nordseng 2003: 370–371), suggest that more such sites in the Oslofjord area will be identified in the years to come.

## Some small things forgotten

Inspired by this new knowledge on Viking-Age leadworking, I have started a reinvestigation of lead finds from the Oslofjord area. The study particularly investigates a group of lead adornments – a category which has been neglected for a long time. They are hardly

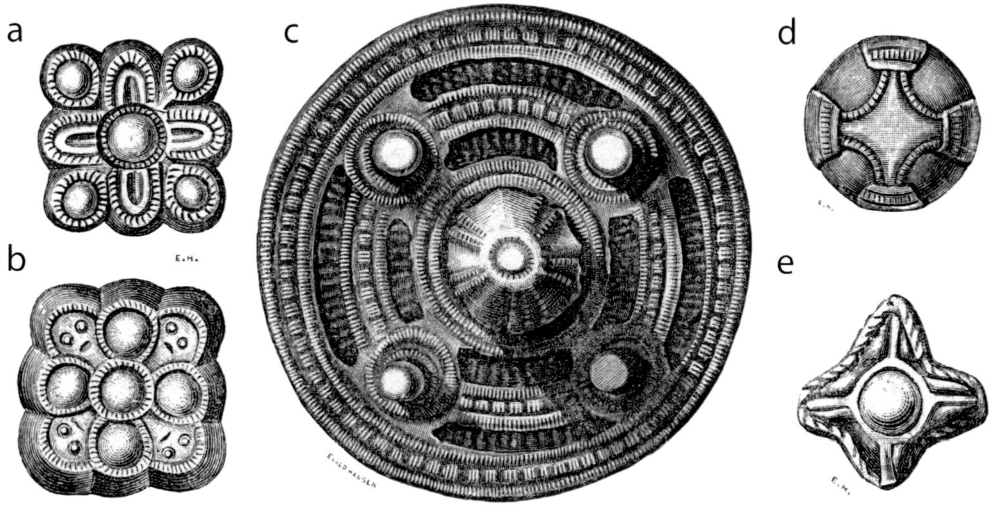


*Fig. 12.2. Lead mounts from Gokstad, a selection of types (drawings from Rygh 1885).*

mentioned in discussions of Viking-Age metalworking before 2010, despite the fact that we have had a noteworthy collection for quite some time: 64 decorative lead mounts from the famous ship burial from Gokstad (Fig. 12.2). The large grave mound was excavated in 1880 and the lead mounts were published in Nicolay Nicolaysen's (1882) report from the excavation. Shortly after, the mounts were included in Oluf Ryghs (1885) much used catalogue, *Norske Oldsager*. Thereafter they seem to have been forgotten.

The lead ornaments are not included in Haakon Shetelig's (1920) influential discussion of the Vestfold School, based on woodcarvings from the well-known ship burial from Oseberg. Metalwork from Gokstad and Borre is drawn into his study of craftsmanship in the Oslofjord area, but he explicitly states that he has only included the objects of copper alloy and those in the animal style (Shetelig 1920: 227). The lead mounts are not mentioned by Bjørn Hougen (1934) in his studies of the Gokstad find, despite the fact that he was inspired by some newly discovered objects, including lead mounts, found when the mound was reconstructed. They are not discussed in the publication celebrating the 100th anniversary of the Gokstad excavation either (Wexelsen 1981). This stands in contrast to some of the mounts of copper alloy from Gokstad (Fig. 12.3), which are more frequently brought into discussions of Viking-Age craft and style (Graham-Campbell 1980; Hougen 1934; Müller-Wille 2001; Shetelig 1920; Wilson 1995).

The lead adornments from Gokstad can be divided into several distinct types, based on their shape and stylistic characteristics (Fig. 12.2). Fifty-nine were found together during the excavation in 1880, inside the grave chamber within the ship (Nicolaysen 1882: 46, 50–51). Another five were found in 1928–1929 when the mound was reconstructed, demonstrating that some objects were missed by Nicolaysen and his team. This is hardly surprising, as his

*Fig. 12.3. Copper alloy mounts from Gokstad, a selection of types (drawings from Rygh 1885).*

excavation targeted the ship, and the burial had been plundered, most likely in the second half of the 10th century (Bill and Daly 2012). Nevertheless, it serves as a reminder that the group could have included more mounts at the time of burial.

Two of the types are far more numerous than the others, with respectively 22 and 17 mounts (Figs 12.2b and 12.2d). Within most types the mounts are almost identical, suggesting that they were cast in the same mould (Pedersen *et al.* in prep). One mount (Fig. 12.2c) differs from the others with a gilt copper-alloy sheet behind an openwork lead plate, while all the others are cast in lead. Stylistic elements suggest that all the objects belonged to one set. The mount with the copper-alloy sheet has three copies in lead, while the other motifs fluctuate from type to type (Fig. 12.2). Therefore, the stylistic elements suggest that all the mounts were produced by one hand or within one group of craftspeople, with the possible exception of the mount that seems to have been copied.

### Graves with lead mounts

The lead mounts from Gokstad have close parallels in a few Norwegian grave finds, all located in the Osloford area (Fig. 12.1). The most noteworthy are 21 mounts of four different types found in a chamber grave from Haugen, Rolfsøy, the only find from the eastern side of the fjord. The mounts are all of lead, and are similar, but not identical, to the types from Gokstad (Brøgger 1922: fig. 12). Another closely related, but poorly preserved mount comes from the ship burial from Borre (Brøgger 1916: fig. 29). Finally, a grave at Nes, Kvelde, Hedrum, yielded eight mounts of a type also found in Gokstad (Nicolaysen 1886). Thus, three graves west of the Oslo fjord have almost identical mounts.

Again, the groups of lead mounts might have been more numerous. The ship burial at Borre was destroyed before Nicolaysen arrived in 1852 (Brøgger 1916: 1–2). The objects from Haugen were first collected by the archaeologists three years after the grave was discovered by a local farmer in 1864 (Brøgger 1922: 20), and it is mentioned in the museum catalogue that more mounts were actually found (C4188–4197; Aarsberetning 1867: 59–62).

Adornments of lead are rarely found in graves in the Oslofjord area, or elsewhere in Norway. There are only a handful graves with lead ornaments, including crosses, in addition to the mentioned graves (Pedersen 2010: 260). The group of closely related mounts makes up the majority of the lead adornments known from Norwegian grave finds. Lead weights and fishing equipment of lead are found in some graves (Pedersen 2008; Tansøy 2001), but otherwise burial practices seem to exclude objects of lead. This is particularly evident at Kaupang, where no ornaments of lead have been found in the graves encircling the town, despite the fact that several different types are known from the settlement area, including some characteristic pendants (Fig. 12.4a). Moreover, different types of lead weights dominate in the settlement area at Kaupang, while lead weights are absent in the local graves (Pedersen 2008: fig. 6.3).

### Lead adornments in Scandinavia and beyond

The search for parallels in other parts of Scandinavia and beyond is a work in progress. So far two sites with exactly the same type of mounts have been identified. One of the types from Gokstad is found in Hedeby, Denmark (Anspach 2012: Taf. 9.70, Capelle 1968: Taf. 23.2), while another type is found in Domburg in the present day Netherlands (Capelle 1976: pl. 19.326). They are both single finds from settlement contexts, and perforated, as opposed to the mounts from Gokstad, thus suggesting that they have been reused. Therefore, it seems more likely that these mounts arrived from the Oslofjord area than the other way round. Nevertheless, at both sites the mounts belong to a larger collection of lead objects, attesting to a local use of simple ornaments and dress accessories of lead or copper alloys (Anspach 2012; Capelle 1968: Taf. 23, 1976: Taf. 15, 19).

Lead adornments are found in a few graves in Scandinavia, for example in the ship burial from Ladby (Sørensen 2001: 81). They are also found in settlement contexts elsewhere in Scandinavia. Most noteworthy are the close parallels to some lead pendants from Kaupang (Fig. 12.4a). The same type of pendant is also found in Birka (Serning 1956: fig. 10), Ribe (Feveile 2006: Tavle 53), Hedeby (Anspach 2010: Taf. 9.78–79) and in Truso in Poland (Auch *et al.* 2012: fig. 48). The number of lead ornaments from settlement sites is steadily growing, especially in Denmark, due to comprehensive metal-detecting activities (Dobat 2010; Henriksen 2000). Lead adornments are also found elsewhere in Europe, none of exactly the same types as the Oslofjord collection, but some rather similar, in particular a mount from Gnezdovo, Russia (Hedenstierna-Jonson and Holmquist Olausson 2006: 39.24). Disc brooches are a dominant type in Western Europe, but the group also includes pendants, some mounts and finger rings (Capelle 1976; Wamers 1994).

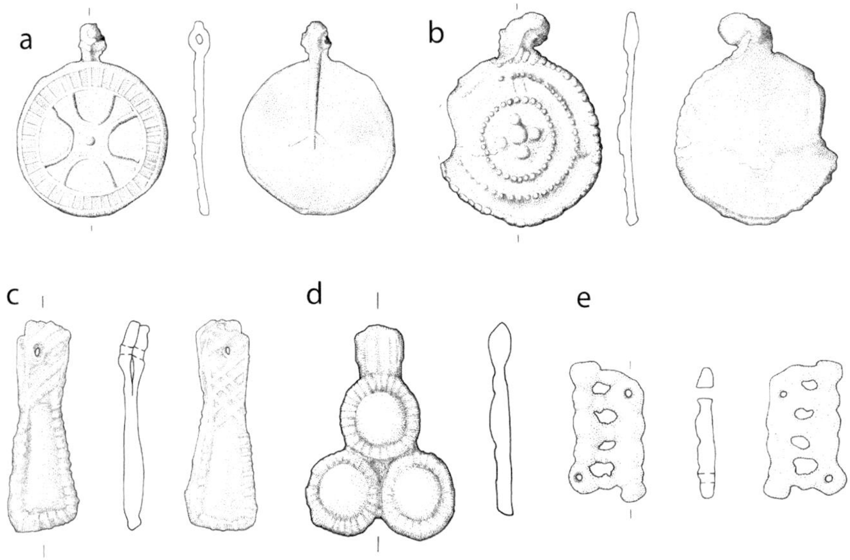


*Fig. 12.4. Lead adornments from Kaupang, a selection of types. Drawings: © Bjørn-Håkon Eketuft Rygh, Kaupang Excavation Project, University of Oslo.*

## Horse harnesses and dress accessories

The lead mounts from Gokstad were found along with mounts of copper alloy and a horse bit, and have been interpreted as decorative mounts for a horse harness (Rygh 1885: 32). Three of the lead mounts were attached to a leather strap when they were found, but the brief report provides no additional information on the mounts (Nicolaysen 1882: 51). The horse harness exhibited at the Viking skip museum is thus more of a construction than a reconstruction. All the mounts in Haugen are reported to have been found together in the corner of the grave chamber (Aarsberetning 1867: 59–62). They have also been interpreted as belonging to a horse harness, and a horse bit was also found in the grave, although at an unknown location (Brøgger 1922: 23–24; Stylegar and Nordseng 2003: 358–359). Likewise, the mounts from Nes were found with some bones from a horse (Nicolaysen 1886: 34). As the ship burial from Borre contains a horse harness with a larger series of gilt copper alloy adornments mounted on leather straps (Brøgger 1916: figs 13–14), it seems highly possible that the lead mounts from all the graves were used in the same way as in Gokstad and Haugen – to adorn horses.

The adorned horses belonged to persons in the uppermost strata of society, with the possible exception of Nes, where the mounts were found with some poorly preserved iron artefacts. The ship burials from Gokstad and Borre are among the wealthiest graves in Scandinavia, and the buried persons have been interpreted as chieftains or petty kings (Brøgger 1916; Myhre 2003). The individual buried in the chamber grave from Haugen has also been interpreted as a man from the uppermost strata of society (Stylegar and

Nordseng 2003: 361), but both the number of artefact types and the construction of the grave indicate a level slightly below the ship burials. The burials at Gokstad, Haugen and Borre are all dated to the same period of time, around AD 900 (Bonde and Christensen 1993: 582; Brøgger 1922: 29; Myhre 2003: 53). Therefore, it is possible that these persons and their horses might even have met.

Lead can be interpreted as an affordable raw material, based on the large amounts of lead at Kaupang, and well in correspondence with interpretations of lead ornaments from Western Europe (Wamers 1994: 197). Still, the mounts could have looked more impressive than they actually were, as a horse harness would only have been observed, by most people, from a distance. Lead could have been taken for silver, and the imitations of press sheet work and filigree decoration (Brøgger 1922: 24) might have fooled the more distant observers. A gilded decorative horse head with unknown function from Kaupang (Pedersen 2010: fig. 4.111), some silver coated lead buttons from a grave in Stengade, Denmark (Brøndsted 1936: fig. 74), and the silver coating observed on the mounts from Nes (Nicolaysen 1886: 34) point in a similar direction.

The graves seem to suggest that ornaments of lead were mainly used by horses, but the material from Kaupang demonstrates a wider use of the material. The functions of the lead adornments at Kaupang are difficult to interpret, as they are found individually, and none in a context that provides information on their use; none is of the same type as any of the mounts from the graves, and the only artefact interpreted as a mount is of a completely different character (Fig. 12.4e). Some can be interpreted as pendants (Figs 12.4a and b), based on insular and continental counterparts (Roesdahl *et al.* 1981:105, YD104; Wamers 1994: 73) and similar types in copper alloy from graves (Petersen 1928: figs 157–163). Thus, at least some of the lead adornments at Kaupang are dress accessories. None have any counterparts in the grave material, suggesting that dress accessories of lead were more effectively excluded from the graves than the lead mounts.

## Local production

The lead pendants at Kaupang are undoubtedly a result of local production. Two are miscast, and the site has also produced a mould for pendants of a slightly different type (Pedersen 2010: figs 4.35, 4.104.a.v and 4.107). Thus, it seems likely that most, or all, of the lead adornments at Kaupang were produced by the non-ferrous metalworkers at the site. The production of the lead pendants can be dated rather precisely, as the mould and a miscast pendant is found in contexts dated to AD 805/810–840/850. The other objects could not be dated more precisely.

The production of pendants does not demand great skills, access to specialised tools or specialised raw materials other than lead. However, a technical finesse points towards metalworkers with considerable skills and knowledge. Both the pendants and the mould demonstrate that the loop was produced when the object was cast, with the help of a small iron rod in a transverse groove in the mould. Moreover, the mould itself points to a rather sophisticated access to raw materials. It is made of a volcanic tuff brought to Kaupang from quite some distance, most likely from the Continent. Kaupang is the only site in Norway where the tuff has been identified, and it is used for yet another tool: a die for the production of small decorative nails of silver or gold (Pedersen 2010: fig. 4.33.a.i). It seems highly likely that this specific raw material was used by one group of non-ferrous metalworkers. In addition, the two types of tools suggest that this group mastered different techniques and metals – just like the other non-ferrous metalworkers at the site.

With leadworking in mind, it seems relevant to investigate if the lead mounts from the graves in the Oslofjord area are results of a local production. Earlier researchers, like Shetelig (1920) and Hougen (1934), seem to have assumed they were not, as the mounts were excluded from their discussions of local style and craft. Leadworking has, more generally, been seen as one of the characteristics of the non-ferrous metalworking in insular areas, including Viking towns like Dublin and York (Bayley 1992; Wallace 1987: 204, 212).

More recently, Wladyslaw Duczko (2004) and Bjørn Myhre (2013) have argued that the horse equipment in the ship burials in the Oslofjord area served to highlight close ties with the political elite in Central Sweden and the Rus area. They both point to the many similarities between the ship burials in the Oslofjord area and elite burials in Sweden, Russia and Ukraine. Works in the Borre style are emphasised, but the eastern parallels of the lead mounts are also mentioned (Myhre 2013: catalogue 1). However, the identical types from Hedeby and Domburg, as well as the leadworking at Kaupang, demonstrate that Viking worlds were more complex than the elite wanted them to appear. Moreover, the Kaupang material testifies to local production of mounts for horse harnesses, and even a type in the Borre style, known from the local ship burials. Among the tools from Kaupang is a lead mould for wax models, used to produce mounts of exactly the same type as a gilt copper alloy mount found during the reconstruction of the Gokstad mound (Pedersen 2010: 105–106). So, not all these objects were brought to the Oslofjord area as a result of the establishment and maintainance of alliances.

The stylistic analyses of the lead mounts from Gokstad suggest that they were produced by one hand or by a group of craftspeople operating together, with a copied mount as a possible exception. Scientific analyses have been carried out in order to investigate the raw material, and 39 mounts were sampled for lead isotope analyses (with MC-ICPMS; Pedersen *et al.* in prep.). The interpretation of the results was carried out independently of the archaeological interpretation, but produced strikingly similar results, also pointing to a set produced together. The lead isotope ratios fell into six distinct groups, interpreted as six types of raw material. However, five of the groups are linked together, as two most likely are the result of a deliberate mixing of another two (Pedersen *et al.* in prep.). Thus, it seems most likely that the mixing took place during the casting process. Moreover, all mounts of one type were produced by one type of raw material, while two or three types of mounts were cast from one type of raw material. There is only one exception to this: a few mounts that fell into a less distinct group. All in all, it seems most likely that the mounts were produced by one hand or group, at one site, and that the mixing of raw materials took place at the site where all the raw materials were in use (Pedersen *et al.* in prep.).

The access to lead of different types corresponds well with the artefact assemblage at

Kaupang, taking into account the reused containers and ingots of different shapes. When the scientific analyses of the mounts from Gokstad were initiated, a key question was to investigate the relationship between the leadworking at Kaupang and the lead mounts at Gokstad. It was then considered highly likely that the lead mounts might have been produced at Kaupang. The scientific analyses of the Gokstad mounts have not produced results that can support this hypothesis (Pedersen *et al.* in prep.), but in the meantime the source situation has changed, as demonstrated above. Leadworking was carried out at several different sites in the late 9th century, and Heimdaljordet now stands out as a more likely place for the production of the Gokstad mounts. Thus, extending the lead isotope analyses to the workshop assemblage from Heimdaljordet seems like a promising avenue for future research. The striking similarities of the lead mounts from the graves, in particular the ones on the western side of the fjord, indicate a common origin, and future lead isotope analyses may reveal whether or not they are made of the same raw material as the Gokstad ones.

### A new picture emerging

A new picture of non-ferrous metalworking in the Oslofjord area is emerging. There is no doubt that lead was used extensively by the non-ferrous metalworkers at Kaupang and at the nearby Gokstad complex, and it seems highly likely that lead was also worked at several other sites by the Oslo fjord. In consequence, leadworking formed an integral part of non-ferrous metalworking in Viking-Age Norway, and was far from unique for Kaupang.

The strictly limited amount of lead adornments in the graves reflects a burial practice where dress accessories of lead might not be included and where other ornaments of lead are rare. It is in the graves of the uppermost elite that the use of adornments in lead could be observed, and then only in the form of harnesses for their horses. Whether this reflects a wider scope of action for the elite, a tighter social control of dress accessories or other circumstances needs to be explored in the future. As affordable fashion without ethnic or regional bonds (Wamers 1994: 197) the dress accessories might have been irrelevant in the burial ritual. They could have been part of the urban material culture that united traders and craftspeople with different cultural, social and ethnic backgrounds (Gaut 2011: 255–257).

The identification of leadworking at different sites within the Oslofjord area provides a new understanding of metalworking in Viking-Age Norway. Kaupang stood out as a unique place in Norway until the discovery of Heimdaljordet, but now it seems highly likely that even more sites with similar finds will show up in the years to come. The new finds clearly indicate that craftspeople worked at several different sites within a restricted area, sketching a new social stage. Whether a metalworker was actually operating at more than one site, is a question to be followed up in the forthcoming studies of the workshop assemblage from Heimdaljordet and other sites. The tool for wax models found at Kaupang suggests that they did. It demonstrates the production at Kaupang of a type of mount only known from Gokstad. With Heimdaljordet in mind, it is possible that the slightly different mount was produced by the same hand, but within the Gokstad complex. If so, the relationship between the craftspeople and the elite might have been different from that frequently assumed. It has often been taken for granted that the craftspeople were subordinate to the elite, and had to fight for the elite's attention and favour. The different sites with evidence of non-ferrous metalworking could suggest that it may have been the other way round: that the elite were dependent on attracting craftspeople to their estates. After all, they were dependent on precious gifts to maintain power, and the metalworkers produced such gifts. We must assume that the different local rulers in the Oslofjord area competed against each other in all possible ways. Moreover, as people in Scandinavia accumulated wealth as a result of Viking raids, even more groups could have requested the skills of the non-ferrous metalworkers, providing them with a larger social room to manoeuvre in.

The lead adornments also invite a discussion of the background of the metalworkers operating in the Oslofjord area. Shetelig (1920) identified a Vestfold school behind the artworks from Oseberg, Gokstad and Borre, working within a Scandinavian tradition, and with animal motifs as their characteristics. The evidence from Kaupang demonstrates that at least some craftspeople worked with completely different motifs. The lead pendants, for instance, have a motif with origins in the Frankish area (Pedersen in press b). Maybe some non-ferrous metalworkers grew up, or lived outside the Oslofjord area? One of the types of lead mounts from Gokstad is especially noteworthy in this respect, as two eyes and a mouth were stamped with a punch after the mount was cast (Fig. 12.2b). Despite sticking to another ornamental style, the non-ferrous metalworkers seem to have flirted with the local(s). Could this be a foreign non-ferrous metalworker who paid tribute to the local style, or is it an attempt of a local to sneak in a well-known motif even when an object in a foreign style was ordered?

## To be continued…

This is hardly the last word on leadworking in Viking-Age Norway, as more knowledge is expected to be added in the years to come. It is reasonable to assume that intensified rescue management excavations and increasing metal-detecting activity will unearth more finds, both finished products and manufacturing waste. Secondly, a greater awareness of lead adornments as a relevant find category, should result in more lead finds being acknowledged as Viking-Age artefacts and delivered to the museums. Thirdly, more information could be extracted from existing museum collections. For instance, the use of lead isotope analyses to investigate similarities and differences in the use of raw materials could be extended to the workshop waste from Heimdaljordet, other lead mounts in the Oslofjord area, and similar mounts found elsewhere in the Viking worlds.

## *References*

Aarsberetning

1867. Oversikt over de til Universitetets Samling af nordiske Oldsager i 1867 indkomne Sager, ældre end Reformationen. *Foreningen til norske fortidsminners bevaring. Aarsberetning* 1867: 34–72.

Anspach, Birte
2010. Die bleifunde von Haithabu. In *Stüdien zu Haithabu und Füsing*, edited by Claus von Carnap-Bornheim, pp. 13–128. Die ausgrabungen in Haithabu, Vol. 16. Wachholtz, Neumünster.
Auch, Michał, Mateusz Bogucki, Beata Jurkiewicz and Macej Trzeciecki
2012. Ślad osadniczy z późnego okresu wędrówek ludów na stanowisku Janów Pomorski 1. In *Janów Pomorski Stan 1. Wyniki ratowniczych badań archeologicznych w latach 2007–2008*, Vol. 1:2, edited by Mateusz Bogucki and Marek Jagodziński, pp. 9–232. Museum of Archaeology and History in Elbląg, Elbląg.
Bayley, Justine
1992. *Anglo-Scandinavian Non-Ferrous Metalworking from 16–22 Coppergate*. The Archaeology of York: The Small Finds, Vol. 17. Council for British Archaeology, York.
Bill, Jan and Aoife Daly
2012. The plundering of the ship graves from Oseberg and Gokstad: an example of power politics? *Antiquity* 86: 808–824.
Bill, Jan and Christian Løchsen Rødsrud
2013. En ny markeds- og produksjonsplass ved Gokstad i Vestfold. *Nicolay* 120: 5–12.
Bonde, Niels and Arne Emil Christensen
1993. Dendrochronological dating of the Viking Age ship burials at Oseberg, Gokstad and Tune, Norway. *Antiquity* 67: 575–583.
Brooks, Howard, Nina Crummy and Marion M. Archibald
2004. A medieval lead canister from Colchester High Street: hoard container, or floor safe? *Medieval Archaeology* 48: 131–142.
Brøgger, A. W.
1916. *Borrefundet og Vestfoldkongernes graver*. Videnskapsselskapets skrifter II, Hist.-filos. Klasse, Vol. 1. Jacob Dybwad, Kristiania.
1922. Rolfsøyætten: Et arkeologisk bidrag til vikingetidens historie. *Bergen museums aarbok, hist.-antikv. række* 1920–21: 3–42.
Brøndsted, Johannes
1936. Danish Inhumation Graves of the Viking Age. *Acta Archaeologica* 7: 81–228.
Capelle, Torsten
1968. *Der Metallschmuck von Haithabu. Studien zur wikingischen Metallkunst.* Die Ausgrabungen in Haithabu, Vol. 5. Karl Wachholtz Verlag, Neumünster.
1976. *Die frühgeschichtlichen Metallfunde von Domburg auf Walcheren.* Nederlandse oudheden.
Dobat, Andres
2010. Füsing. Ein frühmittelalterlicher Zentralplatz in Umfeld von Haithabu/Schleswig. In *Stüdien zu Haithabu und Füsing*, edited by Claus von Carnap-Bornheim, pp. 131–256. Die ausgrabungen in Haithabu, Vol. 16. Wachholtz, Neumünster.
Duczko, Wladyslaw
2004. *Viking Rus. Studies on the Presence of Scandinavians in Eastern Europe.* The Northern World, Vol. 12. Leiden, Brill.
Feveile, Claus
2006. *Ribe Studier. Det ældste Ribe. Udgravninger på nordsiden af Ribe Å 1984–2000*, Vol. 1.2. Jysk Arkæologisk Selskabs skrifter, Vol. 51. Jysk Arkæologisk Selskab, Højbjerg.
Gansum, Terje
1997. Jernaldermonumenter og maktstrukturer. Vestfold som konfliktarena. In *Konflikt i forhistorien*, edited by Ingrid Fuglestvedt and Bjørn Myhre, pp. 27–40. AmS-Varia, Vol. 30. Arkeologisk museum i Stavanger, Stavanger.

Gaut, Bjarne

2011. Vessel glass and evidence of glassworking. In *Things from the town. Artefacts and inhabitants in Viking-Age Kaupang*, edited by Dagfinn Skre, pp. 169–279. Kaupang Excavation Project Publications Series, Vol. 3. Norske Oldfunn 24. Aarhus University Press, Århus.

Graham-Campbell, James

1980. *Viking Artefacts: A Select Catalogue*. British Museum, London.

2011. *The Cuerdale Hoard and Related Viking-Age Silver and Gold from Britain and Ireland in the British Museum*. British Museum Research Publication, Vol. 185. British Museum, London.

Hedenstierna-Jonson, Charlotte and Lena Holmquist Olausson

2006. *The Oriental Mounts from Birka's Garrison. An Expression of Warrior Rank and Status*. Antikvarisk arkiv, Vol. 81. Kungl.Vitterhets Historie och Antikvitetsakademien, Stockholm.

Henriksen, Mogens Bo

2000. *Detektorfund – hvad skal vi med dem? Dokumentation og registrering af bopladser med detektorfund fra jernalder og middelalder*. Skrifter fra Odense Bys Museer, Vol. 5. Odense Bys Museer, Odense.

Hougen, Bjørn

1934. Studier i Gokstadfunnet. *Universitetets Oldsaksamling Årbok* 1931–1932: 74–112.

Jouttijärvi, Arne

2007. Kobberlegeringer fra Kaupang. Heimdal-archaeometry. Report in the archive of the Museum of Cultural History, University of Oslo.

Khazaei, Houshang and Camilla Haugan

2013. Kufiske dirhemer fra Rygge. Electronic document, http://www.khm.uio.no/om/aktuelt/nye-funn/2011/kufiske-dirhemer-fra-rygge.html, accessed Desember 16, 2013.

Loveluck, C. P.

1998. A high-status Anglo-Saxon settlement at Flixborough, Lincolnshire. *Antiquity* 72: 146–164.

Müller-Wille, Michael

2001. Tierstile des 8.–12. Jahrhunderts im Norden Europas. Dendrochronologie und kunsthistorische Einordnung. In *Tiere – Menschen – Götter. Wikingerzeitliche Kunststile und ihre neuzeitliche Rezeption*, edited by Michael Müller-Wille and Lars Olof Larsson, pp. 215–250. Vandenhoeck and Ruprecht, Göttingen.

Myhre, Bjørn

2003. Borregravfeltet som historisk arena. *Viking* 66: 48–78.

2013. Viken – Sveariket – Rus-riket. Viken omkring år 900 i lys av en nytolking av Borre-funnet. *Viking* 76: 151–180.

Nicolaysen, Nicolay

1882. *Langskibet fra Gokstad ved Sandefjord*. Alb. Cammermeyer, Kristiania.

1886. Udgravninger i Kvelde (Hedrum) 1885. *Foreningen til norske fortidsminners bevaring. Aarsberetning* 1865:22–44.

Pedersen, Unn

2008. Weights and balances. In *Means of Exchange. Dealing with Silver in the Viking Age*, edited by Dagfinn Skre, pp. 119–195. Kaupang Excavation Project Publication Series, Vol. 2 and Norske Oldfunn, Vol. 23. Aarhus University Press, Århus.

2010. *I smeltedigelen. Finsmedene i vikingtidsbyen Kaupang*. Ph.D. dissertation, Department of Archaeology, Conservation and History, University of Oslo.

in press a. Noe for enhver smak – smykkeproduksjon i vikingtidsbyene. In Inn i fortida – ut i verden – i museet!, edited by Jon Anders Risvaag, Terje Brattli and Ragnhild Berge. Acta Archaeologica Nidarosiensia, *Vitark* 9. Fagbokforlaget, Trondheim.

in press b. Urban craftspeople at Viking-Age Kaupang. In *Everyday Products in the Middle Ages: Crafts, Consumption and the Individual in Northern Europe c. AD 800–1600*, edited by Gitte Hansen, Steven Ashby and Irene Baug. Oxbow Books, Oxford.

Pedersen, Unn and Lars Pilø
2007. The settlement: artefacts and site periods. In *Kaupang in Skiringssal,* edited by Dagfinn Skre, pp. 179–190. Kaupang Excavation Project Publication Series, Vol. 1 and Norske Oldfunn, Vol. 22. Aarhus University Press, Århus.

Pedersen, Unn and Christian Løchsen Rødsrud
2013. Nye vektlodd fra Vestfold. *Nicolay* 119: 53–59.

Pedersen, Unn, Tom Andersen and Siri Simonsen
In prep. Lead ornaments from the Viking ship burial, Gokstad, Norway.

Petersen, Jan
1928. *Vikingetidens smykker*. Stavanger museum, Stavanger.

Roesdahl, Else, James Graham-Campbell, Patricia Connor, and Kenneth Pearson
1981. *The Vikings in England and in their Danish homeland*. The Anglo-Danish Viking Project, London.

Rygh, Oluf
1885. *Norske Oldsager*. Alb. Cammermeyer, Christiania.

Serning, Inga
1956. *Lapska offerplatsfynd från järnålder och medeltid i de svenska lappmarkerna*. Nordiska museet: Acta Lapponica, Vol. 11. Hugo Gebers, Stockholm.

Shetelig, Haakon
1920. Vestfoldskolen. In *Osebergfundet bind III*, edited by A.W. Brøgger, Hj. Falk and Haakon Shetelig, pp. 8–334. Den Norske Stat, Kristiania.

Skre, Dagfinn
2007. Towns and markets, kings and central places in south-western Scandinavia *c*. AD 800–950. In *Kaupang in Skiringssal,* edited by Dagfinn Skre, pp. 445–469. Kaupang Excavation Project Publication Series, Vol. 1 and Norske Oldfunn, Vol. 22. Aarhus University Press, Århus.
2008. Dark Age towns: the Kaupang case. Reply to Przemysław Urbańczyk. *Norwegian Archaeological Review* 41: 194–212.
2011. The inhabitants: activities. In *Things from the Town: Artefacts and Inhabitants in Viking-Age Kaupang*, edited by Dagfinn Skre, pp. 397–415. Kaupang Excavation Project Publications Series, Vol. 3. Norske Oldfunn 24. Aarhus University Press, Århus.

Stylegar, Frans-Arne and Per G. Nordseng
2003. Del II Mot historisk tid. In *Øst for Folden*, edited by Ellen Anne Pedersen, Frans-Arne Stylegar and Per G. Nordseng, pp. 278–512. Østfolds historie, Vol. 1. Østfold fylkeskommune, Sarpsborg.

Sørensen, Anne C.
2001. *Ladby: A Danish Ship-grave from the Viking Age*. Ships and boats of the North, Vol. 3. Viking Ship Museum, Roskilde.

Tansøy, Birgit
2001. Fisket på Kaupang i vikingtid. Hovedfagsoppgave, Department of Archaeology, Conservation and History, University of Oslo.

Wallace, Patrick F.
1987. The economy and commerce of Viking Age Dublin. In *Der Handel der Karolinger- und Wikingerzeit*, edited by Klaus Düwel, Herbert Jankuhn, Harald Siems and Dieter Tiempe pp. 200–245. Untersuchungen zu Handel und Verkehr der vor- und frühgeschichtlichen Zeit in Mittel- und Nordeuropa, Vol. 4. Vandenhoeck and Ruprecht, Göttingen.

Wamers, Egon
1994. *Die Frühmittelalterlichen lesefunde aus der Löhrstrasse (Baustelle Hilton II) in Mainz.* Mainzer Archäologishe Schriften, Vol. 1. Archäologische Denmalpflege, Mainz.
Wexelsen, Einar
1981. *Gokstadfunnet: Et 100-års minne.* Sandefjordmuseene årbok 1979–80. Sandefjordsmuseene, Sandefjord.
Wilson, David M.
1995. *Vikingatidens konst.* Signums svenska konsthistoria, Vol. 2. Signum, Lund.
Williams, Gareth and Barry Ager
2010. *The Vale of York Hoard.* British Museum, London.
Øye, Ingvild
2011. Textile tools from Kaupang. In *Things from the Town. Artefacts and Inhabitants in Viking-Age Kaupang,* edited by Dagfinn Skre, pp. 339–379. Kaupang Excavation Project Publication Series, Vol. 3 and Norske Oldfunn, Vol. 24. Aarhus University Press, Aarhus.

Chapter 13

# Isotopic analysis of silver from Hedeby and some nearby hoards. Preliminary results

*Stephen Merkel, Andreas Hauptmann, Volker Hilberg and Robert Lehmann*

*Abstract*

Silver played an important role both as a material of status and as a medium for exchange in the Viking Age. Hedeby was at the frontier between the monetized kingdoms of the West and the hacksilver/bullion economy of Scandinavia and the Baltic. Fueled by the influx of newly mined and recycled silver from the Middle East, Central Asia, and Europe, mints were irregularly maintained at Hedeby and across Denmark in the 9th–11th centuries. A diachronic study was undertaken to examine the flow of silver as a raw material at Hedeby from the 10th–11th centuries with the use of elemental and lead isotope analysis. Sampling of coins was done by Laser Ablation Inductively Coupled Plasma Mass Spectrometry, allowing for precise and accurate analyses with limited damage to the objects. The minting campaigns at Hedeby provide an excellent chronologic mirror to the changing sources of silver.

## Introduction

In the Viking Age, silver was one of the most widely used forms of durable, movable wealth and became an important medium of exchange. The need for silver and other valuables can be tied to the development of long-distance trading networks, which not only conveyed material goods from distant lands, but also brought about cultural interaction and the exchange of ideas over large geographic areas (Sindbæk 2011; Skre 2011; Steuer 2004).

Silver, compact and valuable, lends itself well to long-distance travel and is easily recycled, alloyed, and refined. It could remain in circulation for centuries, as in the case of Sassanian Drachmas in the Abbasid Empire (Heidemann 2011: 454), but constant loss and an ever increasing reliance on silver for the currency in many parts of the medieval world meant that new silver was actively being sought, mined and distributed (Patterson 1972).

The silver used in Viking-Age Scandinavia arrived by various means, but most, if not all, came from lands outside Scandinavia. There are a number of famous and prolific mining regions that supplied the early medieval world with silver such as Carolingian Melle (Téreygeol 2002), the Ilak of Samanid Transoxania in modern-day Uzbekistan (Buryakov 1974), and the Ottonian/Salian Harz Mountains in Germany (Klappauf 1993). While these are the large-scale mining regions, the 'giants' of silver production, the real picture of medieval silver production is much more complex.

There is a multitude of factors that impact the productivity of mines and the distribution of their products. The rise and fall of mines is not only linked to the availability of ore, but also to the technological capabilities, economic/political stability, and availability of fuel. Our knowledge of mining during the early medieval period is not complete, nor will it ever be. With a focus on the large well-published mines we risk the danger of underestimating the role of small or decentralized operations and mines that are unknown or entirely lost to archaeology through more recent workings.

The material science analysis of silver objects can give us a picture that historical and archaeological evidence alone cannot. The field of archaeometry is a sub-discipline of archaeology, and its methods can provide new strands of evidence to support or supplement archaeological/historical interpretations and can be used to find inconsistencies in the record.

Lead isotope analysis is a relatively untapped resource in the study of Viking silver. Due to the lack of comparable studies, this project is exploratory in nature; we aim to find the benefits and limitations of this technique in combination with trace elemental analysis to investigate silver production, trade, and re-use in the Viking Age. Coins, jewelry, and hacksilver found at Hedeby and some nearby hoards from the late 9th–11th centuries were analyzed in order to identify any chronological trends in isotope and elemental composition. The project was designed to examine how silver objects and coins are interconnected by comparing the different types of silver objects available at Hedeby with the Hedeby coins and other Danish coins. These coinages form the backbone of this study; since they are thought to be produced at Hedeby and other Danish mints, they can potentially give information about the silver stock at different points in time.

## Minting at Hedeby

Minting at Hedeby in the 9th and 10th centuries is a widely accepted hypothesis and is based on the distribution and concentration of coin finds. The typology is illustrated by Ralf Wiechmann (2007: Abb.1a–b), but a few examples of the Hedeby coinage are presented in Figure 13.1. Brita Malmer (1966, 2002) developed the typology and distribution of the combination group (KG) series coins. The first minting at Hedeby (KG3) is thought to have taken place around the year AD 825 and was stylistically based on Frisian imitations of the Carolingian Dorestad coinage (Malmer 1966: 204–209). Minting resumed in the first decades of the 10th century with the KG7, which is stylistically related to the earlier KG3. The precise dating of the KG7 is not settled, but is thought to be between AD 900 and 920 (Wiechmann 2007). The KG8 and KG9 are further elaborations on the design of KG7 and are attributed to the 950s–980s (Malmer 2002; Wiechmann 2007).

*Fig. 13.1. Examples of Hedeby/ Danish coins analyzed in this study. From left to right, top to bottom: KG7, KG9, KG10a and penny of Hardeknut. Photo: Stephen Merkel, © Landesmusem Schloss Gottorf.*

In the 980s and 990s, the KG10 Cross coinage of Harald Bluetooth replaced the Carolus-Dorestad motif coinage, and recent findings suggest minting occurred at Hedeby (Moesgaard 2012). The distribution and chronology of the Årstad 95/96 coinages also indicate that Hedeby was minting between AD 1015 and 1035 and typologically represent the transition in Denmark between the earlier half-bracteate and the later penny type coinage (Wiechmann 2013). In the 1030s the style of coinage in Denmark radically changed taking a more nationalistic character with mints having individual symbols (Malmer 2002: 129). Under the reigns of Hardeknut (1035–1042), Magnus (1042–1047), and Sven Estridsen (1042–1074) coins were minted at Hedeby and other Danish towns (Gullbekk 2000; Hauberg 1900; Jonsson 1994: 223–227), but minting under Knut the Holy (1075–1086) is more obscure.

## Hedeby and the trade of silver

The town of Hedeby developed into a trading and manufacturing center, which was not only a focal point of royal power, but also functioned as a hub for Baltic and North Sea traffic (Hilberg 2009; Kalmring 2010; Steuer 1987). The finding of weights and scales, silver ingots, hacksilver fragments, locally made coins, and foreign coins from as far as Afghanistan attests to the importance of silver as an exchange medium and the complexity of the local and supra-regional transfer of silver.

Although coin-use was widespread in many of the silver-using lands in Europe, North Africa, and Asia, coins are astonishingly rare in southern Scandinavia before the later 9th century. The custom of trading with weight adjusted rings and ingots, known as the Aurar

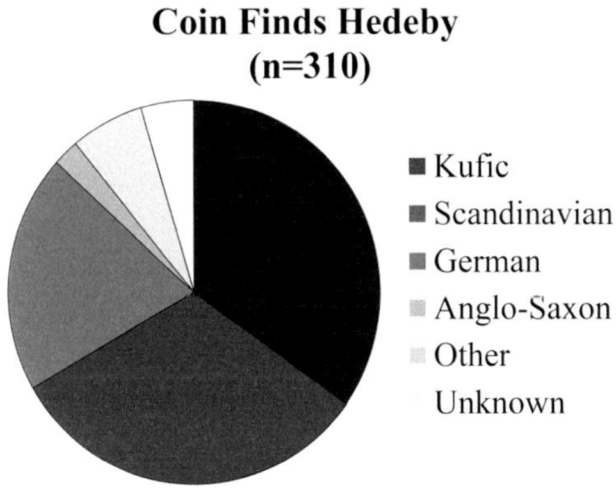


*Fig. 13.2. Breakdown of coin finds from Hedeby. Coin counts are based on the work of Wiechmann (2007) and Hilberg (2011).*

System, may be partially responsible for this discrepancy (Coupland 2007: 15–20; Kilger 2008a). The Aurar System was used in southern Scandinavia in the early Viking Age, and perhaps earlier, but a drastic change occurred with the introduction of a normalized weight system and the establishment of the hacksilver economy around the turn of the 10th century (Kilger 2008a).

One possible consequence of the collapse of the Aurar System in southern Scandinavia at the end of the 9th century is that coins and coin fragments were no longer being melted down to form ingots and rings in such numbers as before (Kilger 2008a: 324). Archaeologically speaking, coins are invaluable due to their inscriptions and stylistic peculiarities that allow them to be geographically and chronologically placed, and, with the development of the hacksilver economy, coins can be seen in the archaeological record in increasing numbers.

By looking at the breakdown of coin finds from Hedeby, three foci become evident: Kufic, early Scandinavian, and German coins (Fig. 13.2). Viking Age Anglo-Saxon/Hiberno-Norse coins are particularly uncommon in Schleswig-Holstein before the end of the 10th century (Wiechmann 1996: 88). For example, seven coins are known from Hedeby (Hilberg 2011; Wiechmann 2007), and there are three from the overwhelmingly Islamic Giekau Hoard (*terminus post quem* 921, Wiechmann 1996: 240), but the hoards of List and Lübeck of the early 11th century have numerous specimens. Carolingian coins are also rare in southern Scandinavia (Garipzanov 2008; Wiechmann 1996: 80–81), and French coins from middle 10th–11th century are rarer (Wiechmann 1996: 83).

Two broad trends can be seen in the coin finds of Scandinavia: one from the Islamic world in the east from the early 9th to the mid-10th century (Kilger 2008b: 211–212; Metcalf 1997; Noonan 2001) and the second from the Anglo-Saxons and the Ottonians/Salians in the west in the second half of the 10th into the 11th century (Blackburn 1993; Hatz 1974, 1983).

Dirhams coming from the Islamic world are diverse and do not constitute a single movement, but waves from various regions at different times (Kilger 2008b; Metcalf 1997: 310–312; Wiechmann 1996: 77–78). It is clear that the eastern trade routes were the major arteries for the flow of Kufic coins. Abbasid dirhams dominate in the 9th century, but by the late 9th century, Samanid dirhams begin to be minted in Central Asia and Khorasan and have a major presence in the hoards and coin finds of the Baltic in the 10th century. German coins appear in Hedeby starting with the mid-10th century Sachsenpfennig, which is thought to be minted in Magdeburg. The Sachsenpfennig predate, but might overlap with, the minting of the Otto-Adelheid-Pfennig, which is closely tied to silver production in the Harz Mountains (Zwicker *et al.* 1991). Coins from the Cologne region and Frisia produced at the end of the 10th into the 11th century also found their way to Hedeby.

## The archaeometry of Viking-Age silver

Viking-Age silver has been the focus of a number of analytical studies, which form an important basis for further study. The analysis of silver has often been achieved through non-destructive means such as X-ray Fluorescence and Microprobe Analysis (Ilisch *et al.* 2003; Kruse and Tate 1992; Metcalf and Northover 1985), but destructive techniques such as Atomic Absorption Spectrophotometry and analytical cupellation have also been used (McKerrell and Stevenson 1972; Metcalf and Northover 1988: 116). These tools can reveal information not only about silver purity, but also elemental relationships among various types of objects.

The groundbreaking study by Hugh McKerrell and Robert Stevenson (1972) demonstrated that there are several distinguishing characteristics between types of Viking-Age silver. These differences in chemistry either relate to the ore minerals used to produce the silver or to technological traditions or practices.

Silver-containing minerals have formed in a number of deposits around the world. Silver can occur in nature as metallic silver, which can be remarkably pure. More often, silver minerals are found mixed with sulphur, gold, antimony, arsenic, copper, bismuth, iron, lead, and many other elements. During the smelting and refining processes most of these elements are separated from the silver; gold, bismuth, and lead are the major exceptions. Cupellation, a high temperature process where noble metals are separated from metallic lead, was used for the production of silver in the medieval world (Meyers 2003). It is not possible to separate gold from silver with this process and bismuth and lead are very difficult to remove completely as has been found through experimental investigations (McKerrell and Stevenson 1972; Pernicka and Bachmann 1983: 595). The use of gold and bismuth contents in distinguishing sources of early medieval silver was discussed by several early researchers (Kraume and Hatz 1967: 36; McKerrell and Stevenson 1972: 202–203; Metcalf 1972: 413–416) and has continuously been used since.

Elements such as tin, zinc, and mercury found in silver reflect technological traditions. These elements are typically removed by the cupellation process and thus reflect anthropogenic alteration of the alloy after refining (Pernicka and Bachmann 1983). Their presence indicates intentional processes such as the use of brass or bronze as an alloying agent in silver or application of mercury surface treatments. There are ties between the Carolingian and the Anglo-Saxon silver in that brass was often used in alloying the silver, especially in the debased coinage of the mid-9th century at the time of Charles the Bald

(McKerrell and Stevenson 1972: 205; Metcalf and Northover 1985: 161–162, 1989: 114–115; Sarah 2010: 233).

Bismuth in Samanid silver from mints in Transoxania and Afghanistan has been the topic of a number of studies (Cowell and Lowick 1988; Eniosova and Mitoyan 2008; Ilisch *et al.* 2003; McKerrell and Stevenson 1972). Bismuth, an impurity which considerably increases the hardness and brittleness of silver (Zwicker *et al.* 1991: 72–73), can typically be found in quantities above 0.5% in Samanid silver, and, in some cases where the silver was poorly refined, can be greater than 10% (Ilisch *et al.* 2003). This silver is unusual in comparison to silver produced in Europe and elsewhere in the Islamic world at this time.

A great deal of information can be obtained through the analysis of trace elements. Some characteristics relating to both technological traditions and the geology of silver sources can be defined. When speaking in generalities, the analyses show that differentiation is possible, but due to differences in the various analytical techniques the resolution can be unsatisfactory or incompatible for direct comparison. With advancements in mass spectrometry and laser ablation techniques, particularly in the area of lead isotope analysis, an entirely new dimension can be brought to the discussion.

**Lead isotope analysis and its application in archaeology**

The use of lead isotope analysis in archaeology is in constant transition, and its success is tied to the adoption of technological innovations as well as an ever-growing awareness of the method's capabilities and limitations (Gale and Stos-Gale 2000; Pollard and Gale 2009). The increasing application of multi-collector ICP-MS in Archaeology (Niederschlag *et al.* 2003), and newly developed laser ablation techniques (Lehmann 2011; Ponting *et al.* 2003), have led to great improvements in the instrumental precision and accuracy, speed of preparation, processing time, and the cost of analysis. A major advantage of laser ablation is that it ablates a microscopic area of an object so that fresh, non-corroded metal can be analyzed with very little visible damage to the original object. Additionally, its semi-non-destructive nature means that the restricted access to sampling precious metal objects is gradually becoming less of an obstacle in archaeometallurgical research.

To briefly go into the chemistry and theory behind lead isotope analysis, there are four stable isotopes of lead, three of which derive from the radioactive decay of uranium and thorium. It has been shown in a number of studies that the ratios between the isotopes of lead are unaffected by metallurgical processes like smelting and cupellation (Gale and Stos-Gale 2000: 525–528). It is therefore clear that a connection can be made from the ore to the finished object via the lead isotope signature. Since the signature of various ore deposits can overlap, the lead can only be confidently used to rule out sources that do not match. In theory, with a combination of analytical methods and archaeological information, lead isotope analysis can produce positive results, but, in practice, it can be quite challenging.

As simple as it may be, the lead isotope ratios in the silver only informs about the lead in the silver. Medieval silver typically has up to one percent of lead, but a distinction needs to be made between the origins of the lead and the silver. Lead metallurgy is intimately intertwined with silver metallurgy: silver and lead ore often occur together geologically. Lead was needed during smelting to act as a silver collector and was used in the refining stage to purify the silver. If old or impure silver was refined, or purified, the isotope ratio reflects the lead used during the cupellation process, effectually breaking the link between the silver origin and the end-product. If silver is recycled, or mixed with other silver, then the isotope ratio reflects this mixture, but there is a relationship to the original composition. When silver from two or more sources are mixed together, the silver becomes homogenized and the isotope ratios are averaged. This means that the new ratio must fall between the two or more original ratios. When the metal is mixed on a large scale, lines will form between the different sources reflecting the various proportions of metal from each source. These lines are called 'mixing lines' (Klein 2007: 144–146; Stos-Gale 2001: 58–60).

While lead isotope analysis is primarily used in archaeology for provenance studies to link metal objects to their prospective ore deposit (Gale and Stos-Gale 2000), this is not the only use. In more complex systems it can be used as a qualitative/quantitative tool to explore interrelationships between metal objects and to explore technological questions regarding the recycling and refining of silver. The technology used in the past impacts the lead isotope signature in important ways, and these principles must be kept in mind while interpreting the lead isotope signatures of silver objects. The goal of this study is not to pin-point the sources of each metal supply, but to look at broader trends and relationships in coinages and silver objects that may have chronological and archaeological significance.

## Methodology

The sampling strategy reflects the range of object types found at Hedeby, but three areas of focus were selected to reflect the three largest groups of coins: Kufic, German, and Scandinavian coins of the tenth and eleventh centuries (Table 13.1). The objects themselves mostly come from excavation and metal-detecting campaigns at Hedeby, but some supplementary examples were taken from the Schleswig harbor excavations and from hoards in Schleswig-Holstein (Wiechmann 1996), namely the Steinfeld Hoard (*t.p.q.* 920–950), the Giekau Hoard (*t.p.q.* 922), the Waterneverstorf I Hoard (*t.p.q.* 976), the List Hoard (*t.p.q.* 1003), and an unpublished West Slavonic hoard (*terminus ante quem* 985) curated in Tübingen. Coins were selected with a priority for securely attributed types and dates.

A total of 158 coins and 15 jewelry objects were analyzed at the Leibniz Universität Hannover with laser ablation inductively coupled plasma mass spectrometry (LA-ICP-MS). Nanosecond-LA-ICP-Quadropole-MS was used to characterize the major, minor and trace elements. All silver objects were analyzed by Portable X-ray Fluorescence (pXRF) to compare the elemental results of the LA-ICP-MS. A Neptune Femtosecond-LA-ICP-Multi-Collector-MS was used to obtain lead isotope abundances and to correct the mass bias Neptune Femtosecond-LA-ICP-Multi-Collector-MS was used to obtain lead isotope abundances, and to correct the mass fractionation, a thallium isotope standard (NIST SRM 997) was measured simultaneously following the previously devised methods (Begley and Sharp 1997; Longerich *et al.* 1987; Rehkämper and Halliday 1998; Walder *et al.* 1993).

| **Silver coins** | **Date range** | **No.** |
|---|---|---|
| Abbasid Dirhams | 776–872 | 11 |
| Saffarid Dirhams | 878–884 | 1 |
| Samanid Dirhams | 892–990 | 37 |
| Unknown Dirhams | ? | 1 |
| Khazar/Volga Dirham imitations | 870–941 | 10 |
| Byzantine Miliaresia | 963–989 | 3 |
| Saxon/Cologne/Frisian Denars | 950–1040 | 40 |
| Anglo-Saxon Pennies | 942–1025 | 5 |
| Hiberno-Norse Pennies | 997–1003 | 5 |
| Hedeby/Danish Half Bracteates & Denars | 900–1086 | 41 |
| **Non-minted Objects** | | |
| Silver ingots/frag. | 9th–10th century | 6 |
| Hacksilver | 9th–10th century | 12 |
| Silver jewelry | 800–1100 | 15 |
| Lead | 800–1100 | 6 |
| Cupellation waste | 850–1100 | 4 |
| Pewter coins | 9th–10th century | 4 |

*Table 13.1. List of objects analyzed in this study and approximate date ranges of production.*

The interference of $^{204}$Hg with $^{204}$Pb was corrected through the measurement of $^{202}$Hg. For further information concerning the analytical methodology refer to Lehmann (2011).

Further ingots, hacksilver, lead, and cupellation waste were destructively sampled and analyzed at the Goethe Universität Frankfurt am Main with a Neptune ICP-Multi-Collector-MS for lead isotope analysis and elemental analysis was performed at the Deutsches Bergbau-Museum, Bochum, with an ICP-MS Thermo Scientific Element XR. Silver samples were dissolved in nitric acid for major, minor, and trace elemental analysis. Gold content was measured separately using Aqua Regia as a solvent. For the lead isotope analysis an internal thallium standard (NIST SRM 997) was used to correct for mass fractionation, and $^{202}$Hg was measured to correct mercury interference. For sample processing and instrumental set-up in Frankfurt refer to Klein *et al.* (2009). In order to insure the data compatibility between the laboratories the same lead isotope standards were used (NIST981), and both data sets were rectified to the values obtained by Todt *et al.* (1996). Additionally, as a control, two hacksilver objects were analyzed in three labs with all instruments.

## Preliminary results and discussion

The isotope ratios in addition to the elements gold, bismuth, zinc, tin, lead, and copper were used to compare the objects to one another and to analyses published. The main focus of this study is to observe the changes in the silver stock used in the Hedeby/Danish coins of the 10th and 11th centuries; therefore the discussion of the results will follow chronologically.

### *Hedeby KG7 (AD 900–920)*

The Malmer KG7s are the earliest Scandinavian coins involved in this study. Ten specimens were analyzed which form a relatively homogeneous group elementally and isotopically.

Their purity is high, above 90% silver, and the coins contain traces of zinc and tin. The gold contents are between 0.2% and 0.4% and the bismuth contents are below 0.2%. The most closely related silver to the KG7 is found in the bar ingots and many hacksilver objects (wires, bars, arm and neck ring fragments) also have a nearly identical range of isotope ratios and elemental compositions. A large Permian spiral ring terminal (Spiral ring Type Sa I after Stenberger 1958: 125) is also in this group which itself weighing 50 g likely belonged to a larger type ring weighing 200–400 g.

Besides the hacksilver and ingots, the next nearest group to the KG7 is a portion of the Khazar and Volga-Bulgharian dirham imitations and two dirhams from Iran. These dirhams and dirham imitations date from the late 9th century and early 10th centuries and match isotopically, but have a wider spread of gold and bismuth contents. The silver of the KG7 is distinctly different from the contemporary Samanid dirhams in gold and bismuth contents.

Western sources for the silver may be possible because one Carolingian silver fitting of the first half of the 9th century matches the KG7 silver group. However, the contemporary Carolingian and Anglo-Saxon coins of the late 9th century from the Cuerdale Hoard, in which a KG7 coin was also found, do not match with the KG7 silver group because of their higher gold contents (Metcalf and Northover 1988).

The isotope ratios from several ore deposits in Iran, Anatolia, and Bulgaria (Berthoud 1979; Chegini *et al.* 2000: 309; Stos-Gale 2004) overlap with the KG7 group and overlap slightly with ore from the Carolingian mine of Melle (Téreygeol *et al.* 2005) and other deposits in southern France (Baron *et al.* 2006; Bode *et al.* 2007). Although Melle was ravaged by the Vikings in 848 and thought not to have recovered (Blanchard 2001: 513–514), the evidence based on the mining archaeology and charcoal presented by Téreygeol (2013) indicates that mining industry was resilient and remained strong until the 10th century.

Based on the evidence at hand, an eastern source of the KG7 and related ingots and hacksilver is possible. It is clear that the KG7 silver group is a mixture of high quality silver that predates the widespread recycling of Samanid silver. On the basis of this new information it can be suggested that the KG7 could be dated earlier, or that it may have taken a decade or more for the newly arriving silver from Central Asia to be melted down and to become fully incorporated into the silver stock.

### *Hedeby/Danish KG8-10 (AD 950–985)*

A group of ten Hedeby/Danish coins of the KG8-10 type were analyzed. A lapse of around 30 years occurred between the minting of the KG7 and the KG8 (Wiechmann 2007: 185–187). During this time, Samanid silver dirhams from the mints of As-Shash, Samarkand and Balkh flowed into the Baltic via eastern trade routes, an importation of silver that must have been immense (Noonan 2001). There is a gradual switch from hoards being dominated by Abbasid dirhams to Samanid dirhams in the first quarter of the 10th century (Noonan 2001: 147–158). While it is believed that the flow of Samanid silver into the Northern Lands happened very quickly, within a decade of minting, it is evident that

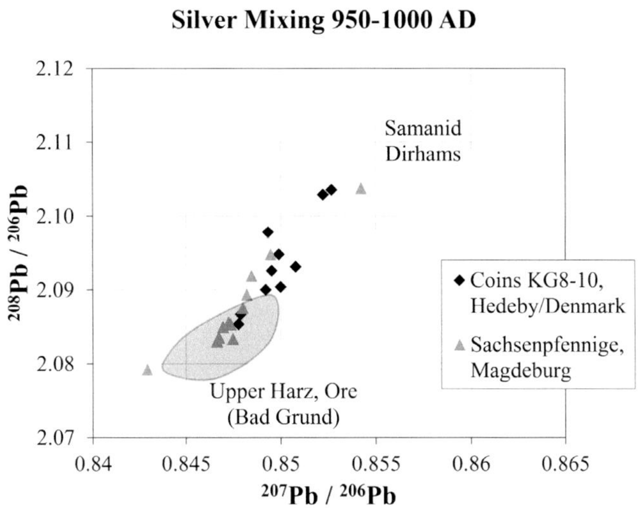


*Fig. 13.3. The isotopic relationship of the KG8-10 coins to the Sachsenpfennige compared to Bad Grund ore deposit in the Upper Harz (Purple field, after Lehmann 2011) and Samanid dirhams (Green Field). Some coins have isotopic ratios more similar to Samanid dirhams or Harz ore, while others may be a mixture of both. The analytical error (2σ) is smaller than the symbol.*

there was large variation of how they circulated in Scandinavia. Many coins circulated for decades before being deposited in hoards (Noonan 2001: 212–213). This must also be true for the recycling of imported silver.

The KG8-10 group has a wide variation of compositions and seems to reflect a transition period, but, with such a small sample size, no chronologic differences could be noticed within the group itself. This group is certainly a mixture of silver from two or more sources because a faint mixing line forms between the compositions more typical of Samanid dirhams and another source, possibly reflecting newly mined silver from the Harz Mountains (Fig. 13.3). The KG8-10 group mirrors the range of contemporary Sachsenpfennige in both composition and isotope ratio, though the Sachsenpfennige – some probably also a mixture of eastern and Harz silver – lean towards more local (Harz) silver resources. The Sachsenpfennige were probably minted in Magdeburg, an important town on the Ottonian Empire's eastern border. It is thought that imported eastern silver was re-coined at Magdeburg (Spurrford 1988: 68; Steuer 2004: 125; Zwicker *et al.* 1991: 76), and this could explain why so few dirhams are found west of the border (Steuer 1987: 129–131).

The year of 968 is often associated with the 'discovery' of the silver deposits in the Harz Mountains (Steuer 2004: 133–134), but archaeological evidence indicates that copper, lead, and silver were being produced already in the ninth century (Alper 2003: 19–25, 353). The growth and development of mining is attributed to the organization brought by royal control of the resources first with the Carolingians and then following with Saxonian emperors. Between 965 and 968 the Archbishop of Magdeburg, in addition to having minting privileges, gained control of the mint of Gittelde in the western Harz (Alper 2003: 22–23; Mehl 2011: 30), reflecting a close relationship between Magdeburg and the Harz.

Not only do the coins from Samanid Central Asia have distinctively high bismuth and low gold contents, but they also have a range of isotope compositions characterized by high $^{208}Pb/^{206}Pb$ in relation to $^{207}Pb/^{206}Pb$ and are quite different from deposits in western and central Europe except for the Cevenne in southern France (Baron *et al.* 2006; Bode 2008; Bode *et al.* 2007; Lehmann 2011; Rohl 1996; Téreygeol *et al.* 2005). There is a positive correlation between the high $^{208}Pb/^{206}Pb$ isotope ratios and higher bismuth contents of the KG8-10 group as well as hacksilver fragments and Volga Bulghar dirham imitations, re-enforcing the observation that silver, which is isotopically more similar to Samanid silver, also has higher bismuth contents like Samanid silver.

The KG8-10 and Sachsenpfennige on the other end of the spectrum matches isotope ratios of the vein deposits from the Upper Harz such as near Gittelde, where there are extensive early medieval workings and smelting remains (Klappauf 1993: 254). The evidence for newly-mined Harz silver is not only due to the isotope ratios, but also due to the trace elements that show both low gold and bismuth contents. Not all of the coins of the KG8-10 group comply with this interpretation. One KG10 coin has a composition more in line with what is known about Anglo-Saxon silver due to the high gold and zinc content (Ilisch *et al.* 2003; Kruse *et al.* 1992; McKerrell and Stevenson 1972; Metcalf and Northover 1986, 2002). The majority, however, conform to the interpretation that Harz silver, Samanid silver, and perhaps the earlier silver stock were mixed, but more work is necessary to look at this issue in detail, particularly the chronology.

### *Danish coins of the 11th century (AD 1000–1086)*

Although the mining in the Harz gained momentum in the years around 970, the great influx of German silver into the North occurred in the last decade of the 10th century. At the same time coins from Anglo-Saxon England began to flow eastward into Scandinavia (Ilisch 1981: 135). The Otto-Adelheid-Pfennig (OAP) is one of the most common coin types found in Scandinavia and was exported in large numbers (Hatz 1974: 41–47; Hatz 1991). All but one OAP match the isotope ratios of the Upper Harz, but the elemental analysis indicates that at least two distinct silver sources were used, both possibly originating in the Harz Mountains, *i.e.* Upper Harz and Rammelsberg (Zwicker *et al.* 1991: 75).

To represent 11th century Danish minting, coins of the Årstad 95/96 types, Hardeknut, Sven Estridsen, and Knut the Holy were analyzed. No longer are any traces of Samanid silver seen in the elemental composition or the isotope ratios. These coins are all relatively low in gold and bismuth. There is a divide between the coins of the Årstad/Hardeknut, which are high quality silver, and those of Sven Estridsen and Knut the Holy that are nearly all debased with brass. The debasement of the coins of Sven Estridsen and Knut the Holy has been noted previously by Gullbekk (2000).

The coins of the early group (Årstad/Hardeknut) fit isotopically with the Otto-Adelheid-Pfennige, the Upper Harz ore and some of the Anglo-Saxon and Hiberno-Norse pennies, but there is a shift in isotope signatures in the debased second group (Estridsen/Knut the Holy). The addition of up to 40% brass may certainly have an effect on the isotope ratios. Interestingly, the isotope signatures of brass-making crucible slag from medieval production centers of Dortmund and Soest (Krabath *et al.* 1999: 436) as well as lead-zinc ore from the Aachen-Stolberg and Sauerland regions (Bode 2008; Krahn and Braumann 1996) match the ratios of the debased coins of Sven Estridsen and Knut the Holy. The brass used in the coinage may have come from Lotharingia and Westphalia, regions thought to be producing brass in the Early Middle Ages.

## Conclusions

In the void of comparable studies, care must be taken not to over-interpret the findings, and a number of blind spots exist to be explored further. It must be re-emphasized that the use of lead isotope analysis in archaeology can only be reliably interpreted in a negative sense. A match in isotope data does not prove that the correlation is meaningful, but with a combination of elemental data and archaeological/historical evidence, interpretations can be made more confident.

This study touches upon several themes in Viking-Age silver research: changing silver sources, time of circulation, and recycling practices. Based on the analysis of Hedeby/Danish coins there are four phases over the course of the 10th into the 11th century. The Hedeby KG7 of the early tenth century is the earliest coin type analyzed and is closely related to hacksilver, ring fragments, ingots, and Khazar/Volga-Bulgharian dirham imitations. Although it is thought that Samanid silver flowed into the Baltic shortly after it was minted in Central Asia and Afghanistan, traces of this silver in the coins from Hedeby only become apparent after the minting of the KG7. In the second half of the 10th century the Hedeby coinage seems to be a mixture of Samanid silver and newly mined silver from the Harz Mountains via the Sachsenpfennig, Otto-Adelheid-Pfennig, or other forms. In the 11th century no trace of Samanid silver could be found in the Danish coins analyzed. Danish coinage of the second half of the 11th century reflects adulteration with brass that may be of continental origin.

One important absence is that of Anglo-Saxon England, both in the coin finds from Hedeby and in the elemental signatures of the Hedeby and later Danish coins. The few Anglo-Saxon and Hiberno-Norse coins of the 10th and 11th century and Anglo-Saxon style silver objects analyzed in this study all have a notable gold content, typically between 0.2% and 0.6%, high zinc content, and almost always a low bismuth content which complies well with the published literature. Isotopically, they are often indistinguishable from the Otto-Adelheid-Pfennige. The gold and zinc contents of the Anglo-Saxon coins in the tenth as in the eleventh century seem to indicate that different silver sources and technical traditions were in use.

The lead isotope analysis of Viking-Age silver is in an early stage with ample opportunity for further research. The analyses, although relatively small in number, show that there are chronological differences in elemental and isotopic composition of silver. As more is studied, the interpretation of analytical data will improve and enrich our understanding of mining, trade and manufacturing in the early medieval period.

*Acknowledgments*

We would like to thank the Leibniz Association for the funding to carry out this study and Claus von Carnap-Bornheim of the Landesmuseen Schloss Gottorf for his support. Sabine Klein at the Goethe University Frankfurt am Main is acknowledged for analytical work as well as Michael Bode at the Deutsches Bergbau-Museum, Bochum, and Daniel Fellenger in Hannover. Dr Lutz Ilisch of the Universität Tübingen identified the recent dirham finds and his careful determination made this study possible. We would also like to thank Christoph Bartels, Arne Windler, Moritz Jansen and two anonymous reviewers and useful comments. This paper is based on the doctoral research of Stephen Merkel, and all data collected, values obtained for reference materials, analytical procedures and the object catalogue will be published upon the completion of the thesis in 2014–2015.

*References*

Alper, Götz
2003. *'Johanneser Kurhaus'. Ein mittelalterlicher Blei-/Silbergewinnungsplatz bei Clausthal-Zellerfeld im Oberharz.* Materialhefte zur Ur- und Frühgeschichte Niedersachsens, Vol. 32. Marie Leidorf, Rahden/Westfalen.

Baron, Sandrine, Jean Carignan, Sarah Laurent and Alain Ploquin
2006. Medieval lead making on Mont-Lozère Massif (Cévennes, France): tracing ore sources using Pb Isotopes. *Applied Geochemistry* 21: 241–252.

Begley, Ian S and Barry L. Sharp
1997. Characterisation and correction of instrumental bias in inductively coupled plasma quadrupole mass spectrometry for accurate measurement of lead isotope ratios. *Journal of Analytical Atomic Spectrometry* 12(4): 395–402.

Berthoud, Thierry
1979. *Etude par l'analyse de traces et la modélisation de la filiation entre minerais de cuivre et objets archéologiques du Moyen-Orient.* Unpublished Ph.D. dissertation, Université Pierre et Marie Curie, Paris.

Blackburn, Mark
1993. Coin circulation in Germany during the Early Middle Ages: the evidence of single-finds. In *Fernhandel und Geldwirtschaft*, edited by Bernd Kluge, pp. 37–53. Jan Thorbecke, Sigmaringen.

Blanchard, Ian
2001. *Mining and Minting in the Middle Ages, Vol. 1. Asiatic Supremacy, 425–1125.* Franz Steiner, Stuttgart.

Bode, Michael
2008. *Archäometallurgische Untersuchungen zur Blei-/Silbergewinnung im Germanien der frühen Römischen Kaiserzeit.* Ph.D. dissertation, Mathematisch-Naturwissenschaftlichen Fakultät, Westfälischen Wilhelms-Universität Münster. Electronic document, http://miami.uni-muenster.de/servlets/DerivateServlet/Derivate-4815/diss_bode.pdf, accessed September, 30 2013.

Bode, Michael, Andreas Hauptmann and Klaus Mezger
2007. Rekonstruktion frühkaiserzeitlicher Bleiproduktion in Germanien: Synergie von Archäologie und Materialwissenschaften. In *Bleibergbau und Bleiverarbeitung während der römischen Kaiserzeit im rechtsrheinischen Barbaricum*, edited by Walter Melzer and Torsten Capelle, pp. 105–124. Soester Beiträge zur Archäologie, Vol. 8. Westfälische Verlagsbuchhandlung Mocker and Jahn, Soest.

Buryakov, Jurij
1974. *Guornoye dyelo i myetalloorguiya sryednyevyekovoguo Ilaka* [*Mining and Metallurgy in Medieval Ilak*]. Izdatelstvo Nauka, Moskva.
Chegini, Naser, Morteza Momenzadeh, Hermann Parzinger, Ernst Pernicka, Thomas Stöllner, Rasool Vatanddoust and Gerd Weisgergber
2000. Preliminary report on archaeometallurgical investigations around the prehistoric site of Arisman near Kashan, western Central Iran. *Archäologische Mitteilungen aus Iran und Turan* 32: 281–318.
Coupland, Simon
2007. *Carolingian Coinage and the Vikings: Studies on Power and Trade in the 9th Century*. Ashgate Variorum, Surrey, England.
Cowell, Michael R. and Nicholas M. Lowick
1988. Silver from the Panjhir Mines. In *Metallurgy and Numismatics*, Vol. 2, edited by W. Andrew Oddy, pp. 65–74. Royal Numismatic Society, London.
Eniosova, Natasha and Robert Mitoyan
2008. Arabic coins as a silver source for Slavonic and Scandinavian jewellers in the tenth century AD. In *Proceedings of the 37th International Symposium on Archaeometry 12th-16th May*, edited by Isabella Turbanti-Memmi, pp. 579–584. Springer, Berlin.
Gale, Noel H. and Zofia Stos-Gale
2000. Chapter 17: lead isotope analyses applied to provenance studies. In *Modern Analytical Methods in Art and Archaeology*, edited by Enrico Ciliberto and Giuseppi Spoto, pp. 503–584. Chemical Analysis Series, Vol. 155. Wiley, Hoboken, New Jersey.
Garipzanov, Ildar
2008. Carolingian coins in Early Viking Age Scandinavia (*c.* 754–*c.* 900): chronological distribution and regional patterns. *Nordisk Numismatisk Årsskrift* 2003–2005: 65–92.
Gullbekk, Sven
2000. Myntforringelse I Danmark og innføring av monopolmynt under Sven Estridsen (1047–1074). *Nordisk Numismatisk Årsskrift* 1994–1996: 111–129.
Hatz, Gert
1974. *Handel und Verkehr zwischen dem Deutschen Reich und Schweden in der späten Wikingerze*it. Kungliga Vitterhets Historie och Antikvitets Akademien, Stockholm.
1983. Finds of English medieval coins in Schleswig-Holstein. In *Studies in Numismatic Method*, edited by C. Brooke, B. Stewart, J. Pollard and T. Volk, pp. 205–223. Cambridge University, Cambridge.
Hatz, Vera
1991. Die Otto-Adelheid-Pfennige in den schwedischen Funden der Wikingerzeit. In *Otto-Adelheid-Pfennige, Untersuchungen zu Münzen des 10.-11. Jahrhunderts*, edited by Gert Hatz, Vera Hatz, Ulrich Zwicker, Noel Gale, and Zofia Gale, pp. 25–57. Commentationes de Nummis Saeculorum IX–XI in Suecia Repertis, Nova Series, Vol. 7. Royal Swedish Academy of Letters History and Antiquities, Stockholm.
Heidemann, Stefan
2011. The Circulation of North African Dirhams in Northern Mesopotamia: The Dirham Hoard of Tall al-Bī'a/al-Raqqa (t.p.q. 186/802). *Revue Numismatique* 167: 451–470.
Hilberg, Volker
2009. Hedeby in Wulfstan's days: a Danish emporium of the Viking Age between East and West. In *Wulfstan's Voyage*, edited by Anton Englert and Athena Trakadas, pp. 79–113. Maritime Culture of the North, Vol. 2. Viking Ship Museum, Roskilde, Denmark.

2011. Silver economies of the 9th and 10th centuries AD at Hedeby. In *Silver Economies, Monetisation and Society in Scandinavia, 800–1000*, edited by James Graham-Campbell, Søren M. Sindbæk, and Gareth Williams, pp. 203–226. Aarhus University, Aarhus.

Hauberg, Peter
1900. *Myntforhold og Udmyntinger i Danmark indtil 1146*. Bianco Lunos Bogtrykkeri, Copenhagen.

Ilisch, Lutz, Sönke Lorenz, Willem Stern and Heiko Steuer
2003. *Dirham und Rappenpfennig. Mittelalterliche Münzprägung in Bergbauregion.* Zeitschrift für Archaeologie des Mittelalters Vol. 17. Dr. Rudolf Habelt, Bonn.

Ilisch, Peter
1981. German Viking-Age Coinage and the North. In *Viking-Age Coinage in the Northern Lands: The Sixth Oxford Symposium on Coinage and Monetary History,* Part I, edited by Mark Blackburn and D. M. Metcalf, pp. 129–146. BAR International Series, Vol. 122(i). British Archaeological Reports, Oxford.

Jonsson, Kenneth
1994. The Coinage of Cnut. In *The Reign of Cnut: King of England, Denmark and Norway* edited by Alexander R. Rumble, pp. 193–230. Leicester University Press, London.

Kalmring, Sven
2010. *Der Hafen von Haithabu*. Die Ausgrabungen in Haithabu, Vol. 14. Wachholtz, Neumünster.

Kilger, Chistoph
2008a. Wholeness and holiness: counting, weighing and valuing silver in the early Viking period. In *Means of Exchange: Dealing with Silver in the Viking Age*, edited by Dagfinn Skre, pp. 253–326. Kaupang Excavation Project Publication Series, Vol. 2. Aarhus University Press, Aarhus.
2008b. Kaupang from afar: aspects of the interpretation of dirham finds in northern and eastern Europe between the Late 8th and early 10th centuries. In *Means of Exchange: Dealing with Silver in the Viking Age*, edited by Dagfinn Skre, pp. 199–252. Kaupang Excavation Project Publication Series, Vol. 2. Aarhus University Press, Aarhus.

Klappauf, Lothar
1993. Zur Archäologie des Harzes im frühen Mittelalter: Eine Skizze zu Forschungsstand und Aussagemöglichkeiten. In *Bernward von Hildesheim und das Zeitalter der Ottonen*, Vol. 1, edited by Michael Brandt and Arne Eggebrecht, pp. 249–257. Bernward, Hildesheim.

Klein, Sabine
2007. Dem Euro der Römer auf der Spur – Bleiisotopenanalysen zur Bestimmung der Merallherkunft römer Münzen. In *Einführung in die Archäometrie*, edited by Günther Wagner, pp. 140–150. Springer, Berlin.

Klein, Sabine, C. Domergue, Y. Lahaye, G. Brey and H. von Känel
2009. The lead and copper isotopic composition of copper ores from the Sierra Morena (Spain). *Journal of Iberian Geology* 35(1): 59–68.

Krabath, Stefan, Dieter Lammers, Thilo Rehren and Jens Schneider
1999. Die Herstellung und Verarbeitung von Buntmetall im karolingerzeitlichen Westfalen. In *799 Kunst und Kultur der Karolingerzeit*, edited by Christoph Stiegemann and Matthias Wemhoff, pp. 430–437. Philipp von Zabern, Mainz.

Krahn, L. and A. Braumann
1996. Lead isotope systemics of epigenetic lead-zinc mineralization in the western part of the Rheinisches Schiefergebirge, Germany. *Mineralium Deposita* 31: 225–237.

Kraume, Emil and Vera Hatz
1967. Silberanalysen deutscher Münzen des 10. Jahrhunderts. *Hamburger Beiträge zur Numismatik* 21: 35–38.

Kruse, Susan E. and James Tate
1992. XRF analysis of Viking Age Silver Ingots. *Proceedings of the Society of Antiquaries of Scotland* 122: 295–328. Edinburgh.
Lehmann, Robert
2011. *Archäometallurgie von mittelalterlichen deutschen Silberbarren und Münzen.* Ph.D. dissertation, Naturwissenschaftliche Fakultät, Leibniz Universität Hannover. Electronic document, http://edok01.tib.uni-hannover.de/edoks/e01dh11/646461346.pdf, accessed September, 30 2013.
Longerich, H. P., B. J. Fryer and D. F. Strong
1987. Determination of lead isotope ratios by inductively coupled plasma-mass spectrometry (ICP-MS). *Spectrochimica Acta, Part B* 42:39–48.
Malmer, Brita
1966. *Nordiska Mynt före år 1000.* CWK Gleerup, Lund.
2002. Münzprägung und frühe Stadtbildung in Nordeuropa. In *Haithabu und die frühe Stadtentwicklung im nördlichen Europa*, edited by Klaus Brandt, Michael Müller-Wille and Christian Radtke, pp. 117–132. Wachholtz, Neumünster.
McKerrell, Hugh and Robert B. K. Stevenson
1972. Some analyses of Anglo-Saxon and associated oriental silver coinage. In *Methods of Chemical and Metallurgical Investigation of Ancient Coinage*, edited by E. Hall and D. M. Metcalf, pp. 195–209. Royal Numismatic Society, London.
Mehl, Manfred
2011. *Münz- und Geldgeschichte des Erzbistums Magdeburg im Mittelalter*, Vol. 1. Verlag Manfred Mehl, Hamburg.
Metcalf, D. M.
1972. Analyses of the metal contents of medieval coins. In *Methods of Chemical and Metallurgical Investigation of Ancient Coinage*, edited by E. Hall and D. M. Metcalf, pp. 384–434. Royal Numismatic Society, London.
1997. President's address Viking-Age numismatics 3. What happened to Islamic dirhams after their arrival in the northern lands? *The Numismatic Chronicle* 157: 295–335.
Metcalf, D. M. and J. P. Northover
1985. Debasement of the coinage of southern England in the age of King Alfred. *The Numismatic Chronicle* 145: 150–176.
1986. Interpreting the alloy of the later Anglo-Saxon coinage. *British Numismatic Journal* 56: 35–63.
1988. Carolingian and Viking coins from the Cuerdale Hoard: an interpretation and comparison of their metal contents. *The Numismatic Chronicle* 148: 97–116.
1989. Coinage alloys from the time of Offa and Charlemagne to *c.* 864. *The Numismatic Chronicle* 149: 101–120.
2002. Sporadic debasement in the English coinage, *c.* 1009–1052. *The Numismatic Chronicle* 162: 217–236.
Meyers, Pieter
2003. Production of silver in antiquity: ore types identified based upon elemental compositions of ancient silver artifacts. In *Patterns and Process*, edited by Lambertus van Zelst, pp. 271–288. Smithsonian Center for Material Research and Education, Suitland, Maryland.
Moesgaard, Jens C.
2012. Hedeby og den danske kongemagt I 900-tallet: Mønternes udsagn. In *KUML 2012 Årbog for Jysk Arkæologisk Selskab*, edited by Jasper Laursen and Ingrid Nielsen, pp. 111–136. Aarhus University, Aarhus.

Niederschlag, E., E. Pernicka, Th. Seifer, and M. Bartelheim
2003. The determination of lead isotope ratios by multiple collector ICP-MS: a case study of Early Bronze Age artefacts and their possible relation with ore deposits of the Erzgebirge. *Archaeometry* 45(1): 61–100.
Noonan, Thomas
2001. Volga Bulghāria's tenth-century trade with Sāmānid central Asia. *Archivum Eurasiae medii aevi* 11: 140–218.
Patterson, C. C.
1972. Dwindling stocks of silver, and their relevance to studies of the metal contents of silver coinage. In *Methods of Chemical and Metallurgical Investigation of Ancient Coinage*, edited by E. Hall and D. M. Metcalf, pp. 150–152. Royal Numismatic Society, London.
Pernicka, Ernst and Hans-Gert Bachmann
1983. Silbergewinnung in Laurion, III. Das Verhalten einiger Spurenelemente beim Abtreiben des Bleis. *Erzmetall* 36(12): 592–597.
Pollard, A. Mark and Noel Gale
2009. What a long, strange trip it's been: lead isotopes and archaeology and response. In *From Mine to Microscope*, edited by Andrew Shortland, Ian Freestone, and Thilo Rehren, pp. 181–196. Oxbow Books, Oxford.
Ponting, M., J. Evans and V. Pashley
200.3 Fingerprinting of Roman mints using laser-ablation MC-ICP-MS lead isotope analysis. *Archaeometry* 45(4): 591–597.
Rehkämper, M. and A. N. Halliday
1998. Accuracy and long-term reproducibility of lead measurements by multiple-collector inductively coupled plasma mass spectrometry using an external method for correction of mass discrimination. *International Journal of Mass Spectrometry* 181: 123–133.
Rohl, B. M.
1996. Lead isotope data from the Isotrace Laboratory, Oxford: *Archaeometry* Data Base 2, galena from Britain and Ireland. *Archaeometry* 38(1): 165–180.
Sarah, Guillaume
2010. Charlemagne, Charles the Bald and the Karolus monogram coinage: a multi-disciplinary study. *The Numismatic Chronicle* 170: 227–286.
Sindbæk, Søren
2011. Silver economies and social ties: long-distance interaction, long-term investments – and why the Viking Age happened. In *Silver Economies, Monetisation and Society in Scandinavia AD 800–1100*, edited by James Graham-Campbell, Søren Sindbæk, and Gareth Williams, pp. 41–66. Aahrus University, Aahrus, Denmark.
Skre, Dagfinn
2011. Commodity money, silver and coinage in Viking-Age Scandinavia. In *Silver Economies, Monetisation and Society in Scandinavia AD 800–1100*, edited by James Graham-Campbell, Søren Sindbæk, and Gareth Williams, pp. 67–92. Aarhus University, Aarhus.
Spurrford, Peter
1988. *Money and its use in medieval Europe*. Cambridge University, Cambridge.
Stenberger, Mårten
1958. *Die Schatzfunde Gotlands: Der Wikingerzeit*. Kungliga Vitterhets Historie och Antikvitets Akademien, Stockholm.
Steuer, Heiko
1987. Der Handel der Wikingerzeit zwischen Nord- und Westeuropa aufgrund archäologischer

Zeugnisse. In *Untersuchungen zu Handel und Verkehr der vor- und frühgeschichtlichen Zeit in Mittel- und Nordeuropa,* Teil IV, edited by Klaus Düwel, Herbert Jankuhn, Harald Siems, and Dieter Timpe, pp. 113–197. Vandenhoeck and Ruprecht, Göttingen.

2004. Münzprägung, Silberströme und Bergbau um das Jahr 1000 in Europa – wirtschaftlicher Aufbruch und technische Innovation. In *Aufbruch ins zweite Jahrtausend,* edited by Achim Hubel and Bernd Scheidmüller, pp. 117–149. Jan Thorbecke, Ostfildern, Germany.

Stos-Gale, Zofia

2001. The impact of the natural sciences on studies of *hacksilber* and early silver coinage. In *Hacksilber to Coinage: New Insights into the Monetary History of the Near East and Greece,* edited by Miriam Balmuth, pp. 53–76. Numismatic Studies, Vol. 24. American Numismatic Society, New York.

2004. Lead-isotope analysis of glass, glazes, and some metal artifacts. In *Serçe Limani: An Eleventh-Century Shipwreck, Volume 1: The Ship and Its Anchorage, Crew, and Passengers,* edited by George F. Bass, Sheila D. Matthews, J. Richard Steffy and Frederick H. van Doornick, Jr, pp. 453–467. Texas A and M University Press, College Station, Texas.

Téreygeol, Florian

2002. Frühmittelalterlicher Bergbau und Silberproduktion von Melle in Frankreich. *Der Anschnitt* 54(6): 253–266.

2013. How to quantify medieval silver production at Melle? *Metalle* 20(2): 80–86.

Téreygeol, Florian, Stefan Hoelzl and Peter Horn

2005. Journée Archéologique de Melle: Le monnayage de Melle au haut Moyen Age, état de la recherche. *Association des Archéologues de Poitou-Charentes Bulletin de liaison et d'information* 34: 49–56. Poitiers.

Todt, W., R. A. Cliff, A. Hanser and A. W. Hofmann

1996. Evaluation of a 202Pb–205Pb double spike for high-precision lead isotope analysis. In *Earth Processes: Reading the Isotope Code,* edited by Stanely R. Hart and Asish Basu, pp. 429–437. Geophysical Monograph, Vol. 95. American Geophysical Union, Washington, DC.

Walder, A. J., I. D. Acell, P. A. Freedman and I. Platzner

1993. Lead isotope ratio measurement of NIST 610 glass by laser ablation inductively coupled plasma mass spectrometry. *Spectrochimica Acta B*48: 397–402.

Wiechmann, Ralf

1996. *Edelmetalldepots der Wikingerzeit in Schleswig-Holstein: vom 'Ringbrecher' zur Münzwirtschaft.* Wachholz, Neumünster.

2007. Haithabu und sein Hinterland – ein lokaler numimatischer Raum? Münzen und Münzfunde aus Haithabu (bis zum Jahr 2002). In *Das archäologische Fundmaterial VIII,* edited by Kurt Schietzel, pp. 182–278. Ausgrabungen in Haithabu, Vol. 36. Wachholtz, Neumünster.

2013. Byzantinische Treppen und englische Kreuze – Zwei Münztypen des 11. Jahrhunderts – geprägt in Haithabu?. In *Kulturwandel im Spannungsfeld von Tradition und Innovation,* edited by Sunhild Kleingärtner, Ulrich Müller, and Jonathan Scheschkewitz, pp. 145–160. Wachholtz, Neumünster.

Zwicker, Ulrich, Noel Gale and Zofia Gale

1991. Metallographische, analytische und technologische Untersuchungen sowie Messungen der Bleiisotope an Otto-Adelheid-Pfennigen und Vergleichsmünzen meist aus dem 9.–11. Jahrhundert: Ein Beitrage zur Münzprägung der sächsischen Kaiser. In *Otto-Adelheid-Pfennige, Untersuchungen zu Münzen des 10.–11. Jahrhunderts,* edited by Gerd Hatz, Vera Hatz, Ulrich Zwicker, Noel Gale and Zofia Gale, pp. 59–146. Commentationes de Nummis Saeculorum IX–XI in Suecia Repertis, Nova Series, Vol. 7. Royal Swedish Academy of Letters History and Antiquities, Stockholm.

*Chapter 14*

# Vikings in Poland. A critical overview

*Leszek Gardeła*

*Abstract*

Over the many decades of Viking-Age research significant attention has been devoted to the travels and interactions of the Norsemen with various peoples of the early medieval world. However, the contacts with their West Slavic neighbours, especially from the area of today's Poland still remain understudied, and wider discussions of these notions are practically non-existent in the major monographs on the Viking Age. Yet the Old Norse written accounts and other texts imply that these contacts were long-lasting and multifaceted. Likewise, archaeological excavations conducted in various areas of Poland have also demonstrated evidence for the presence of early medieval Scandinavians or their material culture in these lands. Therefore, this paper attempts to provide a critical overview of the past and current views on the notion of early medieval Scandinavians in Poland, and to discuss the different roles which they may have played while living among the Slavic communities.

## Vikings in Poland: A brief history of research and reception

Between the 8th and 11th centuries the people commonly known as 'Vikings' travelled widely around the early medieval world, reaching places as far away from their original homelands as the coasts of North America, the magnificent city of Constantinople and the fierce rivers of Rus'. Over many years in historical and archaeological research significant attention has been devoted to the multiple expeditions of the Norsemen, especially to the West and East, but their interactions with their Slavic neighbours on the southern coast of the Baltic Sea have remained largely understudied. In the majority of compendia on the 'Viking world' the Slavic lands – and especially the West Slavic area of what is today the territory of Poland – have been substantially disregarded (*e.g.* Brink and Price 2010; but *cf.* Skov and Varberg 2011). Hence, the mutual relations between the Western Slavs and Scandinavians are often misunderstood, misinterpreted or simply ignored. The reasons for this neglect are manifold, but it appears to have largely resulted from lack of communication between Scandinavian, Anglo-Saxon and Polish scholars – probably stemming from the fact that the majority of works on the presence of the so-called 'Vikings' in Poland were published in Polish, and generally were very difficult to acquire from bookshops or libraries in other countries.

Since the beginnings of the 19th century there has been a growing interest in Scandinavian-Slavic interactions among Polish historians, antiquarians and archaeologists (*e.g.* the classic, yet in many regards very controversial, works of Szajnocha 1858 and Wachowski 1914). As part of this process, from the 1920s onwards, a number of archaeological finds which seemed 'different' from what was then regarded as typically 'Slavic' have been interpreted as possible traces of Scandinavian presence (*e.g.* Kostrzewski 1921, 1946: 87; Łowmiański 1957). Over the next years, increasing numbers of similar discoveries were made at different categories of archaeological sites, including settlements, strongholds and cemeteries. These discoveries were often used and abused in strengthening ideologically driven archaeological arguments concerning the 'superiority' of Germanic peoples – especially among some German scholars in the period before and during the Second World War.

Many controversies regarding the notion of Vikings in Poland have also arisen with regard to the document known as *Dagome iudex* (Holtzmann 1918; Schulte 1918). *Dagome iudex* lists the territories under the rule of the Polish Prince Mieszko I that were placed under the 'protection' of the Apostolic See (*e.g.* Labuda 2002: 177–200). On the basis of its beginning words, some scholars argued that Mieszko I actually came from Scandinavia and that his original name was *Dagr* (or *Dago*, *Dagobert*, *Dagome*, *Dagone*). In the early 20th century the 'Normanist' arguments for his foreign origin were put forward to suggest that the Polish state may have emerged in a similar way as argued for that of the Rus' – through an active involvement of Scandinavian immigrants. In more recent times, however, these ungrounded arguments have been dismissed by the world of academia (*e.g.* Żak 1968), but on occasion they still resurface in mass media leading the general public to misinformation and false assumptions.

In addition to the controversies around *Dagome iudex*, a theme which was widely discussed among Polish and German academics for many decades was the notion of *Jómsborg* – a stronghold that allegedly housed the famous Viking brotherhood, and which, according to the Old Norse *Jómsvíkinga saga* (Blake 1962; Hollander 2000), was located somewhere on the Baltic coast, within the area of today's Poland. Despite intensive efforts (especially by German archaeologists before and during the Second World War), the fortress of *Jómsborg* has never been found. Today, most scholars tend to believe that it probably never existed in the way the saga described it. Rather, they suggest that *Jómsborg* should be identified with the early medieval town of Wolin – an important and multicultural port-of-trade (Morawiec 2009, 2010).

In the 1960s an attempt was made to collect and thoroughly analyse the growing corpus of archaeological evidence and to interpret the various roles which Scandinavians may have played among West Slavic communities, particularly in Poland. This resulted in the publication of a massive three-volume synthesis entitled *Importy skandynawskie na ziemiach zachodniosłowiańskich od IX do XI wieku* (*Scandinavian Imports in the West Slavic Lands from the 9th to the 11th Century*) by Jan Żak (1963, 1967a, 1967b) – a Polish archaeologist who worked at Poznań University. Soon after its publication, Żak's monograph was regarded a ground-breaking study and he was praised for his diligent synthesis of the available sources as well as their thorough assessment. Unfortunately, although Żak's monograph became very influential in Poland, due to linguistic reasons (it was written in Polish) it did not have a very large impact on Scandinavian and Western European archaeology and today it remains generally unknown outside Poland.

Since the publication of Żak's monograph, many further discoveries shedding new light on the presence of Scandinavians in early medieval Poland have been made in different parts of the country. These have come especially from the trade and administrative centres located on the southern coast of the Baltic Sea – *e.g.* Wolin, Kamień Pomorski or the famous Truso (in the Slavic-Prussian border-zone), but also from a number of early medieval cemeteries, settlements and strongholds (*e.g.* Górecki 2002; Kola and Wilke 2000). Some Scandinavian-style objects have also been discovered accidentally (in silver hoards or as stray-finds) or by amateur metal detectorists.

Yet it is not only the physical corpus of data that has changed since Żak's time. During the last 50 years the research paradigms and ways of understanding and presenting the past have also developed in European archaeology – shifting away from the traditional culture-historical models (employed in many works of the aforementioned Jan Żak and his colleagues), to processual or post-processual approaches. In Poland, these advancements were much slower than elsewhere in Western Europe, and even today the traditional culture-historical style of presenting the past is still prevalent in the discussions of allegedly Scandinavian finds. Indeed, a fresh approach to this material is not only desirable, but necessary to avoid further confusion or misinformation. Likewise, there is a great urge for a new and open dialogue between the Polish, Scandinavian, British and other scholars of the Viking Age. This paper is intended as a small step in that direction.

## New discoveries and controversies

Over the last decade or so, in the Polish academic milieus, discussions on the presence and role of Scandinavians in these lands between the 8th and 11th centuries have become very lively (*e.g.* Duczko 2000, 2012), and in 2011 and 2013 two conferences devoted to various aspects of the Viking Age in Poland were organised in Wrocław and Wolin respectively (Stanisławski *et al.* 2013). This growing interest in the Viking Age among Polish scholars is – in my view – not only fuelled by the current research trends in international academia, but also largely influenced by the great popularity of the Vikings in mass media. In this context, it is worth highlighting the fact that Poland currently hosts some of the largest Viking re-enactment festivals in the world (*e.g.* the annual Festival of Slavs and Vikings in Wolin), which attract thousands of visitors each year. All this is indeed very exciting, but at the same time the 'obsession' with the Vikings may (and does) give rise to a range of problems and controversies that could ultimately lead to dramatically distorting our perception of the past.

During the last 50 years, new excavations conducted at various early medieval sites in Poland have produced a range of puzzling discoveries including single artefacts or spectacular silver hoards, but also graves with furnishings that are relatively rare in this area. Consequently, among some Polish archaeologists, there has been a growing tendency to regard many of these foreign-looking artefacts (especially weapons, horse gear and some types of jewellery) and unusual grave constructions (*i.e.* chamber-graves) as evidence for Scandinavian presence and/or ethnicity of their owners. While such interpretations are certainly attractive, and over the last years they have received significant coverage in mass media and popular scientific publications, the manner of their presentation is highly sensationalist and frequently without solid academic grounding. It is often the case that even in 'professional' archaeological literature, the alleged 'Viking graves' or 'Viking finds' from Poland are discussed without setting them in a wider theoretical and comparative context (see valuable critique of similar unscientific approaches in Duczko 2012: 63–64). In result, a number of Polish archaeologists have falsely labelled certain artefacts as 'Scandinavian imports' without really conducting any thorough studies of the Viking-Age culture, and by basing their interpretations on completely ungrounded (and in fact naïve) arguments. Because such arguments have now been repeated numerous times – both in the academic literature and in mass media – they have become almost dogmatic and are very difficult to overcome.

Moreover, it is worth noting that in Polish archaeology there is still an anachronistic tendency to regard the grave contents or grave structures as direct reflections of the roles which the deceased may have played during their lives – *i.e.* graves are often seen as 'mirrors' of the social status and ethnic identities of the deceased. Consequently, graves with weapons or other artefacts that appear even vaguely similar to those found in early medieval Scandinavia are immediately regarded as belonging to 'Viking warriors or mercenaries' (*e.g.* Kara 1991, 1992a, 1992b). During the last decade or so, Anglo-Saxon and Scandinavian academics have moved away from similar reductionist views and sophisticated their understandings of past mortuary practices (Price 2008a, 2008b, 2010; Sayer and Williams 2009; Svanberg 2003; Williams 2006). In my opinion, their nuanced and innovative perspectives on broadly understood 'archaeology of death' should certainly be included in the ongoing debates on Scandinavian/Viking presence in Poland. Likewise, it is essential to define what we really mean by the elusive terms 'Scandinavians', 'Vikings', 'Norsemen' and how they should be understood in this particular, Polish context (*e.g.* Urbańczyk 2008).

The above-mentioned general lack of sophisticated theoretical discussions and analyses leads many Polish scholars, and consequently the general public, to problematic conclusions and misunderstandings regarding Scandinavian-Slavic interactions in the early medieval period. There is a necessity, therefore, to look at both the archival and new archaeological materials from a wider perspective and in a more comprehensive and critical way than before. Questions need to be asked about what may have attracted Scandinavians to come to the area of Poland (the notion of 'pull and push'). Where exactly did they originate from and where did they first arrive? Were they only transient, or did they choose to settle permanently? Were these visits peaceful or violent? Did the Scandinavians come as hostile warriors, mercenaries and outcasts or as friendly merchants, crafts-workers, adventurers and explorers? What ideas, technologies or artefacts did they bring with them or begin to produce while living in the Polish lands? How did they express or manifest their identities through material culture, everyday habits, beliefs and funerary rituals? And lastly, what was the nature of their interactions with the Slavic societies and with the emerging elites and rulers of the rising Piast dynasty?

These and many more questions arise when we attempt at seriously exploring the Scandinavian-Slavic interactions, and it is obvious that they cannot all be answered in this brief article. Below, however, on the basis of selected archaeological evidence (and with particular focus on funerary material), I shall attempt at providing a concise, yet critical overview of some of the key issues related to the notion of Scandinavian presence in Poland and their contacts with the Slavic communities in these lands.

### Scandinavian–Slavic interactions

The area of today's Poland has been visited by people from Scandinavia many centuries prior to the Viking Age. From the beginnings of the 1st millennium AD various traces of their presence – in the form of distinctive graves, cemeteries, settlements, hoards and single finds – are visible especially in the area of Pomerania and the Vistula River estuary (*e.g.* Duczko 2010: 200–202). These interactions continued in further centuries and in the Viking Age they acquired a whole new dimension. Apart from archaeological evidence, the multifaceted contacts between the Scandinavians and Slavs are also well attested in the available written accounts – especially in Old Norse sagas and Latin texts (*e.g.* Morawiec 2009, 2010, 2013). Most of these sources are of course biased in one way or another because they were written down many years (or even centuries) after the events which they claim to describe. However, they should not be immediately dismissed. Since it is not possible to explore these textual accounts in great detail here, it should suffice to highlight the dynastic contacts between the members of the Piast dynasty and the ruling elites of Denmark, Norway and Sweden.

According to some sources, the sister of Bolesław the Brave became the wife of Eric the Victorious and later of Svein Forkbeard (Morawiec 2013: 84–85). Moreover, the majority of scholars agree that the renowned Cnut the Great was a son of a Slavic Princess (whose actual name, unfortunately, remains unknown) who was the daughter of Mieszko I and Dobrawa (Morawiec 2013: 86). The strong contacts between the Scandinavians and Slavs are also clearly visible in the sphere of trade and exchange as evidenced by various goods imported from Scandinavia and discovered in the area of Poland and *vice versa*, by Slavic finds in the area of Denmark, Norway and Sweden, especially of pottery (*e.g.* Roslund 2007). Slavic presence in Scandinavia is also attested by other categories of finds such as, for example, burials, distinctive jewellery, knives and their decorated scabbards. Traces of Slavic settlements in Scandinavia have also been identified through the analysis of place-names (on related notions see Naum 2008; Stanisławski 2012: 124).

### Scandinavians in the ports-of-trade on the Southern Baltic coast

From the 8th century onwards a range of so-called 'emporia' – lively places of intercultural trade and exchange – were beginning to be established on the coasts of the Baltic and the North Sea. The Scandinavians had a great influence on their emergence and development and as merchants or crafts-workers they were also their frequent visitors. In Western academic literature, places such as Hedeby (Haithabu), Birka and Kaupang are well known, and have been given significant scholarly attention. Much less familiar are similar sites within the area of Poland, or elsewhere in Eastern Europe (*e.g.* Bogucki 2004, 2010). While in this short paper it is impossible to discuss and problematise the nature of these localities in great detail, I will only concentrate on their most important features and aim at providing some representative and recent bibliographical references.

The region in the vicinity of the Oder River estuary is among the places in Poland where a significant number of artefacts of Scandinavian origin have been found. Especially prominent in that area was Wolin (Filipowiak and Gundlach 1992; Morawiec 2009, 2010; Stanisławski 2012; Stanisławski and Filipowiak 2013; see also a discussion of the most recent discoveries from Wolin, including Scandinavian objects, in Janowski 2014).The town was founded at the end of the 8th century or the beginning of the 9th century. In the period between the late 9th and 10th centuries Wolin was as significant and lively as Birka and Hedeby. It has been argued that in the 11th century it was probably the largest town in the Baltic, with an estimate of 6000–8000 inhabitants (Filipowiak 1958: 49; Skov 2011: 119). Wolin is described in a range of Old Norse, Latin and Arabic sources. As mentioned above, it has also been (somewhat problematically) associated with the great fortress of *Jómsborg* – so vividly portrayed in the Old Norse *Jómsvíkinga saga*. The German cleric Adam of Bremen considered Wolin to be a real melting pot of cultures, inhabited by pagan Slavs, 'Greeks', Saxons and other 'barbarians'. The information provided by Adam matches the archaeological discoveries from Wolin, especially with regard to the multicultural status of the town. The archaeological finds which have been excavated there since the 1930s include numerous objects analogous to those from Sweden, Gotland, Norway, Denmark and even (in terms of their decoration) the British Isles. Based on archaeological evidence it has recently been argued, however, that despite a number of Scandinavian finds, Wolin was mostly inhabited by the Slavs.

Another important place of trade where Scandinavian finds have been discovered is Kamień Pomorski, which is located *c.* 25 km to the north-east from Wolin (Duczko 2012: 66). The earliest Scandinavian imported goods that arrived there around the end of the 9th century were Norwegian soapstone vessels, but the town is also well known for a magnificent reliquary – the so-called Caminn Casket. This Mammen style masterpiece dates from the 10th century and was probably manufactured in Denmark. Interestingly, a bone with two runic inscriptions has also been found there (Fig. 14.1: i–j; Duczko 2012: 66).

Around 85 km to the north-east from Kamień Pomorski lies Kołobrzeg, a town famous for salt mining and salt trade (Leciejewicz and Rębkowski 2000). The salt was exported from Kołobrzeg to different places within the area of Pomerania, and even as far as Greater

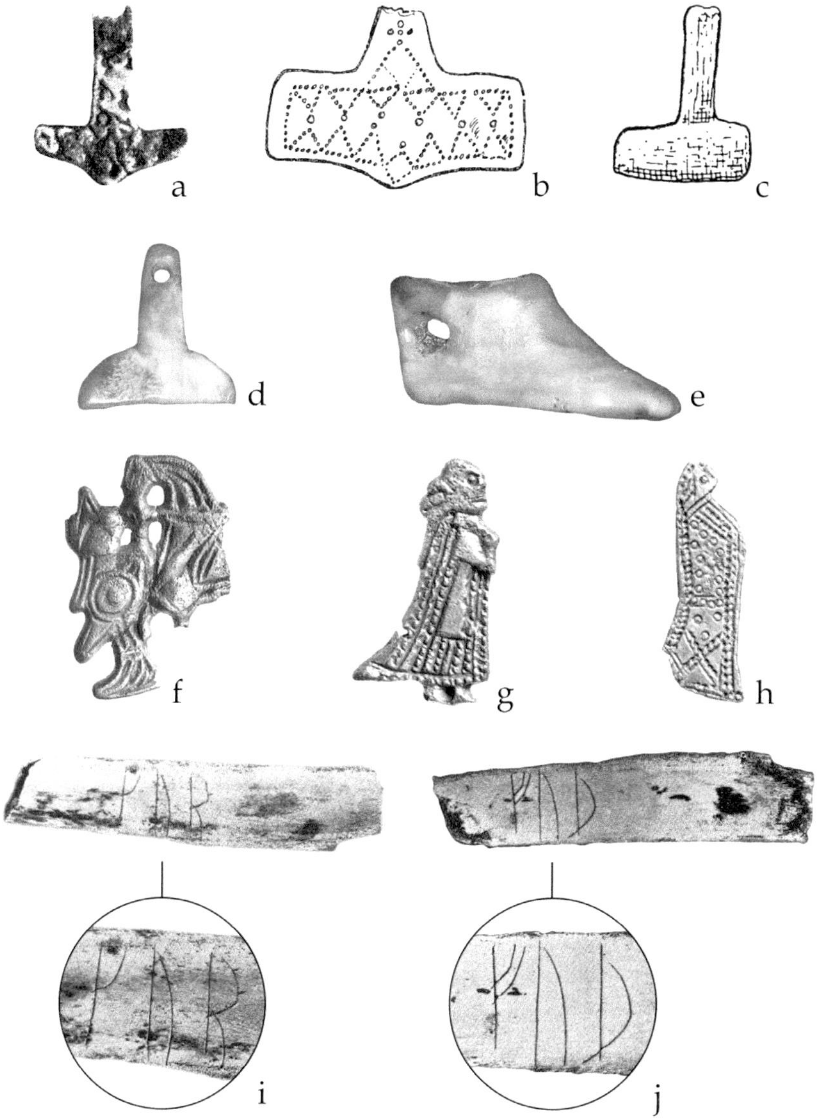

*Fig. 14.1. a. Thor's hammer from Wolin, Poland. Reproduction: Leszek Gardeła (after Żak 1963: 261); b. Thor's hammer from Łupawa, Poland. Reproduction: Leszek Gardeła (after Żak 1963: 283); c. Thor's hammer made from amber from Gdańsk, Poland. Reproduction: Leszek Gardeła (after Żak 1963: 288); d. Thor's hammer made from amber from Wolin, Poland. Reproduction: Leszek Gardeła (after Stanisławski and Filipowiak 2013: illus. 28); e. Foot/shoe-shaped amulet(?) from Wolin, Poland. Reproduction: Leszek Gardeła (after Stanisławski and Filipowiak 2013: 29); f. So-called 'Valkyrie-pendant' from Truso/Janów Pomorski, Poland (after Jagodziński 2010: 106); g. Anthropomorphic pendant from Truso/Janów Pomorski, Poland (after Jagodziński 2010: 158); h. Anthropomorphic pendant from Truso/Janów Pomorski, Poland (after Jagodziński 2010: 158); i–j. Bone with two runic inscriptions* ***kur*** *and* ***fuþ*** *from Kamień Pomorski, Poland Reproduction: Leszek Gardeła (after Żak 1963: 274).*

Poland or Silesia. It is not unlikely that it also reached the southern parts of Scandinavia, such as Sweden and Denmark. Moreover, the excavations at a nearby cemetery in Świelubie suggest that some of the Scandinavian incomers may have lived in this area on a more permanent basis, and were buried in cremation graves with very characteristic Viking-Age jewellery (Fig. 14.2; Łosiński 1972).

Large amounts of Scandinavian finds have also been identified at Truso, a port-of-trade in the Slavic-Prussian borderland. Truso was first mentioned in the 9th century account of the Anglo-Saxon sailor Wulfstan who travelled there by sea from Hedeby (Englert and Trakadas 2009). After many years of searching, the remains of the town of Truso were finally successfully identified in 1982 by the Polish archaeologist Marek Jagodziński. Truso has been excavated ever since and the results have been published in a range of articles, a recent monograph (Jagodziński 2010) and in a new series of publications entitled *Studia nad Truso/Truso Studies* (Bogucki and Jagodziński 2012a, 2012b, 2012c). The town is located on the shore of lake Drużno near Janów Pomorski and it has been estimated that during the time of its prosperity it covered an area of nearly 15 ha. It is likely that it was fortified and had a rampart. The buildings found on the site belong to different types, including the so-called 'long-houses' of Scandinavian type. In the harbour area, archaeologists have recovered remains of clinker-built boats and iron rivets, which suggest that boat repairs were also conducted there. Since the end of the 8th century Truso was thriving with merchants and crafts-workers – there were blacksmiths and skilled jewellers as well as specialists working with amber, glass, antler and bone. Like other emporia of that time, it was a multicultural town inhabited by Prussians, Slavs and Scandinavians. It appears, however, that the majority of Truso's inhabitants were actually of Scandinavian origin, as implied by the finds of typical Viking-Age artefacts in very large quantities (including objects which may be interpreted as amulets – Fig. 14.1, f–h). Interestingly, it seems that many of these objects were not imported, but rather manufactured on site (as suggested by finds of various tools for their production, *e.g.* hammers, crucibles, unfinished products). According to the latest research, it was quite possibly the Danes who influenced the establishment of Truso. This is implied by the types of archaeological artefacts found at the site, but also the very plan of the town, which resembles some of the main ports-of-trade in Jylland, such as Hedeby and Ribe.

## Viking burials in Poland?

Let us now shift our attention to the notions of death and archaeological traces of mortuary behaviour, which may potentially be associated with early medieval Scandinavians in Poland (*e.g.* Jankuhn 1934; Janocha 1974; Kara 1991, 1992a, 1992b, 2001, 2013; Kostrzewski 1921; Krzyszowski 1995; Rajewski 1937; Ratajczyk 2011; Żak 1957).

Before the formal adoption of Christianity – which happened in 966 when Prince Mieszko I and his retinue received baptism – the dominant burial rite in Poland involved cremation. After the introduction of the new religion, cremation was gradually abandoned, and from then onwards inhumation became the standard and official burial rite. At the inhumation cemeteries in Poland the dead were usually interred in a supine position

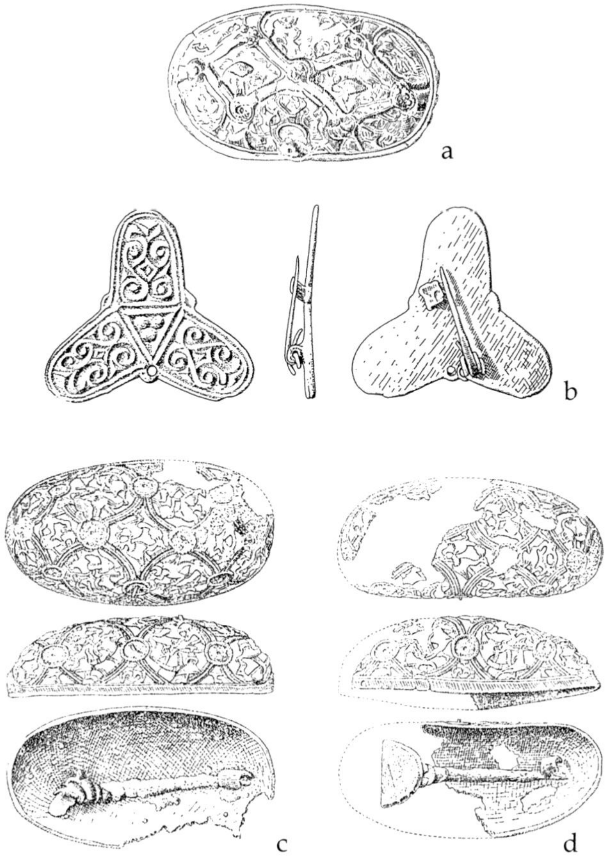


*Fig. 14.2. a. Oval brooch from grave mound 1 in Świelubie, Poland. Reproduction: Leszek Gardeła (after Łosiński 1972: 249); b. Trefoil brooch from grave mound 10 in Świelubie, Poland. Reproduction: Leszek Gardeła (after Łosiński 1972: 250)' c–d. Two oval brooches from grave mound 24 in Świelubie, Poland. Reproduction: Leszek Gardeła (after Łosiński 1972: 252).*

and aligned east–west (Buko 2008; Rębkowski 2011). The graves from late 10th and 11th century Poland were, however, occasionally furbished with different kinds of artefacts such as weapons, jewellery, ceramic, wooden or metal vessels *etc.* Depending on the region or local customs, there existed different variants of burials, but in a general sense the funerary diversity in early medieval Poland was not as large as in Scandinavia or elsewhere within the Viking world (*e.g.* Price 2010; Svanberg 2003).

In this context it is vital to consider whether the Scandinavian immigrants to Poland ever buried their dead in these lands, and, if so, which forms of burial they practiced. Did their burials differ from those of the Slavs, and, if so, in what way? What funerary practices or 'technologies of remembrance' did they bring with them from their homelands? Can we observe any traces of 'hybridisation' within the forms of the graves, their furnishings, or internal and external constructions? Did they combine features that were characteristic for the pagan Slavic and Christian traditions with those from Scandinavia? Were the Scandinavians who died in the area of Poland buried there by their own people, or by the Slavs and, if so, in a 'Slavic way'? Did any of the Slavic mourners attempt to make some

*Fig. 14.3. Map showing the major archaeological sites in Poland mentioned in the article. Illustration: © Leszek Gardeła.*

references to Scandinavian burial traditions while burying the Scandinavian dead? Many of these questions are indeed difficult to answer, but by taking into our interpretative frame the comparative evidence from other areas of Europe (especially the British Isles or the Rus'), in the future it may be possible to reach interesting conclusions on the 'Viking way of death' in early medieval Poland.

Over the last twenty years some Polish scholars have argued for the presence of burials of Scandinavian immigrants in various areas of Poland, including Greater Poland, Western Pomerania, Central Pomerania, Eastern Pomerania and Central Poland (Fig. 14.3). Recently, particular attention has been devoted to the so-called 'chamber-graves' that have been discovered over the last decade or so in different parts of the country. Let us briefly review and critically asses some of these earlier hypotheses.

*Greater Poland*

According to certain scholars, Greater Poland is an area where a significant number of *allegedly* Scandinavian artefacts have been recovered from funerary contexts. These were discovered at early medieval cemeteries in Luboń (currently the district of Dębiec in Poznań), Łubowo, Ostrowąż, Sowinki and Skokówko (Kara 1992). The finds from these sites – mainly including weapons (axes and spearheads), but also parts of wooden buckets and balance-weights – have been interpreted as belonging to Scandinavian men who died in these lands. In a number of articles Michał Kara (1991, 1992a, 1992b) has also suggested that these men served as elite mercenaries in the retinues of the Polish Prince Mieszko I and his son Bolesław the Brave. Kara's views have been widely accepted by Polish archaeologists and uncritically repeated numerous times in various academic and popular publications (*e.g.* Buko 2008: 404–408; Górecki 2002: 134). However, a closer look at the corpus of material evidence on which Kara based his assumptions leads to drastically different conclusions. Firstly, it must be observed that a lot of these finds were discovered in the period before the Second World War (often accidentally and by amateurs) and that they were originally published in a manner which is rudimentary by today's standards (*e.g.* Kostrzewski 1921; Rajewski 1937; but see the reports from the more recent excavations in Sowinki near Poznań, which are relatively well published, Krzyszowski 1995). Secondly, in the majority of cases, precise cemetery plans and particular grave plans are lacking, and therefore little can be said about the actual form of burial, the alignment of the body as well as the positioning of the accompanying objects. Moreover, the finds recovered from a number of these sites disappeared during the Second World War and could not be retrieved; today, they are only known from very poor quality illustrations and/or black-and-white photographs.

The finds that do exist in museum archives and which have been argued by Kara (1991, 1992a, 1992b) to be of Scandinavian provenance include, for example, an elaborate axe that was discovered at an early medieval cemetery in Luboń (Fig. 14.4). This iron axe has a T-shaped blade decorated with silver- and copper-inlaid geometric patterns. In the mid part of the blade there is an inlaid representation of an animal, probably a horse. Despite the fact that the ornamentation of this axe does not even vaguely resemble any of the characteristic Viking-Age art styles, Kara (1992a: 39) wrote that this is a 'Danish axe' dated to the late 10th century or the beginning of the 11th century. This view is completely unsubstantiated. Analogous axes are *extremely* rare in Denmark and, to my knowledge, only four such objects have been discovered there – at Trelleborg in Sjælland, Rosenlund in Funen as well as Over Hornbæk and Lindholm Høje in Jylland (Nielsen 1991; Nørlund 1948; Paulsen 1956: 156–167; Roesdahl and Wilson 1992: 256; see also an important discussion in Pedersen 2002: 30–31 with arguments for these objects' foreign provenance). The occurrence of such an axe at Trelleborg is not very surprising in the light of the most recent research: On the basis of strontium isotope analyses it has been argued that Slavs lived in that area

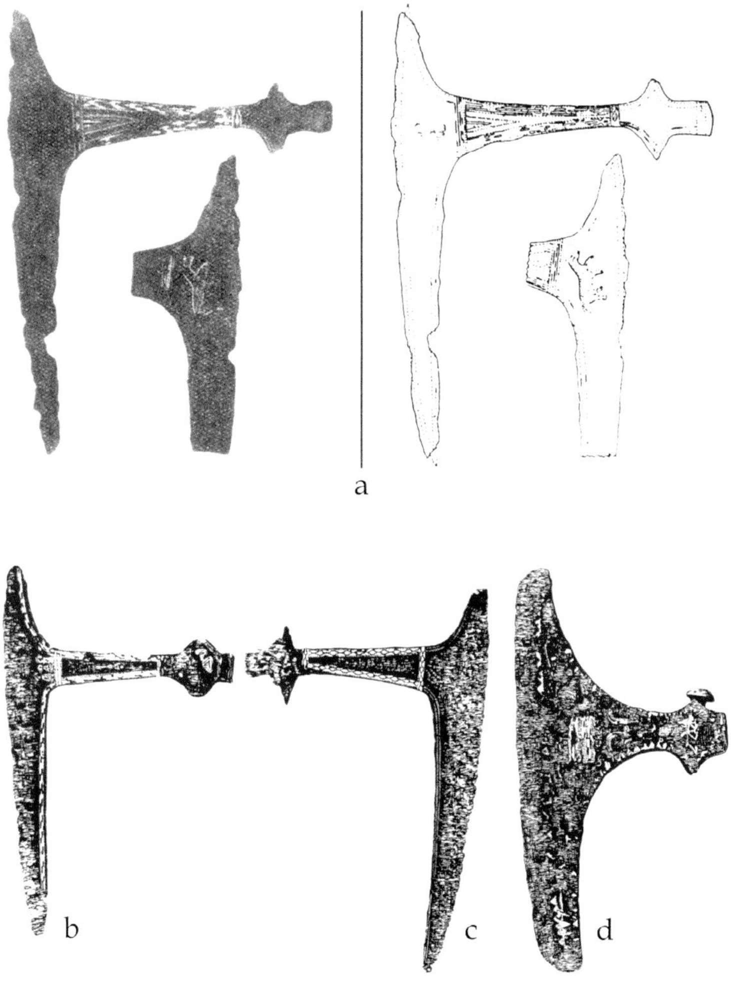


*Fig. 14.4. a. Axe from Luboń (Poland) shown from both sides. Notice the animal figure – probably a horse. Photograph reproduced after Kostrzewski 1949: 300. Drawing after Paulsen 1956: 158; b. Axe from Lund (Sweden). Drawing after Paulsen 1956: 160; c. Axe from Lunow (Germany). Drawing after Paulsen 1956: 157; d. Axe from Trelleborg (Denmark). Drawing after Paulsen 1956: 166.*

and may have served the Danish King Harald Bluetooth (Price *et al.* 2011). From my own experience I know of no examples of axes similar to that from Luboń from Viking-Age contexts in Norway, Iceland or the British Isles. In Sweden, one such axe has been found in Lund in Skåne (Paulsen 1956: 156–167). Very recently another axe of this type has also been discovered in a re-excavated chamber grave at Birka. After consultations with its discoverers (Charlotte Hedenstierna-Jonson and Fredrik Svanberg, pers. comm. 2013) we agreed that it is clearly not of Scandinavian type and its origin should rather be sought somewhere on the southern coast of the Baltic (for similar views regarding earlier finds of such axes see Pedersen 2010: 206), probably in the West Slavic lands where the majority of analogous objects have been discovered. It is vital to note that from the province of Greater Poland, and from the relatively near vicinity of Luboń itself, there are at least three similar objects – from Ostrów Lednicki, Łubowo and Włostowo (as mentioned, in fact, by Kara 1992a: 35; see also Nadolski 1954: 255). Parallels are also known from Meklemburg and Brandenburg and the former Ostpreussen areas on the southern coast of the Baltic Sea (Paulsen 1956: 156–167). The case of the axe from Luboń is just one of many examples of archaeological misinterpretations regarding alleged Scandinavian/Viking finds (and their owners) from Poland, which represents more of a wishful thinking rather than solid argumentation.

### *Western Pomerania*

Some of the graves that were excavated at the Western Pomeranian cemeteries were also argued to belong to Scandinavian immigrants (Duczko 2002: 31–33). In earlier archaeological studies, just as with the graves from Greater Poland, this assumption was predominantly based on the study of their artefactual assemblages (*e.g.* in Wolin), which, as we have seen above, is highly problematic. However, in the case of the graves from the cemetery at Świelubie (near Kołobrzeg), other factors were also taken into consideration, *i.e.* the form of burial which probably involved cremation in a wooden vehicle – perhaps a boat or a body of a wagon (Łosiński 1972: 246–253). The finds from the cremation graves at Świelubie – which actually include objects that can be firmly associated with Viking-Age art styles (*e.g.* oval and trefoil brooches, see Fig. 14.2) – may imply that the deceased who were buried with them were in fact of Scandinavian origin.

### *Central and Eastern Pomerania*

A range of graves that have been (again, rather problematically) interpreted as belonging to Scandinavians have also been discovered in Central and Eastern Pomerania.

In 1900, during the construction of a narrow gauge railway, an intriguing early medieval cemetery was discovered in the town of Ciepłe (Kara 2001; Żak 1957). The cemetery (which has recently been re-excavated, Ratajczyk 2011) included some richly furnished inhumation graves with elaborately decorated weapons and horse-riding gear. All graves were flat and the dead were buried in a supine position aligned east-west. In particular, the lavishly equipped male inhumation grave V was the subject of a long debate among Polish and German archaeologists. The deceased was buried in a coffin and judging by the wide repertoire of objects that accompanied him, we may assume that the coffin was placed in what could be regarded as a chamber-grave (Sikora 2013: 138). Over the years, various scholars have tried to unravel the ethnicity of the deceased man, mainly by concentrating on tracing the provenance of the objects that accompanied him. Among the most spectacular finds from grave V were: a sword, a spearhead, two stirrups, two bowls (one bronze and one made from wood), fragments of horse harness, a bronze beam of scales and ten iron weights plated with bronze. In an extensive article, Żak (1957) critically dismissed the previous views (expressed both by German and Polish scholars) suggesting Scandinavian provenance of the finds from Ciepłe. As Żak (1957: 174) argued, among the grave finds there is not a single object that could be regarded as a Scandinavian product. The same could be said about the funerary rite, which represents more of a Christian influence, rather than one that would be characteristic for Viking-Age Scandinavia. In my view, the more recent efforts of Kara (2001) – who once again argued for a Scandinavian nature of the finds from grave V – remain unconvincing. Sadly, further specialist analyses of the various objects from grave V from Ciepłe are impossible, since they all disappeared during the turmoil of World War II.

Among the problematic graves which have been attributed to Scandinavian immigrants is also one alleged 'ship burial' that was found on top of a mountain known as Góra Chełmska near Koszalin (Duczko 2000: 33; Janocha 1974). Unfortunately, the grave was very poorly preserved, which hampers any detailed interpretations. However, it is worth noting that no finds of Scandinavian provenance were discovered there. In a recent article, Sikora (2012: 96) suggested that judging by the shape of the alleged 'boat' it is more likely that the deceased was actually buried in something like a sledge. In my view, this interpretation seems very plausible indeed.

Apart from the controversial funerary evidence outlined above, it is worth noting that in Elbląg (near Truso), in the years preceding the outbreak of World War II, graves of females containing Scandinavian-style jewellery, including bronze chains, open-work brooches, box brooches, oval brooches as well as bracelets, knives and glass beads were discovered (Jagodziński 2010: 42). The finds from Elbląg indeed bear similarity to artefacts recovered from Viking-Age archaeological sites in Scandinavia.

### *Central Poland*

In discussions on the alleged presence of Scandinavians in Central Poland, the early medieval cemetery in Lutomiersk (a village near Łódź) has always played a very important role (Nadolski *et al.* 1959). The majority of graves at this site were inhumations, but an unusually large number of cremation graves was also found. Many of the graves from Lutomiersk included grave goods in the form of weapons (spearheads, arrowheads, axes and swords), horse-riding gear, wooden buckets and jewellery. The original excavators and authors of subsequent reports and specialist analyses have argued that a range of artefacts from the Lutomiersk cemetery had a Northern or Eastern European provenance. Among such finds were stirrups, horse-bits, ceramic eggs and various types of spearheads. It is not unlikely that the people buried at this site came from the territories of Rus'. The available medieval written accounts may offer some ideas as to the circumstances which could have led to the presence of such men in the area of Poland. The well-known *Povest' vremennykh let* mentions that at the time of the rule of Bolesław Chrobry (Bolesław the Brave), there were internal conflicts in Rus', which forced some of its inhabitants to migrate from their homelands. Perhaps the graves from Lutomiersk belong to such immigrants?

## The problematic chamber-graves

In discussing alleged Scandinavian graves on the southern coast of the Baltic, it is also worth devoting some space to the problem of early medieval 'chamber-graves' in Poland and the identities of the individuals who were buried within them. The last decade has seen a growing amount of discoveries of such funerary structures. Chamber-graves have been found at a range of early medieval cemeteries, for example in Bodzia, Cedynia, Dębczyno, Dziekanowice, Kałdus, Kraków-Zakrzówek(?), Napole, Ostrowite and Pień (*e.g.* Janowski 2011; Wrzesiński 2010) (Fig. 14.4). In almost all cases (perhaps with the exception of Bodzia, Kara 2013), the deceased were laid in a supine position. Most of the graves included only one individual, while others contained the skeletal remains of two people (Dziekanowice, Kałdus and Bodzia). A number of scholars have earlier suggested that several of these chamber-graves may have belonged to Scandinavians (*e.g.* Buko 2008; Chudziak 2003). More recently, however, these views have been questioned, and it has been argued that despite the presence of a wooden chamber, other details differ significantly from their Scandinavian counterparts (Gardeła 2013; Janowski 2011). For example – in contrast to the Viking-Age chamber-graves from Sweden, Denmark or Norway – the Polish chamber-graves generally lack weapons, animal offerings, external structures in the form of mounds or stones, and the dead are nearly always buried in a supine position. The idea of a chamber-grave in the Polish lands should therefore probably be associated with the emerging ruling elites and their desire to manifest power through spectacular funerals, rather than with Scandinavian immigrants.

## Poland and the Viking World(s)

As we have seen, wider explorations of the presence of Scandinavians in early medieval Poland have great potential and may significantly sophisticate our understanding of the Viking world(s). The brief survey of archaeological sources demonstrates that the contacts between the Scandinavians and Slavs were both long-lasting and multifaceted. Objects originating in Scandinavia and/or decorated in typical Viking-Age styles (*i.e.* Borre, Mammen, Ringerike) have been discovered especially in the ports-of-trade on the southern coast of the Baltic (*e.g.* Wolin, Kamień Pomorski and Truso). These finds bear witness to extensive trade networks and exchange of goods, but may also imply a more permanent habitation of immigrants from the North in the Slavic lands. However, still much has to be done in the field of mortuary archaeology, and in developing ways of identifying the burials of Scandinavians. While it is undoubted that such people were buried in the Polish lands (for example in the cemeteries in Świelubie or Elbląg), the previous interpretations regarding the presence of 'Viking mercenaries' in the retinues of Slavic rulers are based on very weak evidence (*e.g.* the problematic graves from Greater Poland discussed above).

The notion of 'Vikings in Poland' certainly has to be theorised, and so far there have been practically no attempts at doing so, perhaps with the exception of the aforementioned early works of Żak from the 1960s, which in many regards are now largely outdated. To some extent theoretical considerations are also introduced in the recent work of Joanna Wojtkowiak (2013). In dealing with such issues, we should definitely pay much more attention to the various and complex facets of intercultural interactions, migrations, ethnicity and identity. It could be very fruitful to draw our theoretical and methodological inspirations from the important works in social sciences (*e.g.* Bourdieu 2003), enriched by theories on 'cultural memory' (*e.g.* Assmann 1995; Connerton 1989) and phenomenology – all of which offer the potential for sophisticating our understanding of how past societies may have acted and reacted in the world, and especially in foreign environments. In future considerations of the notion of Scandinavians/Vikings in Poland, these concepts could substantially contribute to examining and assessing how certain skills and values may have been embodied and manifested by the Norse men and women who migrated to this area of Europe. In this context, it must be mentioned that the theoretical approaches proposed above have been successfully employed in several recent studies of early medieval migrations, ethnicity and social identities (*e.g.* Hillerdal 2009; Naum 2008) with specific regard to Slavic-Scandinavian relations in Bornholm or Rus' – it is high time to test them also in Poland.

With regard to Scandinavian-style objects found in funerary and settlement contexts in Poland the future debates would also benefit from incorporating the recent theoretical developments in artefact studies (*e.g.* considerations of artefact biography or personhood, Fowler 2004) and archaeology of death (*e.g.* the notion of 'remembrance' and funerary practices as a form of 'performance' or 'ritual drama', see Price 2008b, 2010; Williams 2006).

In this paper, I have sought to present and critically assess only a small fraction of the available archaeological evidence, and I hope it is clear that this material certainly deserves a more thorough, interdisciplinary study. Such a study, however, should not be conducted in complete isolation from the recent theoretical advancements and comparative research of Scandinavian, British, German and Eastern European scholars, as was unfortunately often done before. Open-minded scholarly collaboration and mutual awareness of the latest advancements in Viking-Age research in different academic milieus in Europe has a tremendous potential to redefine and sophisticate our perception of this important period in our shared history, not only in Poland, but also with regard to the much wider Viking world(s).

*Acknowledgements*

I wish to warmly thank Charlotte Hedenstierna-Jonson, Andrzej Janowski, Jakub Morawiec, Fredrik Svanberg and Roman Gardeła for their valuable comments which helped me to improve this article. I also thank the organisers of the *Viking Worlds* conference in Oslo in 2013. Special thanks to Marek Jagodziński, Władysław Łosiński and Błażej Stanisławski for their kind permission to reproduce images from their publications.

*References*

Assmann, Jan

1995. Collective memory and cultural identity. *New German Critique* 65: 125–133.

Blake, N. F. (translator)

1962. *Jómsvíkinga saga. The Saga of the Jomsvikings.* Thomas Nelson and Sons, London, Edinburgh, Paris, Melbourne, Johannesburg, Toronto and New York.

Bogucki, Mateusz

2004. The Viking-Age ports of trade in Poland. *Eesti Arheoloogia Ajakiri* 8(2): 100–128.

2010. Viking-Age emporia around the Baltic Sea – a cul-de-sac of European urbanization? In *Making a Medieval Town. Patterns of Early Medieval Urbanization*, edited by Andrzej Buko and Mike McCarthy, pp. 151–165. Institute of Archaeology, University of Warsaw, Warszawa.

Bogucki, Mateusz and Marek Jagodziński (editors)

2012a. *Janów Pomorski Stan. 1/Site 1. Wyniki ratowniczych badań archeologicznych w latach 2007–2008. Archaeological Rescue Excavations in 2007–2008. Tom I:1 Od paleolitu do wczesnego okresu wędrówek ludów. Vol. I:1 From the Paleolithic to the Early Migration Period*, Studia nad Truso/Truso Studies. Muzeum Archeologiczno-Historyczne w Elblągu, Elbląg.

2012b. Janów Pomorski Stan. 1/Site 1. *Wyniki ratowniczych badań archeologicznych w latach 2007-2008. Archaeological Rescue Excavations in 2007–2008. Tom I:2 Od późnego okresu wędrówek ludów do nowożytności. Vol. I:2 From the Late Migration Period to the Modern Era*, Studia nad Truso/Truso Studies. Muzeum Archeologiczno-Historyczne w Elblągu, Elbląg.

2012c. Janów Pomorski Stan. 1/Site 1. *Wyniki ratowniczych badań archeologicznych w latach 2007–2008. Archaeological Rescue Excavations in 2007-2008. Tom I:3 Analizy. Vol. I:3: Analysis*, Studia nad Truso/Truso Studies. Muzeum Archeologiczno-Historyczne w Elblągu, Elbląg.

Bourdieu, Pierre

2003. *Outline of a Theory of Practice*. Cambridge University Press, Cambridge.

Brink, Stefan and Price, Neil (editors)

2010. *The Viking World*. Routledge, London.

Buko, Andrzej

2008. *The Archaeology of Early Medieval Poland. Discoveries – Hypotheses – Interpretations*, East Central and Eastern Europe in the Middle Ages, 450–1450, Vol. 1. Brill, Boston.

Chudziak, Wojciech

2003. Wikingerzeitliche Spuren des Skandinavischen Brauchtums in Kałdus (Ostpommern). *Archäologisches Korrespondenzblatt* 33(1): 145–156.

Connerton, Paul

1989. *How Societies Remember*. Cambridge University Press, Cambridge.

Duczko, Władysław

2000. Obecność skandynawska na Pomorzu i słowiańska w Skandynawii we wczesnym średniowieczu. In *Salsa Cholbergiensis. Kołobrzeg w średniowieczu*, edited by Lech Leciejewicz and Marian Rębkowski, pp. 23–44. Wydawnictwo Le Petit Café, Kołobrzeg.

2010. Posłowie. In Marek Jagodziński. *Truso. Między Weonodlandem a Witlandem*, pp. 199–204. Muzeum Archeologiczno-Historyczne w Elblągu, Elbląg.

2012. Wikingowie i wczesnośredniowieczna Polska. In *Swoi i obcy w kulturze średniowiecza. Wykłady popularno-naukowe zorganizowane w ramach VII Festiwalu Kultury Słowiańskiej i Cysterskiej w Lądzie nad Wartą w dniach 18–19 czerwca 2011 roku*, edited by Michał Brzostowicz, Maciej Przybył and Jacek Wrzesiński, pp. 61–69. Fundacja 'Unia Nadwarciańska', Muzeum Archeologiczne w Poznaniu, Starostwo Powiatowe w Słupcy, Poznań-Ląd.

Englert, Anton and Athena Trakadas (editors)
2009. *Wulfstan's Voyage. The Baltic Sea Region in the Early Viking Age as Seen from Shipboard*, Maritime Culture of the North, Vol. 2. The Viking Ship Museum, Roskilde.
Filipowiak, Władysław
1958. Wolin – największe miasto Słowiańszczyzny zachodniej. In *Szkice z dziejów Pomorza. Pomorze średniowieczne*, edited by Gerard Labuda, pp. 36–72. Książka i Wiedza, Warszawa.
Filipowiak, Władysław and Heinz Gundlach
1992. *Wolin Vineta. Die tätsachliche Legende vom Untergang und Aufsteig der Stadt*. Hinstorff, Rostock.
Fowler, Chris
2004. *The Archaeology of Personhood. An Anthropological Approach*. Routledge, London.
Gardeła, Leszek
2013. Dead or alive? Chamber graves and their inhabitants in the Old Norse literature and Viking-Age archaeology. In *Scandinavian Culture in Medieval Poland*, edited by Błażej Stanisławski, Sławomir Moździoch and Przemysław Wiszewski, pp. 373–394. Institute of Archaeology and Ethnology Polish Academy of Sciences, Wrocław.
Górecki, Janusz
2002. *Gród na Ostrowie Lednickim na tle wybranych ośrodków grodowych pierwszej monarchii piastowskiej*, Biblioteka Studiów Lednickich, Vol. VII. Muzeum Pierwszych Piastów na Lednicy, Poznań.
Hillerdal, Charlotta
2009. *People in Between. Ethnicity and Material Identity – a New Approach to Deconstructed Concepts*, Occasional Papers in Archaeology, Vol. 50. Institutionen för arkeologi och antik historia, Uppsala Universitet, Uppsala.
Hollander, Lee M. (translator)
2000. *The Saga of the Jómsvíkings*. University of Texas Press, Austin.
Holtzmann, R.
1918. Böhmen und Polen im 10. Jahrhundert. Eine Untersuchung zur ältesten Geschichte Polens. *Zeitschrift des Vereins für Geschichte Schlesiens* 52: 1–37.
Jagodziński, Marek F.
2010. *Truso. Między Weonodlandem a Witlandem/Truso. Between Weonodland and Witland*. Muzeum Archeologiczno-Historyczne w Elblągu, Elbląg.
Jankuhn, Herbert
1934. Der Wikingerfund aus Libau in der Provinz Posen. *Altschlesien* 5: 309–317.
Janocha, Henryk W.
1974. Wyniki prac badawczych prowadzonych w latach 1961 i 1962 na Górze Chełmskiej (Krzyżance) koło Koszalina, cz. 2. *Materiały Zachodniopomorskie* 20: 31–167.
Janowski, Andrzej
2011. Early medieval chamber graves on the south coast of the Baltic Sea. In *Der Wandel um 1000. Beitrage der Sektion zur slawischen Frühgeschichte der 18. Jahrestagung des Mittel- und Ostdeutschen Verbandes für Altertumsforschung in Greifswald, 23. bis 27. März 2009*, edited by Felix Biermann, Thomas Kersting, Anne Klammt, pp. 257–267. Beiträge zur Ur- und Frühgeschichte Mitteleuropas, Vol. 60. Beier and Beran, Archäologische Fachliteratur, Langenweissbach.
2014. *W wolińskim porcie/In Wolin's port*. Wolin: Muzeum Regionalne im. Andrzeja Kaubego w Wolinie, Urząd Miejski w Wolinie.
Kara, Michał
1991. Z badań nad wczesnośredniowiecznymi grobami z uzbrojeniem z terenu Wielkopolski. In *Od plemienia do państwa. Śląsk na tle wczesnośredniowiecznej Słowiańszczyzny Zachodniej*, edited

by Lech Leciejewicz, pp. 99–120. Śląskie Sympozja Historyczne, Vol. 1. Polska Akademia Nauk, Komitet Nauk Historycznych, Uniwersytet Wrocławski, Centrum Badań Śląskoznawczych i Bohemistycznych, Wrocław-Warszawa.

1992a. Siły zbrojne Mieszka I. Z badań nad składem etnicznym, organizacją i dyslokacją drużyny pierwszych Piastów. *Kronika Wielkopolski* 62(3): 33–47.

1992b. The graves of the Armed Scandinavians from the Middle and the Younger Viking Period from the Territory of the First Piasts' State. In *Death and Burial. A Conference on Medieval Archaeology in Europe. 21st–24th September 1992 at the University of York. Pre-printed papers*, Vol. 4, pp. 167–177. Medieval Europe, York.

2001. Frühmittelalterliches Grab eines bewaffenten Kaufmannes aus dem Ort Ciepłe (Warmhof) in danziger Pommern in Lichte einer erneueten Analyse, *Acta Universitatis Lodziensis. Folia Archaeologica* 23(1): 113–144.

2013. Wybrane groby z uzbrojeniem z cmentarzyska w Bodzi pod Włocławkiem – przyczynek do studiów nad obecnością „wikingów" w państwie pierwszych Piastów, *Studia nad dawną Polską* 3:117–132.

Kola, Andrzej and Gerard Wilke

2000. *Mosty sprzed tysiąca lat. Archeologiczne badania podwodne przy rezydencji pierwszych Piastów na Ostrowie Lednickim.* Uniwersytet Mikołaja Kopernika w Toruniu, Toruń.

Kostrzewski, Józef

1921. Cmentarzysko ze śladami kultury wikingów w Łubówku, w pow. gnieźnieńskim. *Przegląd Archeologiczny* 1(3–4): 140–147.

1946. Germanie przedhistoryczni w Polsce. *Przegląd Archeologiczny* 7: 65–89.

1949. *Kultura Prapolska.* Prace Instytutu Zachodniego, Vol. 11. Instytut Zachodni, Poznań.

Krzyszowski, Andrzej

1995. Ein reiches Gräberfeld aus dem 10./11. Jh. in Sowinki bei Poznań. *Slavia Antiqua* 36: 49–71.

Labuda, Gerard

2002. *Mieszko I.* Zakład Narodowy Imienia Ossolińskich Wydawnictwo, Wrocław, Warszawa, Kraków.

Leciejewicz, Lech and Marian Rębkowski (editors)

2000. *Salsa Cholbergiensis. Kołobrzeg we wczesnym średniowieczu.* Wydawnictwo Le Petit Café, Kołobrzeg.

Łosiński, Władysław

1972. *Początki wczesnośredniowiecznego osadnictwa grodowego w dorzeczu dolnej Parsęty (VII–X/XI w.).* Zakład Narodowy Imienia Ossolińskich, Wydawnictwo Polskiej Akademii Nauk, Wrocław-Warszawa-Kraków-Gdańsk.

Łowmiański, Henryk.

1957. *Zagadnienie roli Normanów w genezie państw słowiańskich.* Państwowe Wydawnictwo Naukowe, Warszawa.

Morawiec, Jakub

2009. *Vikings among the Slavs. Jomsborg and the Jomsvikings in Old Norse Tradition.* Studia Medievalia Septentrionalia, Vol. 17. Fassbaender, Wien.

2010. *Wolin w średniowiecznej tradycji skandynawskiej.* Avalon, Kraków.

2013. *Knut Wielki. Król Anglii, Danii i Norwegii (ok. 955–1035).* Avalon, Kraków.

Nadolski, Andrzej

1954. *Studia nad uzbrojeniem polskim w X, XI i XII wieku.* Acta Archaeologica Universitatis Lodziensis, Vol. 3. Zakład Imienia Ossolińskich we Wrocławiu, Łódź.

Nadolski, Andrzej, Andrzej Abramowicz and Tadeusz Poklewski
1959. *Cmentarzysko wczesnośredniowieczne w Lutomiersku pod Łodzią.* Acta Archaeologica Universitatis Lodziensis, Vol. 7. Łódzkie Towarzystwo Naukowe, Łodź.

Naum, Magdalena
2008. *Homelands Lost and Gained. Slavic Migration and Settlement on Bornholm in the Early Middle Ages.* Lund Studies in Historical Archaeology, Vol. 9. Lunds Universitet, Lund.

Nielsen, Bjarne Henning
1991. Langbladsøksen, *Skalk* 1991(2): 9–13.

Nørlund, Poul
1948. *Trelleborg,* Nordiske Fortidsminder, Vol. IV, I. Det Kongelige Nordiske Oldskriftselskab, Copenhagen.

Paulsen, Peter
1956. *Axt und Kreuz in Nord- und Osteuropa.* Rudolf Habelt Verlag, Bonn.

Pedersen, Anne
2002. Scandinavian weaponry in the tenth century: the example of Denmark. In *A Companion to Medieval Arms and Armour,* edited by David Nicolle, pp. 25–35. Boydell Press, Woodbridge.
2010. Viking weaponry. In *The Viking World,* edited by Stefan Brink and Neil Price, pp. 204–211. Routledge, London.

Price, Neil
2008a. Dying and the dead: Viking Age mortuary behaviour. In *The Viking World,* edited by Stefan Brink and Neil Price, pp. 257–273. Routledge, London.
2008b. Bodylore and the archaeology of embedded religion: dramatic license in the funerals of the Vikings. In *Belief in the Past. Theoretical Approaches to the Archaeology of Religion,* edited by Kelley Hays-Gilpin and David S. Whitley, pp. 143–165. Left Coast Press, Walnut Creek, California.
2010. Passing into poetry: Viking Age mortuary drama and the origins of Norse mythology. *Medieval Archaeology* 54: 123–156.

Price, Thomas D., Karin M Frei., Anders S. Dobat, Niels Lynnerup and Pia Bennike
2011. Who was in Harold Bluetooth's army? Strontium isotope investigation of the cemetery at the Viking Age fortress at Trelleborg, Denmark. *Antiquity* 85: 476–489.

Rajewski, Zdzisław A.
1937. Wielkopolskie cmentarzyska rzędowe z okresu wczesnodziejowego. *Przegląd Archeologiczny* 6(1): 28–86.

Ratajczyk, Zdzisława
2011. Nowe odkrycia na cmentarzysku z okresu wczesnego średniowiecza w Ciepłem, gm. Gniew, stanowisko 6. In *XVII Sesja Pomorzoznawcza. Vol. 1. Od epoki kamienia do wczesnego średniowiecza,* edited by Mirosław Fudziński and Henryk Paner, pp. 572–576. Muzeum Archeologiczne w Gdańsku, Gdańsk.

Rębkowski, Marian
2011. *Die Christianisierung Pommerns. Eine archäologische Studie.* Universitätsforschungen zur prähistorischen Archäologie, Vol. 197. Habelt, Bonn.

Roesdahl, Else and David Wilson
1992. *From Viking to Crusader. The Scandinavians and Europe 800-1200.* The Council of Europe, København.

Roslund, Mats
2007. *Guests in the House. Cultural Transmission between Slavs and Scandinavians 900 to 1300 AD.* The Northern World, Vol. 33. Brill, Leiden.

Sayer, Duncan and Howard Williams (editors)
2009. *Mortuary Practices and Social Identities in the Middle Ages. Essays in Burial Archaeology in Honour of Heinrich Härke.* University of Exeter Press, Exeter.
Sikora, Jerzy
2012. Wczesnośredniowieczne pochówki szkieletowe jako przejaw barbarzyńskiej mentalności? Przykłady pomorskie. In *Barbarzyńcy u bram. Monografia oparta o materiały z VI Międzynarodowej Sesji Naukowej Dziejów Ludów Morza Bałtyckiego. Wolin 05-07 sierpnia 2011*, edited by Maciej Franz and Zbigniew Pilarczyk, pp. 88–103. Mare Integrans. Studia nad dziejami wybrzeży Morza Bałtyckiego. Wydawnictwo Adam Marszałek, Toruń.
2013. Akulturacja, wymuszona chrystianizacja czy migracja? Problem genezy wczesnośredniowiecznej inhumacji na Pomorzu. In *Migracje*, edited by Wojciech Dzieduszycki and Jacek Wrzesiński, pp. 135–146. Funeralia Lednickie, Vol. 16. Stowarzyszenie Naukowe Archeologów Polskich, Poznań.
Skov, Hans
2011. Jomsborg and the Wends. In *Aros and the World of the Vikings. The Stories and Travelogues of Seven Vikings from Aros*, edited by Hans Skov and Jeanette Varberg, pp. 118–120. Moesgård Museum, Højbjerg.
Skov, Hans and Jeanette Varberg (editors)
2011. *Aros and the World of the Vikings. The Stories and Travelogues of Seven Vikings from Aros.* Moesgård Museum, Højbjerg.
Schulte, Lambert
1918. Beiträge zur ältesten Geschichte Polens. *Zeitschrift des Vereins für Geschichte Schlesiens* 52: 38–57.
Stanisławski, Błażej
2012. *Garncarstwo wczesnośredniowiecznego Wolina.* Instytut Archeologii i Etnologii Polskiej Akademii Nauk, Wrocław.
Stanisławski, Błażej and Władysław Filipowiak
2013. *Wolin wczesnośredniowieczny. Część 1.* Origines Polonorum, Vol. VI. Fundacja Na Rzecz Nauki Polskiej, Instytut Archeologii i Etnologii Polskiej Akademii Nauk, Wydawnictwo Trio, Warszawa.
Stanisławski, Błażej, Sławomir Moździoch and Przemysław Wiszewski (editors)
2013. *Scandinavian Culture in Medieval Poland.* Institute of Archaeology and Ethnology Polish Academy of Sciences, Wrocław.
Svanberg, Fredrik
2003. *Death Rituals in South-East Scandinavia AD 800–1000. Decolonizing the Viking Age 2.* Acta Archaeologica Lundensia, Vol. 24. Almqvist and Wiksell International, Stockholm.
Szajnocha, Karol
1858. *Lechicki początek Polski.* Nakładem Karola Wilda, Lwów.
Urbańczyk, Przemysław
2008. Nordmannowie, Normanowie i Norwegowie. *In Przez granice czasu. Księga jubileuszowa poświęcona Profesorowi Jerzemu Gąssowskiemu.* Acta Archaeologica Pultuskiensis, edited by Andrzej Buko and Władysław Duczko, pp. 489–497. Instytut Antropologii i Archeologii Akademii Humanistycznej im. Aleksandra Gieysztora, Pułtusk.
Wachowski, Kazimierz.
1914. *Jomsborg. Normannowie wobec Polski w X w. Studyum historyczne*, Prace Towarzystwa Naukowego Warszawskiego, Vol. II. Wydział Nauk Antropologicznych, Społecznych, Historii i Filozofii. Druk Rubieszowskiego i Wrotnowskiego, Warszawa.
Williams, Howard
2006. *Death and Memory in Early Medieval Britain.* Cambridge University Press, Cambridge.

Wojtkowiak, Joanna

2013. *Skandynawskie wpływy kulturowe w Wolinie (IX–XI wiek).* Chronicon, Wrocław.

Wrzesiński, Jacek

2010. Kto wierzy w Odyna? Czyli zagadkowe groby w państwie Piastów. In *Religia ludów Morza Bałtyckiego. Stosunki polsko-duńskie w dziejach.* Mare Integrans. Studia nad dziejami wybrzeży Morza Bałtyckiego, edited by Michał Bogacki, Maciej Franz and Zbigniew Pilarczyk, pp. 51–61. Wydawnictwo Adam Marszałek, Toruń.

Żak, Jan

1957. Czy grób uzbrojonego jeźdźca z Ciepłego, pow. tczewski, jest grobem skandynawskim? *Archeologia Polski* 1: 164–180.

1963. *'Importy' skandynawskie na ziemiach zachodniosłowiańskich od IX do XI wieku (Część katalogowa).* Prace Komisji Archeologicznej Tom VI – Zeszyt, Vol. 1. Poznańskie Towarzystwo Przyjaciół Nauk, Poznań.

1967a. *'Importy' skandynawskie na ziemiach zachodniosłowiańskich od IX do XI wieku (Część analityczna).* Prace Komisji Archeologicznej Tom VII – Zeszyt, Vol. 1. Poznańskie Towarzystwo Przyjaciół Nauk, Poznań.

1967b. *'Importy' skandynawskie na ziemiach zachodniosłowianskich od IX do XI wieku (Część syntetyczna).* Prace Komisji Archeologicznej Tom VII – Zeszyt, Vol. 2. Poznańskie Towarzystwo Przyjaciół Nauk, Poznań.

1968. Czy państwo polskie zawdzięcza swe powstanie Normanom? *Z Otchłani Wieków* 35(2): 130–131.